A CONSTITUTIONAL HISTORY OF INDIA

1600-1935

A CONSTITUTIONAL HISTORY OF INDIA

1600-1935

BY

ARTHUR BERRIEDALE KEITH,

D.C.L., D.LITT., F.B.A.

OF THE INNER TEMPLE, BARRISTER-AT-LAW, AND ADVOCATE OF THE SCOTTISH BAR; REGIUS PROFESSOR OF SANSKRIT AND COMPARATIVE PHILOLOGY AND LECTURER ON THE CONSTITUTION OF THE BRITISH EMPIRE AT THE UNIVERSITY OF EDINBURGH; FORMERLY ASSISTANT SECRETARY TO THE IMPERIAL CONFERENCE

GYAN

Published by

Gyan Publishing House
5, Ansari Road
Daryaganj, New Delhi-110002
Phone: 011-47034999, 9811692060
E-mail: books@gyanbooks.com

Distribution Network
gyanbooks.com
India, USA, Canada, UK, Australia, France

ISBN : 978-81-212-2176-4 (HB)
First Published, 1936

2nd Impression 2021

Printed at: Gyan Press, Delhi.

A
Constitutional History of India
Author: Arthur Berriedale Keith

A CONSTITUTIONAL HISTORY OF INDIA 1600-1935

ARTHUR BERRIEDALE KEITH
D.C.L., D.LITT., F.B.A.
OF THE INNER TEMPLE, BARRISTER-AT-LAW, AND ADVOCATE OF THE SCOTTISH BAR; REGIUS PROFESSOR OF SANSKRIT AND COMPARATIVE PHILOLOGY AND LECTURER ON THE CONSTITUTION OF THE BRITISH EMPIRE AT THE UNIVERSITY OF EDINBURGH; FORMERLY ASSISTANT SECRETARY TO THE IMPERIAL CONFERENCE

METHUEN & CO. LTD. LONDON
36 Essex Street W.C.

In Memoriam

MARGARET STOBIE KEITH

AND

MARGARET BALFOUR KEITH

PREFACE

It was the aim of the greatest among the early British administrators in India to train the peoples of India to govern and protect themselves, as Sir Thomas Munro wrote in 1824, rather than to establish the rule of a British bureaucracy. The method which they contemplated was doubtless that carried out with the most conspicuous success in Mysore, which, thanks in the main to the efforts of Sir Mark Cubbon as resident, was handed back to Indian rule in 1881 with the assurance that a tradition of sound government had been created which could be operated without detailed British supervision. Elsewhere this ideal proved impossible of accomplishment; the necessity of securing justice and order led to the progressive extension of direct British sovereignty and the evolution of that splendid instrument of government, the Indian Civil Service. That service, however, brought with it British political ideas and made English the official language of the higher functions of government. The result was inevitable; with steadily increasing strength the Indian intelligentsia has demanded the fulfilment of self-government, not in the form contemplated by Munro and his contemporaries, but in that of British Parliamentary institutions. To men deeply imbued with the fundamental principles of democracy, such as Lord Morley of Blackburn, these demands seemed inconsistent with the structure of Indian society, which is founded on the basis of social inequality and racial and religious diversity. But the services of India in the war elicited a formal declaration on August 20th 1917 of the policy of the British Government as involving steps to the gradual realization of responsible government in India as an integral part of the British Empire.

It is possible to condemn the declaration as an ill-considered piece of war propaganda; it seems clear at least that Lord Curzon did not realize that the pledge involved parliamentary government of the British type. But, whether the adoption of the policy was wise or not, it is clear that it had to be honoured, and the constitution of 1919 was the method suggested by Mr. Montagu and Lord Chelmsford to inaugurate the process of change. Whether the system of dyarchy on which it was based was workable may be doubted; the insight into it which I derived from membership of Lord Crewe's Committee on the Home Administration of India satisfied me that, for the reasons pointed out in my report (Cmd. 207) as a member, radical alterations in the principle of control would be essential if the principle of responsibility was to be tested. Naturally enough, considerations of caution prevailed, and the constitution as enacted and as operated effectively negatived any real test of the capacity of Indian ministers to work responsible government. It is the essential merit of the Act of 1935 that it recognizes the failure of the Act of 1919 and presents, so far as Indian social conditions permit, the possibility in the provinces of true responsible government. It would, of course, be absurd to ignore the difficulties of operating the system under Indian conditions, which necessitate reserving large powers of intervention to the governors, but the task is at least not impossible as it was under the Act of 1919.

In the federal government also the semblance of responsible government is presented. But the reality is lacking, for the powers in defence and external affairs necessarily, as matters stand, given to the governor-general limit vitally the scope of ministerial activity, and the measure of representation given to the rulers of the Indian States negatives any possibility of even the beginnings of democratic control. It will be a matter of the utmost interest to watch the development of a form of government so unique; certainly, if it operates successfully, the highest credit will be due to the political capacity of Indian leaders, who have infinitely more serious difficulties to face than had the colonial statesmen who evolved the system of self-government which has now culminated in Dominion status.

Since this book was written, the British Government has taken the necessary decisions regarding the separation of Sind and Orissa from their present union with Bombay and Bihar. The new provinces during the period of transition will have a distinctive form of government. Each will be governed by a governor without either an executive or a legislative council, and without any form of dyarchy. A measure of aid will be afforded by advisory councils of not more than twenty-five and twenty members respectively, nominated by the governor, of whom not more than three will be officials. The governor may choose one or more of the council to assist him in such manner as he thinks fit. Legislation rests with the governor-general in council under the procedure provided in the Government of India Act (s. 71) for special areas; finance with the governor, who, however, is required to submit his statement of revenue and expenditure and proposals for appropriation to his council, but only for general discussion. Revenue Commissioners are provided for the two provinces, and arrangements are made for allocation of officers, and apportionment of property, assets and liabilities as between the provinces; in the case of Orissa the matter is complicated by the fact that certain areas are transferred from Madras and the Central Provinces to constitute with the Orissa Division of Bihar and Orissa the new province.

Reductions are necessarily made in the size of the Legislative Councils of the diminished provinces; that of Bombay is reduced to ninety-five members (sixty-seven elected): that of Bihar loses ten elected and two nominated official members, that of Madras two elected members. The High Court at Patna becomes the High Court for the whole of the newly constituted Orissa.

The new arrangements are obviously suited only for a brief transitional period; it is hoped that the necessary delimitation of constituencies under the Act of 1935 and the investigations of financial conditions will be carried out in time to permit of inaugurating provincial autonomy by bringing Part III of the Act into operation in 1937; federation will be necessarily slower in reaching fruition. The selection of Commander A. D. Cochrane, M.P., as the governor of Burma marks the preparation for the inauguration there of the new régime; the precedent indicates that under the changed conditions the chance of members of the Indian Civil Service attaining governorships is greatly reduced, necessarily involving a further decline in the attractiveness of a service which has conferred great benefits on India, but which inevitably must lose authority under the new régime.

For purposes of convenience the original Government of India Act, 1935 (25 & 26 Geo. V, c. 42) has been reprinted as the Government of India Act, 1935 (26 Geo. V, c. 2) and the Government of Burma Act, 1935 (26 Geo. V, c. 3), and the section references in this book refer to these Acts accordingly. The Government of India Act, without date, to which reference is occasionally made, is the Act of 1915 consolidating earlier legislation, as reprinted by direction of Parliament with alterations under amending legislation passed before the Act of 1935. When the latter Act takes full effect, the earlier legislation will pass away, together with the historic system which it represents. The vital change between the Act of 1935 and 1919 is thus formally attested; if it was possible to fit the changes then made as amendments into the substance of the old system that was out of the question with the Act of 1935.

In this sketch of the constitutional history I have necessarily concentrated attention on those matters which appeared to me of special significance as bearing on the evolution of self-government. After the earlier periods administrative and judicial details have, therefore, been passed over. Brevity also has dictated curtailment of discussion; otherwise I should have desired to deal fully with the views of the apologists for the action of Warren Hastings, and the defenders of the remarkable and in my opinion quite untenable claims put forward by the rulers of the Indian States.

A. BERRIEDALE KEITH

THE UNIVERSITY OF EDINBURGH
February 12th 1936

CONTENTS

A CONSTITUTIONAL HISTORY OF INDIA
1600–1935

CHAPTER I

THE COMPANY BEFORE PLASSEY; ITS CONSTITUTION, RELATION TO THE INDIAN STATES, AND THE ADMINISTRATION OF ITS SETTLEMENTS AND TERRITORIES

1. THE CONSTITUTION OF THE COMPANY

THERE was little to suggest the acquisition of dominion in India in the début of the Governor and Company of Merchants of London trading into the East Indies to whom Queen Elizabeth, after much hesitation, granted a charter of incorporation on December 31st 1600. The aims of the Company were essentially commercial. Trade with the East was essential in order to obtain those spices necessary to render palatable the limited foodstuffs available under the primitive agricultural conditions of the day and other products prized for their utility or beauty in the West. The traditional route passed through the dominions of the Sultan of Turkey, and Elizabeth in 1581 granted a charter to the Levant Company to trade with these dominions under the terms of the concessions made by the Sultan in 1579, when he granted privileges of trade and residence, with exemption for most purposes from Turkish criminal and civil jurisdiction, to English subjects. The Company sought to extend its trade to India, and in 1592 secured a fresh charter authorizing them to trade to India overland through Ottoman territories.

Serious difficulties, however, were placed by the Sultan in the way of the development of overland trade, while the discovery of a practical passage to India by the Cape of Good Hope suggested a new line of approach. Political conditions favoured action. The Bull of May 1493 of Pope Alexander VI had assigned India to Portugal in its division between that country and Spain of the undiscovered non-Christian world; and subsequent treaties between these countries had recognized with modifications the allocation. Since 1580 the sovereignty of Spain had been extended over Portugal, and the Portuguese rights over Indian territories had passed to the Spanish Crown.

But the Reformation had undermined the validity of Papal dispositions, and the revolt of the Netherlands involved the decision to strike a determined blow at Spain through depriving her of the monopoly of Eastern trade. The ambition and courage of Dutch merchants in association were displayed to great advantage in the expeditions of 1595–6 and 1598–9 to Java, and, if they were not to find a Dutch monopoly replacing that of Spain, early action by the merchants of London was plainly necessary. At a meeting at Founders' Hall under the auspices of the Lord Mayor on September 22nd 1599, the vital resolution was arrived at to form an association to trade direct with India. In securing this end the Levant Company was clearly much interested; the first governor of the Company which received the royal charter in 1600 when all hope of peace with Spain had been abandoned was also governor of the Levant Company.

In these circumstances all that was contemplated by the merchants, and their more aristocratic associates who supported them at Court, was the creation of an association to carry on trade by dispatching ships to Indian territories and by founding therein trading stations with the permission of the local rulers, on lines similar to those on which trade was conducted with the Ottoman dominions. There could be no question, as in the case of the patent granted to Sir Humphrey Gilbert in respect of Newfoundland,[1] of the assumption of sovereignty over newly discovered lands. But the Crown was entitled in the view of the lawyers of the day to regulate by the prerogative foreign trade and the actions of its subjects beyond the realm, and on the basis of these powers the royal charter was issued. It conferred corporate character and juristic personality on the Earl of Cumberland, and the 217 knights, aldermen, and burgesses with him associated, granted them essential commercial privileges, and provided them with authority to govern themselves and their servants.

The Company was authorized freely to traffic and trade 'into and from the East Indies, in the countries and parts of Asia and Africa, and into and from all the islands, ports, havens, cities, creeks, towns, and places of Asia and Africa, and America, or any of them, beyond the Cape of Bona Esperanza to the

[1] Keith, *Const. Hist. of First British Empire*, pp. 37 f.

Streights of Magellan'. This right was to endure for fifteen years, but might be determined on two years' warning, if the trade did not appear profitable to the realm; otherwise a renewal for a further fifteen years was contemplated. It was to be an exclusive right, but the company might grant licences to trade. Unauthorized traders, on the other hand, were to be liable to forfeiture of their goods, ships and tackle, and to imprisonment and such other punishment as might seem meet and convenient for so high a contempt of the 'prerogative royal, which we will not in that behalf have argued or brought in question'. The legality of the grant of such a monopoly was not then seriously in question; it is part of the genius of the common law that it accords with essential economic and political conditions, and at that date the successful prosecution of trade with the East demanded the concentration of authority in the hands of a single body which could deal with native princes, regulate sailings, and contend against rival European traders. It is significant that in 1602 the Dutch traders consolidated their forces in the Dutch East Indies Company, which rapidly developed into a power able to dictate to the State the terms on which it was to be aided. Strengthened by this help, it was successful in its competition with the London Company for control of the Spice Islands, which formed the prime object of interest to both; the failure of James I to afford adequate protection or to avenge the massacre of English traders at Amboyna in 1623 resulted in the virtual exclusion of the London Company and its restriction to the Indian peninsula, with decisive results for the future of British rule.

The constitution of the Company was simple, falling within the type of 'regulated companies' as opposed to 'joint-stock companies'. In such companies members were subjected to certain regulations and enjoyed certain privileges, but traded on their own capital. In practice the Company in its early days functioned as a syndicate with a concession for the Indian trade, which it worked by forming minor groups from among its members who found the capital for each separate voyage, and whose liability was normally limited to the voyage for which they had subscribed, though they might be forced to contribute to a further venture if fresh capital could not be raised from a new group of subscribers. After 1612 the subscribers threw their contributions into a joint stock, though not yet on a permanent basis, the joint stock being formed for a series of voyages only.

Membership of the Company was accorded in the charter to those who had purchased a share in the first voyage, and was granted subsequently to such persons as took up shares in later voyages, the amount contributed varying from time to time. Membership could also be claimed by the sons of members on reaching the age of twenty-one. Further, membership could be secured through service or apprenticeship and the payment of a small sum on admission. Or members might be admitted in return for a fixed cash payment, usually of a hundred pounds, and membership was from time to time conferred on distinguished individuals who were deemed likely to be able to aid the Company.

The control of the Company's business was democratic in principle. The Company was authorized to elect annually a governor and twenty-four committees, the precursors of the later directors, who were to have the direction of the Company's voyages, the provision of shipping and merchandises, the sale of merchandise brought to England, and the managing of all other things belonging to the Company. Other officers were soon added, including a deputy governor, secretary, and treasurer. In general the governor and committees managed the general detail of the voyages, but they called together a general meeting of the members when they deemed it necessary.

To the Company were conceded certain limited powers of a legislative character, based on those recognized at the time as appropriate for municipal and commercial corporate bodies. The Company might assemble themselves in any convenient place, 'within our dominions or elsewhere', and there hold court for the Company and its affairs, and might 'make, ordain, and constitute such and so many reasonable laws, constitutions, orders, and ordinances, as to them or the greater part of them being then and there present shall seem necessary and convenient for the good government of the said Company, and of all factors, masters, mariners, and other officers, employed or to be employed in any of their voyages, and for the better advancement and continuance of the said trade and traffick'. They were further authorized to impose such pains, punishments, and penalties by imprisonment of body or by fines and amerciaments as might seem necessary or convenient for the observation of such laws and ordinances. Both laws and punishments must be reasonable and not contrary or repugnant to the laws, statutes or customs of the realm of England. It will be seen that the power given is essentially a power of minor legislation, forbidding any fundamental alteration of the principles of English law, and limited drastically by the character of the punishments which could be inflicted in respect of contraventions. The limited character of the Company's authority is clearly marked in the earliest copy of such laws extant, that printed in 1621. They deal chiefly with the management of the Company's meetings and its officers in England, the administrative arrangements in the East, whereby Bantam in Java and Surat were made the principal factories, and the employment of shipping. They assert in accordance with the charter the illegality of private trade and order factors to seize goods so shipped and to send them home, and they require—an ominous hint of evils to come—that all presents made by foreign princes, rulers, or commanders to members of the Company shall be brought into the general account of the Company.

It is important to contrast the terms of this grant with those made to the companies or individuals who contemporaneously were seeking to establish themselves in the newly discovered Western lands. The charter of Charles I to the governor and company of the Massachusetts Bay in New England confers on the general meeting of that company the right to elect officers and admit members, but the legislative power is in wider terms, 'to make Lawes and Ordinances for the Goode and Welfare of the saide Company and for the Government and Ordering of the saide Landes and Plantasion and the People inhabiting and to inhabit the same'. There is here unmistakably a definite power to legislate for and govern territory, which is not contemplated in the case of the London Company. It was understood in the widest sense by the people of Massachusetts when the charter was, by resolution taken in

London, with the acquiescence of the Crown, carried to the plantation, and despite the restriction that the laws and ordinances should not be contrary or repugnant to the laws of England, there was enacted a code of legislation which in certain vital respects went in severity towards dissident members of the community beyond English law. In the same spirit it was held in the colony that it was entitled to execute the fullest powers of penal jurisdiction, and it was not until 1683–4 that the Crown felt itself strong enough to secure the forfeiture of the charter on the score that the colony had usurped power not granted to it, as in the imposition of taxation on English imported goods.[1]

The powers of the London Company were manifestly unequal to the situation unless supplemented, but the Crown made good this defect by a further exercise of prerogative. For each voyage the Crown granted to the 'General' in command of the vessel the right to inflict punishment for capital offences, such as murder or mutiny, and to put in execution martial law.[2] At this time the extent and the authority of the Crown's right to authorize martial law was quite uncertain, and it was plainly necessary that there should be authority to maintain discipline during long voyages. The position of the Company itself became better defined in May 31st 1609 when James I granted a fresh charter making that of Elizabeth perpetual, subject, however, to the right of the Crown to determine it on three years' notice on proof of injury to the public. This was followed up by a royal grant of December 14th 1615, authorizing the Company itself to issue commissions to their captains with the important proviso that in capital cases a verdict must be found by a jury. The power, it will be seen, was intended to cover the case of the maintenance of discipline on board ships, but as soon as the Company established on the Indian coast trading settlements the question of maintaining discipline inevitably arose. In their transactions with the natives of India the Company's servants were of course subject in the absence of agreement to the contrary to the control of the native ruler, but it was not to be expected that the local authority would

[1] Keith, *Const. Hist. of First British Empire*, pp. 26–32, 101–8. Cf. *Advocate-General of Bengal v. Surnomoye Dossee* (*Ranee*) (1863), 2 Moo. P.C. N.S. 22.

[2] *Lellington's Case* (1616), Kaye, *Admin. of E.I. Co.*, p. 66.

concern itself with disputes arising among the members of a foreign settlement. The difference between the local systems of law, whether Hindu or Muhammadan, and English law was inevitably such as to render it natural that local authorities would not concern themselves with the disputes *inter se* of tolerated intruders.

James I, therefore, on February 4th 1623, extended the power of the Company by authorizing it to grant commissions to their presidents and chief officers for the punishment of offences committed by the Company's servants on land, subject to the same provision for trial by jury in capital cases, thus, at last, placing the Company in the position to provide more or less effectively for the due government of its servants, both on the high seas and in India.

It is unnecessary to consider the adverse conditions which in the later part of James's reign and in that of Charles I affected the prosperity of the Company, whose interests, as already noted, after 1623 were perforce concentrated on the Indian peninsula as a result of the greater strength of their Dutch rivals, backed as they were by the whole force of the State. The Company suffered also from the doubtful faith of Charles I, who granted to Sir William Courteen and his associates a licence to trade with the East Indies in 1635. The rival company is best known from its settlement at Assada in Madagascar; its success was limited, but it depressed severely the fortunes of the London Company. It was to Cromwell that the Company owed some alleviation of both external and internal difficulties. Their just claims against the Dutch were recognized by the treaty of Westminster 1654 which awarded them £85,000 compensation for the massacre of Amboyna and for the illegal exclusion from the trade with the Spice Islands. Moreover, the Dutch were required to restore the island of Pulo Run in the Bandas, which would have afforded the Company a renewed opportunity of competition in the trade in cloves. The island, however, was finally assigned to Holland by the Treaty of Peace of 1667. Moreover, Cromwell borrowed £50,000, which was never repaid. On the other hand, he imparted decisive strength to the Company by bringing about the merger with it of what was left of Courteen's association, the separate stocks of the Company being united in a single joint stock. Cromwell's charter is lost, but there is no doubt that it virtually, on October 19th 1657, reconstituted the Company in the form in which it was established by the charter of Charles II on April 3rd 1661.

Under the charter the Company was established on a regular permanent joint-stock basis, and voting power at its meetings was accorded to each member on the basis of one vote for every £500 subscribed by him. To the Company thus reorganized, and enjoying the royal favour largely through the influence of the famous economic expert Sir Josiah Child, the King accorded wide powers which recognized the extent—to be noted later—of the Company's effective authority in India. It was recognized that the Company owned fortresses and not merely trading factories. They were authorized to send ships of war, men, and ammunition for the security of their factories and to erect fortifications and supply them with provisions and ammunition free of export duty, and to transport volunteers to garrison them. They might choose commanders and officers and give them commission under their common seal or otherwise to make peace or war with any non-Christian people in any places of their trade for the advantage and benefit of the Company and their trade. They were to exercise power and command over their fortresses and to appoint governors and other officers. They might govern their employees in a legal and reasonable manner and punish them for misdemeanour and fine them for breach of orders.

The trading monopoly of the Company was reaffirmed; they might seize unlicensed persons and send them to England, where they might suffer such punishment as the laws would allow.

In addition to the authority over their servants a general judicial authority was given to the governor and council of each factory 'to judge all persons belonging to the said governor and Company or that shall live under them, in all causes, whether civil or criminal, according to the laws of this kingdom, and to execute judgment accordingly'. In any place where there was no governor the chief factor and council were empowered to send offenders for punishment, either to a place where there was a governor and council or to England. The same power to send persons as prisoners to England was accorded by the charter in the case of appeal being made against their sentence by persons in the employment of the Company, when punished by its officers. But even at this period[1] there already existed grave doubt as to the possibility of taking punitive proceedings in England in respect of actions happening outside that country.[2] The chief advantage of this provision lay in effect in the recognition which it accorded to the expulsion from India of unruly servants.

The extended authority, both political and judicial, accorded to the Company by the charter of Charles II was further reinforced on the occasion of the transfer to the control of the Company of the island of Bombay, which was ceded by Portugal by the marriage treaty of 1661. Portugal had held the island in full sovereignty and the King at first proposed to govern it as a royal ceded colony. But the King soon found that his new possession was likely to be more trouble than profit, and by charter of March 27th 1668, he transferred the island to the Company to be held of the Crown 'as of the Manor of East Greenwich in free and common Soccage' for the annual rent of ten pounds, which was actually paid to 1730. The prerogative of the Crown to govern a ceded colony was absolute,[3] subject to the international obligation of respect for the terms of cession, and the King accordingly was in the position to confer on the Company full sovereign rights over the territory and the inhabitants of the island as well as over the servants of the Company. The Company, therefore, were authorized through their general court or court of committees to make laws, orders, ordinances, and constitutions for the good government of the port and island and of the inhabitants thereof. They were authorized by their governors and other officers to exercise judicial authority. Moreover, they were to have power and authority of government and command in the island with power to repel any force which should attempt to inhabit precincts without licence or to annoy the inhabitants. The Company

[1] Cf. for Newfoundland, Keith, *Const. Hist. of First British Empire*, pp. 120, 171.

[2] Pointed out in *Young's case* in 1670 by the Company; *English Factories in India*, 1668–9, p. 253 n.1.

[3] *Calvin's case* (1608), 7 Co. Rep. 1; *Campbell* v. *Hall* (1774), 1 Cowp. 204; Keith, *Ind. Hist. Quart.*, xv., 57 ff.

were also empowered to take into their service such of the King's officers and soldiers on the island as might be willing to volunteer, thus forming the nucleus of the Company's first European regiment, or Bombay Fusiliers. Recognition of the control necessary in respect of military forces was accorded by empowering the principal governor of the island 'to use and exercise all such powers and authorities in cases of rebellion, mutiny, or sedition, or refusing to serve in wars, flying to the enemy, forsaking colours or ensigns, or other offences against law, custom, and discipline military, in as large and ample manner, to all intents and purposes whatsoever, as any captain-general of our army by virtue of his office has used and accustomed, and may or might lawfully do'.

The definite establishment of the political authority of the Company was further marked by the grant by charter of October 5th 1676 of the power of coining money at Bombay to be called rupees, pices, or such other name as the Company might think fit, such coinages to be current in the East Indies but not in England. The charter is of special interest as marking the complete sovereignty of the Crown over Bombay, and the necessity therefore of a royal charter for the exercise of the prerogative right of coinage. In Madras, on the other hand, a mint had already been established for the coinage of pagodas by the Company, but under the authority derived from the Company's Indian overlord.

Further extension of the Company's authority was shortly to be granted in consequence of the decision taken on the instigation of Sir Josiah Child to extend the power of the Company on the analogy of Dutch East Indies Company, and to create an Empire in India. By charter of August 9th 1683 the Company were given full power to declare and make peace and war with any of the heathen nations of Asia, Africa and America within the charter limits, to raise, arm, train, and muster such military forces as seemed requisite and necessary, and to execute martial law for the defence of their forts, places, and plantations against foreign invasion or domestic insurrection or rebellion. This remarkable grant was accompanied by a proviso reserving to the Crown the power of making peace and war 'when we shall be pleased to interpose our royal authority therein', and 'the sovereign right, powers, and dominion over all the forts, places, and plantations'. We have here expressed in unmistakable fashion the essential rule that the acquisition of sovereignty by subjects of the Crown is on behalf of the Crown and not in their own right.

The charter also made important provision regarding the judicial arrangements of the Company. It was clearly necessary that something should be done to strengthen judicial administration, and accordingly the charter provided for the establishment of a court of judicature to consist of one person learned in the civil law and two assistants to be appointed by the Company. The court was to determine cases of forfeiture of ships or goods for trading contrary to the charter, and mercantile and maritime cases concerning persons within the charter limits, and cases of trespasses, injuries, and wrongs done on the high seas or within the charter limits.

The favours of Charles II were renewed by James II in 1686 (April 12th) with certain additions. They were expressly authorized to appoint admirals and other sea-officers in any of their ships within the charter limits, with power for these officers to raise naval forces and exercise within their ships on the other side of the Cape of Good Hope in the time of open hostility with some other nation the law martial for the defence of their ships. The charter also accorded to the Company a general power within their forts to coin any species of money usually coined by native princes, such coin to be current within the charter limits. The judicial provisions for the charter of 1683 were likewise repeated, with some modifications. But a very important innovation was made in the decision to permit the Company to extend constitutional government in its Indian territories by the establishment of a municipal constitution for Madras. The decision must have been influenced by the precedent of Tangier, which had been granted such a constitution by Charles II in the hope of encouraging mercantile activity, and constitutionally the determination is noteworthy in two respects. It marks the development of the territorial character of the Company's rule in Madras, and it signalizes the readiness of the Crown to accord the fullest power to the Company. Normally so high a prerogative would have been exercised directly, but the Company had found that difficulties had arisen from the claims of officers appointed under the powers of the charters of 1683 and 1686 to judicial office to be royal rather than Company's officers, and accordingly the Company was authorized by the King on December 11th 1687 to grant a municipal charter to Madras. The grant was inseparably bound up with the new policy of the acquisition of political sovereignty and the creation of sources of revenue based thereon; it was intended largely to increase the revenues of Madras, and it was hoped that the creation of a municipality on a generous basis would facilitate the increase of taxation.

The project of Empire was rudely dissipated as soon as the Company in 1686 seriously matched its strength with that of the Mogul Empire, and the discredited Company was faced with a grave attack on its position as the result of the revolution of 1688, which was naturally prejudicial to the fortunes of a body which under the governorship of Sir Josiah Child since 1681 was identified in the public eye with the cause of reaction. Its legal privileges as regards monopoly of trade had just been exposed to judicial examination in the *cause célèbre* of *The East India Co.* v. *Sandys*,[1] in which the Company brought an action against Mr. Sandys on the ground that he had traded to the East Indies without their licence. This long-drawn-out case ended in a decisive affirmation by Jeffreys, L.C.J., of the validity of the monopoly. It could be supported on many grounds. The King, as a good Christian, must be deemed to be ever at war with infidels; it lay with him clearly to relax, if he chose in favour of the Company only, the normal rule that his subjects might not trade with the enemy. Or, more generally, it was the King's absolute right to regulate all import and export trade whatever, and this included the power to decide by whom it might be carried out. Stress was also laid on the fact that the legislation under James I (1624), which struck at monopolies, was so framed as not to affect the London Company's Indian trade. In fact, as noted above, the monopoly when it was granted could be supported on the broad ground of public advantage, and the bitterness of the attack upon it

[1] 10 St. Tr. 371. Cf. *Skinner* v. *East India Co.* (1667), Hargrave, Hale, *Jurisdiction of the House of Lords*, pp. ciii ff.

was largely due to the change in the political situation and the conflict of interested personalities. The rivals of the Company formed themselves into an association which struggled against the Old Company both in Parliament and in the City. Petitions were presented by both to Parliament, which resolved in 1691 that the trade with the East Indies was profitable to the nation, and that it would be best carried on by a joint-stock company with wide privileges. It seems clear that the view of the majority of the Commons favoured the maintenance of monopoly, but its enjoyment by a body in which the newly formed association would be merged in the existing Company; but this project failed owing to the unwillingness of Sir J. Child to accept as adequate the terms offered. The House of Commons therefore requested the Crown to give the requisite three years' notice of the determination of the charter, but before this could take effect the Company, apparently by oversight rather than of fixed purpose,[1] incurred a forfeiture by failing to pay a new tax imposed on joint-stock companies. The Crown was, however, not inclined to press matters against the Company, Sir J. Child being lavish in gifts to certain of its advisers, and on October 7th 1693 a charter was granted, confirming its existing charter but subject to the acceptance by the Company of such further regulation as might be imposed. The policy of the Government was directed towards giving effect to the wishes of the Commons, as indicated in the resolution of 1691 and the Bill founded thereon, which had failed through the intransigence of Sir J. Child.

Accordingly, a supplementary charter of November 11th 1693 opened the way to the wide increase of membership of the Company by adding £744,000 to the capital and forbidding any individual to subscribe more than £10,000. To prevent the gathering of voting power into the hands of a clique, while one vote was given for each £1,000 subscribed, the maximum voting power was restricted to ten votes. The qualification of the governor and deputy governor was fixed at £4,000, that of each committee at £1,000. A subsequent charter of April 13th 1698 varied these rules; it reduced the amount required for a vote to £500, and the total votes of any member to five, but

[1] As suggested by Hunter, *Hist. of British India*, ii, 310.

doubled the qualification of the committees. By a charter of September 28th 1694 the principle of rotation of office was made compulsory. Neither governor nor deputy governor was to continue in office for more than two years, eight new committees must be elected each year, and, to increase the control of the general court of members, it must be specially summoned to meet within eight days on the request of six members holding £1,000 stock. The renewal of the Company's powers was expressly made subject to the maintenance of the right of the Crown to determine its privileges on three years' notice.

Under the new charters the way was open for the introduction of new members, and it was provided that any merchant might join the Company on payment of five pounds. But naturally these changes left the former members in effective control, and their rivals were in no wise satisfied. The Company was far from conciliatory; it immediately put its renewal of authority to the test by arranging for the detention of the *Redbridge*, while lying in the Thames, ostensibly bound for Spain but alleged to be meditating a voyage beyond the Cape of Good Hope. This action so irritated the Commons that on January 19th 1694 it resolved that 'all the subjects of England have equal right to trade to the East Indies unless prohibited by Act of Parliament'. A resolution of Parliament, of course, was not necessarily law, still less that of one House, but the view of the Commons naturally encouraged the interlopers to persevere in their trade, while the Company urged its local representatives to exercise to the full their rights to seize offending vessels under the charter.

The conflict thus raging was determined by the power of the purse. Mindful of the precedent of Cromwell's raid on the assets of the Company, Montagu, the Chancellor of the Exchequer, sought aid thence, to find that he could have £700,000 as the return for a legalized monopoly. This was insufficient, and in any case Montagu was on the side of those who desired to favour the plans of the new association. Accordingly, he arranged for the issue of a loan for £2,000,000 at 8 per cent. Subscribers could be individuals or corporate bodies, but all were to be united in a new corporation, the

General Society, each member of which was to be free to trade to India to an extent not exceeding the amount he had advanced to the Government. This part of the plan met the views of those opponents of the Company who desired in place thereof the establishment of a regulated company on the model of the Levant Company. But the view of the Commons that a joint-stock company was necessary was also provided for; all or part of the members of the General Society might unite under a royal charter for trading in common, surrendering the right to separate trade.

The scheme was rendered operative by an Act,[1] following the precedent set by Montagu in 1694 when the Bank of England was established in consideration of a loan of £1,200,000, and by two charters. The first of these, dated September 3rd 1698, incorporated the General Society as a regulated company; the second, September 5th 1698, incorporated most of the members of the Society as a joint-stock company, 'the English Company trading to the East Indies'. The English Company was to have a monopoly of joint-stock trading, subject until September 29th 1701 to the concurrent right of the London Company, whose rights were to terminate on notice of three years. But the Old Company had secured £315,000 of the stock issued, and was the largest single holder in the English Company; its position in India was entrenched, its influence at home very strong, and in 1700 it procured an Act of Parliament[2] permitting it to continue trading until the improbable event of the repayment by the Government of the £2,000,000 loan. It was therefore in a position to negotiate on advantageous terms with the New Company. Lord Godolphin exerted his influence and the authority of the Crown to secure agreement, and on July 22nd 1702 an Indenture Tripartite between the Queen and the Companies attested an accord. The Old Company was to maintain its separate existence for seven years, but thereafter to surrender its charter. In the meantime the trade of the two companies was to be carried on jointly in the name of the English Company by twenty-four managers, half selected by either Company, while the English Company was to be renamed 'The United Company of Merchants of England

[1] 9 & 10 Will. III, c. 44.

[2] 11 & 12 Will. III, c. 4.

trading to the East Indies'. This body was to operate under the terms of the charter of September 5th 1698, and it was only by the Charter Act of 1833 that it received the shorter name of the East India Company, by which, however, it is convenient to designate the united body.

The agreement proved to have certain obscurities affecting chiefly the financial relations of the two companies, and it was necessary for intervention by the Crown and Parliament to adjust the issues. By an Act of 1708[1] the Company was required to advance £1,200,000 without interest, making in effect the debt of the Crown £3,200,000 at 5 per cent, and was given in return the continuance of its privileges at least until March 25th 1729. Matters in dispute were to be arbitrated by Godolphin, whose award was issued on September 29th. On May 7th 1709 the Queen accepted the surrender of the Old Company's charters, and the United Company attained sole control, the managers becoming the first directors under its charter. Its position was further strengthened by an Act of 1711,[2] which provided that its rights were not to determine on the repayment of the £2,000,000 loan, and successive Acts[3] extended the duration of its rights to 1780 at the cost of further loans and reduction of interest on existing loans. At the same time Parliament fulfilled its duty of protecting the Company's monopoly now legally operative by strengthening from time to time the legislation penalizing interlopers,[4] and by countering the effort of the Emperor Charles VI to maintain the Ostend Company chartered by him in 1722 as a rival in the Indian trade.[5]

The constitution of the Company as defined by the charter of 1698 was essentially similar to that of the Old Company, though by adoption of more modern terminology the committees were now styled directors. The qualification for directors was fixed at £2,000 stock; election was to be annual by the general court, in which only those with £500 stock could vote, no member having more than one vote. The general court must meet at least four times a year; a special meeting

[1] 6 Anne, c. 71. [2] 10 Anne, c. 35.
[3] 3 Geo. II, cc. 14, 30; 17 Geo. II, c. 17; 23 Geo. II, c. 22.
[4] 5 Geo. I, c. 21; 7 Geo. I, st. 1, c. 21; 9 Geo. I, c. 26; 5 Geo. II, c. 29.
[5] Roberts, *Hist. of Brit. India*, pp. 64–9.

must be convened by the directors if requested by at least nine members duly qualified to vote. The carrying on of the business of the Company was entrusted to the court of directors, subject to the by-laws, constitutions, orders, rules or directions of the general court. That court had also power to make reasonable by-laws, constitutions, orders and ordinances for the purposes of the Company, including the raising of money, the declaration of dividends, and the good government of the trade and of the agents, factors, and other officers concerned in the same, with power to inflict reasonable punishment by imprisonment, fines, or the like for breaches of their enactments. But their by-laws must not be contrary to the laws of England and must be made in due form.

At the same time the charter contemplated the exercise of sovereign powers in India by the Company, for it continued the powers given by the Stuarts of rule and government of their forts, factories, and plantations, with authority to appoint governors and officers who should as directed by the Company raise, train and muster military forces for the defence of their forts, factories, and plantations, 'the sovereign power and dominion over all the said forts, places, and plantations, to us, our heirs and successors, being always secured'. The charter further continued in operation the provisions of the charters of 1683 and 1686 for the erection of courts of judicature to deal with specified classes of causes. In essence the New Company was maintained by William III in the powers of the Old, and this régime remained unaltered under Anne and her Hanoverian successors.

Changes, however, were introduced in the judiciary, as a result, it appears,[1] of the fact that the Company in England found itself liable to suit in certain cases in part as the result of the non-existence of fully organized judiciaries in the settlements. The Company had authorized the local councils to take possession of the assets of deceased servants and to dispose of them for cash for the benefit of their heirs, but difficulties sometimes arose from this practice, as in the case of a certain Mr. Woolaston, who brought several actions in respect of the estate of his deceased son. Another cause of difficulty was the

[1] Fawcett, *First Century of British Justice in India*, pp. 215, 216.

assertion of the right to attach the goods of servants for alleged debts to the Company; this led not rarely to Chancery causes in which the action of the local councils was censured as arbitrary and illegal and decree given against the Company where on balance the servant was creditor of the Company. Hence, apparently, the Company changed its attitude from that which it had adopted under Charles II and James II. It no longer insisted that courts should be established under its authority and control, but secured a royal charter of September 24th 1726 which authorized the setting up of mayor's courts in the three chief settlements, Madras, Bombay, and Calcutta, and gave them testamentary jurisdiction, which would be recognized in English courts. Moreover, a regular system of appeal from these courts to the governor and council, and thence to the King in Council marked, together with the regulation of criminal jurisdiction and the use of juries, the definite establishment of justice on a duly ordered basis. Of equal significance was the authority given to the governors and councils of the settlements to make by-laws and ordinances for the several corporations and to impose reasonable pains and penalties in case of breach, provided that the by-laws and penalties were not contrary to the laws of England, and had been duly confirmed by the court of directors before they took effect. The Crown thus established in India itself a subordinate power of legislation, which was destined to supersede the authority in this regard vested in the Company itself. Plainly in the long run it was desirable that legislation for Indian conditions should be enacted in India, subject to the control of the Company, or later the Crown, but it is noteworthy that the Company was destined to lose that power of legislation which it at first appeared to be given, and which corresponded to the power of the Crown to legislate by Order in Council for conquered or ceded colonies.

On the other hand, the charters expressly recognized once more the right of the Company to appoint generals and other officers for their forces on sea and on land, with authority to raise such forces and in time of war or open hostility to exercise martial law. It seems doubtful if this repetition of existing authority was wholly satisfactory to the Company, as it had complained of the lack of authority to keep the military forces which served it in due order.

The charter of 1726 was put in abeyance by the French conquest of Madras in 1746, and to remove doubts of its validity on the recovery of the town by the treaty of Aix-la-Chapelle of 1748 it was surrendered and a new charter issued in 1753 (January 8th) which embodied certain improvements on the former instrument. The charters for Bombay and Calcutta, therefore, were also surrendered and replaced. But of much greater constitutional importance was the decisive aid accorded by Parliament to the Company as regards the control of its forces in 1754.[1] The need for such action had become acute with the development of an Indian army as opposed to the small European forces which had been controlled by the Company. In 1748 a small force of sepoys was raised at Madras, following the example set by France four years earlier, while a European force was formed from sailors borrowed from the British ships on the coast and from men smuggled on board the Company's ships sailing from England, both bodies of troops being placed under the command of Major Lawrence with a commission from the Company. Clearly the control of such forces demanded further powers than those given by the charters to the Company, but in England itself it had been made clear that the Crown had no prerogative power to govern effectively troops in time of peace. Hence recourse to Parliament was necessary, and the Act of 1754 made provision for the Indian forces of the Company on lines similar to those of the English Mutiny Acts. The Act laid down penalties for mutiny, desertion, and other military offences; it permitted the Company, on the authority of the King, to authorize their governors and councils and commanders-in-chief to set up courts martial for the punishment of military offences. Further, the King might make articles of war for the better government of the Company's forces. It is significant also that, at the same time as these wide powers were conferred, the precaution was taken of making oppression and other offences committed by the presidents or councils in India cognizable and punishable in England, a provision which, if of minor practical efficacy,

[1] 27 Geo. II, c. 9. The Company had issued Military Regulations in 1748.

was at least testimony to the feeling of responsibility for the due government of India by the Company.

The successes of Clive, culminating in the battle of Plassey in 1757, evoked further royal grants. The recovery of Calcutta had been effected by the co-operation of the Company's forces from Madras with the British Navy, and it had been agreed by those commanding to divide their booty into two halves, the one of which was retained by the captors, the other deposited to await the King's pleasure. By charter of September 19th 1757 the moiety of booty reserved was granted by the Crown to the Company, save only that any part thereof which was captured from the King's subjects should be returned on payment of salvage. A more important charter of January 14th 1758 established generally the principle that the Company might keep any booty taken in wars legitimately waged in the charter limits against the enemies of the Company or the King, subject to the right of the King to distribute the booty at his discretion when royal forces took part in the operations concerned. It was further provided that the Company[1] might by treaty with any Indian prince or government restore, cede, or dispose of any fortresses, districts, or territories acquired by conquest from any Indian prince; in the case of territories acquired from the subjects of any European power the licence of the Crown was made requisite for any dealing of this kind.

These charters are of special interest, as they rest on the doctrine that acquisition of territory by conquest necessarily vested not merely the sovereignty but also the property therein in the Crown, while peaceful acquisition gave the Crown the sovereignty only but not proprietary rights.[2] But it was felt proper to grant the right to cede conquered territory as a logical and necessary complement of the right to make war and peace which the Company had enjoyed under successive charters.

2. THE COMPANY AND THE NATIVE PRINCES

It was natural that the Company should direct its first endeavour to establishing trade relations with India to the

[1] *Lachmi Narain* v. *Partab Singh* (1878), I.L.R. 2 All. 1; *Damodhar Gordhan* v. *Deoram Kanji* (1876), 1 App. Cas. 332.

[2] Opinion of law officers, Dec. 24th 1757 (*C.H.I.*, v, 593).

Spice Islands, and that it should have sought to follow the line of action suggested by the foundation of the Levant Company. That Company was established to take advantage of the concessions granted by the Turkish Sultan in 1579,[1] which in effect exempted the servants of the Company from local jurisdiction and authorized them to manage under their own law their relations *inter se*. Such a system was almost inevitable under the circumstances of the time, when even in Europe the idea of a territorial law applicable to every person within a given area was only slowly becoming definite. Both Muhammadan and Hindu law were definitely religious in origin and character and could not easily or with any justice be applied to European merchants, and the native princes had no interest in insisting on attempting to apply them. The Europeans might, without injury to the native State be allowed to govern themselves according to their own laws. Obviously a local ruler could not be expected to tolerate disorderly conduct or injuries inflicted on his subjects, and it is significant that the charter of 1605 of James I to the Levant Company avoids ascribing criminal jurisdiction proper to the Company's consuls in the East, and this branch of their jurisdiction seems to have been of later development.[2]

In the light of these facts it is easy to understand the terms of the charter of privileges which Captain Lancaster obtained from the King of Achin on his first voyage. It confers on the English traders the privilege of enjoying their own laws with exemption from compulsion to accept the local law or faith. It authorizes disposal of property by will or on intestacy by the law declared by the chief of the factory, thus excluding the regular practice of the confiscation by the sovereign of the property of a merchant dying in his territory. It authorizes the chief factor to execute justice, both criminal and civil, as between the merchants and servants, but it assumes that offences committed against natives will be punished by the local authorities, merely exempting the goods of the Company from seizure as punishment for the misdeeds of their servants.

[1] Cf. *The Laconia* (1863), 2 Moo. P.C. N.S. 161; and *The Indian Chief* (1800) 3 Rob. Adm. at p. 28; *Advocate-General of Bengal* v. *Surnomoye Dossee* (1863) 9 Moo. Ind. App. at 428, 429.

[2] Cf. Wood, *History of the Levant Company* (1935), pp. 39 ff.

The Company, however, was not fated to effect much in the Spice Islands, and in India its contacts were with subordinates of the Mogul Emperor, who were not in the least inclined to treat on the basis of equality with the English merchants, especially as the influence of the Portuguese was exerted energetically against them. Hence the effort of James I through William Hawkins to obtain permission for regular trade from the Emperor ended in 1611 in failure, though Jahangir had at first shown much favour to Hawkins during his stay at Agra. Force, however, extorted local respect, and the authorities at Surat agreed to grant trading privileges which an imperial firman confirmed. A more important effort to secure a treaty settlement was made by the King through Sir Thomas Roe, sent as ambassador in 1615–19.[1] He found that the Emperor was not prepared to conclude a treaty, and in the end he had to content himself with obtaining what was requisite in the way of permission to trade and to manage the affairs of the factory independently of local interference, in the form of a grant from Prince Khurram, the viceroy of Gujarat. Failure to effect more was inevitable, so weak was the Company, and so engaged in conflicts with the Portuguese and later in disputes with its former allies, the Dutch. It was not therefore surprising that Roe found it impossible to secure leave to settle in Bengal or Sind, and that the first settlements had to be confined to Surat, Agra, Ahmadabad, and Broach, the chief factor at Surat being given authority over the other settlements and the style of president, while the control of trade with the Red Sea ports and Persia fell also under him. Further expansion became possible with the growing decline of Portuguese power and influence at the Mogul Court as the result of Dutch attacks. In 1635 the Viceroy at Goa gladly concluded with the English president at Surat a truce, which was confirmed by the Anglo-Portuguese treaty of 1642, concluded after the emancipation of Portugal in 1640 from Spanish control. Finally Cromwell in 1654 extracted from the Portuguese Government a formal recognition of the right of trade with Portuguese ports in the East Indies, and the marriage treaty of

[1] *The Embassy of Sir Thomas Roe* (ed. Foster); Foster, *The English Factories in India*, 1618–21, p. viii.

Charles II in 1661 guaranteed Portugal against the loss of its few remaining possessions to the Dutch. Cromwell also in 1654 secured definite peace with Holland, though too late to save the English share in the Spice Islands. Pulo Run was surrendered in 1667, Bantam in 1682, and Bencoolen in Sumatra, settled in 1686, was handed over under the treaty of 1824 when Malacca became British.

Though Surat figured largely in the history of English trade on the coast, the Company was not destined to secure territorial authority there. Its operations had to be carried on on the basis of the permission of the local authorities confirmed by the Emperor and subject to imperial sovereignty. The same conditions prevailed within those areas in which the Emperor had effective authority and even in the lesser Muhammadan states. The first real territorial authority which was acquired in India was obtained from a Hindu prince. In 1611 the Company, following the example of the Dutch, had started a factory at Masulipatam, the chief port of the kingdom of Golconda. But trade advantages were found to be superior in the Hindu territory to the south, and in 1626 a subsidiary settlement was formed at Armagaon, which was the first fortified post of the Company in India. But it proved unsatisfactory, and in 1639 a grant was obtained from the local chief of Wandiwash, who empowered the English Company to build a fortress, to mint money, and to govern Madras, on condition that half the customs and revenues of the port should be paid to the grantor.[1] The English removed from Armagaon in 1640, and in September 1641 the new station, named Fort St. George, superseded Masulipatam as the English headquarters on the Coromandel coast. In 1645–7 the surrounding district was overrun by the forces of Golconda, but the grant made by the Hindu raja was continued in operation by the new ruler. The division of the customs, however, caused difficulty; in 1658 it was agreed that an annual payment of 380 pagodas should be accepted as the King's share. In 1672 the amount was increased to 1,200 pagodas, when it was expressly laid down that no local authority should be maintained at Madras, but that it should be wholly under the English with unrestricted power of command, government, and justice.[2] This grant remained effective

[1] Love, *Vestiges of Old Madras*, i, 17. [2] Ibid., i, 345.

when in 1687 Golconda was conquered by Aurangzib. The position therefore was that the English power of government was plenary, but that the sovereignty of the Fmpire was fully recognized by the payment of a substantial quit rent. The Company obtained also in 1693 the grant of three villages adjoining Madras, and under the administration of Thomas Pitt five more were added in 1708, but were resumed by local officials in 1711. In 1717, however, confirmation of the right to these villages was obtained by the mission of John Surman[1] to the Emperor Farrukhsiyar, who also confirmed the Company's established privilege of freedom from dues in the province of Hyderabad. The quit rent of Madras remained payable and the Emperor's supremacy was attested by the pattern of the rupees, which the Mogul authorities permitted the Company to coin at Madras.

The situation in Madras, with the decline of the authority of the Emperor, became more and more in effect one of dependency on the local representative of the Mogul, the nawab of the Carnatic, who was in theory subordinate to the subadar of the Deccan.[2] The outbreak of war with France resulted in the conquest of Madras in defiance of the prohibition of the nawab, and though the latter's position was recognized by Dupleix the real control rested in French hands. On the restoration of the town by treaty with France in 1748, the Company might no doubt have asserted its full sovereignty, but they contented themselves with his renouncing, in 1752, the quit rent, whereupon the English tenure of Madras and the limited area around its walls became absolute, but the rest of the country remained under the nominal sovereignty of the Emperor and the effective rule of the nawab, whose power, however, was essentially dependent on his support by the Company.

In Bombay, on the other hand, as we have seen, the Company had obtained from the King, who was its absolute sovereign by virtue of its cession by Portugal, full powers of government, and Bombay was indisputably British territory.

From Masulipatam trade had been carried to the seaports of Orissa and factories established in 1633 at Hariharpur and

[1] Wilson, *Early Annals of Bengal*, ii, pt. ii.

[2] The Nizam-ul-mulk, 'regulator of the state', Asaf Jah in 1724 had withdrawn to Hyderabad to establish a dynasty there nominally under the Emperor.

Balasore, while in 1650–1 a settlement was made at Hugli and later extended to Patna and Kasimbazar. But no effective sovereignty could be obtained. The agents of the Company had to content themselves with efforts to secure exemption from transit duties and customs in consideration of an annual payment of 3,000 rupees, and in 1656 they obtained from Shah Shuja a grant freeing them from demands on these accounts. The factors were especially interested in the concession which applied to their private trade as well as to that of the Company, while the latter bore the burden of the payments to the local authorities. Efforts to obtain imperial confirmation of the governor's grant met with comparatively little success, though in 1678 apparently he renewed the grant with the approval of the Emperor, and two years later a firman was obtained from Aurangzib himself. The failure of the local officials to pay respect to this grant and the interference with the Company's trade in the important commodity of saltpetre were a prime cause of the determination in 1686 of the Company on the instigation of Sir Josiah Child to make war on the Mogul. The result of this rash enterprise was the realization of the weakness of the Company, and on the initiative of the Bombay authorities peace was restored in 1690; and in February 1691 an imperial grant was made of freedom from all dues in consideration of the payment of 3,000 rupees per annum in lieu. Under this pacification the English settlement was established in August 1690 at Sutanati, the site of the future Calcutta. In 1696 a local rebellion afforded the factors an excuse for fortifying the factory, and in 1698 the Company purchased at the cost of 1,200 rupees a year the right of zamindar over the three villages of Sutanati, Calcutta, and Govindpur. The fortified factory was named Fort William in honour of the King, and in 1700 became the seat of a presidency. As zamindar the Company was entitled to collect the revenue and exercise civil judicial authority. It appears also that by the judicious exercise of bribery the Company was able to exercise criminal jurisdiction over Muhammadan and Hindu subjects of the Empire without interference either by the local faujdar of Hugli or his superior authority, the nazim at Murshidabad.

The uncertain and not wholly satisfactory condition of

English rights in India as they existed in 1698 led to an effort by the New Company to establish relations on a more regular basis. The directors dispatched on a mission to Aurangzib with the authority of the Crown a special ambassador, Sir William Norris. It was contemplated that he should obtain from the Emperor formal concessions for trade and the right to exercise jurisdiction over their settlements, as in the case of the Ottoman dominion. For this purpose the representatives of the New Company were given rank as King's consuls and claimed authority as such over all Englishmen in India, including the representatives of the Old Company. The latter inevitably used their influence with the Indian authorities to defeat the efforts of Sir William Norris, while they carried on a bitter rivalry at their headquarters with the new-comers. The net result was the complete failure of the mission of Sir William Norris, who died *en route* home in 1702, and the abandonment once more of the effort to assimilate conditions in India to those prevailing in the Ottoman territories.

The United Company, therefore, had to content itself with the process of obtaining concessions by imperial grant in lieu of the formal treaty aimed at by Norris, and in practice each presidency normally had to negotiate with the local authorities separately. But in 1714–17 a definite and not unsuccessful effort was made by the mission of Surman already referred to, to secure from the Emperor a general settlement. Surman in fact procured from Farrukhsiyar three firmans addressed to the rulers of Gujarat, Hyderabad, and Bengal. A composition of 10,000 rupees was accepted for customs and dues at Surat; the rupees coined at Bombay by the Company were to be valid in the imperial dominions. The position at Madras was regularized as above described, and the right to trade free of dues in Bengal subject to the annual payment of 3,000 rupees was established. Moreover, they were to be allowed to settle where else they pleased and to acquire fresh villages in the vicinity of Calcutta. But at this time the value of an imperial firman had come to be very slight with the decline of imperial power, and it proved impossible to secure from the local governors, whose position approached more and more closely to that of effective sovereigns, the villages which it was desired to acquire. Nor was it possible even to secure the right to mint coins. But a vital change was effected by the events which led to the defeat of Siraj-ud-daula and his acceptance in February 1757 of a formal treaty which confirmed the privileges of the Company, and gave it the right to coin money and to fortify its town, which had proved fatally exposed to capture. The position was further consolidated under the terms[1] on which Mir Jafar was raised to the nawabship of Bengal. He was required to recognize English sovereignty in Calcutta; to grant lands sufficient to enable the Company to maintain a military force; to meet the cost of the troops used to support him; and to accept the residence of a servant of the Company at his durbar. The twenty-four parganas, whose acquisition had been approved by the firman of 1717, now at last passed into the hands of the Company as zamindar,[2] paying a quit rent to the nawab who in 1759 assigned it to Clive. The Company naturally took exception to this abnormal position under which they paid rent to their own servant, but, after stopping payment in 1763, they sanctioned the resumption of the grant, first until 1775 and then for ten years more.

The substitution of Mir Kasim by a fresh accord as nawab in 1760 brought further territorial powers to the Company, which received the districts of Burdwan, Midnapur, and Chittagong free of all payment. It must, therefore, be assumed that by this date the sovereignty over Calcutta, the twenty-four parganas, and the three districts, was definitely British, subject to whatever value might be attached to the vague claims of the Emperor to be paramount sovereign in India.[3]

3. THE GOVERNMENT OF THE COMPANY'S SETTLEMENTS AND TERRITORIES

(a) THE EXECUTIVE GOVERNMENT

In the early days of the activities of the Company there was little need for elaborate organization. The Company had

[1] Keith, *Speeches and Documents on Indian Policy*, i, 10 ff.

[2] The Emperor confirmed the nawab's grant in 1759, and again in 1765 (ibid., i, 24, 25).

[3] Cf. Lord Stowell in *The Indian Chief* (1800), 3 Rob. Adm., at p. 28; *Mayor of Lyons* v. *East India Co.* (1836), 1 Moo. Ind. App. 175, 272, 273.

merely trading stations without territorial sovereignty, and it was only gradually that wider authority came to be exercised at Madras, Bombay, and Calcutta under the varying conditions dictated by the different sources of its power. The general principle of the control of the business of the factories was the rule of a council, the chief member of which was styled governor or president. The policy of the Company varied from time to time regarding the principle on which control should be exercised. Surat and Bantam were at first selected to be the chief centres of the Company's affairs, other factories being made dependent upon them, but this arrangement was later varied, until in the period of depression in 1657 the determination was taken to have but one presidency, Surat, to which Fort St. George, Bantam, Hugli, and Persia alike should be made subordinate. Surat, however, suffered from the disadvantage that territorial power there could not be obtained, and accordingly, when the policy of securing political authority was resolved upon, it was decided to terminate the dependence of Bombay on Surat. In 1686 John Child, who had been made president of Surat and governor of Bombay four years earlier, was created captain-general, admiral and commander-in-chief of the Company's forces in all its possessions as well as director-general of all mercantile affairs. His headquarters were normally to be Bombay, which from May 1687 superseded Surat as the headquarters of the western presidency, but he was empowered to visit Madras and Bengal to regulate affairs there. It was expressly explained that the high titles were intended to give the Company's general the same pre-eminence and authority as was enjoyed by the general of the Dutch Company at Batavia, whose political policy was being adopted by the London Company. On the failure of Sir John Child's efforts and the disasters in Bengal, the Company's projects were modified. After Child's death the post of captain-general and commander-in-chief was given in 1693 to Sir John Goldsborough, but his headquarters were fixed at Madras, while Sir John Gayer was to act as his lieutenant-general and governor of Bombay. Gayer in 1694 succeeded to the style of general on Goldsborough's death, but remained at Bombay, while Higginson, president at Madras, became lieutenant-general.

The latter title, however, disappeared in 1698 when the redoubtable Thomas Pitt was appointed governor of Madras, and, after being held by successive governors of Bombay, the title general was dropped in 1715, when the new post of president and governor of Bombay was created. In 1700 the independence of Calcutta was recognized by the appointment of a president and governor of Fort William, terminating the vicissitudes of the supreme control of the Bengal posts. The three presidencies now stood on a like footing, subject only to the co-ordinating power of the Company, which naturally at so great a distance was able to do little to bring about a concerted policy.

The position of the president differed considerably from that of the governor of a Crown colony, because collegiate rule was encouraged by the Company, and the president was not normally entitled to overrule his colleagues. The number of members of council varied from time to time and place to place. In 1674, for instance, Madras had a governor who was first member of council, a book-keeper, a warehouse-keeper, and a customer who collected customs, rents, and taxes. In Bombay the president was aided by an accountant, a warehouse-keeper, who registered the European goods sold and the Eastern goods purchased; a purser marine who gave an account of imports and exports, paid porters and seamen, and supervised ships' stores; and a secretary who recorded proceedings, wrote letters, and kept the Company's seal. The higher officers of the Company, who constituted the council, had normally worked their way up from the position of writers through that of factor, obtained after five years' service, to senior factor, reached after three years' further service, and to that of merchant. Naturally for effective action and decisions such a body was seldom well suited, and Clive had to insist, when faced with the task of government, on being given effective authority to act without the necessity of carrying with him the whole body of the council at Fort William. It is significant of the Company's distrust of autocracy in any form that the original resolution taken by the Madras Council on the eve of the dispatch of Clive to Calcutta would have associated with him two deputies to constitute a council to determine the political conduct of the expedition. The project was dropped simply because of the opposition to it of a member of the Calcutta council, whose objection was based on the wholesale supersession of that body, with the fortunate result that sole authority was given by Madras to Clive. Fortunately, as a forerunner of the later difficulties between Crown and Company's officers, Colonel Adlercron, commander of the royal regiment which had come to India with Admiral Watson, had disqualified himself from the command of the expedition to relieve Calcutta by refusal to accept in advance the division of the prospective plunder on the basis laid down in the Company's instructions, and to undertake to return when required by the Madras Council.

The absence of authority by the president was probably on the whole disadvantageous to the interests of the Company. This was revealed in a marked form in 1762, when Vansittart entered into an agreement with Mir Kasim to regulate on an equitable basis the dues on the internal trade. The agreement authorized the officers of the nawab to determine disputes, and this deprivation of the right of acting as judges in their own cause induced the council to reject an arrangement in itself meritorious and led to the conflict with Mir Kasim and his replacement by Mir Jafar.

The control exercised by the chief authorities in the presidencies over the factories subordinate to them is shown by the correspondence to have been close and continuous, as in the case of Bombay, when its government was supervised by the president and council at Surat. But the presidencies themselves were subject to a very close control by the Company, so far as that could be exercised, through the medium of correspondence. The Company had, of course, the supreme right of dismissing or removing from the offices which they occupied any of its officers as well as of punishing them. Moreover, it could remove from India any persons engaging in trade without its licence, and so could prevent dismissed officers from trading after their dismissal. But it was difficult to make effective the exercise of its powers, and it was by no means always possible for the Company to secure the effective carrying out of its directions.

(*b*) JURISDICTION AND LEGISLATION IN BOMBAY

Great constitutional interest attaches itself to the judicial arrangements operative in this period, the changes in which display a gradual evolution of the rule of law in the affairs of India. The system can be followed most clearly in the case of Bombay, because Bombay was, from the first, subject to the unfettered sovereignty of the British Crown and judicial arrangements were not affected by derivation from two sources.

In the first years of Bombay under the direct control of the Crown the chief concern of the government was military protection, for the island was threatened by the hostility of Aurangzib and the Maratha Sivaji and also from the Portuguese and Dutch settlements. In these circumstances it was natural that the island should have been subject to martial law regulations, which could properly be enforced under conditions akin to war proper. Apparently those which were in operation were adopted from the set issued by Peterborough for the garrison of Tangier in 1662. The adaptation may have been made by Henry Gary, who became governor of the island on the death of Sir Gervase Lucas in 1667. Otherwise the island appears to have continued under the existing Portuguese law. The island had been since its cession by the Sultan of Gujarat in 1534 under Portuguese rule, and it would have been difficult for the governor, H. Cooke, who received it from the Portuguese in 1665 to introduce forthwith English law. As he explained on December 23rd 1665, the maintenance of the civil law gave great satisfaction, as the Portuguese on the mainland had often possessions on the island and vice versa. The garrison was governed by martial law, and liberty of conscience was accorded to all persons. Prior to the occupation judicial cases had not been dealt with in the island but carried to the judge at Thana or to the higher court at Bassein. Cooke therefore had to establish a justice of the peace to examine causes with the bailiff and to report to Cooke, who gave the final decision, a rough and ready mode of procedure which resulted in the probably well-founded accusation that Cooke accepted bribes. His successor Lucas did not alter his arrangements, but put a stop to the exercise by Portuguese landlords of powers of coercion over their tenants, taking upon himself, as royal governor, sole power of punishment, either in his own right or through the justices of the peace. Gary, his successor, also tried cases personally, but he urged the appointment of a judge advocate trained in the civil law. It seems, however, that the courts martial dealt not only with Englishmen and military offenders, but might also punish natives accused of capital offences, such as wife murder.

The maintenance of the Portuguese law was of course entirely in accord with English law in its application to conquered and ceded territories, the rule being as recognized in *Calvin's case*[1] by the judges of James I and asserted as indisputable by Lord Mansfield in *Campbell* v. *Hall*[2] that the laws of the conquered or ceded territory remained unaltered until replaced by the command of the sovereign, so far, of course, as such laws were not incompatible with the substitution of English for Portuguese sovereignty. It is curious, therefore, that in 1845 it was judicially held[3] that neither Portuguese law nor Portuguese courts survived in Bombay after the session of 1661.

With the transfer of the island by the charter of 1668 to the government of the Company the position was completely changed. The charter, as already noted, gave to the Company through the court of committees power to legislate and by their governors and other officers to exercise judicial authority, and it was required that their laws should be consonant to reason and not repugnant or contrary to the laws of England. Moreover, they were to be as near as may be agreeable to such laws, and the courts and their proceedings were to be like those used and established in England. It is clear, therefore, that the Crown did not contemplate any deviation from the principle which had been acted upon in the case of Jamaica in 1661–4[4] that English law and English judicial procedure should be applied to a ceded territory.

The orders from the Company reached Sir George Oxenden, president of Surat, in September 1668, and he himself visited

[1] 7 Co. Rep., 1 *a*.

[2] (1774), 1 Cowp. 204.

[3] *Advocate-General* v. *Richmond*, Perry, Or. Cas. 573; cf. *De Silveira* v. *Texeira*, Morley, *Digest*, i, 349.

[4] Keith, *Const. Hist. of First British Empire*, pp. 127–31.

the island in January 1669. In accordance with instructions from the Company he established the executive government under a deputy governor and council, but the current belief that he enacted codes for the civil and military administration of the island rests on a misunderstanding. The laws and ordinances of war which then were operative in the island had clearly been in force before his arrival, and so far from enacting them he expressed grave doubt as to their effectiveness and warned the deputy governor of Bombay, who claimed that they authorized a court martial to pass sentence of death on a military officer for alleged mutinous conduct, that the powers given rested only on the prerogative and that a man might be prosecuted for condemnation by court martial. Oxenden's doubts were natural. No state of war proper could be held then to exist, and the extent of the right of the Crown to authorize punishment of such offences as mutiny or desertion by courts martial in time of peace was wholly doubtful.[1] James II had in 1685 asserted the right to punish drastically by courts martial so long as the insurrection of Monmouth was raging, but he had instructed recourse to the civil courts the moment warfare had ceased, and this was in accord with the spirit of the Petition of Right of 1628 and the contemporary debates in the House of Commons, which showed that it was held in legal circles under Charles I that even soldiers under the common law could not in time of peace be dealt with by martial law, a system essentially intended for the government of armed forces when war was raging. It might be claimed that the authority of the Crown was greater when outside England, but Oxenden's caution was justified, nor was it lessened by the fact that so far as he knew the laws in question had not been formally issued by the King. Despite his objection, however, he could not absolutely prohibit their use; a revised edition which mitigated the extreme severity of the original articles, the death penalty being excised from some twenty-five articles, was prepared apparently in Bombay and accepted by the Company. It continued to be operative for many years. At an uncertain date there were adopted, and were enforced in 1729 at any rate, selections from the articles of war which were

[1] Anson, *The Crown* (ed. Keith), ii, 203.

issued in 1717 in England under the authority of the Mutiny Act of that year.[1] These articles were applied in 1747 by the Madras government to their forces,[2] and in 1748 the regulations framed by the Company itself provided that military offences should be tried according to the rules, customs, and articles of war in His Majesty's service.

As already noted it was not until 1754 that the position of martial law in India was brought into accord with that in England by the passing of an Act of Parliament, based on the analogy of the English Mutiny Act, which removed any doubt as to the authority of the Crown by the prerogative to authorize the Company to punish by courts martial offences against military law committed by its officers and soldiers in time of peace.

Only after the death of Oxenden in July 1669 did there arrive in India laws[3] which were enacted by the Company under the charter for the government of Bombay. These laws were drafted by Thomas Papillon, the rival of Sir Josiah Child, and by the Company's solicitor. Their draft was revised by the Court of Committees and the Solicitor-General and duly engrossed and sealed. They were taken to Bombay by Aungier in January 1670. Translated into Portuguese and the coast dialect of Marathi, they were published in February. As the first important legislative work of the Company their contents are of special interest. Their first section dealt with religious observances, requiring attendance at public worship in accordance with English law, but freedom of religious belief, observances, and customs was granted not merely to Roman Catholics, as required by the Treaty of Cession (Art. xi), but generally to all inhabitants, and fine or imprisonment might be inflicted for the use of abusive or contemptuous language about another person's religion.

Section 2, regarding the administration of justice, confirmed the existing rights provided for the impartial administration of justice, laid down the principle of trial and conviction by a jury of twelve men before deprivation of rights or the infliction of corporal punishment, and forbade commitment to prison without specific warrant.

[1] 4 Geo. I, c. 3, s. 40. [2] Wilson, *Hist. of Madras Army*, i, 48.
[3] Fawcett, *First Century of British Justice in India*, pp. 18–28.

By Section 3 provision was made for the establishment of a Court of Judicature for the decision of all suits in criminal matters under a judge appointed by the governor and council, trials to be by jury of twelve Englishmen unless one party to the dispute was not English when half the jury was to be non-English. There was to be a right of appeal from the court to the governor and council, which was constituted the supreme court for the island. Authority was also given for the appointment of justices of the peace and constables, for the maintenance of order, apprehension of criminals, etc.

Section 4 provided for the registration of transactions relating to houses or land, and Section 5 laid down miscellaneous penalties for the chief crimes. In many cases the Company mitigated the severity of English law, notably in the case of robbery. The same characteristics are marked in Section 6 touching military discipline and the prevention of disorder and insurrection. Mutiny, sedition, insurrection, or rebellion could be punished by death, but other offences were treated lightly; even a soldier who slept on duty could only be fined or imprisoned. Offences were to be tried not by courts martial but by the governor and council, or by a jury. Unfortunately the temperate character of the laws in this regard raised bitter complaint locally, with the result that the president and council gave permission for resort on necessary occasions to the Articles of War. The two codes, therefore, continued to subsist side by side; in point of fact the more drastic remained in operation, when, less than fifty years later, the laws of the Company had passed out of remembrance.

The need of a judiciary was sufficiently indicated by the episode which was the immediate cause of Aungier's visit to Bombay. Young, the deputy governor, had quarrelled with his chief military assistant and had endeavoured to secure his condemnation to death by court martial, an action disapproved by Oxenden, and he had assaulted and confined the wife of his leading member of council, whose death later was asserted by her friends to be due to his violence. Aungier convened a grand council of thirteen persons in all to investigate the charges, which were found not to be proved, and the only action taken was to send home the parties to the controversies.

But, as the Company pointed out, it was not possible to deal with the matters involved, including the allegation of murder, in England,[1] and Young was actually permitted to serve in Persia, where his insane action elicited orders for his removal which was anticipated by his death.

Aungier was not in a position immediately to supersede the system of the administration of Portuguese law in Portuguese by local experts, but he set up benches of justices at Bombay and Mahim, including besides natives of Bombay the English customs officer at each place to deal with minor disputes, up to 200 xeraphins[2] in value, and petty offences. Appeal lay to the deputy governor and council, who sat weekly and who heard major cases and matters affecting the government of the island and the Company's interest therein. The superior court employed juries for the more important felonies at least, and applied the Company's laws; in the inferior courts Portuguese law was probably still effective. Englishmen were subjected to the jurisdiction of the superior court, and the Company itself and its officers were not exempt from its jurisdiction, though it was clear that the Company was not likely to suffer wrong from a court of its own servants. Appeal to the president and council at Surat was discouraged. This system was well adapted to lead up to the formal introduction from August 1st 1672 of English law and the setting up of the Court of Judicature as directed by the Company. Bombay was now divided into four Hundreds in imitation of English subdivisions of counties, and justices of the peace appointed, now English in lieu of Portuguese, for them, with power to hold preliminary investigations on the strength of which indictments were preferred before the court. The justices also assisted the judge, who in 1678 was renamed chief justice, apparently to indicate that his position was reduced to that of *primus inter pares*. The court from 1672 dealt summarily and without appeal with civil causes under twenty xeraphins, and petty quarrels. In other civil causes juries were duly employed and paid; attorneys were allowed to practise; English procedure, including arrest and imprisonment, was followed, and English substantive law,

[1] Foster, *English Factories in India*, 1668–9, p. 253, n. 1.
[2] A Portuguese coin worth about 1*s.* 6*d.*

including statûte law, applied as closely as possible. Appeals to the governor and council were discouraged, and after 1677 apparently out of use. The court also undertook probate and administration work, and registered deeds affecting immovables, and, anticipating English legislation of 1854, bills of sale of goods.

Criminal jurisdiction was exercised monthly in general sessions, juries were used for major offences, but minor infractions against religion and morals were punished without jury trial. For theft the death penalty was sometimes inflicted, as in 1674–5, but the Company in 1677 definitely disapproved of it. Capital sentences were considered by the governor and council, who might refer to the president and council at Surat, and in many cases were remitted for good cause. English common and statute law was applied freely to make good defects in the Company's laws. This was doubtless, as in civil cases, just and proper under the charter. To the credit of Child it should be put that he was reluctant to permit the execution of persons accused of witchcraft, thereby showing himself in advance of the sentiments of the day. The court on the English analogy asserted control of punch-houses, which had to be licensed by the council, the making and mending of highways, and the fixing of prices, a power still exercised as late as 1727.

The regularity of the position of the court was established in 1677 when an appeal against the attachment of certain property was considered by the Privy Council Committee for Trade and Plantations. The committee held on June 12th that the Company were right in contending that the issue involved was one to be decided by the Bombay Court by the verdict of a mixed jury as provided in the Company's laws, and the matter was ended amicably by submission by the complainant, Alvaro.

In a few cases of special importance trial took place by the governor and council with a jury. Thus Captain Shaxton, deputy governor, was thus tried for complicity in the mutiny of his company in accordance with the Company's laws in 1674; found guilty on several counts he took exception to the court as interested parties, so that it merely referred the matter to the Company. The soldiers concerned were tried by martial law, on the ground that by mutiny they had put themselves outside the laws of the Company. It seems probable that the chief weakness of the court lay in the fact that the judge was dependent on the good will of the council, as was seen in the dismissal of Niccolls in 1677, but there is no clear proof of injudicious interference with the court by the council. Under Gary in 1679 it reversed a decision of his as to the grant of administration in respect of a piece of land belonging to a widow dying intestate without relatives, but that was a just assertion of the right of the Company under the charter of 1668 to escheats, which would normally fall to the Crown.[1]

Keigwin's rebellion from December 1683 to November 1684 interrupted the orderly development of the court and inaugurated a period of innovation both in judiciary and in the law. As mentioned above, Charles II had granted a new charter (August 3rd 1683) providing for the erection of a court for maritime causes of all kinds, including all cases of trespasses, injuries, and wrongs, done or committed upon the high seas or in Bombay or its adjacent territory, the court to be held by a judge learned in the civil law assisted by two persons chosen by the Company. The causes heard were to be determined by the court in accordance with the rules of equity and good conscience and the laws and customs of merchants by such procedure as the judges might direct. The officer sent out was Dr. St. John, and this zealous judge succeeded in securing authority from the governor to act also as chief justice of the Court of Judicature, which remained necessarily in being, for the authority of the Admiralty Court did not cover all civil business, for instance, matters affecting houses and lands, and probably did not extend to the punishment of offences other than those connected with interloping. The Company certainly at the outset took the natural view that the new court was essentially a court to deal with what ranked in English law as Admiralty causes. St. John, however, was not acceptable to John Child at Surat, and his work as chief justice ceased in 1685 (March 27th) and he was removed from the Admiralty Court two years later.

But before this Sir Josiah Child had shown a new interpretation

[1] Cf. *Joanna Fernandez* v. *De Silva* (1817), Morley, *Digest*, i, 214.

of the rights and purposes of the Company, fortified in his view by the terms of the charter of 1686, under which he claimed that the Company had become a sovereign state in India.[1] From a series of letters sent to the presidencies it is clear that he arrogated to the Company absolute power to legislate and exercise jurisdiction at its pleasure. Ignoring the terms of the charter of 1668, it was laid down (July 28th 1686) that the law for Bombay was not to be found in statute books of English law, where it was still the custom of the court to seek it, but such law as the King or the Company might lay down, and such temporary by-laws as the general and council at Surat might find cause to make, until disapproved by the King or the Company. Moreover, it was asserted that under the charters of 1683 and 1686 the people of Bombay were to be governed by the law martial and the civil law, which only was proper to India. On February 3rd 1687 Surat was required to enact by-laws for Bombay, and it was reiterated that common law was quite unsuited for India, including, doubtless, in that term English statutes of general character. It was also made clear[2] that in Sir J. Child's view the letters of the Company ought to be deemed binding as law on all its servants in India. To strengthen the position the post of deputy governor of Bombay was conferred on Sir John Wyborne as an expert in the government of Tangier, in conformity with which Bombay was to be governed. *En route* he was commissioned to try by martial law the planters and others concerned in the mutiny of 1684 at St. Helena, and the Company asserted that it had the royal commission to govern both St. Helena and Bombay by martial law. It is, however, obvious that the claims made by the Company were invalid. The King had not the power to authorize the use of martial law in civil matters, and, though the Company could make laws, it had to be done in due form not by mere letters, and the laws made were not to be repugnant to English law. It would not, therefore, have been possible for the Company itself to confer the power to govern by martial law, and the whole episode is suggestive of the

[1] Hunter, *History of India*, ii, 304.

[2] To Surat July 14th 1686; to Madras April 8th 1687. Cf. the Madras Charter, December 30th 1687 as to martial law; it gives power to the president and council to make temporary by-laws.

period of prerogative run mad which preluded the revolution of 1688.

In point of fact civil jurisdiction was never confined to the Admiralty Court by the Company. The Court of Judicature was temporarily held also by Dr. St. John as chief justice, but he failed entirely to meet the wishes of the two Childs, for, fortified by the fact that he held a commission from the King as well as from the Company, and embittered by the Company's refusal to continue him in charge of the Court of Judicature, he set up extravagant claims of judicial independence. In *Thorburn's case*,[1] where the Court of Judicature, under the new head John Vaux, had condemned him, he argued that the court had no right to try a mercantile cause, his jurisdiction being exclusive, but this was clearly an impossible claim, and appears to have been negatived. In the case of *Day* v. *King*,[2] tried in the Admiralty Court, he strove to establish his right to pronounce the decision against the views of his two assistants, and he denied that an appeal lay to the governor and council. Both claims were patently absurd, the first running counter to the rule of the charter that the determination of the court was to be that of the majority, the professional judge being one thereof, and the latter ignoring the general appellate jurisdiction given to governor and council by the Company's laws of 1669. Moreover, he claimed the right to try military offenders, and asserted that he had been promised the control of the Court of Judicature, so that, if his pretensions had been accepted, he would have been sole judge, a dangerous contingency, for we find him sending to prison on his own authority an alleged servant.[3] On the other hand, while the Company, anxious over the rebellious spirit of the territory as seen in Keigwin's rebellion (1683–4) and the loss of trade from interloping, might be excused for objecting to any *imperium in imperio*, it was obviously undesirable that Sir J. Child should insist that the judges must obey the general and council 'as it becomes all under command'. Dr. St. John was permitted to remain in control of the Admiralty Court until 1687, when he was dismissed; first Sir J. Wyborne, and from 1688 to 1690

[1] Fawcett, *First Century of British Justice in India*, p. 142. [2] Ibid., p. 145.

[3] Sir John Child properly objected, quoting the saying, 'I will not be judge in my own case.' Cf. Keith, *Const. Hist. of First British Empire*, p. 350.

Vaux, succeeded him. The latter was at the close of his office a pluralist, acting on military service during the Sidi's invasion, as member of council and as judge. His departure to win Aurangzib's forgiveness marked the end of both courts for the time being, for John Child's death deprived Bombay of any person capable of resuscitating an effective administration to aid recovery from the injuries inflicted by the war.

Neither court could be restored for years, and justice was administered in a rough and ready way by the governor and council, whose action could be authorized under the charter of Charles II. But much doubt existed as to the power to punish unless on confession, especially in the case of murders, and the Company returned no reply to Sir John Gayer's appeal in 1702 for power. Sir N. Waite, the chief representative of the New Company who took charge in 1704, Gayer being confined at Surat, took some action. He and the deputy governor shared jurisdiction; Waite and the council heard civil and criminal causes, but most of the work was done by the deputy, while crimes resulting in death were investigated by the coroner, whose office dates from 1672, the governor and council awarding punishment. From 1708 when Aislabie, the deputy, succeeded Waite, the same system of delegating authority to the deputy prevailed until 1712, when the council itself resumed sittings, only shortly after to permit the former practice to be resumed. Only under Charles Boone in 1716 was orderly judicial procedure restored, and so completely had the charter of 1668 and the laws of 1669 been forgotten that application was made for power to try pirates and murderers. The Company's reply is significant; it sent out the charter and advised the council to remove from the island any who refused to obey the laws in force.

The new arrangements established a Court of Judicature mainly composed of the Company's servants, but including four Indians, representing the Hindus, Muhammadans, Portuguese Christians, and Parsees, though for cases between English persons three English justices must sit. The jury system was not revived, and only in the punishments inflicted is there much evidence of remembrance of the terms of the laws. The law of England was not unknown and was applied where appropriate, and even some knowledge of international law can be traced. Rough and ready methods of obtaining confessions were not unknown, and summary punishment was awarded for perjury or contempt of court. Both in criminal and civil matters the court exercised a wide jurisdiction, but in cases where a capital sentence could be imposed, such as murder or rape, the court referred for sentence to the governor and council. To that body appeals presumably lay, but appear to have been rare.

The Court of 1718–28 differed essentially in its basis from that of 1672–90, for the latter was definitely constituted by the laws of the Company, while the former was established by order of the governor and council, approved by the Company only. No doubt it was legally enough constituted, but the fact that capital sentences were passed by the governor and council only may be explained by the rather informal character of the court's creation. Again the earlier court used juries, and its judges might be, as in the case of Niccolls and Gary (1675–83), outsiders, while the later court was essentially a Company's court, the bench consisting mainly of members of council. But it was undoubtedly an improvement on the haphazard system of 1690–1718, and it paved the way for the introduction of the Mayor's Court in 1728 under the charter of 1726. That court was based on the principle of the Mayor's Court introduced into Madras under the charter of 1687; it had been considered in 1688 whether it should be extended to Bombay, but Child was doubtless opposed, and, though not formally adopted by Boone, it inspired part of the system of 1718. But the new plan rested on a royal charter, indicating, as noted above, the feeling that royal authority was necessary for a court if its judgments and grants of probate and administration were to be recognized by English courts. Further, the charter granted legislative power to the governor and council. Sir J. Child had asserted that the power to make by-laws was vested in the general and council of Surat, but we find that little had ever been done in this regard. The Bombay Council itself laid down regulations as to public-houses, gaming, and other minor matters, but its regulations were largely analogous to those under English law, and we have no evidence of any serious claim to possess legislative authority proper.

The Letters Patent of September 24th 1726 provided for the establishment of a municipal corporation, the mayor to be elected annually from the aldermen by the mayor and aldermen, of whom there were to be nine, seven and the mayor being English. The aldermen were to hold office for life, vacancies being filled by the mayor and aldermen from the leading inhabitants. They could be removed from office by the governor and council for reasonable cause, but subject to appeal to the King in Council.

The mayor and aldermen were constituted a court of record, the mayor and two aldermen being authorized to hear all suits of a civil character arising in Madras or the factories subordinate to it. Its process was to be based on English law and to be executed by a sheriff chosen annually by the governor and council, but no juries were used. Appeal lay to the governor and council, with a further appeal to the King in Council where the sum involved was over 1,000 pagodas.[1]

Criminal justice was given to the governor and five senior members of council who were to have the same powers as English justices of the peace. They were to hold Quarter Sessions four times a year, and were also given the powers of Commissioners of Oyer and Terminer and Gaol Delivery, but might not try cases of high treason. Procedure was to be by indictment as in England, and thus both petty and grand juries became regular; the latter had only been known sporadically under the Court of 1672–90.

As a corollary to the creation of municipal bodies it was decided to grant legislative power for the better government and regulation of the corporations, and the governor and council were empowered to make such regulations and impose pains and penalties for their breach, provided that by-laws and punishments were not contrary to the laws of England, and both had been confirmed by the Court of Directors before they took effect.

The court was expressly authorized to grant probate and

[1] A gold coin worth about three rupees, current in Madras; its use in regard to Calcutta is due to this fact.

letters of administration in case of intestacy. Moreover, in 1727 (November 17th) it was provided by supplementary Letters Patent that the fines levied by the court should go to the Company. This principle had long been operative in practice, but clearly under a royal grant the claims of the Crown would have been paramount but for the express provision thus made.

The charter of January 8th 1753 which superseded those of 1726 and 1727 contained some improvements. The aldermen were on vacancies occurring to be chosen by the governor and council. The jurisdiction of the Mayor's Court was restricted to matters where the value was over five pagodas. On appeal the governor and council could execute their decision if the court failed to act. Evidence by Christians was to be on oath, and in the case of Indians in such a form as should most bind their consciences. Special provision was made for cases against the Company or brought by it. The court might frame rules of practice subject to control by the Company. A Court of Requests, composed of at least three commissioners out of a larger number chosen by the governor and council, was established to deal with suits of value up to five pagodas. All members of council were made justices of the peace. Moreover, the Company systematically examined through its legal advisers the reports of the proceedings of the courts and pressed on them the duty of conformity to English law.

It is, of course, obvious that it would have been impossible to insist on the government of natives in Bombay in regard to their civil rights by English law, and from the first this fact was recognized in various forms. Aungier, on the suggestion of the Company in 1673–4, recognized the authority of panchayats, or caste representatives, over all inter-caste disputes which were submitted to them by agreement, though otherwise matters must be determined by the court. It is clear that the court had to apply caste rules in such cases. The panchayats were also given duties of watch and ward and reporting all sorts of offences to justices of the peace. Moreover, they were bound to look after the estates of orphans. Under the system of 1718 we find the chowghulas, headmen, and vereadores of the several tribes of inhabitants recognized as empowered to decide caste and communal disputes as an inferior court, whence appeal lay to the Court of Judicature. The latter were a legacy of Portuguese times, and were elected by the landowners; they were used to muster militia and collect taxes and seem to have superseded the panchayats in charge of orphans' estates. Issues were often referred to them for report by the court, and in the case of Muhammadans the kazi and chowghulas played a similar part. The kazi seems to have had a minor jurisdiction in cases of inheritance and the like. For Hindus reference might be made to caste headmen or merchants for opinions. So strengthened, the court could revise even a sentence of the casting out of caste of a panchayat.

The Mayor's Court asserted naturally enough like power, but this led to dispute in 1730 with the council, which denied its right to deal with issues of religion or caste, and dismissed the mayor from his post as secretary to the council as punishment for his insistence on his judicial independence. But the Company very properly upheld the authority of the court against the council, and the mayor and aldermen as grand jurymen were able to express freely their views to the governor and council, using their power to refuse to find true bills of indictment to press their views on the due method of swearing Hindus. These conflicts had their effect in the Letters Patent of 1753, where suits between natives were to be determined by the court only on submission by the parties. But it appears that this rule was ignored at Bombay in practice, even if it were legally binding there.[1]

(c) JURISDICTION AND LEGISLATION IN MADRAS

The position in Madras was vitally affected by the fact that authority there as regards the natives was essentially derived from Indian suzerains, while that over Englishmen rested on the Company's charters. A regular judicature over the latter dates only from 1666, though the necessary power was accorded in the charter of 1661. In 1665 the Company pointed this out to the governor, and a grand jury duly indicted, and a mixed petty jury found guilty, a murderer.[2] Streynsham Master, who

[1] Denied by Perry, J., in 1843 (*Perozeboye* v. *Ardaseer Cursetjee*); see Morley, *Digest*, Intr., p. clxix; ii, 343.

[2] Love, *Vestiges of Old Madras*, i, 404, 405.

became governor in 1678, reformed the court on the Bombay model, and it sat with juries to hear civil and criminal causes save minor matters, following English law. In 1686, however, it was superseded by the Court of Admiralty, which in Madras fared far better than in Bombay, partly because in 1687 there was appointed as judge advocate Sir John Biggs, who was a protégé of the Company and enjoyed its favour. The court served also as the Supreme Court, and when a corporation was instituted in 1688 under the charter given by the Company, appeal was made to lie to the court and not to the governor and council.

The creation of a municipal corporation, as noted above, was motived by the desire to secure general acquiescence in taxation, a strike and no co-operation movement having greeted the imposition of a house tax in 1686. The corporation was composed of an English mayor and twelve aldermen, of whom the three senior must be English, but the others were to be of any nationality, a Frenchman, two Portuguese, three Hindus, and three Jew or Armenian merchants being among those first appointed by the Company. Thirty of the 120 burgesses were to include the heads of the castes. In fact, the institution did not work as desired; it neither raised taxes nor founded municipal institutions, but it was of considerable importance judicially. The mayor and aldermen were constituted a civil court, while the mayor and the three senior aldermen were justices of the peace with criminal jurisdiction. Appeal lay to the Admiralty Court where the value exceeded three pagodas, or in criminal cases the offender was sentenced to lose life or limb. Its power to inflict sentences of death was disputed, but conceded in 1712[1] by the council. Appeal lay to the Admiralty Court when that existed from 1688 to 1689 and 1692 to 1704, and in the interim to a temporary court of the governor and four justices. After 1704 Admiralty jurisdiction was apparently exercised by the governor and council, who tried pirates and interlopers as pirates under the Piracy Act of 1699[2] by special commission. It also heard appeals from the Mayor's Court, and while it lasted the Admiralty Court, under the instructions

[1] Love, *Vestiges of Old Madras*, ii, 174, 175.

[2] 11 Will. III, c. 7. For interlopers being tried as pirates by Admiralty Courts, see Wheeler, *Madras*, i, 320; Anderson, *The English in Western India*, p. 257.

of the Company to Pitt as governor in 1698 to hear appeals in cases of not less value than one hundred pagodas.

In the Admiralty Court, in criminal jurisdiction, and in the Mayor's Court, juries seem to have been employed, but in civil causes juries seem not to have been employed in the Admiralty Court, the charters of 1683 and 1686 ignoring them, and certainly they were unknown to the Mayor's Court.

To the jurisdiction of these courts natives, it is clear, were regarded as subject probably from the time when they became effective, and by the eighties cases of hanging major Indian offenders are frequent; Europeans were often suffered to escape with branding on the hand, doubtless because of the English legislation as to benefit of clergy, which seems to have been accepted also in Bombay and Calcutta in the eighteenth century; when applied to Indians at Calcutta the additional penalty of expulsion across the river was often added. The source of this control of Indians was unquestionably the cession of authority by successive overlords, none of whom were especially strong, and all of whom were prepared to meet the wishes of the English for a consideration. At first naturally native disputes were left to the Indian adigar, or town governor, who administered justice according to long-established usage at the town house or choultry. About 1654 this practice was varied, two Englishmen being appointed to sit. In the reform system of Streynsham Master three justices were appointed, two to be a quorum, with authority in respect of small misdemeanours, breaches of the peace, and actions of debt to the value of fifty pagodas or under, unless the parties agreed to a larger amount. Appeal lay to the governor and council with jury trial there. The court proved to have a long life; in 1688–9 aldermen replaced the magistrates, but the work proved to require special justices, who continued to impose sentences of whipping, fines, imprisonment, and the pillory. In 1727 the Madras Council purported to create a Sheriff's Court, with appeal to the Mayor's Court if the value at stake exceeded five pagodas, but this attempt to supersede the Choultry Court was disapproved by the Company, who were no doubt justified in holding that the council had no authority thus to act. The need for a court of the type proposed was recognized, as in the case of Bombay, by the charter of 1753, but it seems to have superseded this side of the choultry jurisdiction only in 1775, and, despite doubts cast by the Advocate-General at Madras in 1788 on the legality of the constitution of courts for the trial of matters affecting Indians, the Choultry Court continued to exercise a minor criminal jurisdiction until it was abolished in 1800.

The major courts erected under the authority of the Company were superseded by the Mayor's Court, established under the charter of 1726, which was on the same lines as that granted to Bombay. The new court soon showed a praiseworthy inclination to defend its judicial powers. It insisted on committing to prison two merchants in 1736 for refusing to take the pagoda oath, i.e. an oath in a temple, and, to calm the indignation of the Indian residents, the governor had to intervene and secure the release of the men on parole. The Company censured the spirit of the court, warning them that they would not allow those who failed to show proper deference to remain in their limits, but they also insisted that, so long as they acted within their charter rights, they should receive the support of the governor.

The question of the law to be applied to natives by the court naturally arose. The Company was insistent on due observation of English law in the court, but it was anxious to favour the continued recognition of any peculiar customs of the Indians. Hence, when the castes of Madras appealed to the Company its reply of February 12th 1731 insisted that disputes between natives should be decided among themselves according to their own customs, or by justices or referees to be appointed by themselves, or otherwise as they thought fit. If, however, they desired the court to decide, it must do so by English law, and the same rule must apply in differences between natives and subjects of England where either party was obstinate and determined to go to law. The decision is interesting, and, in view of the terms of the charter, no doubt inevitable. In the charter of 1753 jurisdiction of the court in matters between natives was made to depend on their submission. But this seems in practice to have caused little change, and the awkward position arose that the natives of Madras had no very effective substitute for the Mayor's Court. The Choultry Court, or that of Requests had a very limited authority, and, though in 1770 the idea of establishing a special court to deal with cases of native law was discussed, it resulted in action only in 1795, when a Court of Cutcherry was erected, only to be superseded by the Recorder's Court of 1798, in which an arrangement existed adapted to secure due regard for Indian law in cases affecting natives of India.

(*d*) JURISDICTION AND LEGISLATION IN CALCUTTA

In its early days Bengal fell far short of Madras or Bombay in the character of its organization, executive and judicial alike. The settlements in the Bay were too unimportant as a rule to be considered worthy of the presence of a governor and council at any point, and the judicial authority given by the charter of 1661 authorized trial only by a governor and council. The establishment of a Court of Admiralty never became effective; when war was declared on the Empire the officer in command of the naval expedition was given a commission (January 1686), but prize business alone was transacted, and no court seems ever to have sat under later commissions of 1688 and 1693. After Charnock's establishment at Sutanati in 1690 the position was clearer, but in 1693, owing to piracies in the Red Sea, the privileges of the Company were placed in abeyance by the Emperor, and the idea of setting up a Court of Judicature was dropped, the local council being instructed in 1698 to send prisoners for trial to Madras. At the close of 1699, however, Bengal was declared a presidency and the governor and council thus became possessed of full judicial authority. In 1704 they established a committee of three members for the decision of minor causes, but the sittings of this body seem to have been irregular.

Over Indians the Company had acquired jurisdiction by the purchase of the three villages, Sutanati, Govindpur, and Calcutta, which gave it the rights of a zamindar.[1] Under the régime then existing in Bengal, a zamindar was wont to exercise a wide criminal jurisdiction, whipping, fining, and imprisoning

[1] Wilson, *Early Annals of the English in Bengal*, i, 163.

at discretion. The Company took full use of this authority, and a member of council regularly held a Zamindari Court for both civil and criminal business. Holwell, famous as the survivor and historian of the Black Hole, was collector of Calcutta from 1752 to 1756, and acted as magistrate; he tells us that the procedure was summary; in causes of property appeal lay to the president and council, while in capital sentences the president was required to confirm the judgment of the infliction of the lash until death.[1] It is clear that by this time the necessity under which an ordinary zamindar lay of submitting sentences of death for confirmation to the local faujdar at Hugli and the nazim at Murshidabad had been got rid of, but the detail of the mode of inflicting a death sentence confirms the assertion of Bolts, which has wrongly been disputed,[2] that hanging was prohibited for Muhammadans by decree of the Emperor. It seems, however, that at least on one occasion Muhammadan members of a party of criminals were spared lest the nawab be induced to assert his rights of supervision.

What, however, is interesting is that this Court of Cutcherry dealt also with disputes between Europeans and Indians of European descent, a position attacked by the Mayor's Court in 1755–7. As a result, in 1758, the Company ordered the constitution of two separate courts. The former dealt with all criminal causes, consisting of a quorum of three justices, the members of council sitting in rotation, each sitting for a month in turn as the acting justice to dispose of slight offences with an appeal to the quorum. When dealing with Europeans this court was clearly the governor and council under the charter; when dealing with natives it was a Zamindari Court. But it seems that the quorum of three was not persisted in, and by 1772 Bolts[3] describes the Zamindari Court as held by one of the council or of the Company's servants sitting alone. Over Europeans presumably criminal jurisdiction in serious cases would be exercised under the charters of 1726 and 1753 by the Court of Quarter Sessions thereby created, which used juries.

The second court dealt with civil matters exceeding twenty rupees in value; it was composed of five of the servants of the

[1] Wilson, i, 220. [2] *C.H.I.*, v, 590.
[3] *Considerations on Indian Affairs*, i, 80.

Company below the council, with appeal to the president and council where the amount in dispute exceeded a hundred rupees. It seems, however, that it tended to evade decisions and to refer really difficult cases to arbitration by Indian merchants, who resented this tax on their time.

Beside these courts was that called the Collector's Cutcherry, which was simply the mode in which the Company exercised the coercive powers of the zamindar as collector of land revenue over the tenants or farmers of the revenue.[1] Its practice of ordering whipping of delinquents was merely in accord with native practice, as was the complete injustice of allowing punishment to be inflicted at the discretion of an interested party who acted as judge in his own cause.

The charters of 1726 and 1753 established in Bengal the courts also set up in Bombay and Madras, the Court of Quarter Sessions, the Mayor's Court, the Court of Requests from 1753, and the governor and council as Court of Appeal from the Mayor's Court. But naturally for Indians the three courts of the Zamindari persisted. The Mayor's Court exhibited like those of the other presidencies a measure of independence sufficient to arouse the Company's displeasure, and it fulminated also against the same spirit among the attorneys, whose activities in all three presidencies undoubtedly pointed the way to the emancipation of justice from any excessive executive control, an ideal expressed admirably in 1672 by Aungier but one slow to develop under the rather jealous eye of the Company.

The development of commerce and government alike had undoubtedly reached a stage at which the servants of the Company could not suffice without training for the purposes of a judiciary, and the time was ripe for far-reaching changes. One obvious defect in the systems which had prevailed was the absence of provision for Indians as judges; under the charters of 1726 and 1753 Indians could serve as jurors in the Sessions Court, but only if Christians, a restriction removed only in 1826. The Bombay Court of Judicature from 1718 to 1728 had admitted Indians, though hardly as fully equal to European justices; a like system had been tried at Madras from 1687 to 1692, and the original intention of the Madras municipality was

[1] Bolts, op. cit., i, 80.

to include Indian aldermen, but this plan failed wholly to materialize. Small wonder therefore if the question of how to give just effect to Indian law where Indians were concerned remained to be solved. Calcutta indeed felt least the inconvenience, for the exclusion of cases between Indians by the charter of 1753 mattered little to a presidency in which these cases were capable of disposal by the Zamindari Court of Cutcherry.[1]

[1] Legally, however, the right to judge natives in the Zamindari Courts instead of the Charter Courts was doubtful, as Warren Hastings pointed out (Monckton-Jones, *Warren Hastings in Bengal*, pp. 157, 158), and the Mayor's Court in 1773 was asked to exercise jurisdiction over a zamindar on a visit (pp. 328, 329). For the injustice of punishment by English law of natives for acts legal by Hindu or Muhammadan law, see Verelst in Kaye, *Admin. of E.I. Co.*, p. 324, and the successful petition of 1765 against the execution of Radhacharan Mitra for forgery (p. 325).

CHAPTER II

THE DIWANI, THE EXPLOITATION OF BENGAL, DYARCHY, AND ANARCHY

1. THE GRANT OF THE DIWANI

WITH Plassey and the following arrangements with successive nawabs of Bengal, the real authority had passed into the hands of the Company. When its unreasonable demands regarding freedom of private trade from dues and the right to act as judge in its own cause had driven Mir Kasim to revolt and open war, a new treaty with Mir Jafar provided further limitations on the nawab's power. He was to limit his forces, to receive a permanent resident at the durbar, and not to levy more than 2½ per cent duty on English trade, while compensation was to be paid for all losses, public and private, due to the disputes with Mir Kasim. This accord still left room for some independence on the nawab's part. He appointed Nandakumar as his chief minister, and his attitude during the war with Mir Kasim and his allies, the nawab of Oudh and the Emperor, was deemed dubious. So at his death in 1765 the position was strengthened by the grant of recognition to his son Najm-ud-daula only on condition that he agreed to appoint a minister as deputy subadar with the management of affairs, whom he was not to displace without the sanction of the Company. The position of the Company was thus definitely assured in fact though not in law. Clive indeed was indignant that the council had acted thus definitely without his assent, for by 1764 he had secured control of the Company and had decided to assume the governorship of Fort William in order to restore confidence. Public opinion in England had viewed with just reprobation the establishment of Mir Kasim in 1760, and the contest with him, provoked by indefensible claims, and redeemed only by the success of Munro at the decisive battle of Baksar (October 22nd 1764). Utter confusion prevailed both in the domestic and the external relations of the Company. Vansittart had found his prudent projects rejected by the council, and corruption raged among the Company's servants, who had violated the instructions of the Company in taking large presents on the accession of the new nawab.

Clive's solution for the situation as regards the nawab of Oudh and the Emperor alike was of the highest importance in determining the future history of India. He himself in his earlier stay in India[1] had contemplated the possibility of the direct assumption by the Crown and had approached Pitt on the subject, but without result, and his own views were now set on a different solution. He decided to secure the position of the Company as the *de facto* authority in such a way as would shield it from claims either by foreign powers or by the Crown, to provide it with a faithful ally, and to bring the Emperor into the position of a grateful pensioner. He rejected, therefore, definitely any idea of restoring imperial power, such as had been involved in Vansittart's suggestion of the grant to the Emperor of Oudh, which he restored to the nawab on payment of fifty lakhs and the cession of Kora and Allahabad. The Emperor was promised a tribute of twenty-six lakhs, and the districts ceded by Oudh. In return he regularized the position of the Company in Bengal by bestowing upon it formally the diwani, covering the whole of the financial administration, including the collection of land revenue and customs, and the civil government. The diwani had hitherto rested with the nawab, who was also in control of the military government and criminal law, the combination of powers marking the decline of the former principles of the Empire. Now it was definitely detached from him as a matter of theory. But Clive did not contemplate the actual taking over of the authority and its execution by the servants of the Company. His idea was very different. The actual administration was left in the hands of the four deputies of the nawab, and in his final directions to the Calcutta Council (January 16th 1767) he insisted that, while the nawab was but a name and a shadow, policy required that he should be venerated and be encouraged to show resentment at any lack of respect by foreign nations. His office should be used to repel any foreign efforts at control, and genuine grievances should be adjusted through him. While the

[1] January 7th 1759; Keith, *Indian Policy*, i, 13 ff.

revenues belonged to the Company, the territorial jurisdiction must be exercised through the chiefs of the country acting under him and the presidency in conjunction. If the mask were thrown off, foreign powers would be able to complain directly to the British Government, which might be compelled to look closely into matters with results likely to embarrass the Company. It was not forgotten that, by the Letters Patent of January 14th 1758, the Company's authority in case of war to deal with lands acquired from any foreign power was subject to the approval of the Crown. The Company shared the views of Clive; on May 17th 1766 it definitely urged that the control of the Company should be confined to superintendence of the collection of the revenue and of its transfer from the treasury of the nawab to that of the Company, and it was only by experience that it could be realized that the system of dual control was utterly inefficient. Moreover, time had to elapse before the servants of the Company could gain sufficient experience to be able to take over charge of the administration, and, before that happened, the country was fated to suffer enormously from their rapacity.

2. THE WORKING OF DYARCHY

Clive had fully realized the danger of plunder of the province following in his own footsteps. But, undeterred by reminders of his past, he insisted on the servants of the Company signing the new contracts ordered by the Company forbidding the acceptance of presents and supplementing their existing covenants.[1] On the other hand, he recognized that the salaries paid were far too low, and tried to solve the problem of private trade and due remuneration by establishing a Society for Trade, which was allowed to work the monopoly in salt, and to pay thence handsome subventions to the principal military and civil officers. The Company treated this step as a disregard for their orders for the abolition of private trade, and the business was stopped in 1768, but the problem was left unsolved. The reputed riches of the country had the

[1] Hence the term 'covenanted' civil service, the practice of a signed contract persisting after its first end had ceased.

result predicted by Clive. Influence was exerted from the royal family downwards to secure posts in India for hangers-on and younger sons of noble or rich families, and the new-comers were intent only on acquiring fortunes. The easily won wealth was brought home and expended on the purchase of seats in the Commons, with the result of offending the territorial magnates, who found themselves outbidden, and disgusting moderate men with the insolence and over-bearing character of the newly enriched ex-servants of the Company.

Clive, though aware of the danger impending, had nothing to suggest to keep it in check. The government of the presidency remained virtually in the same form as before 1756, with the exception that the select committee of the council then instituted for prompt action in emergency was continued as a regular piece of machinery. The council, as laid down in 1770,[1] was to consist, with the governor, of nine members, all of whom were to reside at Calcutta—unless the resident at the durbar were a counsellor—and not to have any other employment. The governor, commander-in-chief, and three senior members constituted a select committee, charged with the conduct of negotiations with the country powers and the issues of war and peace thence arising; but any treaty, whether of commerce or alliance, must be approved by the whole body. The correspondence on such topics was conducted by the governor, but must be submitted to the select committee, and copies sent to the Company. The supremacy of the civil authority was emphasized in 1769; the council could delegate its power to any civil servant, who must be obeyed by the highest officer of the Company's army, and the majority of the council might dismiss officers at its discretion. This insistence on military subordination had been emphasized by Clive when he was confronted with a mutiny of officers on his carrying out the orders of the Company to reduce the allowances paid to them. Nothing but his firmness of character enabled him to quell the mutiny, the great majority of the officers being permitted to remain on after signing three-year contracts which, under the East India Mutiny Act, would

[1] On Hastings' appointment fourteen were named (April 10th 1771).

have rendered them in the event of a fresh insubordination liable to the death penalty.

Supreme as was in theory the council, it was wholly incapable of inducing moderation in the desire of the servants of the Company to enrich themselves, and its own members were inevitably subject to the same urge to attain easy fortunes and to leave a land for which they had no affection. Nor was the position improved by the activity of Parliament which, like the proprietors, desired to share in the plunder. While the proprietors insisted in 1766 on raising the dividend from 6 to 10 per cent and in 1767 demanded 12½ per cent, the outcome of the inquiry by a committee of the whole House of Commons in 1766–7 was the demand of the State for the payment of £400,000 a year for two years from February 1st 1767, in return for which the Company might retain its territorial acquisitions and revenues for that period.[1] Parliament also interfered in the disgraceful business of the management of the dealings in the shares of the Company. It overruled the demands of the proprietors for 12½ per cent,[2] and restricted voting to persons who had held their qualification for six months, while dividends could be declared only at a half-yearly or quarterly court.[3] In 1769 the bargain was continued for five years.[4] The pressure on the Company was thus most serious. Far from sharing in the riches of its servants, its debts were put at £6,000,000, it had an army of 30,000 men to maintain, and it paid £1,000,000 a year in subsidies to the nawab, the Emperor, and other Indian chiefs.

The effect of the demands for money on the unfortunate province were described effectively by the resident at the durbar who lamented on May 24th 1769 the fact that the fine country which had flourished under the most despotic and arbitrary government was verging to its ruin when the English had so great a share in the administration. The governors who succeeded Clive were not men of the calibre necessary to deal with so grave a situation. Verelst, however, secured the appointment in 1769 of supervisors who were to make a full study of the history of their districts, to report on their resources

[1] 7 Geo. III, cc. 56, 57.
[2] 7 Geo. III, c. 49; 8 Geo. III, c. 1.
[3] 7 Geo. III, c. 48.
[4] 9 Geo. III, c. 24.

and the amount of land, to investigate all payments made by the ryots to the zamindars or collectors, to report on manufactures, and, as regards justice, to enforce it when the law demanded, to encourage arbitration in disputes as to real property and to discourage arbitrary fines. They were to examine the credentials of local officials and to see that records were kept locally and returns sent to Murshidabad. It was later determined mainly to make their functions advisory, but the system did not work as hoped. There were many cases of disputes with local officials who resented interference, and unhappily too many of the officers concerned merely regarded their appointments as an excellent mode of acquiring control of the trade of the district and making a rapid fortune. It must be remembered that few officers were available of character or experience. It was in vain that in 1770 were added controlling councils of revenue for Murshidabad and Patna, to which later were added a controlling committee of accounts and a controlling committee of revenue at Calcutta (1771).

The *coup de grâce* to the attempt to carry on on these lines was administered by the appalling famine of 1770, when at least a fifth of the population of Bengal, then perhaps fifteen millions, perished while some of the Company's servants profiteered in necessities and the principal deputy added 10 per cent to the assessments to make good at the expense of the living the losses involved in the wholesale depopulation.

CHAPTER III

THE INTERVENTION OF PARLIAMENT, NORTH'S REGULATING ACT, AND WARREN HASTINGS

1. WARREN HASTINGS IN BENGAL

THE anarchy of Bengal was plainly intolerable, and Parliament was certain to intervene. But the Company was deeply moved by the facts revealed, and every motive of self-interest drove it to seek to establish order before worse befell. As early as 1769 it had dispatched Vansittart with two other experienced servants of the country to India with power to reform, but their ship was lost without trace, and the opportunity was gone, for when in 1772 the Company proposed to entrust a like mission to six supervisors Parliament definitely forbade the act.[1] What the Company could do was to resolve to end the system of dyarchy and to require the president and council to stand forth as diwan, and by the agency of the Company's servants to take upon themselves the entire care and management of the revenues as laid down in the directors' letter of August 29th 1771. The man to accomplish this mission was Warren Hastings, who in April 1772 succeeded Cartier and who had had much experience in Bengal and from 1769 as second at Madras. While the determination to take over formal charge might easily be justified, the method of action was deplorable. Hastings was required to co-operate with Nandakumar in accusations, which were later proved false, against the deputy diwans of Bengal and Bihar, and Nandakumar after all was denied the succession to the office which he had anticipated. In other matters he had a freer hand, and his work for the two years before the intervention of Parliament became decisive was probably the most creditable of his career,[2] for the difficulties to be faced were enormous, and he was deeply handicapped by the necessity of securing funds whence dividends could be paid, and of avoiding too great

[1] 13 Geo. III, c. 9.
[2] Monckton-Jones, *Warren Hastings in Bengal, 1772–4* (1918).

offence to the mass of influential people at whose instigation the civil service had grown out of all proportion to the needs of the occasion, numbering in 1781 no less than 252 members, sons of the first families in the kingdom, aspiring to the rapid acquisition of lakhs and to return home in their prime. When he started his work, the supervisors in the districts, the boards of revenue at Murshidabad and Patna, and the governor and council at Calcutta represented in that order the real hierarchy of power, and it was his essential task to restore authority to the hands entitled to wield it.

The assumption of direct authority involved the disappearance of the offices of deputy diwan, and the useful step of removing the treasury from Murshidabad to Calcutta, thus revealing to Bengal the fact that Calcutta was now the real capital of the country and remedying the undue authority which had been enjoyed by the board of revenue at Murshidabad. At the same time the allowance of the puppet nawab was reduced from thirty-two lakhs at which it had been fixed in 1769 as opposed to fifty-three in 1765 to sixteen lakhs, though careful adjustments seem to have increased the sum available for the nawab's personal pleasures. Much more dubious was the decision, approved but not suggested by the directors, to appoint as guardian of the nawab Mir Jafar's widow. Hastings no doubt was quite pleased that the Munni Begam should leave the youth without administrative experience, since it formed no part of his plans to encourage the nawab to play any effective part in government.

The revenue reforms of Hastings and his colleagues, four of whom formed with him a Committee of Circuit (1772) to determine for five years a settlement of the revenue, were instrumental in establishing the office of collector, an improved version of the former supervisor; in each district a diwan was appointed to aid the collector. The whole council became a committee or board of revenue[1] to audit the accounts of the diwani with the aid of the rai raian, an Indian official who supervised the provincial diwans. The treasury, now at Calcutta, was reorganized, and the office of accountant-general created. But, while improvements in form were

[1] Superseding that of 1771; the boards at Murshidabad and Patna disappear.

made, the essential work of fixing the revenue was badly muddled by adopting the putting up to auction of its collection. If the zamindars had been oppressive, they now were often superseded by unscrupulous adventurers without that connexion with the ryots possessed by hereditary zamindars. The latter in origin may have been mere agents for rent collection, but they had long since struck deeper roots in the system, and some measure of the relation of landlord and tenant had begun to appear. The collectors soon realized the degree of over-assessment, but the board of revenue at Calcutta was obdurate, and the Company destroyed the work of the collectors by ordering in April 1773 their withdrawal and the substitution of some other agency. Their motive seems to have been the view that the collectors were monopolizing the trade of the country. But the decision was unfortunate. The Company then and later knew nothing accurate of the amounts paid to the zamindars by the ryots and of the amounts retained by the latter. The information was mainly in the hands of the hereditary corporation of kanungos, whose business it was to act as registrars of land revenue and to secure that the ryots were not oppressed. These functions they had come to perform in such a manner that the ryots derived no profit from their existence, while they more or less intimidated the zamindars into sharing their profits with them. If the collectors had been persistently kept at work it might have been possible to obtain such an exact knowledge of the system as would have permitted of due protection of the tenant and of the interests of the government; as it was, lack of proper knowledge was to compel acceptance of the permanent settlement of Bengal in which the government and the tenants alike were losers in the interests of the zamindars or tax-collectors.

The president and council, on November 23rd 1773, drew up a scheme which was to have been temporary but was not effectively revised by the Company. A committee of revenue was formed at Calcutta composed of two members of council and three other servants of the Company to supervise the first of the six divisions into which the territory was divided. In the other five provincial councils were set up, apparently in the expectation that the Calcutta committee would ultimately take over their functions. In each district the collector was to be replaced by an Indian diwan; occasional inspections were to be made by commissioners of the board of revenue set up in 1772, and the chiefs of the councils had to swear not to engage in private trade, receiving in lieu the substantial salary of 3,000 rupees a month. The new scheme proved no improvement on the old; the records show defaulting zamindars, absconding farmers, and deserting ryots; the diwans did their work both slowly and badly, and the provincial councils insisted, as had the collectors, that the land was over-assessed, that at Patna suggesting as the only remedy a settlement in perpetuity as the one way of securing stability. Hastings was not a revenue expert, and the problem was unsolved when the régime of the Regulating Act deprived him of the complete ascendancy which in fact he exercised over his colleagues, and which made his position for the two years one of unquestioned though informal authority.

On the other hand, his reforms in judicial matters are of greater note, because, while in the nature of things they had to suffer much change, they were on sound lines at the time and helped to the more efficient execution of justice. Verelst had quite fairly denounced the system of civil and criminal justice under the nawab: 'Every decision is a corrupt bargain with the highest bidder . . . Trifling offenders are frequently loaded with heavy demands and capital offences are as often absolved by the venal judge.' The Company, as holders of the diwani, were responsible for civil justice, as virtual masters of the nawab they were morally reponsible for criminal justice and in the reform scheme regard was had to both duties.

The system of justice existing in Bengal before the Company became responsible was summary and unsatisfactory. The chief criminal court was held by the local zamindar, who had a right to the fines exacted by reason of his tenure; he could pronounce sentence of death, but execution depended on the orders of the government at Murshidabad. The zamindar was also the judge of the civil court, or adalat, taking a fourth or fifth part of the amount recovered. Naturally, in lieu of litigation in this court arbitration was often preferred. The law administered was that of the Koran and the commentators;

where these afforded no guide, local customs and usage were relied on, but these were so ill defined that judgment was largely discretionary. Appeal lay to the similar courts at the capital, but in addition the government could interfere in the course of justice, and could give on complaint a remedy or inflict punishment without any judicial sentence. Moreover, in the districts the peasants were hampered even in seeking justice by the lack of local courts. Corrupt judges and a corrupt government added to the defects of the legal system, and the absence of any register of judicial proceedings rendered appeals most difficult.

Religious causes were not decided by the temporal judges without the aid in cases affecting Muhammadans of the kaḍi, and in those affecting Hindus of a brahman, especially in cases where outcasting might be the result of condemnation. Clearly this rule afforded in inheritance cases a certain security for the observation of justice denied in issues of criminal law.

In revenue cases the jurisdiction had been originally exercised by the zamindar, but some time before the diwani passed to the Company jurisdiction had, doubtless in the interest of the government, been transferred to deputies, naib diwans, with appeal to the chief diwan at Murshidabad.

The forms of justice thus existed, but it is clear that the courts were the instruments of power rather than of justice, useless as means of protection, but apt instruments for oppression. It is significant of the position that the servants of the Company, when they had claims against Indians, not residing under the British flag but in the vicinity of the Company's settlements, used simply to seize and hold them prisoners until they consented to pay, without asking the authority of any officer of the native government, but with its full approval. The government indeed was so complaisant as to overlook cases of seizure of persons who did not fall within this category, and after the Company's acquisition of the diwani both the French and the Dutch exercised like rights, the French at least disputing the demand of the president and council that recourse in such cases must be had to the law courts.

The course of justice was further troubled by the revolution, which placed Mir Kasim in power, for many Englishmen with or without the consent of the Company soon scattered through the interior to seize the trade, and exerted wide influence on the administration of justice, and the overthrow of Mir Kasim led to further encroachments on native authority, the banyans or native agents of the English often controlling the local courts and even acting as judges. The beginnings of better things seem to have followed the appointment of supervisors in 1769, for they were encouraged to observe the maintenance of justice, to discourage arbitrary fines, and the retention of a fourth of the value as a perquisite of the court. It seems that capital and other important cases were referred to the resident at Murshidabad in order that the pleasure of the nawab should be taken, which, of course, in practice meant that of the deputy, who was under effective control by the Company.

For this unsatisfactory state of affairs the remedy proposed on August 15th 1772 provided for the creation in each district[1] of a provincial Court of Diwani—Mofussil Diwani Adalat—for all civil causes including real and personal property, inheritance, caste, marriage, debts, disputed accounts, contracts, partnerships, and demands of rent. Over this court presided the collector and other officers of the Company; cases were heard twice a week in open court. From its decision appeal lay to the Diwani Sadr Adalat at the chief seat of government. In that court the president with at least two members of council sat, aided by the diwan of the treasury, the chief kanungos, and other officers. From this jurisdiction was excepted the right of succession to zamindaris and talukdaris, which remained reserved to the president and council in their executive capacity.

Criminal courts were constituted on a similar basis. In the provincial courts sat the kazi and mufti of the district with two maulvis to expound the law, the Muhammadan criminal law, and decide if the accused were guilty of a breach thereof; but the collector was enjoined to see that evidence was duly submitted and weighed and the decision passed fair and impartial, and given in open court. The proceedings of the

[1] At Calcutta similar courts were set up, the civil replacing the court of 1758 (Chap. I, § 3 (*d*)), the criminal the Zamindari Court for natives, while it was presided over by a member of council who as a justice of the peace could apply English law to Europeans; *Warren Hastings in Bengal*, pp. 327, 328.

provincial Faujdari Adalats were supervised by the Nizamat Sadr Adalat, presided over by the Darogo Adalat, appointed by the nazim, representing the nawab in his capacity of supreme criminal judge, with the aid of the chief kadi, the chief mufti, and three maulvis. The chief and council were to supervise the proceedings of this court. In capital cases the court certified its view to the nazim, but Hastings arranged (1774) for the grant of authority to the darogo to affix the seal of the nazim to warrants of execution, thus giving in effect power to the court to pass final sentences.

Much was also laid down to improve procedure, including due records in each provincial Diwani Adalat and their transmission to the Sadr Adalat. To relieve the ryots from the burden of travelling in search of justice the head farmers of the parganas were empowered to decide without appeal suits up to ten rupees. But the practice of the exercise of jurisdiction by creditors over debtors, as of moneylenders over ryots, was absolutely forbidden. Arbitration by consent as opposed to compulsion under the old system was advocated for partnership debts, disputed accounts, contracts, and the like, while in cases involving marriage, inheritance, caste, and other religious usages the Koran for Muhammadans and the Shastras for Hindu were made binding, the maulvis or brahmans to expound the law and aid in the decision. In cases up to five hundred rupees in value the provincial courts could give final decisions, but thereafter appeal lay. The practice of heavy charges for delivering judgments was stopped, and officials were forbidden to take fees for themselves. The Faujdari courts were not permitted to pass death sentences, but must transmit the evidence with their opinion to the Sadr Court for decision. Any fine over a hundred rupees must be confirmed by the Sadr Court, which alone could decree forfeiture and confiscation of property. Against dacoits great severity was provided; they were to be executed in their own villages, their families made state slaves, and their villages fined, while police officers were to be rewarded for activity in their apprehension. In imposing the death penalty Hastings deliberately went beyond the Koran.

An important clause authorized the collectors to make

subsidiary regulations for the due course of justice and the welfare and prosperity of the ryots as local circumstances might require, the approval of the council being eventually required. This is interesting as a recognition of the right of the Company through its officers to exercise the power of making regulations which appertained to the diwan.

The abolition of the collectorships in 1773 interfered with the judicial arrangements in an unfortunate manner. Their place was taken in each district by the diwans, who reported their proceedings to the provincial council. In each division there was a provincial court, presided over in succession by the members of the council other than the member of the presidency council, but with power to the whole council to revise the proceedings of the superintending member. Appeal lay from the councils to the Sadr Adalat in matters above 1,000 rupees in value. Complaints against the head farmers, diwans, zamindars, and other chief officers were assigned to the provincial councils with appeal to the council of revenue at Calcutta. Complaints against officers of the Faujdari Adalats were to lie to the governor, and by him to be referred to the Nizamat Adalat for inquiry and determination. Clearly, whatever the objections to the combination of revenue collection and jurisdiction in the hands of the collectors, the change suggested by Hastings could serve no useful purpose.

It must be added that Hastings was aware of the desirability of the due ascertainment of Hindu and Muhammadan law and contemplated the issue of codes of both, tentative preparations for this end being set on foot. In one regard, however, his inaction must be censured. When British officers were given oversight over the administration, it was intolerable that they should have been compelled to acquiesce in sentences of mutilation and impalement, and these could have been abolished forthwith.

Of Hastings' commercial reforms, part of which were only made effective later, little need be said. In March 1775 he swept away the abuse of the fraudulent employment of the free passes to exempt the goods of the servants of the Company from dues. The latter were reduced to 2½ per cent, payable by Europeans and Indians alike, and the customs-houses in the zamindaris were swept away, leaving only the central establishments at Calcutta, Hugli, Murshidabad, Patna, and Dacca. Monopolies in salt, betel-nut, and tobacco alone were retained, and the decaying internal trade was definitely stimulated.

In his relations with the nawab, as has been seen, Hastings was utterly indifferent to the maintenance of the fiction of his sovereignty. In this period of his career he was no less opposed to any recognition of effective authority in the Emperor. He had two good excuses for his attitude. The Emperor had most unwisely in 1771 permitted himself to accept the tutelage of the Marathas when, recovering from the disaster at Panipat (1761), they swarmed back to Delhi, and the Company was desperately anxious to save the tribute of twenty-six lakhs of which he was in receipt. Hastings determined not to pay, and so peremptorily declined to do so on the ground of the poverty of the province, denouncing to the directors the folly of aggrandizing an enemy, and he sold Kora and Allahabad, which had been designed as an appanage of the Emperor, for fifty lakhs to the nawab of Oudh. Hastings has been applauded for his action by serious judges,[1] but it clearly was a definite breach of a solemn promise and neither legally nor morally defensible, for the Company should clearly have warned the Emperor in 1771 that his adherence to its enemies would compel it to stop the tribute, if that were its intention. Hastings seems indeed to have gone further, and to have contemplated establishing direct relations between the Crown and Oudh; he must have discussed the project at Benares in 1773 when he visited Shuja-ud-daula, and found him willing to strike his coinage in the name of the King, a decisive feature. He seems in 1777 to have contemplated the possibility of such action as regards Berar also, but the project evidently never matured in his mind.[2] In any case, the British Government would never then have agreed to so decisive an assertion of sovereign power. In the Treaty of Paris in 1763 it made no claim to sovereignty, contenting itself with an agreement with France under which Salabat Jang was recognized as subadar of the Deccan and Muhammad Ali as nawab of the Carnatic. Not until 1769 was

[1] *C.H.I.*, v, 216.

[2] Gleig, *Warren Hastings*, i, 508; ii, 136.

direct action taken by the Crown, and then only in the shape of commissioning the commodore of the squadron, which was to escort the supervisors of the Company to India, as royal plenipotentiary, and sending through him gifts to the Emperor in return for those presented by the latter to the King on his accession. As the Company was not duly informed of the commission, its local councils questioned the authority of the commodore to interfere with their relations with the Indian States, and much friction arose between the Madras Council and Lindsay, and his successor Harland, who even projected the conclusion of a treaty with the Marathas in violation of the subsisting agreement of 1769 with Hyder Ali. The experience then gained would, it may safely be said, have negatived any desire on the part of the ministry to add to its troubles direct responsibility for Indian affairs.

The unquestioned authority of Hastings displayed itself in his conduct of relations with Oudh and his disposition of the Company's military forces. He allowed himself to be induced to support the nawab in the destruction of the Rohilla power in Rohilkhand, an achievement accompanied by the gravest excesses on the part of the nawab's forces. Hastings in this matter is beyond excuse; happily in no later case were British forces placed at the disposal of a despotic ruler for the carrying out of a policy which resulted in the destruction of enlightened rulers in favour of the sovereignty of a dynasty whose government of its unhappy subjects was from first to last indescribably incompetent and unjust.[1] For Hastings the chief gain was the relief to the funds of the Company.

2. THE INTERVENTION OF PARLIAMENT AND THE REGULATING ACT

The period of Hastings' unquestioned authority was now to pass away, for Parliament had at last been driven to intervene with definite authority. It was now patent that the East India Company was no longer merely a company for the extension of commerce, 'but in reality a delegation of the whole power and sovereignty of this kingdom sent into the East'. Such a body

[1] Thompson and Garratt, *British Rule in India*, pp. 128–31.

could not be allowed to remain outside the interest of the state. To leave it to carry on without further control was impossible; even Clive and Hastings, as we have seen, had held that direct relations with the Crown might be desirable. To carry this farther to the logical conclusion of establishing the sovereignty of the Crown, in lieu of that of the Company, was a step too bold to be expected. It would have necessitated the rejection of the sanctity of property rights, one of the maxims most strongly held by the Parliament of the time. It would have placed directly in the hands of the government an enormous mass of dangerous patronage. It would have compelled an immediate definition of the rights of the diwani, for the Crown could not with dignity hold as delegate of the Mogul, and much bitterness would assuredly be caused in India and among European powers if the necessary course of negativing Mogul sovereignty was adopted. There remained, therefore, only the alternative of subjecting in its political aspect the Company to legitimate control, and this step was strongly commended by the current doctrines of constitutional law. There seems no reason to doubt the soundness of the view taken by the law officers on December 24th 1757:[1] in the case of territory granted by Indian princes under peaceful conditions the right of property vested in the donees, but the sovereignty over the inhabitants as English subjects and over the settlements as English settlements vested in the Crown; in the case of territories acquired by conquest the property and the sovereignty alike vested in the Crown. Governor Johnstone,[2] it is true, in the debates on the Bill proposed by the Company in 1772 for the better government of their territories, denied that lands gained by conquest vested in the Crown, asserting therefore that the Company was lawfully owner. But in any case he suggested from his colonial experience that the Crown should grant the lands to the Company as in New England, asserting that foreign states would be perfectly well pleased to have the position regularized in place of the pretence of control by a cipher of a nawab. Clive spoke strongly against the directors, the proprietors, the government, and the administration of the Company in India, and the Bill was decisively

[1] *C.H.I.*, v, 593.

[2] *Parl. Hist.*, xvii, 376 f.

rejected. Instead, Burgoyne secured the appointment of a select committee in April to inquire into the state of affairs in India, alleging that the prime evil was the intermixture of trade and government.[1] In August the Company was forced to beg the government for a loan, despite the fact that in March a dividend of 12½ per cent had been declared, and this elicited the appointment of a secret committee. The two reported from time to time with great rapidity showing such serious errors that Chatham wrote[2] in 1773, 'India teems with iniquities so rank as to smell to earth and heaven,' and Shelburne, with his usual wealth of information, repeated the condemnation of directors, proprietors, the Indian administration, and the government. Parliament was so moved that in December 1772 it forbade the proposed dispatch of supervisors to India as involving expense which the Company could not afford.

The Company in March 1773 renewed an appeal for a loan, and in May Burgoyne resumed his attack, and secured the passing of a resolution,[3] 'That all acquisitions, made under the influence of a military force, or by treaty with foreign princes, do of right belong to the State.' This resolution, as its wording shows, was specially aimed at covering the condition of affairs in Bengal, and, though a resolution of the House could not make law, it is clear that it correctly declared with all the authority of Parliament behind it the existing law. Decisive action by Parliament was forthcoming, though Burke denounced as unconstitutional interference with an established right. The pecuniary needs of the Company were relieved by a loan of £1,400,000 at 4 per cent and the promise to forgo the Company's debt of £400,000 until the new loan had been discharged. The Company was forbidden to declare a dividend exceeding 6 per cent and required to submit accounts half-yearly to the Treasury.[4] But far more important was the accompanying Act imposing new political conditions, the Regulating Act,[5] which Burke denounced as 'an infringement of national right, national faith, and national justice'. This measure altered the constitution of the Company at home, changed the structure of the government in India, subjected in some degree the whole

[1] *Parl. Hist.*, xvii, 454 ff.
[2] *Correspondence*, iv, 276.
[3] *Parl. Hist.*, xvii, 856.
[4] 13 Geo. III, c. 64.
[5] 13 Geo. III, c. 63.

of the territories to one supreme control in India, and provided in a very inefficient manner for the supervision of the Company by the ministry.

To secure continuity in the direction annual election of the whole body of twenty-four directors was terminated, six being elected each year, to hold office for four years, and then to be ineligible for re-election for at least one year. In practice few changes were made, and thus a directorate of thirty members of whom six were temporarily out of office was constituted. Voting power was restricted to holders for at least a year of £1,000 stock and measures were laid down to frustrate collusive transfers in order to multiply votes. The result was to deprive 1,246 of the smaller holders, but the measure failed to improve the quality of the Court of Proprietors or to prevent power being readily purchased by servants of the Company returning with the spoils of the East, especially as holders of £3,000 stock were now given two votes, of £6,000 three, and of £10,000 or over four votes.

For the government of the presidency of Fort William a governor-general and four councillors were appointed by name, Hastings as governor-general, General Clavering, Colonel Monson, Barwell, and Francis. They were given office for five years,[1] and could be removed earlier only by the King on the recommendation of the Court of Directors; a casual vacancy in the office of governor-general was to be filled by the senior member of council, while the Company was to fill any casual vacancy in the members of council with the assent of the Crown, and after five years to have the full patronage. In this body was vested the whole civil and military government of the presidency, and the management and government of all the territorial acquisitions and revenues in the kingdoms of Bengal, Bihar, and Orissa, in like manner as they were or might have been exercised by the president and council or select committee hitherto. The Act thus evaded in the characteristic British manner the danger of definition by reference to a *fait accompli.*

The other presidencies were subjected to Bengal in so far as

[1] Hence apparently the five years' normal tenure of the governor's office in India, and of many minor posts.

no government of such a presidency might give orders for commencing hostilities or declaring war against any Indian power or for concluding any treaty of peace or other treaty with such a power without the previous consent of the governor-general in council, but two vital exceptions were allowed, those of imminent necessity which would render postponement dangerous, and the receipt of special orders direct from the Company. A president and council offending could be suspended by the governor-general and council. Moreover, the governors were to transmit regularly to the governor-general intelligence of all transactions relating to the government, revenues, or interests of the Company.

On the other hand, the governor-general and council were to obey the orders of the Court of Directors and to keep it fully informed of all matters affecting the interests of the Company. In its turn it was to send the Treasury, within fourteen days after receipt, copies of advices received regarding the revenues, and to a secretary of state advices as to civil and military affairs.

These provisions were supplemented by remarkable clauses regulating the judicial arrangements of the presidency. The committee of secrecy in its report of May 6th 1773 had stressed the unsatisfactory character of the existing system under the charter of 1753, since the trial of claims against the Company in the Mayor's Court and of charges against its servants in the Court of Oyer and Terminer and Gaol Delivery was vitiated by the fact that the judges held office subject to removal by the governor and council, from whose action there lay only the dilatory remedy of appeal to the King in Council. Moreover, the judges were supposed to act by English law, of which they were largely ignorant, with the result that they referred for the advice of the Company's counsel before decision—for instance, regarding their ecclesiastical jurisdiction and power of dealing with crimes committed by Europeans not under the Company's flag. In this regard it was pointed out that the charter conferred authority only over the town or district of Calcutta and its subordinate factories, and that there were many of His Majesty's subjects resident in Bengal who did not fall under the jurisdiction of English law.

To meet these difficulties the Regulating Act provided for the erection of a judiciary emanating directly from the Crown, and therefore able to punish the servants of the Company without fear of consequences and to adjudicate on claims against it. The charter of March 26th 1774 gave effect with minor additions to the express provisions of the Act, superseding for Calcutta the provisions of the charter of 1753. The Court was constituted of a chief justice and three puisne judges appointed by the King from barristers of five years' standing, to hold office at pleasure, and their authority was assimilated to that of judges of King's Bench in England. They were empowered to appoint necessary subordinate officers, but the governor-general and council must approve their salaries. With like assent they could regulate court fees. The admission of attorneys and advocates lay in their hands, and they nominated three persons for the office of sheriff when selection was made by the governor-general and council.

The jurisdiction of the court was of the widest possible character, including the functions of a Court of Equity according to the rules of the English High Court of Chancery, so that the same court combined both the common law and the equity jurisdiction. It was also a Court of Oyer and Terminer and Gaol Delivery for Calcutta, the factory of Fort William, and the factories subordinate thereto as if in England, justice being administered through grand and petty juries summoned by the sheriff. As a superior court it was empowered to superintend the Court of Requests and the Court of Quarter Sessions and the magistrates thereof—the governor-general, members of council, and judges being made justices with power to hold Sessions by the Act—and to issue to such courts and officers writs of mandamus, certiorari, procedendo, or error. Further, it was given ecclesiastical jurisdiction over British subjects in Bengal, Bihar, and Orissa, so far as circumstances required, to be exercised as in the diocese of London, and in special it might grant probates and letters of administration, to which was added power to deal with the estates of insane persons. It was also made a Court of Admiralty for Bengal, Bihar, and Orissa and the adjacent dependent territories and islands, and authorized with a jury of British subjects resident in Calcutta to punish treasons, murders, piracies, etc., committed on the high seas within its jurisdiction.

In civil matters appeal lay to the King in Council as in the colonies; it must be brought within six months and the matter must be over one thousand pagodas in value. In criminal causes its consent was required for any appeal.

The jurisdiction of the court, however, was limited in respect of those to whom it was to apply. It had authority over all British subjects resident in Bengal, Bihar, and Orissa, and could hear and determine all complaints against any of His Majesty's subjects for crimes, misdemeanours, or oppressions, and also to entertain, hear, and determine any suits whatsoever against any of His Majesty's subjects in Bengal, Bihar, and Orissa, and any suit, action, or complaint against any person employed by or in the service of the Company or of any of His Majesty's subjects. Clearly many of the inhabitants of the areas mentioned would not fall within its jurisdiction, and a special clause modified this exclusion. The court could hear any suit or action by any of His Majesty's subjects against any inhabitants of India within the territories named on any contract in writing, where the cause of action exceeded five hundred rupees and the inhabitants had agreed in the contract that in case of dispute the matter should be determined in the Supreme Court; in such cases the action might be brought in the first instance in that court, or on appeal from a provincial court. It seems clearly to follow from this enumeration that normally suits by British subjects against Indians could be brought only by consent of the defendant, that suits by inhabitants against inhabitants were not expected to be brought, but presumably could be heard by consent, but that suits lay always against British subjects and persons employed by the Company or any of His Majesty's subjects.

From the jurisdiction of the court were excluded offences short of treason or felony of the governor-general, council, and judges, and their arrest in civil proceedings was forbidden.

Offences of which the court had cognizance were to be tried by a jury of British subjects resident in Calcutta.

The court superseded the Mayor's Court and that of Oyer and Terminer under the charter of 1753, but not those of

Requests and Quarter Sessions, which were to be held as before, the judges being added as justices to the governor-general and council.

Legislative power was granted as in the charter of 1753. The governor-general and council could make rules, ordinances, and regulations for the good order and civil government of Fort William and the subordinate factories; such enactments were to be just and reasonable and not repugnant to the laws of the realm, and reasonable fines and forfeitures[1] could be imposed for their breach. But they were not to have effect until registered in the Supreme Court with its approval;[2] copies must be sent home, to be exhibited at the India House and to be communicated to a secretary of state, and they might spontaneously or on representations being made be cancelled by the King in Council. This procedure substituted the court as the immediate check on hasty legislation, but avoided the long delay of obtaining home approval as required by the charter of 1753.

A series of clauses was aimed at the flagrant errors of the past. The governor-general and council and the judges were not to receive presents or engage in trade save that of the Company. No officer, civil or military, might accept a present from any native prince or power on pain of forfeiting double the amount and being removed from India. No officers engaged in revenue collection were to engage in trade or any of the state monopolies. No subject of His Majesty was to lend money at more than 12 per cent interest. Servants of the Company punished for breach of trust might be removed to England. A dismissed servant could be restored to office only with the assent of three-fourths of the directors and proprietors. Further, the Court of King's Bench in England was given power to punish any offence against the Act or any crime, misdemeanour, or offence against any of His Majesty's subjects or of the inhabitants of India.

At the same time. to recompense the officers for losses under

[1] The power to provide whipping was only given by 39 & 40 Geo. III, c. 79, ss. 18, 19, to two justices.

[2] A parallel may be seen in the one-time requirement that corporations should enter by-laws on record with justices of the peace and have them examined by the chancellor or judges (15 Hen. VI, c. 6; 19 Hen. VII, c. 7); Perry, J., in *Ramchund Ursamul* v. *Glass* (1844), Or. Cas. 360.

a more regular régime, salaries were granted on a generous scale, £25,000 for the governor-general, £10,000 for members of council, and £8,000 for the chief justice.

3. WARREN HASTINGS AS GOVERNOR-GENERAL—EXTERNAL AFFAIRS

Warren Hastings was unfortunate from the first in his colleagues on the council and in the rule that he had no power to override them, though in case of equality he was given a casting vote. The plan adopted was in accord with the existing practice in the presidencies. This differed from the usage in the colonies, where the governor was advised by a council but not effectively controlled by it, having in emergency the right to displace members, and being normally responsible for recommending their appointment.[1] The system might have operated more successfully had the other councillors been men akin in spirit; it could hardly have been desirable in any case. As it was, Clavering, Monson, and Francis came to India under the influence of the general belief in the discreditable character of Indian officers of both races, and Francis at least was animated by dreams of winning the governor-generalship for himself. Hastings could rely on Barwell, who dropped interest in public affairs in order to amass in flat defiance of law and duty an enormous fortune. But, until Monson died on September 25th 1776, the control of the council rested with his opponents. Unquestionably they misused their power to harass needlessly the governor-general, and forfeited any claim to moral sympathy in their treatment of Nandakumar, whom they encouraged to prefer charges against Hastings. The latter apparently could not refute the allegations of a man he hated deeply, and instead resorted to counter-attack, Nandakumar being accused of forgery, committed five years previously, by an Indian, Mohan Prasad. Nothing but racial prejudice can explain the efforts to minimize the part played by Hastings in this matter; twelve days after the committal he prophesied (May 18th) his enemy's death, though the case against him was not tried until June and though, if the judges had done

[1] Keith, *Const. Hist. of First British Empire*, pp. 191 ff.

their duty, they would have refused to try the accused on the plain ground that he was not subject to the criminal jurisdiction of the court. But in fact the judges, seeing that even the twelve British jurors might not be convinced by the evidence for the prosecution, intimidated the witnesses for the defence by cross-examination in a hostile manner. Moreover, it is clear that the provision of the English statute of 1728 making forgery a capital offence was not legally in force in India. Apart from the tentative terms of the charter of 1661, English law was introduced by the charter of 1726. The subsequent charter of 1753 and the Act of 1773 could not possibly be regarded, as they were by Impey, as substantive reintroductions of English law up to their date, and in any case to apply literally an English law was a mere miscarriage of justice. No Indian after him was executed for the crime, and in 1802 the chief justice expressly admitted that it was not capital.[1] The sentence in any event should, as a matter of plain duty, have been respited by the court, but Hastings' private secretary intervened to prevent such action, and the councillors did nothing. No more odious crime has ever been committed by a British court, whether or not on the instigation of a British governor-general. For Hastings it had the invaluable result of showing natives that with him final power lay, and a complete veil was drawn over charges which but shortly before the councillors were pressing against him with such violence that he refused to continue meetings as governor-general and denied that they could act without him.

Monson's death gave Hastings control by his casting vote, but in June 1777 his position was challenged by Clavering, whose incompetence was only equalled by his greed for power, on the score that Hastings' agent had tendered his resignation, which the directors had accepted. Hastings had withdrawn the authority given, and the issue was decided by the Supreme Court in favour of Hastings, who thus owed a fresh debt to Impey. On August 30th Clavering's death gave control definitely to Hastings, for the new-comer Wheler was gradually won over, and Sir Eyre Coote, when he succeeded Clavering

[1] Morley, *Digest*, Intr., pp. xi, xxiii; Thompson and Garratt, *British Rule in India*, pp. 137–9.

as commander-in-chief, was on the whole apt to follow Hastings. Wheler naturally preferred cash to credit, and acquiesced in Hastings' disgraceful treatment of Chait Singh and the begams of Oudh. Francis disappeared in November 1780, as the result of a duel which Hastings most disgracefully had fastened upon him, and for which later he took ample revenge. Barwell had gone home in 1779; in September 1781 and November 1782 Macpherson and Stables were sent to the council. Both had difficulty with Hastings, but their opposition was often justified and they restrained him from several errors. It is clear that he was a most difficult colleague, completely self-satisfied, and extremely jealous lest any credit for anything done should fall to others.

The disunion of council was unfortunate, for the problems to be faced, external and internal, were of the utmost gravity, especially as the governor-general and council were now given a general controlling power over the other presidencies, and in Madras especially there had taken place events which showed the absolute necessity for such control.

The successive governments at Madras were well content to remain on terms of intimacy with the nawab of the Carnatic, whose position France recognized in the treaty of Paris 1763. Clive in his dealings with the Emperor in 1765 was not unmindful of the nawab, and secured a firman exempting him from dependence on the Deccan, and another granting the northern sarkars to the Company at the expense of the Nizam to whose charge they had lapsed after the expulsion of the French, to whom they had earlier been granted. The grant to the Company was resented by the Nizam, and accord was only reached with him in 1766, when Caillaud concluded a treaty with him whereby in return for the tenure of the sarkars, the English undertook to provide a force to aid the Nizam when required, paying nine lakhs in any year when it was not called on, while the Nizam undertook to aid the Company. This was in effect an alliance against Hyder Ali, who had usurped power in Mysore, and with whom Bombay had meditated an alliance. War with Hyder followed; in 1767 the Nizam failed to keep faith, but next year changed his mind, and renewed the treaty of 1766 with a reduction of the British force promised. The successes of Hyder, however, compelled the council to make peace and to accept a defensive alliance. As noted above, the situation was complicated by the appearance of Commodore Lindsay with a squadron sent at the Company's request against a possible French attack, and a commission from the King to treat with the princes of India.[1] He endeavoured without success, as did his successor, to embroil the council with Hyder by aiding the Marathas in their war of 1770–1 with that prince. But Lindsay, aided by the financial influences headed by Paul Benfield, lent his aid to the nawab's demand for the conquest of Tanjore, which was finally carried out in 1773. When the Company disapproved and Lord Pigot was sent out as governor to reverse the policy, he found himself faced by the opposition of the council, backed by Benfield, and when he attempted to suspend the chief councillors, a revolt took place; he was arrested (August 1776) and detained until his death next year in military custody. The guilty councillors were indeed recalled and tried by King's Bench, but escaped with the paltry fine of £1,000, while Benfield, sent back to England, bribed permission to return in 1781.

The power which thus dominated Madras was as usual that of the purse. Instead of striving to reform the administration of the nawab, the councillors under Benfield's influence joined in a system of loans from which the nawab paid off periodically some of his debts to the Company and bribed wholesale the council. In this way the nawab retained full power of misrule, bribing directors and members of Parliament, so that neither the Company nor the government stepped in to end the disgraceful system, which is complete proof of the utter corruption of English political life.

Rumbold, sent in 1779 as governor, added to the misfortunes of the presidency by tactless relations with the Nizam, from whom the Company held the sarkars at nine lakhs, but, as Guntoor was in the hands for life of the Nizam's brother, paid seven only. He irritated the Nizam by obtaining the transfer of Guntoor direct from his brother, and by adding to this injury the insult of asking him to drop any claim for the

[1] The government had the excuse that the Company had allowed in 1768 the French to mount guns at Chandernagore in defiance of the treaty of Paris; *C.H.I.*, v, 277 ff.

tribute. Hastings now intervened, as he was clearly entitled to do, repudiated the suggestion, and appointed as his resident with the Nizam Hollond, the Madras agent whom Madras dismissed for his obedience to Bengal.[1] Hastings, despite protests, forced the return to the Nizam of Guntoor, but not until Hyder had begun war in the middle of 1780, finding that the Company would not renew the alliance of 1769, and in defiance of his protests had seized Mahé on the outbreak of war with France, whose alliance he now sought. Rumbold had gone home before the storm broke, and Whitehill, his successor, and the commander-in-chief Munro, hopelessly mismanaged matters. Hastings had to send Coote with six hundred European troops and fifteen lakhs, and with justice dismissed Whitehill for disobedience regarding the return of Guntoor.

So far Hastings had had to deal with men inferior to himself, but at the close of 1780 Lord Macartney was appointed governor, and, though he came to India with the intention of working with Hastings, he was forced to assert his own views. He could not obey the desire of Hastings to make an alliance with the Dutch, because Holland was at war and he had orders from the Company to seize the Dutch forts. He demurred on his own judgment to the orders of Hastings to cede the sarkars to the Nizam. Further, Coote's independent position in waging war was justly resented by Macartney and his select committee which controlled political relations, for Coote did not discuss his plans and made extravagant demands for transport and supplies. Macartney took the wise step of requiring the nawab to transfer to the Company his revenues for five years, a fifth to be paid to the nawab, and so managed the revenues as to relieve the peasants and secure large sums for the Company. But Hastings, apparently to buy Benfield's interest in London, ordered the cancellation of the arrangement, and in 1783 sought to empower Coote, whom he dispatched to Madras once more, to suspend Macartney, a criminal folly from which his councillors held him back, most fortunately, for Madras was determined to fight the governor-general's project. This was followed up by the conclusion by Macartney of a treaty with Hyder on the only possible basis of mutual surrender of

[1] A. P. Dasgupta, *The Central Authority in British India*, pp. 81 ff.

conquests and restoration of prisoners. Hastings vehemently condemned it and once more vainly desired to suspend its author, though common sense showed that his action was inevitable. Unhappily in 1785 the Company, more susceptible to bribes than Macartney, ordered the cancellation of the assignment, whereupon Macartney very properly resigned rather than carry out so foolish a policy.

A further constitutional issue was raised by Macartney. Stuart, Coote's successor as commander-in-chief of the Company's forces and the King's forces, apparently meditated a repetition of the *coup d'état* against Pigot, so that Macartney arrested him and sent him home, appointing a Company's officer with the rank of lieutenant-general to command the Company's and the royal forces. His right to take the latter step was denied by Sir John Burgoyne, the senior officer, who was than arrested by Macartney.[1] In this action he was probably without legal justification, but the issue was adjusted by the decision that in future royal officers holding commands under the East India Company should receive letters of service authorizing them to exercise their rank only so long as they continued in that service, so that dismissal terminated their authority in India.

In the case of Bombay, Hastings had the opportunity of showing his great superiority in capacity of conception and execution to the other servants of the Company. Bombay had long cast eager eyes on Salsette and Bassein, and advantage was taken of the disputes as to the Peshwaship to seize by force Salsette at the end of 1774, and to enter into an alliance with Raghunath Rao, uncle of the infant Peshwa. The Bengal Council, overruling Hastings, justly censured the action of Bombay as both wrong and contrary to the restrictions of the Regulating Act, and sent Upton to negotiate a new accord, which was signed at Purandhar on March 1st 1776. In the meantime the Company had condoned the alliance with Raghunath, but later properly held that the terms of Purandhar should be kept if the Marathas did their share, which was not the case. A period of confusion followed, resulting in the

[1] The central government admitted its inability to intervene; Dasgupta, op. cit., pp. 250 ff.

unwise and improper decision of the Bombay Council to make war on the Maratha Empire, with the result of disaster and the conclusion by the commander of the beaten force of the convention of Wadgaon in 1779, which both the governor of Bombay and the governor-general legitimately repudiated. Ultimately matters were rectified by Hastings' energy, which procured the funds necessary and found effective leaders. Goddard's successful march across India revealed the strength of the central authority at the expense of the presidency, and he captured Bassein in 1780, while Popham struck a most effective blow by seizing Gwalior, and inducing Mahadaji Sindhia, greatest of the Maratha leaders who were now breaking away from the Peshwa's control, to act as intermediary in securing peace. This was signed at Salbai on May 17th 1782. The treaty is the chief contribution of Hastings to British power in India. It placed relations with the Marathas on a basis which lasted for twenty years, and left the Company visibly the controlling power in Indian politics. All conquests since 1776 were to be restored, the Gaekwad, whose close connexion with the Company was now consolidated, received back his dominions; Hyder Ali was to be required to return all conquests from the Company and the Carnatic, and the Peshwa and the Company undertook that their several allies should remain at peace with one another. No doubt the provision as to Hyder was rendered of minor importance owing to Tipu's later successes, but it seems clear that before his death on December 7th 1782 Hyder had recognized that the Company was to be predominant in India. Certain it is that after Hyder's death the Peshwa's great minister, Nana Phadnavis, felt bound to ratify the treaty which he disliked. Sindhia from this time definitely embarked on that policy of personal aggrandizement in disregard of his duty to the Peshwa, which made him until his death in 1794 the dominant factor in northern India.

Unhappily the wisdom shown in these proceedings by Hastings was sadly lacking in his other transactions with the country powers. The constitutional interest of these transactions, which are condemned even by some of his admirers, is that Hastings enunciated in the most absolute terms the worthlessness of treaties of any kind as a protection to those who were in relations with the Company. His demands on Chait Singh of Benares,[1] which ultimately led to the ruin of that chief and the grave desolation of his former territory under the mismanagement of the Company's resident who drew £40,000 a year in addition to his salary, were flatly contrary to the agreement of 1775, and rested merely on the right which he asserted as inherent in every government to impose such assessment as it judged expedient for the common service, to which the sufficient answer is that the tribute fixed in 1775 was a definite regulation of that right. In the same manner the demand made on the begams of Oudh, and enforced by the cruel imprisonment of their ministers despite the very real objections of the nawab, was flatly contrary to a most definite agreement in 1775.[2] Hastings' excuse was that money was needed for the Maratha war, but he added personal disgrace to official wrongdoing by accepting from Chait Singh £20,000 and from the nawab of Oudh £100,000, in flat contradiction to the Act of 1773. Like Clive, Hastings in money matters was below any decent standard of honesty. From a further deliberate and shameful breach of treaty with Faizulla Khan of Rampur, Hastings was only withheld by the stern condemnation of the Company.[3]

Much might be excused Hastings had he used his power over Oudh, helplessly tied to the Company, whose alliance, as he admitted, had become so much feared that Berar shrank from it, to protect the people. That something should be done he admitted, and visited Lucknow in March 1784 for that purpose, but all that he accomplished was the abolition of the residency at the expense of setting up an agency which interfered as much with the administration as did the residency, but at an increased cost of £48,000 a year. The nawab's finances and government remained in a state of complete disorder and his people in an utterly miserable condition.

More surprising still was the tendency of Hastings towards the latter period of his rule, when he had got rid of Francis, to reverse his policy towards the Emperor, and to contemplate

[1] Thompson and Garratt, *British Rule in India*, pp. 159–62. Oudh ceded sovereignty in 1775.

[2] Ibid., pp. 162–4.

[3] *C.H.I.*, v, 303–5.

the restoration of his power. Francis had revived the idea, and in 1782 Hastings dispatched an agent to establish relations with the Emperor, though with clear instructions not to permit discussion of the tribute or Allahabad. In 1784 at Lucknow he entered into relations with the Emperor's eldest son, who was seeking aid to re-establish his father at Delhi, and in fear of the rise of the Sikhs he seems to have been eager to assist in restoring the imperial authority. Happily his council declined to concur, and he had perforce to desist from an enterprise which the Company had denounced as early as 1768, and which would have united the princes of India against the Company. Instead, Mahadaji Sindhia became dominant at Delhi.[1]

Hastings' misdeeds did not go unnoticed in England, and on May 30th 1782 the Commons had censured his conduct as contrary to the policy and honour of the nation and demanded his recall, which had been frustrated by the Court of Proprietors who, under Hastings' control, forbade the directors to act. The demand of his agent in 1786 for charges led to the famous impeachment, for which Pitt and Dundas voted. Their motives may have been mixed, but obviously the charge against Hastings was black, and his defence insolently assertive. But the procedure was quite out of date when it concerned actions done in India, and only twenty-nine peers took enough interest in the proceedings to vote on April 23rd 1795; on the issues of Chait Singh and the begams six pronounced him guilty; others no doubt shared the general belief that so long a trial was adequate punishment. Indeed the position was most difficult, as it always must be, when a country is asked to punish one who has at cost of much wrongdoing added greatly to its power and dominion.

4. WARREN HASTINGS AS GOVERNOR-GENERAL— INTERNAL AFFAIRS

In the internal affairs of Bengal Hastings and his council, for once normally in accord, were confronted by a struggle with the Supreme Court, due almost inevitably to the circumstances attending the creation of that body. But at first Hastings

[1] *C.H.I.*, v, 306; the apologia at p. 601 is wholly ineffective.

established close relations with Impey. The latter revealed on his proposed impeachment that Hastings in defiance of his oath[1] had given him a copy of Nandakumar's accusation against him and the judges of conspiracy, and must therefore have been on intimate terms with him. In concert with him, Hastings proposed to meet the difficulties which soon revealed themselves in the working of the court by a further inroad on the theoretic position of the nawab. Contemptuous of forms, Hastings would have treated British sovereignty as paramount, and have extended the carefully limited jurisdiction of the Supreme Court over the whole of Bengal, Bihar, and Orissa. Secondly, he would have united the judges of the court with the members of the council in control of the Sadr Diwani Adalat, the final Court of Appeal at Calcutta, and he would have put on a definitely legal basis the authority of the provincial councils.[2] But the majority of council, relying on the policy of the directors and of Clive in favour of maintaining the dual form of government, rejected the proposal, and matters between the court and the government became severely strained.

The Act of 1773 unquestionably aimed at giving an impartial court control over the excesses of the Company's servants. But what were the limits of its power? English law itself was and is uncertain as to the extent to which a court can interfere in the actions of the executive government, and in 1774 the matter was much more obscure than it now is, and the Company's servants might well fear grave interference with their methods of revenue collection. Again the legislation left wholly untouched the nature of the law to be administered in the court. It followed, therefore, that it must be English law as far as it could be adapted to Indian conditions. Further, the legislation gave the court authority over British subjects or subjects of His Majesty, and persons employed by the Company or by British subjects. That was in itself natural enough, but whom did it intend to include in the number of British subjects? We may fairly say that the ordinary native of the provinces was not a British subject at this time. But the residents of

[1] Stephen, *Nuncomar and Impey*, ii, 115.
[2] Gleig, *Warren Hastings*, ii, 14, 35, 50.

Calcutta presumably were British subjects, and a claim might be made out in the case of the residents of the twenty-four parganas and even of Burdwan, Chittagong, and Midnapur. But did Parliament intend to cover such persons? Did it not rather refer merely to European British subjects?[1] Further, what was included in employment by the Company? Did it cover a great native landlord farming the revenues? The court held that it did, and that it covered also natives imprisoned by the collectors, to whom it granted writs of habeas corpus. Again, what was the relation of the court to the provincial courts of the Company already referred to? The council was certain that it was determined to keep the court out of any intervention in criminal justice, and Hastings seems to have concurred for this purpose in recognizing once more the authority in form of the nawab. Muhammad Reza Khan was in 1775 appointed deputy with superintendence of the criminal courts, and the Sadr Nizamat Adalat was moved to Murshidabad from Calcutta, where it was in too close proximity to the Supreme Court.

Conflict between court and council came to a head in three cases. In that of the Raja of Kasijura the court claimed that a zamindar must be held subject to their jurisdiction in a case of a claim for a private debt against him. The council ruled that zamindars were not subject to the jurisdiction of the court, and by use of a force of sepoys took captive the sheriff's officers sent to arrest the recalcitrant zamindar. This negatived the claim of the court that at least any person alleging that he was not subject to its jurisdiction must plead accordingly. The point was a most difficult one, but, though the Company did not disapprove of Hastings' action, it was undoubtedly high-handed and dangerous.

Another series of disputes touched the right of the court to punish English or native officers of the Company for acts of oppression committed in the collection of the revenue. Bitterly as this was resented the right of the Court was clear, and Impey had some justification in declaring that the function

[1] *Ameer Khan, In matter of* (1870), 6 Beng. L.R. 392, 443. The Calcutta Supreme Court so held in *Manickram Chattopadha* v. *Meer Conjeer Ali Khan* (1782), Morley, *Digest*, i, 374; but otherwise *In goods of Bux Alley Gawney* (1782), ibid., i, 383. See i, 89 and reff.

of the court should be to protect the peasants against the exactions of English magistrates acting through native subordinates.

Even more important was the Patna case in which the Supreme Court awarded heavy damages against her nephew and the officials of the Patna Council to Nadera Begam. Jurisdiction was exercised in this private suit on the inadequate ground that the nephew was a farmer of the revenue, but the essential point is that the court thus claimed power to penalize the judicial actions of officers of the Company, and that examination of the facts shows that the judicial work of the council, left to Hindu and Muhammadan legal experts, was discreditably done. On the other hand, it is very dubious if the new court were really able to benefit the natives to any extent, and it is certain that governor and council and 648 British subjects resident in Bengal petitioned the Home Government for relief. As an immediate remedy Hastings, without the approval of the Company, which clearly was requisite, obtained Impey's acceptance of the presidency of the Sadr Diwani Adalat, in the belief that in that office he could control wisely the provincial councils and thus avoid conflict with the Supreme Court.

The appointment of Impey followed on earlier steps to reform the provincial councils. On April 11th 1780 their revenue business was separated from judicial business consisting of suits between private persons, which were assigned to Diwani Adalats presided over by a covenanted servant of the Company, appeal in important causes lying through the chief of the provincial council to the Sadr Diwani Adalat, over which the governor-general and council were to preside. In fact, since the Regulating Act that court had not in practice sat,[1] and on its resumption under regulations of April 11th 1780 it seems to have determined cases on the recommendation of the keeper of the treasury records. This was plainly unsatisfactory, and Impey's appointment certainly gave the court a better head, while he was authorized to superintend generally the new inferior courts. He did this part of his work efficiently, prepared a code of procedure, and had the courts increased to

[1] Stephen, *Nuncomar and Impey*, ii, 189.

eighteen,[1] of which only four were presided over by collectors as judges. But it was a fatal flaw in the project that Impey thus was granted at the Company's pleasure a large salary, so that the House of Commons in May 1782 properly demanded his recall to answer the charge of compromising thus the independence of the Supreme Court, by taking a salary from those whom the court was to maintain in due subordination. But impeachment was delayed until 1787, when on the first charge pressed, that regarding Nandakumar, Impey, a trained lawyer, succeeded in persuading the Commons to refuse to act. In fact, it was inconceivable that legal evidence could have been found to condemn him in that case. He has of course found advocates to whitewash him,[2] but it is sufficient to cite the appeal of Cornwallis that he should not be allowed to return; 'all parties and descriptions of men agree about him'.

In the meantime Parliament, in deference to the appeal of Hastings and the petition from Bengal, had inquired by a committee into the administration of justice, and an Act of 1781[3] effected important changes in the system of 1773. The preamble showed clearly who had won the contest; it asserted the necessity of supporting the government, the importance of the regular collection of the revenue, and the maintenance of the people in their ancient laws. It was enacted that the governor-general and council, jointly and severally, were not to be subject to the jurisdiction of the court for anything done in their public capacity, and their order could be pleaded in justification of his action by any subordinate; this rule was not to apply to matters affecting British subjects; presumably Europeans were meant. But they were still liable in England, and facilities were given for securing certified copies of documents which were to be available in England. This rule differentiates Indian from colonial government; but at the time when it was enacted the view still prevailed that a governor was not subject to legal process in his own colony for official acts.

A further vital change was the rule that the Supreme Court was not to have or to exercise any jurisdiction in any matter concerning the revenue or any act done in the collection thereof

[1] Jud. Reg. III of 1781. [2] *C.H.I.*, v, 247. [3] 21 Geo. III, c. 70.

according to the custom of the country or the regulations of the governor-general and council. Moreover, the extent of its general jurisdiction was precisely defined. It was declared that no one became liable to jurisdiction because of being connected as landowner or farmer of land revenue with the collection of rent, and that persons servants of the Company or of European British subjects should not be subject to such jurisdiction in matters of inheritance or succession to lands or goods or in contract, but only in actions for wrongs or trespasses and in civil suits by agreement to submit. Moreover, due registers of the natives employed were to be kept and none not so registered could be employed. Over all inhabitants of Calcutta the court had jurisdiction, but in cases affecting Hindus and Muhammadans the law and customs of the defendant were to be applied in matters of inheritance and contract. Moreover, the rights of fathers and masters of families by Hindu or Muhammadan law were to be respected, and acts done by the rule of caste must not be deemed criminal.[1] The court was authorized to frame, for approval by the King, suitable forms of process to be used in native causes. In the respect thus shown for native law Parliament followed the rules of 1772 already mentioned.

The Act also recognized the validity of the actions of the provincial councils by forbidding actions in the Supreme Court against judicial officers of the country courts or persons executing their decrees. Those imprisoned in the Patna case were to be released on security being given by the governor-general and council for payment of the damages awarded, as was in fact done, though appeal to the King in Council was expressly permitted by the Act. Moreover, the appellate jurisdiction of the governor-general and council as the Sadr Adalat was recognized, and its continuance authorized, with appeal in civil suits to the King in Council where the value was £5,000 and upwards. It was also authorized to deal with all offences committed in the collection of revenue, and severities beyond what was customary or necessary, but punishment must not extend to death, maiming, or perpetual imprisonment. It

[1] This provision was repealed only in the Government of India Act 1935, s. 301, together with the like rules (37 Geo. III, c. 142, s. 12) for Madras and Bombay.

will be noted that no jury was allowed in such cases, a logical corollary of taking from the Supreme Court its revenue jurisdiction.

The action of Parliament definitely did away with the idea of Hastings of making the provincial courts subordinate to the Supreme Court and bringing the judicial system into a state of unity. Henceforth the two systems remained side by side until a final fusion was achieved after the transfer of authority to the Crown. By direction of the Company in 1782 the governor-general and council resumed their duty of acting as the Sadr Diwani Adalat.

Apart from Parliament Hastings found it necessary to make innovations in the criminal system. The development of crime necessitated more effective prosecution, so that in 1781 the judges of the Diwani Adalats were required to act as magistrates, or in approved cases zamindars, with power to commit for trial to the nearest Faujdari court. The decision is important as it foreshadows the transfer of jurisdiction to European hands.

The question of legislation was also dealt with in the Act of 1781. The Regulating Act had given a limited power of legislation subject to the control of the Supreme Court. But it was clear that this power was not intended to cover legislation for the inhabitants generally of the provinces. The nawab, as effective authority in the provinces, had exercised the power of issuing regulations, and the Company as diwan could doubtless claim a like right, while it controlled the criminal powers of the nawab. Accordingly, in 1772, Hastings, as we have seen, had issued regulations regarding the administration of justice, and in 1780 further regulations were made, which were consolidated in a new code with Impey's aid in 1781. These regulations were not passed under the form provided in the Act of 1773, but their validity was definitely recognized by the Act of 1781.[1] It allowed the governor-general and council to make regulations for the provincial courts and councils; copies were to be sent to the directors and a Secretary of State. They might be disallowed or amended by the King in Council, but were to remain in force unless so dealt with within two years.

[1] 21 Geo. III, c. 70, s. 23.

It must be admitted that the terms of this enactment are modest, but naturally the governor-general and council preferred to rely on their power thus recognized rather than use the machinery of the Supreme Court, though for some time it was justly doubted if the Supreme Court could be regarded as bound by such regulations.[1]

On the vital revenue question Hastings and his colleagues in their capacity as the Board or Committee of Revenue set up in 1772 wrangled incessantly, Hastings and Barwell holding that the land was the property of the sovereign, Francis that it was the property of the zamindars, and none showing proper regard to the rights of the ryot. Once in full power, Hastings insisted on a new plan (February 20th 1781) of administration based on centralization. The provincial councils disappeared in favour of a Committee of Revenue consisting of four officers of the Company and an Indian diwan, who was relieved of control by the rai raian and soon exercised a dangerous power. Collectors were replaced in the districts, but denied all power as to the settlement of revenue; their reports show the ryots miserably oppressed. Moreover, the kanungos were restored in 1781 to their misused authority. Gradually the errors made were put right. In 1782 an office was established to care for the zamindaris of minors, females, and those incapable; in 1783 the collectors were urged to report on the state of the crops, and after Hastings' departure in 1786 the Committee of Revenue was reconstituted as a board under a member of council; the collectors were made responsible for making the settlements; a new division divided the province into thirty-five (in 1787 twenty-three) districts, and the office of chief saristadar was created to bring the land records, hitherto the property of the kanungos, under government control.

One point remains for consideration. How far did Hastings regenerate the civil and military services of the Company? The answer must be that, no doubt in order to retain control over the Company through favours done to proprietors, his disposal of patronage was recklessly generous, increasing the cost of the civil establishment from £251,533 in 1776 to

[1] *Ameer Khan, In matter of* (1870), 6 Beng. L.R. 392, 408; Morley, *Digest.*, ii. 370 ff., 505 ff.

£927,945 eight years later. There were available, beside the offices of governor-general and councillors, one place of £25,000, one of £15,000, and five each of £10,000 and £9,000, sums far in excess of any merits of the young men who formed the service. It was left to Cornwallis to dispense with support purchased at so serious a price at the cost of the much ill-used ryot.

CHAPTER IV

THE ESTABLISHMENT OF ORGANIZED ADMINISTRATION: PITT'S ACT AND CORNWALLIS

1. THE ESTABLISHMENT OF PARLIAMENTARY CONTROL

THE course of events in India necessitated and received close consideration at the hands of the British Government and Parliament, policy being swayed this way and that according to the strength of Hastings' interest in the Company and its relations to Lord North. The dangerous position of affairs in America proved a source of safety to Hastings, for in 1779[1] and 1780[2] Acts were passed to extend for a year in each case the privileges of the Company and to continue the governor-general and council in office, but the weakness of the Company's position was shown by the tentative motion of North in 1780 to pay off the £4,200,000 due to the Company and to notify its dissolution. In 1781, as already noted, a select committee considered the administration of justice in India, a secret committee the war in the Carnatic. The former resulted in the Act of 1781, which readjusted the judicial arrangements in Bengal. It was based on the decision to maintain the authority of the Company, which by another Act[3] was accorded assurance of continuance until three years' notice after March 1st 1791, and placed under a slight measure of further control, being required to submit all outgoing dispatches on political, revenue, and military matters to a Secretary of State. Moreover, a new financial accord was reached. The Company was to pay £400,000 in quittance of all claims of the State up to March 1st 1781, and might pay dividends up to 8 per cent, the State to receive three-quarters of any surplus profits.

The secret committee's report resulted in a series of efforts, following on resolutions moved by Dundas, who had presided over it, in April 1782. Bills of pains and penalties were prepared against Rumbold and Whitehill for misdemeanours as governors

[1] 19 Geo. III, c. 61.

[2] 20 Geo. III, cc. 56, 58.

[3] 21 Geo. III, c. 65. Further financial concessions were made by 22 Geo. III, c. 51; 23 Geo. III, cc. 36, 83; 24 Geo. III, sess. 1, c. 3.

of Madras, but were dropped, through inability to keep a quorum, next year. On May 30th the Commons desired the directors to secure the recall of Hastings and Hornby for action contrary to the honour and policy of the nation, bringing great calamities in India and enormous expense on the Company. But the directors were prevented by the proprietors from carrying out the wishes of the Commons, and, though the government could refuse to allow them to send a dispatch reporting the facts, it could not compel recall. Thus it was made clear that the Company's directors could not control its servants, nor the State the Company, while events in India in the defiance of Calcutta by Madras proved that the main presidency could not control those subordinate to it. It proved naturally that to fly in the face of Parliament was a risky game, and the opportunity of the government came in 1783, when the Company had to apply for financial relief. Dundas in April proposed a Bill which purported to give the Crown full power to recall the principal servants of the Company, and authorized the governor-general to overrule his council and effectively to control the subordinate presidencies, while the zamindars who had suffered from the quinquennial settlement of Hastings were to be restored. He indicated Cornwallis as the saviour of the situation. Naturally, as Dundas was in opposition, it was impossible to proceed with his Bill, but on November 18th Fox introduced two measures. The former dealt specifically with details of administration and was obviously intended to render impossible in future most of the misdeeds of Hastings. The second was a vigorous effort to reform the whole constitution. There was to be a board of seven commissioners named in the Act, irremovable for four years except on an address from either House of Parliament, vacancies to be filled by the King. It would control the revenues and territories in India with power to appoint and remove all servants of the Company. It was to sit in London and Parliament was to have power to inspect the minutes of its proceedings. The commercial business of the Company, on the other hand, would have been carried on by nine (originally eight) assistant directors appointed for five years by the largest shareholders, casual vacancies to be filled by the Court of Directors. Burke's great speech on the Bill denounced the many abuses of the Company's system, and the criticisms against the Bill were largely insincere and ineffective. The opposition denounced the power of patronage, but the commissioners could not have exercised it in a more dangerous manner than it was being in fact exercised, by Hastings' own admission when he spoke of 'a system charged with expensive establishments and precluded by the multitude of dependents and the curse of patronage from reformation. . . . A country oppressed by private rapacity and deprived of its vital resources by the enormous quantities of current specie annually exported in the remittance of private fortunes'.[1] The weakest spot was the vague control of Parliament over the commissioners, but doubtless that could have been adjusted. The Bill was carried by 208 to 108, but defeated in the Lords by George III, who declared as his enemy any peer who should vote for the Bill, and on December 18th the ministry was dismissed. By a tactical error Fox opposed the dissolution which might have condemned the action of the King, and Pitt in due course with royal aid secured a majority, and in August 1784 passed his Act.[2] It rather characteristically borrowed ideas from its predecessor, but it made a vital improvement from the point of view of tactics by leaving in being the patronage of the Company, and it purported not vitally to change its constitution instead of sweeping away the Courts of Directors and of Proprietors. But its essential plan was the same, the control by the British Government of the conduct of public affairs by the Company. Fox had been willing to leave undecided the right to territorial possessions, and the new Act also avoided dealing effectively with this point. It embodied essentially a compromise.

The Act established a Board of Commissioners for the Affairs of India, usually known as the Board of Control. They were to be the Chancellor of the Exchequer, a Secretary of State, and four privy councillors holding office at the royal pleasure, and appointed by the King. This essential difference from Fox's scheme brought the control of the Company into the hands of the Commons. The quorum was three, the president to have a casting vote. They were to control all

[1] Gleig, *Warren Hastings*, ii, 329.

[2] 24 Geo. III, sess. 2, c. 25.

matters of civil or military government of the British territorial possession in the East Indies. Full access was given to the Company's records; its dispatches from India must be submitted to it, and dispatches out could only be sent with its consent and altered at its desire, while it might require its orders to be sent without the directors' concurrence. A committee of secrecy of not more than three members[1] was to be formed from the directors, and orders of the Board requiring secrecy were to be transmitted by the committee without informing the other directors. The Court of Proprietors was forbidden to alter any decision of the directors approved by the Board, and thus lost its effective power, a proper punishment for defying the Commons in 1782. Against possible encroachment by the Board on its commercial business the directors were protected by the right to appeal to the King in Council.

The constitution of the Indian governments was revised. The governor-general was to have three councillors, one of whom was to be the commander-in-chief, who, however, though having second place, was not to succeed in the case of a vacancy pending a new appointment to the governor-generalship. The other two presidencies were placed under governors and three councillors, one to be the local commander-in-chief, but if the commander-in-chief of the Company were present, he took his place, though the latter might sit. The governor-general or governor was given a casting vote. All these officers were to be appointed by the Court of Directors, but councillors only from the Company's covenanted servants in India. Any officer could be recalled by the directors or the King. Resignations of any of the high officials mentioned must be in writing, a provision intended to obviate the confusion over Hastings' resignation in 1777. On a vacancy in the office of governor-general or governor, or if no person had been appointed to act by the directors, the senior councillor was to act.

The power of the governor-general and council over the minor presidencies was to extend not only to transactions with the country powers or war or peace, but also to any other points referred to their control by the Court of Directors.

[1] Usually the chairman and deputy, who were referred to as 'the Chairs'.

Moreover, the presidencies must obey the governor-general unless they had received different orders from the directors, which were not known to the governor-general. In such a case the orders must be sent to the governor-general and council, who were then to issue such instructions as they deemed necessary. This new rule for the first time established a real subordination.

In like manner subordination was enforced on the governor-general and council, it being asserted that 'to pursue schemes of conquest and extension of dominion in India are measures repugnant to the wish, the honour, and policy of this nation'. They were forbidden[1] without the authority of the directors or the secret committee to declare war, or commence hostilities or enter into any treaty for making war against any of the country princes or states or any treaty of guarantee, except where hostilities had actually been commenced or preparations actually made for the commencement of hostilities against the British nation in India or against some of the princes or states dependent thereon or whose territories were guaranteed by any treaty. The governors of the subordinate presidencies were similarly forbidden without the sanction of the governor-general and council or the directors to commence hostilities or make treaties except in sudden emergency or imminent danger, and any treaty thus made was to be subject if possible to ratification by the governor-general and council. Disobedience of the presidencies might be met by suspension. Moreover, the control of the central government was to be made effective by their obligation to send copies of papers of all kinds.

In judicial matters an important principle was laid down. Subjects of His Majesty, whether servants of the Company or not, were made subject to the jurisdiction of Courts in India and Great Britain for crimes of any kind in the territories of the native states.[2]

Efforts were made to restrain the evil practices of the past. To demand and receive a present in the case of an officer of the Crown or the Company was declared to be extortion, disobedience to the Court of Directors' orders a misdemeanour, as also

[1] S. 34. Re-enacted 33 Geo. III, c. 52, s. 42.
[2] S. 44. Re-enacted 33 Geo. III, c. 52, s. 67. See Madras Reg. XI of 1809; Bombay Reg. III of 1809.

any bargain for giving up or receiving any office. The Company was not to release or compound any sentence on a servant nor restore to office one dismissed by a judicial sentence. Officers of the Company might be required on return to declare on oath their fortunes, and after five years' absence save on grounds of health could only be reappointed with the approval of a three-fourths majority of a Court of Proprietors. Proceedings in England in the King's Bench in case of extortion or other misdemeanour might be by rule or information, and a special court of three judges, four peers, and six members of the Commons was to be set up each session to try cases of information for extortion and other misdemeanours. This remarkable provision,[1] which was amended in 1786, naturally never came into use.

Reductions and retrenchments in the establishments, civil and military, were to be made by the directors. In the civil service promotions under the rank of councillor, in the military under that of commander-in-chief, were to be made by seniority save in special cases where the directors were to be informed. Cadets were not to go out under age fifteen or over age twenty-two, or if they had served for a year in the army over twenty-five.

Special powers were given to the governor-general and governors to authorize the arrest of persons suspected of carrying on illicit correspondence with persons in authority, whether in native states or European settlements, but this power seems to have been allowed to remain unused.

The Act, so far as the powers of the government and Company were concerned, had, very wisely, been matured in consultation with the latter, and, though Fox insisted that it undermined the power of the directors, it is clear that they were left with a considerable possibility, which in practice was a reality, of control. The Board was not normally an originating, but a revising body, and enormous influence necessarily rested with those through whose hands the mass of business passed. Moreover, the Board soon passed into oblivion as such; Pitt and Dundas at first attended meetings, later Dundas virtually acted alone, and in 1793 the office of President of the Board was made

[1] Ss. 66–80; 26 Geo. III, c. 57.

salaried, so that, although provision was made that the two junior members need not be privy councillors and might be paid, the management fell in practice to the president, the fiction of a Board surviving in the rule that an *ex officio* member signed also the President's decisions. The president was virtually a secretary of state for India, and Indian affairs became a matter for the Cabinet in the same manner as those colonial issues which were dealt with by a secretary of state.

Amendments of the Act were early found necessary. Cornwallis, appointed governor-general, would not accept the office unless he was given power in case of necessity to override his council,[1] a right attacked by Burke[2] as introducing arbitrary and despotic government, especially as it also permitted the combination of the offices of governor-general and commander-in-chief. Even so a further Act in 1791[3] was necessary to make beyond question his full power. At the same time the requirement of the approval of the King for the person selected as governor-general was abolished,[4] but the King could recall any officer, as was done in Barlow's case, and the provision therefore was of small practical importance. A third Act[5] repealed the absurd provision as to declaration of property and remodelled the court to try extortion. But its important provision dealt with the jurisdiction of the courts. The Supreme Court at Calcutta was given jurisdiction over all criminal offences committed within the limits of the chartered trade, and the court of the governor and council and the Mayor's Court at Madras were given criminal and civil jurisdiction over all British subjects residing in the territories of the Company on the Coromandel coast or in any other part of the Carnatic or the Northern Sarkars or in the territories of the subadar of the Deccan, the nawab of Arcot, or the raja of Tanjore.

An issue of great constitutional difficulty was raised in 1787–8. Prior to 1781 the Crown had paid for royal forces sent in the public interest to India, but in that year an Act[6] had provided that the Company should pay two lakhs a year for each regiment of 1,000 men sent to India at the Company's

[1] 26 Geo. III, c. 16. [2] *Parl Hist.*, xxv, 1274. [3] 31 Geo. III, c. 40.
[4] 26 Geo. III, c. 25. [5] 26 Geo. III, c. 57. [6] 21 Geo. III, c. 65.

request, while authority was also given to the Company to raise European troops and punish deserters. Discussions arose in 1785–6 regarding the strength of the force, and in 1787 the government decided to send out four regiments, offering to let the Company nominate seventy-five officers. The cost annoyed the Company, which desired also to avoid issues of precedence, and it demurred. The government replied by an Act[1] which gave the Board power to send out troops, but fixed the number which might be charged to the Company. Moreover, the Board was expressly forbidden to increase any salary or pension without the concurrence of the directors and notice to Parliament, and the directors were to lay annually before that body an account of its receipts and disbursements.

The Act evoked much constitutional discussion. It was urged for the Company that its own forces were sufficient and cheaper, and that it was wrong that the Crown should have forces for which Parliament did not provide by annual votes. Pitt, for his part, insisted that armed forces should all be under the Crown, and that he would welcome any means of improving the control over armed forces which was so vaguely accorded by the Bill of Rights and the Mutiny Act. Lord Cornwallis was indeed then considering the possibility of amalgamating the royal and the Company's forces, and the constitutional issue was again debated in 1878, when there was almost equal division of the highest legal authorities on the question whether the Crown could properly use her Indian forces as they were used for the protection of Malta in case of the outbreak of war with Russia.[2]

At the close of Cornwallis's régime the Charter Act fell to be renewed. Pitt was in full power, Dundas reputed expert in Indian affairs, war with France occupied every mind, Indian finances seemed less embarrassed, and the new Charter Act of 1793[3] passed with minimal trouble. It was essentially a consolidating measure, and its alteration struck at points of detail. The cost of the staff of the Board of Control and of the members if paid was placed on the Company. Its trade privileges subject to certain restrictions were continued for twenty years. It was

[1] 28 Geo. III, c. 8; Clode, *Military Forces*, i, 270.
[2] See Anson, *The Crown* (ed. Keith), ii, 205 f.
[3] 33 Geo. III, c. 52.

allowed to increase its dividend to 10 per cent; thereafter on various conditions a sum of £500,000 was to be paid to the state, but these conditions never materialized. But the Crown might order the application of the whole of the revenue to purposes of defence if need be without regard to the investment of the Company. The Company must pay the actual expenses of the royal forces serving in India; but matters up to the end of 1792 were adjusted by wiping out all debts.

In India the position of the commander-in-chief was varied by making express appointment by the directors necessary for his being a member of council. The powers of the governor-general over subordinate presidencies were expressed in the widest term so as to apply to the civil and military government in general. His power to override his council was repeated and applied to the governors, but the authority was declared not to apply to judicial matters or taxation or legislation proper.[1] When visiting a presidency the governor-general would supersede the governor and might appoint a vice-president to act in his absence. Departure from India without permission was to be tantamount to resignation in the case of the higher officers. The King's approval was requisite for the appointment of governor-general, governors, and commander-in-chief.

To remove doubts it was provided that the Admiralty jurisdiction of the Supreme Court at Calcutta was to extend to the high seas.[2] Further the governor-general and council were authorized to appoint justices of the peace in any presidency,[3] but they were not to sit unless invited in the Courts of Oyer and Terminer and Gaol Delivery. The sale of liquor was made subject to the grant of a licence, and power was given to levy a sanitary rate in the presidency towns.

2. CORNWALLIS AND EXTERNAL RELATIONS

The Act of 1784, though it undoubtedly treats as subject to British sovereignty territories which were not in that position in 1778 evades, as did that of 1793, the question of the position

[1] 33 Geo. III, c. 52, s. 51.

[2] S. 156.

[3] S. 151. The power was transferred to the governors in council of Madras and Bombay by 47 Geo. III, sess. 2, c. 68, ss. 5, 6.

of the Crown in India. The treaty of Versailles (Article 13) in 1783 is equally guarded. The French factories in Bengal were to be restored, and the King was to take measures to afford France a safe commerce there, and on the Coromandel coast and Malabar. Troubles arose regarding French rights which evoked vague declarations. Thus the committee of secrecy on July 19th 1786 was content to speak of the general controlling power of the Company as diwan.[1] Cornwallis on November 16th 1786 expressed his dissatisfaction with the vague position adopted, and on February 6th 1787 Eden at Paris is found claiming the sovereignty of Great Britain in Bengal, Bihar, and Orissa, and relying on the terms of the treaties of Paris (Article 11) and Versailles in support of this thesis, a view naturally denied by the French. Cornwallis had no experience in Indian ways, and he did not share the respect for tradition which was marked even in Warren Hastings, who had experience of the time when the Company ranked merely as a very minor factor in Indian life.

The position of the Emperor, or as the English called him the King at Delhi, was now essentially a matter of ceremonial. The princes of India normally acknowledged in form his supremacy. They asked his confirmation of their succession, and continuance of their formal titles, and for these they were willing to pay hard cash. They struck their coinage in his name, and on their official seals they described themselves as his humble servants, and in the mosques the prayers were still read in his name. But they never thought of obeying his orders for remitting regular tribute or troops. Their one wish was to carve out dominions for themselves, as had Azaf Jah, the last great wazir who had established himself in Hyderabad (1724). Tipu went further; he declared himself padshah, thus asserting his independence of the Empire, but Muslims as a rule resented such action. Mahadaji Sindhia, on the other hand, apparently aimed at establishing a Hindu Empire. In 1784 he secured control of the Emperor's person, and induced Shah Alam to give the Peshwa the title of Wakil-i-mutlak, vicegerent of the Empire, and to appoint Sindhia his deputy with command of the Mogul forces and charge of the provinces

[1] *C.H.I.*, v, 595 f.

of Agra and Delhi. Vicissitudes of fortune followed, and in 1788 a Rohilla miscreant Ghulam Kadir seized and blinded the Emperor, who was rescued next year by Sindhia. In his extremity the Emperor appealed to Cornwallis, but in vain. The latter replied in civil and respectful terms, dropping, however, the 'jargon of allegiance and obedience' which he deemed absurd, and declining aid. He saw clearly that the Emperor could not be rescued permanently without being given an army or money to pay one, and he held that it was not the duty of a statesman to attempt to restore a vanished Empire.[1] In the same spirit in 1790 he declined to accept the suggestion that the Company should obtain from the Emperor a sanad, or deed of grant, for Surat, whose nawab had died, partly because there was an heir and partly because he was reluctant thus to admit imperial power.[2] Similarly the Company contented itself with recognizing Nasir-ul-mulk's succession in Bengal, without asking imperial approval, and the suggestion of Sindhia for the Emperor in 1792 that the payment of tribute should be made was met with so hot a reply that he hastened to assure the Company that its supremacy in its territories was unquestioned. Cornwallis recognized that he could not expect full acceptance by the princes of the royal family as an equal, but he demanded it from other states. The Company in his view now occupied the position of a major Indian state, under a nominal allegiance, which he disliked to admit, to the Emperor, attested by minor ceremonial which could not conveniently be laid aside.

As regards the princes Cornwallis was as faithful as he could be to the policy of Parliament, but not unmindful of the obligations of honour and humanity. In Oudh he deplored the administration, which was as bad under Sir John Macpherson as under Hastings, and he demanded reduction of the excessive forces maintained by the nawab. He even offered to reduce the tribute from 74 to 50 lakhs if it were punctually paid, but insisted on maintaining two British brigades for security. In the Carnatic and the nawab's monstrous debts Parliament had interested itself by the Act of 1784, but the Board of Control

[1] *Cornwallis Corr.*, i, 295.

[2] Ibid., ii, 22. Since 1759 the Company had held the fort for the Emperor at the nawab's request.

made no proper effort to extirpate the evils of the position, and Cornwallis had to temporize. A treaty of 1787 assigned nine lakhs of pagodas to the state and twelve to the creditors and gave the Company full military power. In 1790 complete control had to be taken in the war, and on its conclusion a new treaty endeavoured to ameliorate the situation by placing under British control the poligars of Madura and Tinnevelly whose resistance rendered revenue collection especially difficult and by reducing by half the assignment for creditors. But Cornwallis was perfectly clear that this was a mere stopgap, and that it was imperative to take over full control.

With a vision unusual in India, Cornwallis realized that India presented a vital point in Anglo-French rivalry and that it was essential to hold in check Tipu, whose plan of overcoming piecemeal the Nizam and the Marathas was obvious. Cornwallis refused to attack, but he maintained friendly relations with the Marathas and with the Nizam, with whom in 1789 a new settlement of the Guntoor area was arranged, and he was prepared for war when Tipu insisted on attacking the raja of Travancore, though the latter was an ally of the Company. Madras as usual was unready to act, and Cornwallis had to exert his full authority to compel action. Treaties were made in 1790 with the Nizam and the Marathas, and after an exhausting struggle Tipu was driven in 1792 to surrender some half of his territory, which was shared by the Nizam, the abiding character of whose relation to the Company was now established, the Marathas, and the Company, which acquired Baramahal and Dindigul. Unhappily Tipu's temperament rendered abiding peace impossible.

Cornwallis by his chivalry to the defeated Tipu won credit, enhanced by his generosity in refusing prize money and by his passion for justice, which made him insist that his army should treat the invaded country with due humanity for non-combatants. His troops, though numerous, some 70,000 in all, were of very inferior quality especially as regards the 6,000 Europeans of the Company's army, the riffraff of the London streets and the gleanings of the jails, officered by ruined youths or greedy seekers for money. The King's troops numbered some 5,500 Europeans, with much better officers; as we have seen, Cornwallis would gladly have amalgamated the forces[1] had this been permitted.

3. THE REFORMS OF CORNWALLIS

The select committee of 1781 had been instructed to aim at securing *inter alia* the happiness of the native population. That issue had been stressed continuously in the following discussions, and certain principles had emerged. The Company therefore was in a position, when it finally secured Cornwallis's promise to act, to lay down, on April 12th 1786, general principles of revenue and general administration, and Cornwallis had the judgment to select men of character and competence such as John Shore, James Grant, Jonathan Duncan, and on the commercial side Charles Grant to guide him. In judicial matters he had the great advantage of the zeal and ability of Sir William Jones, who was as convinced as Hastings of the necessity of the due study of Hindu and Muhammadan law and who was a Sanskrit student of insight and imagination. Cornwallis's own contribution was common sense, a high sense of public duty and loyalty to superior authority, and complete freedom from personal interests. If his indignation at the low standards of the Indians whom he came across rendered him anxious to secure that the higher posts should be in European hands, he also was determined that these Europeans should be worthy of the place assigned to them.

The commercial branch of the Company's business presented urgent need for reform. Supervised since 1774 by a Board of Trade of eleven members under inadequate control by the council, it exercised the function of providing the goods to be sent to England and had allowed contracts for supply to be made with the Company's own servants. It was recast in 1786, and reduced to five members. Cornwallis's inquiries revealed serious wrongdoing by contractors and members, some of whom were punished. In future the board was to work through commercial residents as agents, and regulations were laid down to prevent oppression of the primary producer or the

[1] *Corr.*, i, 251, 341; ii, 316, 572. For Wellesley's demands for 142,000, see Roberts, *India under Wellesley*, pp. 261 ff.

Indian or foreign trader for the benefit of British traders or the Company's servants. The officers employed were properly remunerated and a high standard of probity demanded, and the system was not materially changed so long as the trade endured.

In the general branch of the Company's affairs revenue and justice were inextricably mingled, as has been seen, until under the reforms of 1781 a distinct separation between revenue and judicial functions had emerged. But the directors now demanded economy, simplification, and purification, and as an essential part of these ideals the union of revenue and judicial functions. In 1787 the number of districts was reduced from thirty-five to twenty-three, thus effecting an economy, and later in the year the collectors in charge of districts were again made judges of the courts of Diwani Adalat, appeal lying in important cases to the Sadr Diwani Adalat,[1] while in minor cases up to 200 rupees Indian registers were allowed to act. Revenue cases were excluded from these courts, appeal from the collector lying to the Board of Revenue and then to the governor-general in council.[2] The criminal powers of the collector as magistrate were increased to dealing with cases of affray and inflicting punishment within certain limits, but in more serious cases they committed offenders to the Faujdari Adalats. Collectors were granted salaries of 1,500 rupees a month with about 1 per cent of the revenue collected; they were provided with European assistants on fair pay and forbidden to trade. Their functions were systematically prescribed in a code of June 8th 1789, and in 1790 they were made to preside in courts of revenue, Mal Adalat, with appeal to the council in order to relieve the Board of Revenue. This combination of power in the hands of the collector proved too great and elicited fresh provisions in 1793.

In the meantime Cornwallis had been investigating the conduct of criminal justice, finding that there were defects alike in the law and its administration, which was essentially, as held desirable by Hastings, in Indian hands, the Nizamat Adalat at Murshidabad being controlled by Muhammad Reza Khan; in 1790 he was removed, and the court re-established

[1] Jud. Reg. VIII of 1787. [2] Rev. Reg. XXIII of 1787.

at Calcutta under the governor-general and council aided by the chief kadi and two muftis.[1] The provincial courts presided over by Indians were replaced by four circuit courts presided over by two covenanted servants aided by kadis and muftis; they were to make tours twice a year throughout the districts. Further magisterial powers were given to the collectors, including the custody of prisoners for trial or punishment and the execution of sentences of the circuit courts. Important police reforms were necessary to supplement the judicial changes. Doubtful of his legislative powers, Cornwallis meditated an Act of Parliament, but finally proceeded by regulations pending a decision of that issue. In 1791 superintendents of police were created for Calcutta with functions of maintaining order and arresting criminals. Next year in the districts the zamindars were deprived of police powers; in each district small districts were put under a daroga subject to supervision by the Company's representative. This system was perpetuated and consolidated in the regulations of 1793, which set up a complete organization of civil and criminal justice, of police, of land revenue, and of commercial management. Cornwallis was persuaded that systematic regulation was imperative and that it could not suffice to trust to the character and sense of duty of individuals, and the directors concurred.

The essential change of 1793 was acceptance of the view that revenue administration must be divorced from judicial functions. This was, of course, a complete reversal of the policy hitherto enjoined by the directors and followed by Cornwallis, under which economy and simplification had resulted in the concentration in the collector's hands of the maximum of authority on both sides. But, as he pointed out, it was obvious that, if the regulations for collecting or assessing revenue were transgressed, the fault must be that of the collectors, and they could not be expected as judges to redress wrongs done by themselves. Hence the revenue courts, Mal Adalat, of 1790 disappeared and revenue cases were referred to the district courts, now reorganized as three city and twenty-three zillah courts, each presided over by an English judge.

From these courts appeal lay to four provincial Courts of

[1] Jud. Reg. XXVI of 1790.

Appeal at Calcutta, Patna, Dacca, and Murshidabad without limit of amount. They might also require the subordinate courts to hear causes, and supervise their performance of duty, reporting to the Sadr Diwani Adalat, which or the government could refer causes to them for investigation. The Sadr Court consisted of the governor-general and council; appeal lay to it where the value exceeded 1,000 rupees, with a further appeal to the King in Council where the amount in dispute exceeded £5,000. This court could deal with complaints against judges of the courts subordinate to it. For very minor causes jurisdiction was given to native commissioners up to 50 rupees and registers of the courts up to 200 rupees, subject to appeal to, or revision by, the city or district judge.

In order to make clear the extent of the jurisdiction of the courts, it was provided that their authority extended over all Indians and Europeans not being British subjects, where the property concerned or the defendant in the suit was within the limits of the court's area. European British subjects were compelled to undertake to accept their jurisdiction as a condition of being licensed to live beyond a ten-mile radius round Calcutta, the power to restrain such resistance save under licence having been given by an Act of 1781.[1]

For purposes of criminal jurisdiction the judges of the city and zillah courts were made magistrates with power to apprehend disturbers of the peace and persons charged with crimes and misdemeanours. They could punish minor offences; otherwise commit for trial or hold to bail for the next session of the Court of Circuit. In these four courts the judges of the provincial courts of appeal acted as judges with the aid of the kadi and mufti, half-yearly sessions being held in some zillahs, monthly in others and the cities. Final approval of sentences of death or imprisonment for life[2] was required from the Sadr Nizamat Adalat under the governor-general and council, aided by the chief kadi[3] and two muftis. It had power to consider all matters of criminal justice, including the submission of

[1] 21 Geo. III, c. 65.

[2] Mutilation disappeared under Jud. Reg. XXXIV of 1791; relatives could not pardon (XXVI of 1790, s. 34), nor was prosecution dependent on their action (XL of 1792).

[3] He disappeared under Reg. VIII of 1809.

regulations or enactment. The right of pardon remained with the governor-general and council. The law administered, however, remained Muhammadan law, modified by regulations and shorn of its more barbarous punishments. Cornwallis hoped for improvements from the researches of Jones and ultimately the development of a case law.

The judicial posts now created were filled in the main by the collectors, whose importance had been diminished by the revenue settlement, which disposed of the work of assessment by fixing perpetually the rent to be levied. The desirability of a long-term settlement was laid down by the directors, who were inclined to regard the zamindars as English landlords. Grant held that the land appertained to the state, and that it could fix as it deemed best the rate to be levied and decide freely on the mode of levying; Shore held that the zamindars should be regarded as landlords paying a customary rent; both held that a permanent settlement was premature. But Cornwallis held that permanency was desirable, and in announcing a decennial settlement in 1790 added that it would be permanent, if the directors approved. The decision was taken by the Board of Control in 1792, Pitt and Dundas combining. It is clear that to Cornwallis the chief merit of the system was that it set free the ablest servants of the Company for the judicial service, though the encouragement of the development of the land and the reclamation of the waste were also adduced as reasons. But the issue of protection of the ryots remained unsolved. In 1790 the sair duties of customs and excise collected by the zamindar were abolished as the only way to prevent abuse, and in 1792 and 1793 efforts to restrict the right of zamindars over their tenants were made, but with little success. Two results of the system were soon apparent: the loss to the public of the enhancement of revenue which would have normally ensued, and the divorce of the administration from immediate and effective contact with the ryots which was necessarily secured in any area where the government dealt directly with the cultivators.

Finally must be noted the reorganization carried through all departments, with elimination of unnecessary staff, and the payment of proper salaries without unauthorized gains. The principal offices were allocated to the Company's servants, and no servant was to hold office under two departments. The treasury, paymaster-general's, and accountant-general's offices were reorganized, the duties of the exchequer defined, the customs establishment cut down, the postal service improved. Unfortunately Cornwallis's distrust for native officials, due in part to his coming into contact with inferior men, led to the Europeanizing of the service to a degree which rapidly shut out from any Indian in British territory the prospect of high office, and Parliament lent its sanction to this system in its insistence on limiting such offices to its covenanted European servants. On the other hand must be noted Cornwallis's fearless refusal to make improper appointments even to gratify the future Prince Regent. Almost incredible requests were proffered, a striking testimony to the utter demoralization of the system under Hastings, who had secured the support of the Archbishop of York by giving control of Benares to his son aged twenty-one,[1] and of Sulivan, chairman of the directors, by the grant of the opium contract to his son, who sold it for £40,000.

[1] It is absurd to attach the slightest value to his testimony of Hastings as 'the most virtuous man of the age', as does Davies, *Warren Hastings*, p. 498.

CHAPTER V

THE SUPREMACY OF THE COMPANY IN INDIA AND THE CHARTER ACTS OF 1813–58

1. THE ESTABLISHMENT OF THE COMPANY'S SUPREMACY

Parliament had announced in 1784 its opposition to the extension of dominion in India, and Cornwallis was a loyal servant. But even he had been compelled by force of circumstances to add to the Company's dominions, and it is curious to reflect that at one time he chafed under the necessity of sending large remittances to Bombay, holding that a trading centre there with that at Surat should suffice. In fact, however, the state of India negated the possibility of any cessation in extension of power. India was a complete stranger to the conception of a system of international law regulating the activities of a number of distinct fully sovereign powers. History had accustomed it to the claims of universal sovereignty by the Mogul Emperors. The reality of imperial power had passed away leaving it open for any ambitious officer to seek to establish his power, and the Company had resources which were manifestly certain to give it a great advantage over its rivals. It was now in political matters the agency of a first-class power with resources far superior to those at the disposal of any of its rival competitors for power. The chief drawback to early achievement of paramount authority lay in the moral principles and political maxims of the Home Government, which for long desired to limit dominion in India, and abandoned that policy only when its impossibility became too obvious to be longer ignored.

Shore, whose value as an adviser on revenue issues had secured his succession, though a servant of the Company, to Cornwallis, loyally in the main adhered to the policy of non-intervention, permitting in 1795 the Marathas assembled for the last time in feudal loyalty under the Peshwa to defeat the Nizam at Kharda. But even he, with the approval of the directors, had to strike a new bargain with Oudh, after determining the succession there. The treaty of 1797 not merely increased the tribute to seventy-six lakhs, but placed a British garrison in Allahabad and increased to 10,000 the number of British troops with whom defence was to rest, while the wazir's forces were strictly limited, and he undertook to have no dealings with other powers without the assent of the Company.

With the advent of Lord Mornington[1] the attitude of the central government became definitely one of acquisition of paramount power. In the case of Oudh, Wellesley demanded security for the Company's possessions. He secured it by insisting, in defiance of treaty, on the cession in 1801 by the wazir of the territory which he had acquired and paid for in the Rohilla War; the territory unquestionably profited and the subsidy ceased to be payable, but nothing effective was done for the amelioration of the lot of the people of the rest of Oudh where misrule continued, while the Company's support prevented revolution. The acquisition of full powers would have been wholly justified in the interest of the people; the actual steps taken were those dictated by British interests. In the case of Tanjore in 1799 the full measure of securing from the raja full powers of administration, civil and military, was adopted, a pension of £40,000 being paid in lieu, and the result fully justified the transfer. In that of the Carnatic a pretext for deposing the nawab was forthcoming in correspondence with Tipu alleged to prove disloyalty. This interpretation was denied, but overruled in a completely high-handed manner, and by a very marked exercise of paramount power the succession was accorded in 1801 to a nawab who was content to hand over full control in return for a fifth of the net revenue. Final arrangements were at last made to discharge the nawab's debts,[2] thus rewarding the dishonest servants of the Company for their flagrant disobedience to its orders and their criminal disregard of the welfare of the natives. One justification of the decision is worth noting. The nawab had been made an independent

[1] Roberts, *India under Wellesley*, pp. 116–36. Wellesley ignored international law, holding it inapplicable to the states, but he also ignored the dictates of honesty and equity.

[2] Ibid., pp. 85–100; Pitt and Dundas were responsible for the scandal.

prince free from control by the subadar of the Deccan by the Company, and it rested with them to undo what they had done. In fact, as early as 1780 the old nawab had urged that he should be formally recognized as hereditary prince of the Carnatic with full power of administration and the right to select his successor under the protection of the Company and the English nation, ignoring his suzerain. Further, on his death in 1795 the succession was approved by the Company as paramount, and again in the events of 1801 the Emperor was simply ignored. In the same spirit on the death in 1799 of the nawab of Surat, Wellesley annexed it, adopting the view that, where the Company displaced the Mogul Empire, it had the right to decide the fate of principalities formerly subject to the Emperor. He added also part of Tipu's territory to that of the Company when his victory at Seringapatam in May 1799 established the Company beyond doubt as the paramount power in India. Much of Mysore, however, was handed back on condition of strict vassalage[1] to the Hindu dynasty dispossessed by Hyder. In 1800 the Nizam accepted subordinate alliance, undertook to consult the company on foreign issues and to pay for a subsidiary force by ceding his gains from Mysore in 1792 and 1799.

As against the Marathas a fundamental blow was delivered in 1802–3 when the Peshwa, all the wisdom and moderation of the Maratha government having disappeared with the death of Nana Phadnavis in 1800, accepted the treaty of Bassein, which definitely forced upon him the acceptance of the system of subordinate alliance, which was to prevail henceforth with a short interruption and to form the basis of relations with all states not already bound in this way. In form the treaty provided for a general defensive alliance for the reciprocal protection of the possessions of the East India Company, the Peshwa and their allies. But the Peshwa bound himself to maintain a subsidiary force of not less than six battalions to be stationed within his dominions; not to continue to employ Europeans of nations hostile to the British; to relinquish all claims on Surat; to recognize the arrangements made between

[1] The payment for the subsidiary force could be raised at pleasure, and the administration could, in case of difficulty, be taken over.

the Company and the Gaekwad; to abstain not merely from hostilities but also from negotiations with other states, except in consultation with the British authorities; and to accept British arbitration in any dispute with the Nizam and the Gaekwad. The treaty unquestionably must be accepted as giving the British the Empire of India, for it reduced the head of the Maratha confederation to a position of complete inferiority, and in matters external of absolute subordination, to the British. The merits of the system in British eyes were clear enough. The fidelity of the state concerned was secured by the presence of the subsidiary force maintained at the cost of the state by the Company; the evils of war were kept at a distance from the source of British wealth and power; the military frontier was thrown considerably in advance of the political frontier, which, however, it naturally tended to become. The states for their part usually ceded territory to support the force in lieu of tribute, and thus to a certain extent were safeguarded from constant friction over demands for unpaid sums. Further, they were protected from internal attack, with the result that they could misuse their subjects free from the fear of a rival raising the country against them. In the case of the Peshwa, Baji Rao, the fifteen years which British intervention secured him of continued rule, free from fear of destruction by one of the confederates, were marked by persistent maladministration, and at the same time plotting against the power which had humiliated as well as saved him. Small wonder that the other heads of the Marathas meditated war, but disunion resulted in their defeat in detail. Wellesley by Assaye forced the Bhonsle raja to accept, under the treaty of Deogaon, December 15th 1803, terms similar to those of the treaty of Bassein and to surrender Cuttack, thus making Orissa a reality, while Lake reduced Sindhia to acceptance of subordinate alliance by the treaty of Surji Arjungaon (December 30th 1803), and the Company acquired control of Agra, Delhi, Broach, and other territories. The operations so far completely successful were marred by war with Holkar, who belatedly joined in the fray and defeated Monson, but had to accept alliance in 1805, and with the raja of Bharatpur, who in 1805 repelled Lake, and had to be allowed to retain his stronghold. Moreover, the directors were distressed by the great cost and doubtful if they had not unduly extended their territories, so that they decided to recall the governor-general and entrust Cornwallis, now sixty-six years old and in bad health with making peace. The accords reached (January 7th 1806) with Holkar and (November 22nd 1805) with Sindhia, surrendered a considerable area of the territory conquered, and released the Marathas from any obligation to respect the Rajput chiefs with whom the Company had begun to have relations. But Wellesley had set the example, in so far as he had delivered in April 1805 the raja of Jodhpur to Sindhia when the former declined to accept the conditions on which protection was offered. The Rajput states thus exposed to the Marathas in vain pleaded that, as the Company was now in possession of the paramountcy of the Mogul, it should interfere to keep them safe. The argument is interesting, but Sir G. Barlow naturally rejected it.[1]

In their attitude to the Emperor, Shore and Wellesley were in general accord. In 1797 Shore visited the begam and the two sons of the late Emperor at Benares, and professed humility and submission before these dependents on the bounty of the Company, who in their turn used the language of princes and invested him with a dress of honour. In 1803 the Emperor fell under British control on the defeat of Sindhia before Delhi. Wellesley attached great importance to this event, for impressed or obsessed as he was with the fear of French intrigue he accepted as serious the risk of the carrying out of the suggestion made by one of Decaen's officers that the Emperor might be induced to confer sovereignty on the French in lieu of the British. Henceforth the Emperor was to live under British protection, exercising full sovereign rights within his palace at Delhi. Revenues were assigned to him from a district round Delhi, which, though administered by a British officer, was administered in His Majesty's name, and in which Muhammadan law was administered, subject to the elimination of the punishment of mutilation. No engagement was made with the Emperor, who was to receive all the forms of respect due to the emperors of Hindustan, and from whom Lake had already

[1] Thompson and Garratt, *British Rule in India*, p. 237; Roberts, pp. 289–94. Barlow, however, refused to relieve the Peshwa or the Nizam from their treaties of subordinate alliance.

accepted a dress of honour and a title. He could, therefore, if he pleased, regard the treatment as the outcome of due obedience from a dependent. In fact, the Company had added to its power and prestige by being able to stand out as the agent through whom the theoretic paramount power of the Empire could be exercised. As has been seen, this view immediately commended itself to the Rajput states. The policy which dictated the action taken was generous, and it did something to soften to the Muslim world the resentment felt at the virtual subjections of Bengal, Oudh, and the Carnatic and the destruction of Tipu, all signs of the final passing away of Muslim importance.

It was of course impossible to preserve for long an attitude of indifference to attacks in India on states not allied with the Company. Minto pointed out to the Company that military states such as were the Indian must aim at conquest and glory, and that the issue was whether the British were to maintain neutrality amid havoc, or intervene for the sake of suffering humanity, and the directors admitted that non-interference could not be rigid. But, while Amir Khan was driven from Berar in 1809, he was left to harry all non-allies. Of great importance, however, was Minto's insistence through Metcalfe on the acceptance by Ranjit Singh[1] of British protection of the Cis-Satlej states, Nabha, Sirhind, Faridkot, and Patiala. The position regarding the states was made clear by a proclamation of May 3rd 1809, which promised them exemption from tribute and full exercise of the rights and authorities which they enjoyed in their territories before coming under British protection. The chiefs must assist with grain and other necessaries armies traversing their territories and join the British in full force to repel any attack. But it soon proved necessary to settle peace among the states themselves by paramount authority.

With the advent of Hastings in 1813 the process of bringing all India into effective dependence was resumed. The British Government had finally thrown off any pretence, and in the Act of 1813[2] renewing the Company's privileges had referred to

[1] *Vide* treaty of April 25th 1809; Aitchison, viii, 144.
[2] 53 Geo. III, c. 155, s. 95.

the undoubted sovereignty of the Crown of the United Kingdom over the territories of the Company. In the treaty of Paris next year with France, Article 12 refers frankly to the British sovereignty in India, and Holland in the same year, like France, acknowledged the *fait accompli*. It was urged by Metcalfe at Delhi that the office of Emperor should be abolished, and Hastings disliked the nominal subordination of the Company so deeply that he discarded from his official seal the admission of subordination, and the usual ceremonial presents ceased to be presented in the name of the governor-general since they implied inferiority. He refused to interview Akbar II unless he waived all ceremonial expressing supremacy over the Company's dominions, so that the two did not meet. At the same time by his overthrow of Maratha power he completed in essentials the system of subordinate alliance. In this policy he had the prompting of Metcalfe, whose experience at Delhi filled him with a strong dislike of native rule. He urged the maintenance of powerful forces, the overthrow of rival powers, the acquisition of territory where possible, and the insistence on pecuniary aid from dependent states. Occasion for advance was accorded by the suffering inflicted on Bengal and the Northern Sarkars by the Pindaris, bandit cavalry, often on good terms with Sindhia and Holkar, who seemed likely to follow the career of the Marathas themselves. The directors were induced to remove the ban on action, and the Rajput states were at last taken under protection, the termination of the treaty of 1805 being notified to Sindhia and Holkar. Sindhia accepted the decision in November 1817 and agreements were at once (in 1817–18) made at Delhi with Udaipur, Jodhpur, Jaipur, Kotah, Bhopal, Bundi, and other states on terms of subordinate alliance. Later, on the evidence of further hostility, Sindhia was required by treaty of 1818 to cede Ajmir; Holkar, defeated in battle, by the treaty of Mandasor (1818) surrendered his dominions south of the Narbada, relinquished any claims on the Rajput chiefs, recognized the independence of Amir Khan, made nawab of Tonk by the British, agreed to reduce his army and to maintain a contingent for service with the forces of the Company, and to accept a resident. The raja of Nagpur was deposed and the state was required to cede the Sagar and Narbada territories.

The Peshwa was first compelled in 1817 to relinquish his headship of the Maratha confederation, to cede the Konkan, to abandon the claims he had on the Gaekwad whose independence he recognized, to grant him Ahmadabad for a tribute of four lakhs a year, and to cede to the Company the tribute of Kathiawar. Later, after war, he was deprived of all power, and exiled in 1818, but with an enormous allowance which he seems to have employed in stirring up troubles for the paramount power. The descendant of Sivaji, was recognized as raja of Satara, but on conditions demanding more explicity than usual co-operation with the Company. With the Gaekwad relations were made still more intimate. Already in 1802 Baroda had ceded territory and admitted the Company's right to supervise its political affairs. In 1805 it accepted a further treaty providing for a subsidiary force and for the submission to the Company of any differences with the Peshwa and of foreign policy in general. In 1817 a fresh treaty provided for the increase of the subsidiary force, and the exchange of Ahmadabad for certain other territory.

It was necessary now to settle the regions in which anarchy had prevailed as a result of Maratha inroads and Rajput resurgence. Malcolm settled Malwa on the basis of drawing up agreements between the Maratha overlords, mainly represented by the States of Gwalior, Indore, Dhar, and Dewas, and the Rajput feudatories who claimed, while paying tribute, to be granted tankhas, payments for orderly conduct, which were guaranteed by the paramount power. Thus the duty of securing due performance on either side became a British engagement, and in this way peace was early established. In course of time the actual control of the feudatories became vested in British hands, and only in 1921 was the original system restored in the case of Gwalior by insisting that the feudatories must be regarded as under the suzerainty of the state subject only to British intervention in case of breach of the agreements. To the Muslim state of Bhopal a grant of territory was made in consideration of its loyalty since 1774, while another state, Jaora, was created under the treaty with Holkar.

In Rajputana the agreements with the states provided for their independence internally as distinct units, but prohibited as usual any relations with any other state or foreign power. It was decided that tributes paid to the Marathas be continued but paid through the British Government.

In the case of Oudh the worst aspects of the system of non-intervention appeared. The Company, on the score of the value to the nawab of the establishment of friendly relations with Nepal, insisted on forcing payment of two crores of rupees, but did nothing to compel amelioration of his administration. Moreover, by a mischievous innovation, Hastings in 1818 induced the nawab to accept the style of King, which the Nizam of Hyderabad refused to do, thus alienating the Emperor and wounding Muslim sentiment without securing any real affection from the rather reluctant King.[1] The Nizam's dominions remained in disorder, and a scandal ruined the happiness of the governor-general. A firm, Palmer & Co., obtained permission to lend the Nizam funds at 25 per cent for the payment *inter alia* of the frightfully expensive contingent for which he had to pay, and it was only the exertions of Metcalfe which cost him the friendship of the governor-general, influenced by personal affection for a ward, the wife of one of the partners, which ultimately secured some relief from this scandal.

Against Nepal, Hastings had to wage determined war, which ended in acceptance in 1816 of peace, with the cession of Garhwal and Kumaun and withdrawal from Sikkim and acceptance of a resident at Kathmandu, relations with foreign countries to be subject to British control.

To Amherst (1823–8) belongs the credit of adding part of Burma to the Empire. In this case the government had little choice, for as conquerors of Arakan, Burma made demands on Calcutta and raided British territory. War from 1824–6 brought cession of Arakan, Tenasserim, Assam, Cachar, Jaintia, and Manipur, the payment of an indemnity, and a promise, not kept, to send a representative to Calcutta and to recognize a British resident. A constitutional issue was raised during hostilities regarding Bharatpur, where the resident had sanctioned the succession of a minor to the throne and proposed to maintain him there by force of arms. Amherst demurred to

[1] He was treated on formal terms of equality as late as the treaties of 1831 and 1837. Both he and the Emperor had higher salutes (21 guns) than the Governor-General; Lee-Warner, *Lord Dalhousie*, ii. 230.

the view that recognition involved such intervention, but Metcalfe on succeeding the former resident persuaded him that the paramount power must be prepared to insist on respect for its decisions, and the fort was now at last stormed. Doubtless it was this incident among others which induced Akbar II to accord the governor-general a meeting on the footing of equality; no presents as from an inferior were presented, the Emperor giving Amherst a string of pearls and emeralds, and in correspondence Amherst modified the terminology to recognize superiority, not vassalage or allegiance.

Lord William Cavendish Bentinck came with instructions from home to restrict activity as regards the states, and this instruction led to the unfortunate condition of affairs under which states were allowed to drift into disorder from which there was no rescue save in annexation. Against Coorg, whose raja was murderous and defiant, war was formally declared, and his state annexed (1834). It is interesting to note that the idea of treating the state as in rebellion in the technical sense of the term was not entertained. It was also necessary to take over control of Mysore in 1831 as the peasants revolted against misgovernment. In Jaipur the murder of the assistant to the resident and of the child ruler was followed by intervention, and the appointment of a council of regency for a new child ruler. But in Gwalior, Indore, Udaipur, and Baroda disorder and hostility to the Company were rampant, nor could the governor-general intervene effectively. But the sacrifice of three British subjects resulted in the annexation of Jaintia, and misgovernment of a gross character ended the existence of Cachar. Hyderabad continued in utter disorder, and a minister in Oudh who attempted reform was driven out, in the absence of any aid from the Company. On the other hand Oudh, Hyderabad, and Gwalior proved helpful in the extirpation of thagi, but the central states successfully resisted his efforts to determine opium policy. Policy towards the Emperor was marked in 1835 by the abandonment of the practice of striking the coinage in the nineteenth regnal year of Shah Alam, the rupee now bearing the King's image and superscription.

Auckland's tragic rule (1836–42) was noted for the conclusion of an abortive treaty with Oudh, the deposition, on uncertain accusations of intrigue with Portuguese and Indian authorities, of the raja of Satara in 1839, and the annexation of Karnul in Madras whose nawab was accused of trying to levy war.

In 1840 Jalaun lapsed, and in 1842 the titular nawabship of Surat also lapsed.

Ellenborough (1842–4) felt bound to intervene decisively in Gwalior, where anarchy had steadily developed under the non-intervention policy of the Company, and a huge army of 40,000 men controlled the state. He found justification in the fear that the Sikhs and Marathas might combine, and relied for legal justification on the promise of Gwalior in the treaty of 1804 to accept a subsidiary force, though the treaties of 1805 and 1817 did not contain this stipulation. The state force was drastically limited, and a contingent of the Company's force placed in Gwalior fort, while for ten years British officers governed for the minor prince. Sind, on the other hand, was annexed in 1843 with the express authority of the Company. It is impossible to justify the action taken on any legal plea; its sole excuse must be that the people profited by the change, and the simple and effective administration therein established by Sir C. Napier anticipated that which was to prove decisive later in securing the Punjab. Ellenborough naturally in his strong imperialism meditated the possibility of ending the empty fiction of the Empire by inducing the princes to quit the palace and transfer the title to the Queen,[1] and despite the wishes of the directors he stopped the making of the usual presents in the name of the company.

Sir Henry Hardinge's tenure of office (1844–8) was marked by the two Sikh wars, the outcome of which was the annexation of the Punjab in 1849. Unquestionably there was no option to such action if the British power were to remain paramount in India. Less fortunate was the decision taken in 1846 to establish a distinct Kashmir state under a Hindu prince in subordination.

It will be seen, therefore, that annexation was distinctly in the air when Dalhousie[2] in 1848 became governor-general. The principle had been laid down in 1841 that the Company should persevere in the one clear and direct course of abandoning no

[1] A. Law, *India under Lord Ellenborough* (1926), pp. 92 ff.
[2] Lee-Warner, *Life* (1904); *Private Letters* (1910).

just and honourable accession of territory or revenue, while all existing claims of right were to be scrupulously respected. The difficulty, of course, was to value claims of right, and herein trouble was inevitable. The directors espoused the perfectly tenable view that they should sparingly recognize any political succession due to adoption in the case of a state which was fully dependent, that is created by the Company or held on a subordinate tenure, to the overlordship of which the Company had succeeded. The Indian rule of law thus adopted was well known and in regular use by the Maratha overlords of Rajputs. They recognized adoption only if permitted prior to the ceremony; otherwise escheat was possible, but it was normally not enforced in full, though part of the territory might be withheld, the tribute raised, or the conditions of tenure otherwise varied. The failure of the raja of Satara, who died in 1848, to obtain consent to the adoption he made doubtless gave a formal right to enforce escheat, and the directors approved. But Elphinstone dissented, and, though doubtless technically Satara might be regarded as a state created by the Company, Indian opinion considered rather that it represented the line of Sivaji. Sambalpur also lapsed in 1849. In 1853 the raja of Nagpur died without making any adoption, and Dalhousie urged successfully annexation. He then classified the states as tributary and subordinate, when consent to adoption should be required; as of the Company's creation when adoption should not be allowed; and as independent when the Company had no right to intervene. Nagpur he classed as created by the Company. In vain did Colonel Low plead the maxims of Lord Hastings, Elphinstone, Munro, and even Metcalfe in favour of permitting adoption to continue state rule, on the ground that British rule was unpopular, that annexation denied the aristocracy in the states any outlet for their energies, and that a childless raja was apt to misgovern the subjects who were not to pass to a descendant. But the directors approved an annexation of such obvious military and commercial advantage.

In the case of Jhansi, which won notoriety because of the bitter hostility shown by the rani during the mutiny, the case of the Company was clear. The territory had merely been held by a provincial governor under the Peshwa, who fell under

British control on the disappearance of his sovereign. Jaitpur and Sambalpur in 1849 also lapsed justly.

In another case, that of Karauli, a Rajput state claiming to date from the eleventh century, Dalhousie proposed annexation, and, while ready not to urge the point against the view of Low, insisted that the right to annex was clear. He was overruled by the directors, who quite soundly urged that Karauli was not a dependent state but a protected ally. Dalhousie himself in cases where there was no immediate dependency was not prepared to intervene. Thus in 1852–3 against the wishes of John Lawrence he declined to interfere in a disputed succession in the Muslim state of Bahawalpur, though eventually a rebel established himself there by force of arms. Similarly, though he used all his personal influence against suttee, he could not insist on its abolition at the funeral of the Rajput rulers; in Dungarpur, on the other hand, the crime was punished severely during a temporary British regency.

There remained Oudh, whose wretched princes were so absolutely loyal that no excuse could even be imagined for depriving them of power. In 1837 Auckland made a new treaty which gave power of intervention in case of misrule and the right to employ British officers to remedy abuses. But the directors rejected it, and Auckland failed so to inform the King, and by his carelessness the treaty was long believed by all concerned to be in force. Hardinge in 1847 warned the King that action might be necessary. Sleeman as resident in 1849 and Outram in 1855 concurred in reporting the deplorable misgovernment of the country, though the former was decidedly opposed to annexation as likely to provoke a sepoy mutiny. Dalhousie did not think annexation justifiable in view of the fact that no treaty had been broken. He regarded the situation as governed by international law,[1] so that all he thought right was to persuade the King to hand over the administration while maintaining the sovereignty. But the directors overruled him, and as the King refused to yield he was deposed in 1856, and unhappily there was serious delay in providing suitable allowances for the dependants of the royal family. The disbanded forces of the state became sources of disloyalty,

[1] *Letters*, p. 363 (December 15th 1855).

while the sepoys of the Company's forces, many of whom had homes in Oudh, were deeply perturbed.

As regards the Nizam, Dalhousie was able to take a step of great value to Hyderabad. The misgovernment of the territory was serious, and there was added constant friction over the pay of the contingent due by the state. In 1853 by taking over the administration of the Berars, while leaving the sovereignty in the Nizam, the claim for subsidies was dropped, to the great advantage of the ruler's position though annexation might have been better for his subjects at that time.

No criticism is possible of the decision not to continue the titles of nawab of the Carnatic on the death of the holder in 1855 or the extinction of the title of raja of Tanjore in like circumstances. Nor, despite the infamous deeds of Nana Sahib during the mutiny, can it be made a matter of censure that Dalhousie declined to continue to a mere adopted son the vast pension which the undue charity of Malcolm had promised to the ex-Peshwa, when Baji Rao died in 1851.

Dalhousie's policy, instigated and supported by the directors, thus completed the work of Hastings and of Wellesley. The states of India were brought into definite relations of subordination or annexed, so that there could be no doubt where lay complete power in India. In Burma after provocation leading to war he annexed Lower Burma; the King, unable to sign a treaty of cession, in 1853 intimated his acquiescence in the loss and asked for renewed trade.

Towards the Emperor Dalhousie's view was that natural in a firm believer in the advantage to India of direct British rule. On the death of Bahadur Shah II he urged that the title should be allowed to lapse. The directors were required by the Board of Control to approve, but with so much doubt that Dalhousie accepted the suggestion of reconsideration and agreed with Fakr-ud-din, the heir-apparent, that he should retain the title, if he vacated the palace which was desired as the ideal site for a military depot and accepted a new residence and undertook to treat the governor-general as an equal. On the death, however, of Fakr-ud-din in 1856 this project dropped, the directors were induced to agree that the title should die with the Emperor. In fact it expired before him; tried on the accusation of complicity in the mutiny he was deposed, and died at Rangoon in 1862.

The disappearance of the Emperor was an event of greater importance in Indian history than is commonly admitted.[1] It rendered the direct sovereignty of the Crown natural as well as inevitable, and it rendered the Crown entitled if it so desired to make use of all the Mogul prerogatives which the Emperor still claimed, though he could not effectively make them operative. The tone of the British contentions from this moment is decisively changed. Nothing more is heard of international law as regulating the relations of the Company and the states as under Bentinck and Dalhousie. All are now dependent, because the Emperor had been, or had claimed to be, titular superior of every Indian state.

2. THE CONSTITUTIONAL LEGISLATION OF THE IMPERIAL PARLIAMENT: THE CHARTER ACTS OF 1813–53

The main structure of Indian government as laid down in the Charter Act of 1793 remained unchanged during the long period of European war, but minor measures were enacted by Parliament to meet emergent needs. The earlier attempts to save Indian states from the evil consequences of bad finance were reinforced by an Act of 1797[2] which forbade the lending or raising of loans to or for Indian princes by British subjects without the authority of the Company or the local government. Any person contravening this provision was to be guilty of misdemeanour and his security was to be void. It was under this Act that Hastings gave the consent to loans to the Nizam which ultimately involved him in resignation.

The Act, however, had a far more important effect, for it gave further approval to the system of legislation practised in Bengal. Cornwallis had passed many regulations, consolidated in 1793, with the assent of his council, but not under the precise terms of the Act of 1773. Rather, he acted as inheritor of the

[1] His position *de jure* is underestimated by Dewar and Garrett (*Trans. R.H.S.*, 1924, pp. 130 ff.), whose contentions on points of law are untenable. Buckler (ibid. 160–5) certainly exaggerates his influence on the mutiny.

[2] 37 Geo. III, c. 142.

nawab's legislative power, but he had doubts as to the extent of the authority which could be exercised under the Act of 1781 above referred to and desired further imperial legislation. It came now in a cautious form. Cornwallis in his regulations, No. XLI, had provided for forming into a regular code the regulations enacted for the internal government of Bengal. Parliament endorsed this provision and directed that all regulations affecting the rights, property, or persons of the natives and others subject to the jurisdiction of the provincial courts should be registered in the judicial department, formed into a code and printed with translations, the reasons for each regulation being prefixed. The courts were to be bound by such regulations, and copies were to be sent to the directors and Board of Control.

The Act also reduced to two the number of puisne judges of the Supreme Court at Calcutta, and provided for the creation of Recorder's Courts at Madras and Bombay. Supreme Courts were substituted by Acts of 1800[1] and 1823[2] respectively, with powers discussed later. The Act of 1800 also extended over Benares and other areas annexed to Bengal the authority of the Supreme Court at Calcutta. In 1807[3] the governors and councils of Madras and Bombay were given powers of legislation for these towns and their dependencies similar to those of the Regulating Act, subject to registration and approval by the Supreme Court and the Recorder's Court respectively. In both cases a power to legislate had already been exercised under the charters of 1753, and power to deal with regulations for the Company's Courts as in Bengal was given to Madras in 1800,[4] in view of the fact that Madras had now vast Indian territories within its boundaries.

The constitutional issue of the European military force of the Company was simplified by an Act of 1799[5] which provided that the Crown should take in hand the enlistment of Europeans for service in India and should transfer them from time to time to the Company on its petition. The total number might not

1 39 & 40 Geo. III, c. 79.

2 3 Geo. IV, c. 71.

3 47 Geo. III, sess. 2, c. 68, s. 1. Cf. for early irregularities Mackintosh in Morley, *Digest*, ii, 505 ff.

4 39 & 40 Geo. III, c. 79, s. 11. Bombay's right was recognized by 47 Geo. III, sess. 2, c. 68, s. 3, possibly by 37 Geo. III, c. 142, s. 11.

5 39 Geo. III, c. 109; Clode, *Military Forces of the Crown*, i, 289.

exceed 8,000 or such figure as was specified in the Mutiny Act, while the Company might raise and train not over 2,000 and appoint officers holding also the royal commission. All the men were to be subject to the Mutiny Act until embarked for India, and thereafter to the Indian Mutiny Act.

Searching inquiry preceded the renewal of the Company's charter. The conquests of Wellesley had raised financial difficulties which necessitated applications for relief, and the House of Commons in 1808 appointed a committee of investigation which did its work so well that its fifth report in 1812 is the standard authority on the judicial and police arrangements then in force and on land tenures. Finally, at the end of 1811 Melville intimated the decision of the government that other British subjects must have access with their ships to India. The Company in vain urged that their commercial privileges and their political power were inseparable and that the commercial profits were essential as a source of revenue. Not only was this point disputed, but the continuation of the tea monopoly accorded the one real source of profit. Stress was further laid by the Company on the danger of the admission of persons not under their control into India. It was pointed out, with the approval of Warren Hastings among others, that great injury might be done to the Indians by the presence of such persons, especially as they could be punished for offences only by the Supreme Courts or other courts at headquarters. The solution adopted was licensing entry, subjection to regulations by the local governments, and restrictions on residence.

The Act of 1813[1] therefore continued the Company in the enjoyment of its territorial possessions and revenues, over which the sovereignty of the Crown was now expressly proclaimed,[2] for twenty years; gave the Company a continued monopoly of the China trade and that in tea, but threw open the rest of the trade to British subjects. The commercial and territorial accounts were to be kept apart, full powers of superintendence being assured to the Board of Control. The debt was to be reduced, the dividend to be at the rate of 10½ per cent with five-sixths of any surplus for the state. The patronage of the Company was retained, the Crown to approve appointments of

[1] 53 Geo. III, c. 155. [2] S. 95.

governor-general, governors, and commanders-in-chief, and the Board of Control certain other appointments. The college at Haileybury—opened in 1805—was to be continued, no person to be appointed writer until he had resided there four terms and had duly conformed to the rules of the college. For military purposes the seminary at Addiscombe was to be continued; the Board of Control was to have the right to control these institutions as well as those at Calcutta[1] and Madras.

The number of troops which the Crown might send to India at the cost of India was fixed at 20,000, save on special requisition. In further elucidation of the rights of the Company it was provided that the governments in India could make laws and regulations and articles of war for the native troops and authorize the holding of courts martial.

The governments in India were also authorized with the sanction of the Court and Board of Control to impose taxes on persons subject to the jurisdiction of the Supreme Courts, and to impose imprisonment for failure to pay. This power, of course, was supplementary to that exercised under the authority inherited from the Indian states, which was of doubtful validity in respect of European British subjects.

In view of the influx of traders expected justices of the peace were given jurisdiction in case of assault or trespass committed by European British subjects on natives of India, and in case of small debts due to Indians. British subjects residing, trading, or occupying immovable property more than ten miles from a presidency town were to be subject to the jurisdiction of the provincial courts in civil matters, and special arrangements were made for criminal cases.[2]

Persons desiring to go to India whether as missionaries, a point over which controversy had raged, or as traders, might be licensed for this purpose by the directors or on appeal the Board of Control, with authority to remain so long as they conducted themselves properly but subject to such restrictions as might from time to time be deemed necessary. Unlicensed persons were to be subject to the penalties imposed on interlopers by earlier legislation and to be punishable on summary

[1] Created by Wellesley at the cost of a bitter struggle with the Directors.
[2] See Morley, *Digest*, i, pp. xcvi ff.

conviction in India. British subjects permitted to reside more than ten miles from a presidency town must register with a district court. Possibly in connexion with the influx of undesirables which was feared, or for some other reason, special clauses imposed punishments for theft, forgery, perjury, and coinage offences.

By an innovation the Act sets aside a lakh of rupees each year for the revival and improvement of literature and for encouragement to the learned natives of India, and for the introduction and promotion of a knowledge of science among the inhabitants of the British territories in India. Nor was religion neglected, for provision was made for a bishop of Calcutta and three archdeacons, the bishop to have jurisdiction over the ministers of the Church of England in India, but naturally no attempt was made to establish the church therein.

Curiously enough it became necessary in 1814[1] to enact specifically with retrospective effect that the governments in India might impose customs and other taxation on British subjects, foreigners and any other persons, an indication of the narrow ambit which it seems always to have been the practice to assign to Indian legislative power. In 1815[2] the Indian governments were authorized to extend the limits of the presidency towns and power was given to remove from India persons not being British subjects or natives of India. By a Foreign Enlistment Act of 1819[3] permission to engage in the military service of any potentate in India must be obtained from the governor-general in council or in conformity with his orders.

In 1820,[4] the Company was authorised to raise a corps of volunteer infantry not exceeding 800 from its employees. In 1823[5] the sum of £60,000 was charged on Indian revenues for the payment of pensions of the royal forces serving therein. Another Act[6] consolidated the regulations punishing mutiny and desertion of officers and men of the Company's Indian army. In 1828,[7] the Bombay marine was placed under the Mutiny Act.

[1] 54 Geo. III, c. 105. [2] 55 Geo. III, c. 84. [3] 59 Geo. III, c. 69.
[4] 1 Geo. IV, c. 99. [5] 4 Geo. IV, c. 71, s. 1.
[6] 4 Geo. IV, c. 81. It repeals 27 Geo. II, c. 9. See also 6 Geo. IV, c. 61.
[7] 9 Geo. IV, c. 72.

The rules as to hiring of ships by the Company were codified in 1818,[1] and in 1823[2] a Navigation Act opened expressly the trade with all ports save in China to British vessels in general.

In addition to legislation in 1823–5,[3] regarding salaries and pensions of bishops and archdeacons, an Act of 1819[4] authorized the archbishops and the bishop of London to admit to orders persons intending to serve in His Majesty's foreign possessions, such persons not to be entitled to act in England without further permission, and an Act of 1823[5] allowed the bishop of Calcutta to ordain persons to act in that diocese only, excusing those who were not United Kingdom British subjects from the necessity of taking the oaths requisite in England.

Judicial matters were regulated as regards salaries and pension by the legislation of 1823–6, as regards juries the restriction limiting as regards grand juries and the trial of Christians, the right to act to Christians disappeared finally in 1832,[6] when the appointment of others than covenanted civil servants as justices of the peace was sanctioned. In 1823[7] a supreme court for Bombay was authorized. It is significant of the limited character of the legislative power ascribed to the presidencies that it was felt necessary in 1818[8] to legislate to remove doubts as to the validity of marriages performed by Scots clergymen, in 1828[9] to enact a bankruptcy law, to make the real estate of British subjects dying within the jurisdiction of the Supreme Courts liable for their debts,[10] and to extend certain amendments of English criminal law.[11]

In 1824 it was agreed to take over all the Dutch possessions in India and Malacca in exchange for Bencoolen and the British holdings in Sumatra. Singapore was transferred to the Company by an Act of 1824,[12] and provision for its government made in the following year,[13] when the ceded territory on the Coromandel coast and the Northern Sarkars were placed under Madras.

[1] 58 Geo. III, c. 83. [2] 4 Geo. IV, c. 80.
[3] 4 Geo. IV, c. 71; 6 Geo. IV, c. 85. [4] 59 Geo. III, c. 60.
[5] 4 Geo. IV, c. 71, s. 6.
[6] 2 & 3 Will. IV, c. 117, amending 7 Geo. IV, c. 37. [7] 4 Geo. IV, c. 71.
[8] 58 Geo. IV, c. 84; later regulated by India Acts, III & XV of 1872.
[9] 9 Geo. IV, c. 73. [10] 9 Geo. IV, c. 33.
[11] 9 Geo. IV, c. 74; this accords power to try bigamy committed outside India.
[12] 5 Geo. IV, c. 108. [13] 6 Geo. IV, c. 85.

The Charter Act of 1833,[1] like its predecessor was the outcome of much inquiry and consideration. It was produced at a time when Whig and Liberal principles were politically victorious, when Macaulay was Secretary to the Board of Control, and James Mill, the disciple of Bentham and admirer of his views on legislation and codification, was examiner of correspondence at the India House. It followed from the whole trend of affairs that the trade monopoly disappeared,[2] and the Company was required to wind up its commercial transactions. Its debts were charged on Indian revenues and they were authorized to pay 10½ per cent, but arrangements were made for redemption of the stock at £200 per cent, for which purpose the Company was required to pay two millions to the National Debt Commissioners, to be accumulated at compound interest until it reached twelve millions.

The territorial possessions of the Company except St. Helena, which was vested in the Crown, were continued to the Company for twenty years but 'in trust for His Majesty, his heirs and successors, for the service of the government of India', and the control of the British Government was as before to be exercised through the Board of Control, which was expanded to include the great officers of state, but in fact the President continued to act. The Company received at long last a compendious name, the East India Company; it was relieved from the disability of the Act of 1773 under which any one in its service was ineligible for election as a director, but otherwise the system of control was continued, with special emphasis on the secret committee and on the retention of patronage. Macaulay defended this position and the retention of the Company on the ground that it was not desirable to give so much uncontrolled power to the Crown, for Parliament was incapable of exercising effective supervision over Indian government.

The original proposal was to entrust to the governor-general and councillors the government of India, but that was in the Act reduced to the superintendence, direction, and control of the governor-general in council. Another project of centralization had proposed the abolition of the councils of Madras and Bombay,

[1] 3 & 4 Will. IV, c. 85; in the main operative from April 22nd 1834 (s. 117).
[2] 3 & 4 Will. IV, c. 59, gave power to regulate the trade by Order in Council.

but it was felt sufficient to give the power to abolish or to reduce, and in both cases the number was brought down to two. The council of the governor-general was fixed at four, one for legislation only, while the commander-in-chief or commander-in-chief of the Bengal army might be made an extraordinary member.

It was proposed to divide the presidency of Fort William into two, Fort William and Agra, both under a governor and council, and with Madras and Bombay subject to the governor-general in council, whose orders as to civil or military government were to be obeyed and whose permission was necessary for creating new offices or granting any salary, gratuity, or pension. But the division was postponed by an Act of 1835 which authorized the appointment of a lieutenant-governor of the North-Western Provinces, and the Charter Act of 1853 continued the suspension. The governor-general of India[1] was left governor of Bengal, a position relieved in practice by his appointing under the Act a deputy governor.

Alterations of vital importance were made in the legislative system of India. The aims stated by the government in justifying the measure included the simplification of law, and reform of legislative power rendered the more necessary because it had been decided to open India freely to the entry of British subjects as opposed to the permit system of the past. At the same time it was decided to centralize the wide legislative power to be granted, and to differentiate the function of legislation from that of administration. Hence the addition of a fourth member to the council of the governor-general who was not to be a member of the Company's service; he was in theory entitled only to sit and vote at meetings for the purpose of making laws, but the directors suggested[2] that he should be allowed to sit at executive business meetings as a means of appreciating the great problems to be dealt with, and Macaulay was thus admitted to such meetings. The purpose of his presence was primarily to secure that legal measures should be duly drafted by a professional hand, and Indian legislation henceforth is certainly technically improved.

[1] This style superseded that of governor-general of Bengal.
[2] Ellenborough insisted that they could not direct that he sit; Law, pp. 117, 118.

The Act superseded the existing legislative powers of Madras and Bombay, and greatly extended the powers hitherto vested in the governor-general and council of Bengal. In all three territories power had been given to legislate so as to bind those Europeans and Indians who were subject to the jurisdiction of the Supreme Court by regulations duly registered by the Supreme Courts. But the governments agreed in objecting to this control, and refrained from this procedure, so that their regulations[1] could be made effective only on Indians resident outside the headquarters of each territory and such Europeans as were subject to the control of the provincial courts. This fact explains the curious instances above noted of legislation on local issues for India by the British Parliament. English common and statutory law had been introduced for the guidance of the supreme judiciary by the charter of 1726, but unless specially extended to India subsequent legislation did not apply. For the guidance of the provincial courts, on the other hand, there were bodies of regulations, including the Cornwallis code of 1793 and subsequent regulations down to 1834, for Madras regulations from 1802 to 1834, and for Bombay Elphinstone's code of 1827 embodying legislation from 1799 and additions down to 1834. It was obviously most undesirable to maintain this division of legal enactments and of courts, and the new provisions were calculated to render fundamental change possible. Moreover, it was clearly necessary to remove from dispute the legal authority on which legislation rested.

The difficulties of the position are admirably stated in an opinion of Sir George Grey and Sir Edward Ryan,[2] which was before Parliament when it legislated. They pointed out that the bulk of the Indian territories had really become the possession of the Crown by conquest or cession, and that therein its sovereignty was absolute, the overlordship of the Mogul being merely formal. The Company exercised two sets of powers, those derived from the Crown directly, and indirectly those of the rulers they supplanted which the Crown had acquiesced in their exercising in the judicial and legislative sphere, i.e. by the provincial courts and the regulations. The direct powers

[1] They were unco-ordinated, the governor-general's veto being little used; *Hansard*, 3rd Ser., xviii, 727.

[2] October 16th 1830, in Fifth App. to Third Report of Select Committee.

from the Crown given by Parliament had superseded those of the charters of 1698 and 1726. The indirect powers including that of taxation might be called in question now that India was to be opened to European entry. They drew attention to the extreme confusion which existed regarding the term British subject as used in imperial legislation, and deprecated the confusion caused by the maintenance of two completely distinct judicial and legislative systems, under which the most important powers of the Indian government, including the whole of the criminal law as applied to natives, lay outside the control of any power save the Company and the Board of Control. They strongly recommended remedial measures, justly criticizing the very unsatisfactory terms of the existing charters of justice which purported to carry out the legislation under which they were issued.

The strengthened legislature was put in the position to legislate for all British territories in India with the same effect as Parliament, subject to certain limitations. It could (*a*) repeal, amend, or alter any law in force in the Indian territories; (*b*) make laws for all persons, British or native, foreigners or others and for all courts, chartered or otherwise; (*c*) legislate for all places and things whatsoever in the territories; (*d*) legislate for all servants of the Company within the native states; and (3) make articles of war for the government of the native officers and soldiers in the Company's military service and for the administration of justice by courts martial accordingly. But it might not repeal any provisions of the Charter Act of 1833 or of the Acts punishing mutiny or desertion of officers or soldiers of the Crown or the Company; or affect any prerogative of the Crown, or the authority of Parliament or any part of the unwritten laws and constitution of the United Kingdom whereon might depend the allegiance of any person to the Crown, or the sovereignty or dominion of the Crown over Indian territories. Nor without the previous sanction of the directors might it authorize any save a chartered high court to sentence to death any of His Majesty's natural-born subjects born in Europe or their children or abolish any chartered court. There was also an express saving of the power of Parliament to legislate for India and to repeal Indian Acts, which were to be duly laid before it. Acts of the Indian legislature could be disallowed by the directors subject to the Board of Control, but otherwise were to operate without registration as Acts of Parliament.

It was proposed further that Indian legislation should be consolidated, and codified and that, where possible, general laws should be passed, and judicial systems and policy standardized, and an Indian Law Commission on which Macaulay sat was set up to report on ameliorative measures.

India was opened as regards the area under the Company on January 1st 1800, the Carnatic, Cuttack, and Singapore to British subjects, on condition of entering at a customs-house; for residence elsewhere a licence was still required, but other areas could be opened, and without formal repeal the system of licences was dropped. But the Indian legislature was required to legislate regarding illicit entrance or residence, and this was duly acted upon in Act III of 1864.[1]

It was further enjoined on the legislature to make regulations, in view of the freedom of entry conceded, for the protection of the natives from outrage on their persons, religion, and opinions.[2]

By s. 87 of the Act it was expressly provided that no native or natural-born subject of the Crown resident in India should be by reason only of his religion, place of birth, descent, colour, or any of them be disqualified for any place in the Company's service. This excellent sentiment, however, was not of much practical importance, since nothing was done, despite the views of Munro, Malcolm, Elphinstone, Sleeman, and Bishop Heber, to repeal the provision of the Act of 1793, which excluded any but covenanted servants from occupying places worth over £500 a year. A further reform was projected. The service was to be entered under the system of competition after nomination of four candidates at least for each vacancy, a period of three years' training at Haileybury to follow. But the directors defeated this wise proposal, inducing next year the passing of an Act postponing the operation of the proposal.

Provision was made for increasing to three the bishoprics in

[1] *Alter Caufman* v. *Government of Bombay* (1894), I.L.R. 18 Bombay, 636.

[2] Embodied in Indian Penal Code, ss. 295–8.

India, giving to the bishop of Calcutta metropolitan status subject to the general superintendence of the archbishop of Canterbury. In each presidency two chaplains of the Church of Scotland were to be provided and power was given to appoint ministers of other Christian sects.

Of fundamental importance was the provision requiring the governor-general in council to take into consideration the mitigation of the state of slavery, the amelioration of the condition of slaves, and the ultimate extinction of slavery. They were to submit drafts of legislation for the approval of the directors, and the latter had each year to submit to Parliament the drafts received and their proceedings in respect thereof. Already by the Acts of 1811[1] and 1824[2] engaging in the slave trade had become first a felony, and then piracy, whose penalty was death, and these Acts applied to India, but India was not included in the general legislation of 1833, it being recognized that Hindu and Muhammadan law had to be respected. By Act V of 1843 the necessary action was set on foot.

The Act of 1833 was supplemented by two Acts[3] regarding the conditions of trade to India and China and the tea trade in special. In 1835[4] as noted above, permission was obtained to defer the partition of Bengal, and in 1840[5] the Indian Mutiny Acts were consolidated and amended and power given to the governor-general in council to legislate for the Indian navy. In view of earlier legislation on insolvency a further Act[6] was passed in 1848 which stood until repealed and re-enacted for the presidency towns in 1909 (Act III).

When the extension granted by the Act of 1833 approached its close, the situation was most closely considered. The passage of time had shown a steady growth in favour of the substitution of Crown control in place of that of the Company, but the power of the directors was by no means obsolete. They had still normally the initiative in public business, and, while the appointment of the highest officials tended to pass from their hands, as when Lord Auckland was chosen in 1835 in lieu of Metcalfe, they could recall a governor-general they disliked, as in the case of Ellenborough in 1844, despite the objections of the

[1] 51 Geo. III, c. 23.
[2] 5 Geo. IV, c. 113.
[3] 3 & 4 Will. IV, cc. 93, 101.
[4] 5 & 6 Will. IV, c. 52.
[5] 3 & 4 Vict., c. 37.
[6] 11 & 12 Vict., c. 21.

Queen herself. Moreover, their expert knowledge was obviously a great asset, which could not hastily be dispensed with. The decision therefore carried out in the Act of 1853[1] continued the powers of the Company in trust for the Crown until Parliament should otherwise direct. But it reduced the number of directors from twenty-four to eighteen, and made provision for the election of six by the Crown; of the others, six must, like the Crown's nominees, have served at least ten years in India, thus paving the way for a council of advice essentially expert. The quorum was reduced from thirteen to ten, thus rendering it even possible for the Crown directors to be in a majority. More vital as a sign of change was the taking away of the patronage of the directors and the substitution of competitive examination open to British subjects generally under a scheme prepared by the Board of Control. At the same time the position of President of the Board of Control was increased in importance by being placed on equality with a Secretary of State as regards salary, the reduction to £3,500 from £5,000 in 1831 having rendered the office a stepping-stone to higher positions, and the sanction of the Crown was required for all appointments to the councils in India.

The vexed question of the administration of Bengal was dealt with by authorizing the appointment of a governor, or until that was done a lieutenant-governor, a step taken in 1854. A new presidency might be created, or a lieutenant-governorship, and the latter step was taken for the Punjab in 1859. The former measure was long overdue, for the governor-general[2] in council was overburdened with work, and Bengal did not receive anything like the amount of oversight essential for its development or even for the elementary task of maintaining security of life.

The legislative provisions of the Act were of considerable importance. The legislative member was now given full rank as a member of council with voting power in all business, as desired by Macaulay. At the same time the distinction between the council as executive and as a legislative body was marked by certain changes. Hitherto the governor-general in executive

[1] 16 & 17 Vict., c. 95.

[2] He appointed a deputy, but these changing officers could do little; Curzon, *British Government in India*, ii, 74; Lee-Warner, *Lord Dalhousie*, ii, 246 ff.

business could act with one of the council and had an overriding power in executive business. In legislative business three councillors could legislate in his absence and he could not override them. Now he was given the right to withhold his assent, though not to pass legislation over the dissent of the majority of the council. Secondly the council was increased in size, to consist of the governor-general, the commander-in-chief, the four members of council, a representative of each presidency or lieutenant-governorship selected from civilians of ten years' standing at least by the head of the local government, the Chief Justice of Bengal and another Supreme Court judge; two other civilians might be, but were not, added. The sittings of the council were made public and their proceedings published. The proposal to add unofficial European and Indian members was negatived on the ground[1] that it was impossible to select an Indian or a Muslim properly representative. The obvious solution, however, would have been to have a larger advisory body, for, while the new council was much better equipped in legal and provincial knowledge, it lacked effective spokesmen of Indian or non-official European views. As it was, the new legislature fell rapidly into disrepute with the government, for it adopted parliamentary models, and showed an inclination to inquire into executive business and even to criticize the government in respect of its grants to the Mysore princes.[2] This attempt to cast doubt on the wisdom of the government was as little appreciated in the United Kingdom as in India, and the step taken was remedied in 1861.

The law commission in India established under the Act of 1833 had worked hard, but no important positive enactments had resulted, and on the score of expense it had been reduced to a skeleton organization. Provision was now made for commissioners in England to work into legal form the final work of the Indian commission.

The regulations for open competition were drafted by a committee under Macaulay, and were destined to improve seriously the quality of the service. But they ignored the fact that by establishing this system of entry by examination in

[1] Wood, *Hansard*, 3rd Ser., cxxix, 418 ff.
[2] Proceedings, 1860, pp. 1343–1402.

India a grave obstacle was being placed in the way of entry of Indians to the civil service. Moreover, it was decided[1] to close from 1858 Haileybury as a place of training.

In 1854[2] the system of administration in India was supplemented by an important Act. The growth of Bengal had been remarkable. It included the conquered and ceded provinces which in 1834 were styled the province of Agra, and renamed North-Western Provinces in 1836, being placed under a lieutenant-governor. Assam, Arakan, and Tenasserim were ceded in 1826, small Dutch possessions exchanged in 1824, Serampur bought from the King of Denmark in 1845, the enclave of Darjeeling obtained from Sikkim in 1835 and a portion of Sikkim in 1850. The Act of 1853 had contemplated a new presidency and a further lieutenant-governorship, but these powers were found inadequate, and provision was felt to be necessary for areas which were not suited for creation into a lieutenant-governorship. The solution now adopted was to permit the governor-general in council, with the sanction of the directors and Board of Control, to take under his immediate authority any territory and thereafter to provide for its administration. The officers placed in charge of such districts, to whom were delegated such powers as were not held proper to be reserved to the central authority, were styled in practice chief commissioners, a style recognized by an Act of 1870.[3] Thus when under the Act of 1853 a lieutenant-governor was appointed for Bengal, Orissa, and Assam, Tenasserim was kept in the hands of the governor-general, and Arakan, at first handed over to the lieutenant-governor, was shortly afterwards restored to the governor-general. As a matter of fact the necessities of the case had led, when the Sagar and Narbada territories were acquired, and later when Assam, Arakan, and Tenasserim were occupied in 1824–6 and Pegu in 1852, to the decision of the government to exempt them from the operations of the Bengal regulations, and to govern them as non-regulation areas on simpler lines, employing military as well as civil officers. This practice may have been of doubtful legality; if so, it was now rendered possible to carry out the system legally.

[1] 18 & 19 Vict., c. 53. [2] 17 & 18 Vict., c. 77. [3] 33 Vict., c. 3, ss. 1, 3.

The Act of 1854 further simplified government by taking from the governor-general his now unnecessary style of governor of Bengal, conferring on him in council all powers not allocated to the governments of the areas into which the old presidency was now divided. Further power was given to the government of India with home approval to alter the boundaries of the Indian provinces as held desirable.

3. THE SYSTEM OF ADMINISTRATION

During this period, as already noted, the Company through its Court of Directors still remained an important factor in the system of administration,[1] and controlled personnel, recalling Ellenborough and driving Wellesley to resign. The Board of Control doubtless had paramount power in all save commercial issues, but much depended on the strength of its president who came in practice to represent its authority. Dundas, Pitt's incompetent protégé, was able as a rule to exercise the full authority of a cabinet minister, but the president might as in the case of Minto be left outside the cabinet. Even Castlereagh is found explaining to Wellesley how delicate was his task in handling the directors. Doubtless the president could send dispatches to the secret committee for dispatch to India, and dispatches might be sent from India to that body which could not show them to the other directors. But normally the business was settled between the chairman and the president informally, and only when agreement was reached was a formal draft submitted for the Board's approval. In the case of persistent disagreement the Crown could proceed by application to King's Bench for a mandamus to the Company,[2] but that was necessarily rare. The net result was a distinct improvement on the earlier chaos.[3] The government of India was brought into effective touch with the British Cabinet, but that body was not burdened by the patronage of India, nor was it left to attempt to devise policy without the

[1] Cf. Kaye, *Memorials of Indian Govt.*, p. 483; *Admin. of E.I. Co.*, pp. 129 ff.; Roberts, *India under Wellesley*, pp. 263–88.

[2] Cf. the dispute over Wellesley's college at Calcutta; Roberts, *India under Wellesley*, pp. 157–65.

[3] Its disadvantages are stressed by Curzon, *British Government in India*, ii, 67 ff.

aid of an authoritative body which stood between it and the public.

As regards the government in India, the appointment of Cornwallis marked the decisive preference for sending men from England to fill the office of governor-general. Shore indeed succeeded Cornwallis in 1793 for special reasons, but his management of affairs was not regarded as commending a repetition of the experiment, and the ineffective character of Barlow's tenure of office (1805–7) on the death of Cornwallis on his second visit confirmed the objections. The government at home refused to allow Metcalfe to succeed, sending in lieu the inefficient Auckland, and it was only in exceptional circumstances and after the Mutiny that the rule was departed from.[1] Unquestionably there were advantages in the plan. The noblemen sent from England had a wider grasp of foreign affairs and politics generally than could be expected in the servants of the company; they had higher moral standards, and their views were unquestionably received with far more respect by directors and Board of Control alike than would have been those of former servants of the Company. Applied to the case of the governorships of Bombay and Madras the principle worked worse. With the exception of Bentinck the men who accepted office were second-rate, inferior to Lord Macartney, whose appointment in 1780 to Madras marked the beginning of the system. Dalhousie considered that it might be dropped with advantage, and in some cases it was ignored. Thus for their services in the last Maratha war Elphinstone was given Bombay and Munro Madras, where they both accomplished much valuable work.

The presidency governments were constructed on the basis of the central government, the governor being aided by a council of two civil members to whom was added the commander-in-chief of the local forces. He had the same power to override his council, and until the passing of the Act of 1833 had legislative as well as executive powers, subject in the case of legislation intended to apply to those within the jurisdiction of the Supreme Court to registration therein.

After Cornwallis the subordination of the presidencies to

[1] In Lawrence's case (1864–9); cf. Curzon, ii, 233.

the governor-general was complete. The Act of 1793 made it clear that the governor-general could visit a presidency and there exercise with the local council his authority as with the council of Bengal, and could issue orders to any servant of the Company without previous communication with the local council. Thus Wellesley was not hampered by local resistance when in 1798 he took upon himself the burden of controlling at Madras the preparations for the overthrow of Tipu Sultan.[1] Even he complained of lack of readiness to carry out his orders, and his predecessor Shore found Lord Hobart ordering about the naval squadron on the coast without reference to him, and their quarrel was so serious that Hobart went home and threw up his chance of succession.[2]

If the servants of the Company lost the highest posts available they were amply compensated by the statutory security accorded in 1793, which gave the servants in each presidency a monoply of offices inferior to councillorships. No post with pay of over £500 a year could be awarded to any servant under three years' service, for £1,500 six years were necessary, nine for £3,000, and twelve for £4,000.[3] The figures seem large, but it must be remembered that they were intended to replace the scandalous profits of the past. The new régime had the great merit of reducing the directors' patronage to writerships, and putting an end to the flood of greedy adventurers who visited India to seek employment. Only in areas exempted from the regulation system was it possible to evade the rules of the statutes. But the system shut out Indians from superior office, and this was a serious disadvantage, which was not remedied by declarations of principle such as that of 1833 above referred to, and was perpetuated by the adoption of open competition in England under the Act of 1853.

The special powers of the governor-general in council naturally resulted in the constant tendency to model government even outside Bengal on that system. The history of this period, therefore, is largely taken up with the different reactions

[1] Wellesley so dominated his council as to receive strong disapproval from the directors, and he personally dictated policy to the governors; see Roberts, *India under Wellesley*, pp. 3–8, 279–85; for his control of Lord Clive at Madras, pp. 44–8.

[2] Teignmouth, *Life of Shore*, i, 372.

[3] Reduced by 53 Geo. III, c. 155, s. 82: the periods fell to four, seven, and ten years.

outside Bengal to that model, while in Bengal itself tardily it was realized that the reforms of Cornwallis, necessary as they were at the time, involved disadvantages which had slowly and tentatively to be eliminated.

(*a*) BENGAL

Cornwallis's system was based on the permanent settlement of the revenue, the separation of revenue administration and the judicature, and the employment of Europeans in the higher offices, subjecting them to the control of a complex system of regulations designed to check any misdemeanours. Unquestionably his motives were excellent. The weakness of his plan lay in the fact that recourse to the courts was wholly ineffective as a means of protection to the ryots against the zamindars, while their existence encouraged among the richer Indians a love for litigation not unknown in other lands but accentuated in India. The permanent settlement worked badly at first; litigation choked the courts, and sales of estates became frequent. In 1795 and 1799 it was felt necessary to give zamindars coercive powers over tenants, and in the latter year to authorize the arrest of the zamindars themselves. But only slowly was friction reduced and not until many of the original zamindars had disappeared.

To remedy congestion in the courts various devices were tried, mainly in the direction of increasing the number and powers of subordinate Indian judges, in limiting appeals, and expediting proceedings. In 1801 the Sadr Diwani Adalat was handed over to three judges, thus ending the judicial activity of the governor-general in council;[1] in 1807 the number was increased to four, and in 1811 provision was made to augment the number of puisne judges as need arose.[2] Provision was made in 1797 for hearing appeal cases, when the provincial courts were on circuit, while magistrates were given increased powers in petty cases. But none of these experiments served seriously to improve matters, and only in 1814 were effective steps taken to modify the basis of Cornwallis's system.

[1] Until 1818 he continued to hear appeals from Madras; Madras Reg. V of 1802, ss. 31–6.

[2] Reg. II of 1801; XII of 1811.

In 1814 the directors and the Board of Control raised the question whether it would not be right to give the collectors of revenue some part in civil justice as a means of aiding the ryots, and to associate them with the control of the police and magisterial functions. But there was much reluctance locally to undo the work of Cornwallis and reforms were slow. In 1813–14 the police were reorganized, in 1814 and 1821–31 munsiffs and sadr amins were given wider powers in civil cases, a fifth judge was added to the Sadr Diwani Adalat and the work apportioned among the judges.[1] The number of zillah judges was increased, and slowly some revenue matters were referred to the collectors, in 1819 claims to freedom from assessment, in 1822 rectification of errors at sales. The action of the courts was aided by the definition of the rights of ryots and others in land by Regulation VIII of 1819, though by this time it was impossible satisfactorily to protect the ryot. In criminal justice Regulation IV of 1821 permitted the government specially to authorize collectors to act as magistrates. In 1824 and 1831 steps were taken which led to collectors dealing with summary suits as to rent, though a regular suit could be brought in the civil courts. The collectors worked under the control of the Board of Revenue at Calcutta.

In 1829 commissioners of revenue and circuit were appointed, who controlled the collectors and the judge magistrates, and themselves held courts of sessions, the provincial courts' duties being handed over to them. But in 1831 sessions work was given to the district judges, who handed over their magisterial powers to the collectors. In 1837, however, separation once more took place; each district tended to have a district civil and sessions judge, a collector, and a magistrate; these officers were aided by assistants of the civil service, by deputy collectors, and deputy magistrates, often natives, and at headquarters the collector's office included a treasury. The post of deputy collector was legalized in 1833, that of deputy magistrate in 1843, while Bentinck created the post of joint magistrate to which senior subordinates could be posted to aid the collectors and the magistrates; later these officers became subdivisional officers, being stationed at subdivisions where it

[1] Reg. XXIII of 1814; V of 1831.

was specially desirable to bring justice close to the people and to supervise the police. In a few cases collectors also held magisterial functions. Bentinck, in a desire to extend the services of Indians in the judicial service, established principal sadr amins who could try cases up to 5,000 rupees value, and from them in certain cases appeal lay only to the Sadr Diwani Adalat.

The system was unsatisfactory in operation, and Dalhousie in 1854, the first lieutenant-governor, and Canning in 1857 were at one in a demand for the union of powers in the collector, so that he might take the place occupied by the corresponding officer of the time in Madras, Bombay, and the North-Western Provinces. This preference for patriarchal rule unquestionably corresponded with the need of the time and received effect after the Mutiny. It was not realized by the supporters of the system of Cornwallis that the protection of courts means nothing to persons without the means to make use of their advantages.

As regards the added territories, in 1795 a city and three zillah courts were created for Benares as well as a provincial Court of Appeal. In 1803 the Bengal system was introduced into the ceded area of Oudh, and extended in 1804 to the Duab. In 1831 a distinct Sadr Diwani Adalat was created for the North-Western Provinces. For criminal purposes in 1795 the judges of the Benares city and zillah courts were made magistrates and the provincial court given the power of a Court of Circuit. Over all was extended the jurisdiction of the Sadr Nizamat Adalat. In 1803 in the Oudh districts the seven zillah judges were made magistrates, the provincial court made a Court of Circuit under the Sadr Nizamat Adalat. Similar provisions were made in 1804–5 for the Duab. In 1817 Dehra Dun and Kumaun were brought under the legal system, and in 1831 a separate court of Sadr Nizamat Adalat was set up at Allahabad, with authority over the North-Western Provinces, Kumaun, and the Sagar and Narbada territories.

Cuttack, acquired in 1804, was brought under the judicial system as two zillahs under the Court of Circuit for the Calcutta division.

In addition to these courts, whose powers were extended over all persons in 1836, there existed the courts established under direct parliamentary authority. The jurisdiction of the Supreme Court as it existed in 1853 applied to all persons within the area of Calcutta proper with a population of 413,182. The only limitation was that its ecclesiastical jurisdiction was not exercised in the case of Hindus and Muhammadans beyond the grant of probate of wills. It also applied to all subjects born in the British Islands and their descendants, resident in the presidency or the province of Agra. Further, all persons resident in these areas who kept a house and servants in Calcutta, or carried on business in any place there through agents, were deemed subject to the common law and equity jurisdiction of the court. Indians who had bound themselves by written contract to accept its jurisdiction were subject to it where the cause of action exceeded 500 rupees. Persons who made use of the court thereby subjected themselves to its jurisdiction in the same matter on another side, e.g. if probate was taken out, the person so acting fell under the equity jurisdiction for due administration of the estate. Servants, past and present, of the Company or any British subject were liable in case of wrongs or trespasses, and by agreement in other civil suits, while they were liable in crime, misdemeanour, and oppression to its criminal jurisdiction. The Admiralty jurisdiction applied fully criminally in respect of crimes on the high seas and civilly in respect of the provinces of Bengal, Bihar, and Orissa.

Moreover, the court had jurisdiction in respect of any crimes committed by British subjects at any place within the charter limits or in the territories of Indian states.

The law adminstered in the court was complex. It comprised: (1) The common law as it existed in 1726 so far as not subsequently modified by imperial or local legislation; (2) English statute law under the same conditions; (3) English statutes expressly applied to India, or adopted for India by local legislation; (4) the civil law as followed in the ecclesiastical and Admiralty jurisdictions in England; (5) regulations made by the governor-general in council prior to the Act of 1833 if duly registered in the court, and Acts made under that measure; (6) Hindu and Muhammadan law and usages in cases regarding inheritance and succession to lands, rents, or goods, and all matters of contract and dealing between party and party where a Hindu or Muhammadan was defendant.

It must be added that under each head the law was hard to ascertain,[1] and the judges had also to take into consideration the charter of the court, commissions from the government, circulars from the Nizamat and Diwani Adalats, treaties and arguments from international law. In the Company's Courts the matter was still more confused if possible, though English common and statute law were not regularly in force, for they felt bound in a manner unknown to the Supreme Court by the directions issued from the government and the Appeal Courts. It can easily be understood, therefore, that there was great difficulty throughout this period, even after the Act of 1833 gave full legislative authority and extended the jurisdiction of the Company's Courts, in ascertaining legal issues.

Police also remained inefficient, and an experiment from 1837 to 1854 under which the commissioners ceased to supervise the forces, which were placed under a superintendent, did nothing to improve matters. Not until 1856 was the protection of villages improved by appointing chaukidars subordinate to the district magistrates and paid by a local cess. The country was overrun by thugs and dacoits, who rejoiced in an immunity greatly helped by legal niceties. Special legislation in 1836 was necessary to condemn to life-imprisonment any associate of a band, and Sleeman's efforts gradually diminished the evil. Similar legislation in 1843 and 1851 reduced the curse of dacoity.

Matters were not helped by the financial straits caused by the permanent settlement, the zamindars objecting to pay cesses even for roads or education; customs and excise, the salt monopoly and opium were the other chief sources. The final control rested with the Board of Revenue in subordination to the supreme government.

[1] e.g., how far was English law capable of application in the presidency towns, etc.: *Lyons Corpn.* v. *East India Co.* (1836), 1 Moo. P.C. 175 (rules against land-ownership by aliens not in force); *Advocate-General of Bengal* v. *Surnomoye Dossee* (1863), 2 Moo. P.C. N.S. 22 (English law of suicide inapplicable); *Freeman* v. *Fairlie* (1828), 1 Moo. Ind. App. 305; *Ram Coomar Coondoo* v. *Chunder Canto Mookerjee* (1876), 2 App. Cas. 186 (law as to maintenance and champerty). The application of native law was most complex; Morley, *Digest*, i, pp. cix ff. The Sikhs and Jains had special usages, the Parsees their own practices, which received legislative effect in part in 1837, the Armenians claimed English law. See Eggar, *Laws of India*, i, 26 ff.

(b) MADRAS

Efficient administration of any kind at Madras dates virtually from the acquisition of Dindigul and Baramahal by Cornwallis, for the Northern Sarkars had been carelessly managed by incompetent agents and the Company's jagir was in no better case. A Board of Revenue was set up in 1786, and in 1794 Hobart installed district collectors under the Board in the sarkars, and placed the jagir under a single collector. Efforts were made by the latter, by Place in Baramahal, and by Munro in Kanara, to establish direct relations with the ryots for raising the land revenue, but Bengal in 1798 ordered the adoption of the system there in force. It was therefore in 1802–4 arranged to set up in the sarkars, the jagir, Baramahal, and Dindigul a permanent zamindari system, and the judicial organization of Bengal was brought into force with district judges who were also magistrates and in charge of the police darogas; with provincial Courts of Appeal from the judges, which acted as Courts of Circuit; and a code of regulations which vainly attempted to protect the peasants. Later the system was forced on the poligars of the Carnatic, but gradually its defects became visible, and Bentinck, governor from 1803–7, realized the claims of the ryotwari views of Munro. But the Board of Revenue preferred and experimented unsuccessfully with a plan of village settlements. The way was now open to revert to Munro's views, which included the conviction that the collector should have magisterial and police authority, that local panchayats should as far as possible be used to settle disputes, only appeals and serious criminal cases going to British judges, whose employment in general was too expensive, while legal complications denied justice to the ryots. This policy was adopted in 1818. The collector received magisterial powers and the control of the police, the darogas being disbanded and their work carried out by the collector's revenue staff and village watchmen. Paid munsiffs were stationed at convenient centres to try causes up to 200 rupees, village headmen could try petty civil suits, and panchayats suits of any value on submission.

The zillah courts' judges were given certain criminal powers, but these in the main were conferred on the four provincial courts of appeal as circuit courts. The final court was from 1807 composed of judges presided over by a member of council; as a civil court it was styled the Sadr Adalat, as a criminal court the Sadr Faujdari Adalat. In 1827 the use of native judges was extended for both civil and criminal cases where natives were concerned, while auxiliary judges with jurisdiction also over Europeans and Americans were set up in chosen districts. The introduction of jury trial in the circuit courts was also provided for.

In 1843 the provincial courts were swept away and the zillah courts replaced in part by civil and sessions judges, in part by increasing the powers of the sadr amins.

Reversion to ryotwari settlements in place of zamindari was approved in 1818, and since then the former system has been widely extended. In 1822 the collector was empowered to interfere as a summary arbitrator, but this plan was unfavourably affected by decision of the courts in favour of determining rents on a competitive basis. Other sources of revenue were licence duties, a tobacco monopoly, abolished in 1852, transit dues, abolished in 1844, the salt monopoly, taxation of liquor and drugs, and customs duties.

As in the case of Bengal, Madras had a distinct Supreme Court, which was created by charter of December 26th 1801, under statute[1] to replace the Recorder's Court, consisting of the mayor, three aldermen, and a recorder, created by statute of 1797[2] with jurisdiction similar to that of the Supreme Court at Calcutta. Its jurisdiction extended over the town of Madras, and over British subjects in the narrower sense within the territories dependent on Madras and the territories of princes allied to Madras. The principles of the statute of 1781 affecting the Supreme Court at Calcutta applied to its jurisdiction.

(c) BOMBAY

The extension of the territorial authority of Bombay was slow. The bay islands were yielded by the treaty of Salbai in 1782, Bankot in the south Konkan ceded by the Marathas in

[1] 39 & 40 Geo. III, c. 79. [2] 37 Geo. III, c. 142.

1755, and Surat from 1759 was administered for the nawab by one of the Company's servants; in 1800, on the nawab's death the administration was completely taken over. Shortly after great accessions of territory resulted at the expense of Sindhia, the Peshwa, and the Gaekwad, which were largely augmented after the last Maratha war.

Judicial organization tended to follow the lines of Bengal at first. Thus in 1812–18 for Gujarat there was a Sadr Adalat with criminal judges and magistrates subordinate to it, while it acted as a Court of Circuit and heard appeals in civil causes from the sadr amins who heard cases in the towns. In 1818 the important change was made of giving the collectors magisterial powers and control of the police. In 1827 the Sadr Diwani Adalat, now composed of four judges, and the Sadr Faujdari Adalat, consisting of a member of council and three judges, were removed to Bombay. In the districts there were judges with civil and criminal jurisdiction, subject in Gujarat until 1830 to a Court of Circuit. In 1830 the use of native judges was widely extended, most civil cases going before them; the magisterial powers of the collectors were increased, and they were authorized to take cognizance of civil suits regarding land and to decide issues of ownership subject to appeal to the district court. To secure due administration of justice special commissioners were appointed for Gujarat and the Deccan, who toured these areas.

For Bombay there was under the Act of 1797[1] a Recorder's Court similar to that of Madras which was transformed into a Supreme Court by Act of 1823.[2] It had jurisdiction also over British subjects in the territories dependent on Bombay, and the native states, and its jurisdiction was based on the same principles as that of the Supreme Court at Calcutta. A small causes court for cases up to 175 rupees was set up in 1799, and courts of the senior, second, and third magistrates of police in 1812–30, and petty sessions were held from 1812. The jury system was confined to the Supreme Court's jurisdiction.

In Bombay, as in Madras, the confusion of law applicable was much as in Calcutta, but in 1827 a local code superseded Muhammadan criminal law. Regulations were codified in 1827,

[1] 37 Geo. III, c. 142. [2] 3 Geo. IV, c. 71; Charter, December 8th 1823.

embodying twenty-eight years' earlier work; from 1807[1] regulations registered in the Recorder's, or later Supreme, Court could bind that court.[2]

In Sind after its annexation control was exercised by a commissioner, while the collectors in addition to magisterial powers presided over the administration of justice in the civil and criminal courts.

The land revenue was after a few years of farming out settled on a ryotwari basis, the government appointing the village accountants whose services enabled due assessments to be made. In addition funds were desired from customs, excise, including a tax on salt, fines on succession to property, pasturage fees, and fees for cutting wood on government land.

(*d*) THE NORTH-WESTERN AND OTHER PROVINCES

The North-Western Provinces were formed in 1836 from the territory around Benares ceded by Oudh in 1775; the ceded territories covering most of the modern United Provinces save Oudh, ceded by Oudh in 1801; the conquered territories acquired from Sindhia in 1803; a portion of Bundelkhand then acquired from the Peshwa; the northern hill districts acquired in 1816 from Nepal; and, until 1861 when the Central Provinces were created, the Sagar and Narbada territories ceded by Nagpur (1818) were included therein.

Further territories acquired were the Cis-Satlej states which in 1809 accepted protection, and with the exception of six gradually fell to the Company; the Jalandhar Duab acquired in 1846 after the Sikh war; the Punjab acquired by conquest in 1849; Nagpur and Jhansi which lapsed to the Company in 1853; Berar, assigned by the Nizam, in that year; and Oudh annexed in 1856. The fate of these areas varied. The Cis-Satlej states and the Duab, at first under commissioners, were merged in 1849 in the Punjab. Nagpur was included in the Central Provinces when created, and Jhansi in the North-Western Provinces. Berar remained under a commissioner

[1] 47 Geo. III, sess. 2, c. 68.

[2] The court made extravagant claims of jurisdiction over the natives but was overruled; *Justices of Supreme Court, In re*, 1 Knapp 1; *Moro Ragonath's case*, Mill, *Hist.*, ix, 196; Drewitt, *Bombay in the Days of George IV*, pp. 303–9.

until 1903, when it was attached to the Central Provinces. Oudh was placed under a chief commissioner until in 1877 the charge was amalgamated with the lieutenant-governorship of the North-Western Provinces, the whole being now the United Provinces of Agra and Oudh. The Delhi territory was in 1858 transferred from the North-Western Provinces to the Punjab.

The earlier acquisitions were treated as extensions of Bengal, and the regulations of that presidency were applied thereto with necessary modifications.[1] But the areas taken from Nepal and the Delhi territory were excepted, and later acquisitions remained outside the area of regulations. For them the governor-general issued on his executive authority such orders as he thought fit, and he used such officers as seemed desirable unhampered by the rules in force in Bengal. The local authorities similarly issued rules on their executive authority, and the system was regulated only in 1861 and 1870.[2]

To the regulation districts, the ceded and conquered territories, and the Bundelkhand area were applied the full administrative and judicial regulations of Cornwallis. The collector was confined to revenue functions, the judge and magistrate dealt with civil and minor criminal cases subject to the control of the provincial Courts of Appeal and Circuit, which were subject to the Sadr Diwani and Sadr Nizamat Adalats at Calcutta. In 1829 commissioners of divisions were created, and given the sessions work of the provincial courts; in 1831 separate Sadr Adalats were created at Agra, and in 1833 they took over the civil jurisdiction of the provincial courts, which disappeared. Next the commissioners handed over their criminal work to the district judges who became district and sessions judges, while the collectors took over the magisterial powers of the judges and became collectors and magistrates, there being no reversion here as in Bengal from 1837 to 1859 to separation of functions. In 1831 the powers of the subordinate Indian judges was largely increased to cover most civil litigation in first instance; in 1843 provision was made for the appointment of Europeans and Indians, not in the covenanted service, as deputy magistrates. As in the other

[1] See 39 & 40 Geo. III, c. 79, s. 20. [2] See Chapter VI, § 3 below.

provinces Muhammadan criminal law had to be applied, much modified by regulations and decisions, while in civil causes Hindu or Muhammadan law was applied to the defendant, and custom as regards landed estates.

Revenue administration followed at first Bengal methods, but happily the directors decided by 1811 against permanency and in 1822 onwards sounder principles came to be followed, recognizing the need of a cadastral survey of the land, the recording of rights, a moderate assessment, and protection of tenants. Agreements were made with village communities of the zamindari type, and from 1832 twelve years' continuous occupation was held to justify a permanent and heritable tenure at a rent judicially fixed, and an Act on this basis was passed for Bengal also in 1859. Revenue was also derived from the liquor excise and the opium monopoly among other sources.

In the non-regulation provinces the principle adopted was the concentration in the hands of the district officer, styled deputy commissioner, of the executive, magisterial, and judicial powers, subject to the appellate and supervisional care of the commissioner. Much therefore depended on the personal character, vigour, and integrity of these officers, but responsibility often brought out latent strength, and unquestionably the system afforded greater access to the government for the people and that personal touch which they desired. It was applied with minor success in the Sagar and Narbada territories, but its complete fulfilment is best seen in the Punjab, after final annexation. Under the governor-general full powers of government rested with a board of administration of three members, who controlled the eight divisions under commissioners and the twenty-four districts under deputy commissioners, which again were divided into small areas under Indian tahsildars. Revenue settlement was arranged tentatively, avoiding the errors of Bengal. As a rule the villages were controlled by communities of the zamindari type with whom it was easy to fix terms; in other cases ryotwari tenure was arranged, while where seigniors existed, they were provided for by a fixed rent-charge instead of being made proprietors as in Bengal. Tenant right was safeguarded by giving judicial authority to the settlement officers and by adopting the twelve years' rule of the North-Western Provinces.

In order to secure settled conditions a large body of civil police, 7,000 in number, under the deputy commissioners, was supplemented by 8,000 military police under separate command, and the province was disarmed. The criminal law followed with modifications that of Bengal, while a civil code, not made law, was issued in 1855, embodying much local custom and usage, as a guide to judicial officers. The Bengal regulations were also applied in substance in cases where no special rule applied.

In 1853 the board disappeared, John Lawrence becoming chief commissioner with a financial commissioner and a judicial commissioner, who also controlled the police, education, and local and municipal funds.

In Oudh on annexation a chief commissioner was appointed as a non-regulation province, and a summary settlement of revenue was made. In this Dalhousie pronounced in favour of arrangements not with the talukdars, former revenue-farmers who had acquired a quasi-proprietorial status, but with the subordinate communities, a fact which naturally was reflected in the disloyalty of the talukdars in the Mutiny.

Nagpur from 1818 to 1830, during the new raja's minority, was virtually ruled by the resident, who utilized native institutions and agencies while reforming abuses. Thereafter, until his death in 1853, the raja followed the same lines.

The judicial development of India took place largely without the advantage to be derived from the supervision of the judicial activities by the Privy Council. An appeal in causes where the amount in dispute was over 1,000 pagodas was given by the charters of 1726 and 1753, and this principle was followed in 1773 when the Supreme Court was set up at Calcutta. It was also adopted by the Act of 1797 establishing Recorder's Courts at Madras and Bombay and continued for the Supreme Courts, which superseded them in 1801 and 1823, the limit in the case of Bombay being fixed at 3,000 rupees. But the Crown could grant special leave in any case.

In the case of the Company's Courts the Act of 1781 provided that appeals might be taken from the governor and council when the amount in dispute was £5,000 or over. Rules of procedure were laid down by Regulation XVI of 1797 requiring action within six months, the giving of security for costs, etc. In the case of Madras and Bombay appeal was provided for at least from 1818,[1] but without restriction on the amount at issue. It seems, however, that appeals were few and not very satisfactory in the absence of experience on the part of the agents employed.

In 1833[2] the Judicial Committee was formally constituted as an effective Court of Appeal with provision for the inclusion therein of members with experience of overseas jurisprudence. Rules were provided under the Act, a new set in 1838 reducing the amount at stake to 10,000 rupees. In 1845[3] the practice by which the Company after 1833 managed Sadr Adalat appeals by their agents was stopped, appellants in future instructing their own agents and counsel in England to handle their cases, while the transcript of the record was officially sent to England, where the parties had to take action within two years.

4. THE ARMED FORCES OF THE COMPANY

In the latter part of the seventeenth century the ports of the Company were usually provided with small detachments of European troops under an ensign, while the ships lent a gun-room's crew to work the guns mounted for defence. In 1668 the Company took over the poor remnant of the royal force which had held Bombay, and which formed the nucleus of the 1st Bombay European Regiment. Madras in like manner had a small European and half-caste Portuguese force which grew in 1748 into the 1st Madras Fusiliers. Sepoys had been employed by France from 1721 first at Mahé on the west coast, and from 1744 on the east coast, and in 1748 Lawrence arrived, with a royal commission as major, to command the Company's forces in India. In 1754 the 39th Foot arrived, as well as detachments of Royal Artillery. After Plassey the forces of the three presidencies were reorganized; each had European

[1] Madras VIII of 1818; Bombay V of 1818; Morley, *Digest*, i, pp. cxix ff.

[2] 3 & 4 Will. IV, c. 41.

[3] 8 & 9 Vict., c. 30.

troops and sepoys whose subordinate officers were Indians. Officers for the Company's forces were obtained from various sources, often from the regular army. As the service increased in popularity, the directors took interest in the patronage, and in lieu of local appointments sent out cadets who after training were given commissions. In 1796 a further reorganization of the armies led to the increase of British officers to the loss of Indian subordinates, but the strength of the officers attached to a native regiment was much depleted by detachment for all sorts of purposes—public works, trunk road supervision, service at native courts, surveys, administration and control of native contingents and irregular troops raised in newly annexed territories, etc. These officers returned to their battalions when ordered on active service, or when by seniority they succeeded to the command, for which they were naturally ill fitted. Seniority prevailed for promotion, a fact which explains the feebleness and senility shown by too many of the colonels in the Mutiny. In 1824 a new reorganization divided the native regiments into single battalion regiments, sixty-eight for Bengal, fifty-two for Madras and twenty-four for Bombay. The artillery was converted into brigades and batteries of horse, and battalions and companies of foot, artillery. Madras had eight regiments of regular cavalry, Bengal and Bombay had in addition to eight and three such regiments five and three of irregulars. The Bengal army was largely recruited from Oudh, in that of Madras Muslims, Telingas, and Tamils supplied the most in numbers; they were clearly inferior to the forces of Bengal or Bombay. But in Madras and Bombay less slavish attention was paid to seniority in promotion, and the caste prejudices of the men were less seriously considered than in the case of the Brahmans and Rajputs in the force of Bengal, and the other two armies showed no inclination to join the Bengal army in revolt.

Relations between the Company and its European forces were not marked by anything like the loyalty due from the King's troops. Minor revolts in Bombay in 1674 and 1679 were followed by Keigwin's rebellion in 1683, which ended only by persuasion of the royal admiral sent to reduce the mutineers. The European Bengal Regiment mutinied in 1764, followed by the sepoys, whom Munro sternly suppressed. In 1765 Clive was faced by a mutiny of the officers due to reduction of field allowances, which he firmly repressed. In 1806 the native forces at Madras at Vellore mutinied because they had been forbidden to wear caste marks and ear-rings on parade, and were required to shave their beards and wear shakos in place of turbans, but the revolt was speedily quelled. The Burmese war in 1824 evoked a despairing outbreak at Barrackpur, immediately suppressed. A mutiny among the European officers of Madras in 1809 was with some difficulty repressed. The chief complaint of the officers arose from their inferiority to the officers of the royal regiments and the preference shown to the latter in awarding outside employment.

Reference has been made above to the series of statutes[1] which, superseding the vague powers of the charters, authorized the maintenance of discipline in the forces of the Company, native and European, and the holding of courts martial. The grant of commissions to officers was not regulated by statute,[2] but must be assumed to have been an essential part of the general executive power of the governor-general in council. But such commissions would not convey any power of command over British forces proper, and from 1788–9 this difficulty seems to have been solved by the grant by the commander-in-chief under special authority from the Crown of brevet commissions in the army to all Company's officers.[3]

In addition to the regular forces of the Company it was found expedient to employ other less formal corps to defend newly acquired territory or the possessions of allied princes. Thus Hyderabad had to pay for a contingent of infantry, artillery, and cavalry, officered by Europeans. After 1816 irregular forces of Gurkhas were raised, and in 1838 an irregular force which served in Afghanistan. Of great importance were the irregulars and the corps of guides raised for service from 1846 on in the Punjab.

[1] Beginning with 27 Geo. II, c. 9, and ending with 20 & 21 Vict., c. 66. The inability of the Supreme Court to interfere with regular military court proceedings is laid down *In re Mark Porrett*, Morley, *Digest*, i, 62; ii, 353; 7 & 8 Vict., c. 18.

[2] Cf. *Bradley* v. *Arthur*, 2 St. Tr. (N.S.) at p. 190, per Brougham in argument. Commissions had regularly been given under the Charter régime, and this power doubtless continued.

[3] *Cornwallis Corr.*, ii, 428; Chesney, *Indian Polity*, Ch. XII.

Throughout this period the control of the governor-general over the conduct of military operations is noteworthy. Wellesley planned the campaigns which subdued Tipu and the Marathas,[1] Hastings the operations which reduced the Marathas to subjection, while Auckland had a share in the plans for the Afghan war which ended in disaster. Ellenborough was involved in controversy owing to the instructions given to the commander-in-chief and his generals for the evacuation of Afghanistan, which might have deprived the British arms of the distinction of capturing Ghazni and Kabul,[2] and was actually engaged with his commander-in-chief in the Gwalior operations. Hardinge went so far as to serve under the same officer in the Sikh war, but had in view of his initial failures to apply for his recall; in fact he was given, but did not find it necessary to use, a letter of service giving him authority to exercise his superior rank as lieutenant-general over the commander-in-chief.[3] Dalhousie[4] was emphatic in asserting his political control of his successive commanders, forcing Napier to resignation, and asserting his right to dismiss if he deemed it necessary, thus remaining true to the traditions of 1772.[5] Such independence inevitably was only possible in view of the slowness of communications of the time. In acting, of course, the governor-general required to carry his council with him, and it seems that even Auckland succeeded in winning them over to his policy,[6] while Ellenborough was suspected of undue proclivity to accept military advice and to value too little the principle of civil authority.

The marine forces of the Company trace their origin to 1613, when at Surat a squadron was formed to protect their ships from Portuguese and pirates alike. Its size gradually increased, while after the cession of Bombay there was begun there the construction of small craft to protect the Arabian Sea and the Persian Gulf traffic. In 1686 the squadron's headquarters were

[1] Roberts, *India under Wellesley*, pp. 54, 212.
[2] His defence is given in Law, *India under Lord Ellenborough*, pp. 121 ff.
[3] Hardinge, *Viscount Hardinge*, pp. 104, 105.
[4] See Curzon, *British Government in India*, ii, 207 ff. Lee-Warner, i, 303 ff.; ii, 257 ff.
[5] Cf. Monckton-Jones, *Warren Hastings in Bengal*, 1772-4, p. 154.
[6] *C.H.I.*, v, 498.

moved to Bombay; an officer was annually appointed admiral to control the Bombay marine, while men were supplied by drafts from England. An early example of the co-operation of the British Navy is found in the unsuccessful expedition of 1722 in which the fort of Alibag was attacked with the aid of four English ships under Commodore Mathews. Conflicts with Portuguese, Marathas, and the Sidi of Janjira led to the increase of the marine, and in 1735 the Bombay Council determined to fix at Bombay their shipbuilding yard under the control of Navji Nasarvanji Wadia, whose family connexion with the great dockyards constructed from 1754 to 1810 lasted until 1885. In 1756 the marine in conjunction with Admiral Watson's royal force and Clive's troops captured Angria's Fort Gheria, and lent valuable aid in the capture of Chandernagore. Its services during war with the Marathas were recognized by the revision of its regulations in 1798, when its functions were declared to be protection of trade, suppression of piracy, and general war service, convoy of transports and conveyance of troops, and marine surveying. It was placed under a superintendent, a civilian, with four officers, constituting a Marine Board. In 1827 a royal warrant gave its officers rank with those of the Royal Navy within the charter limits, another warrant from the Admiralty empowered the flying of the Union Jack and pennant, and an order was issued that the superintendent should be an officer of the Royal Navy. In 1828 the marine was made subject to the Indian Mutiny Act.[1] In 1830 the title of Indian Navy was recognized, and in 1848 the title commander-in-chief replaced that of superintendent of marine, and the pennant of the Royal Navy was superseded by a red flag with a yellow cross, having in the corner near the mast the cognizance of the Company, a yellow lion and crown. Its services were many and honourable not merely in Indian waters but at the capture of Aden in 1839, and in New Zealand in 1846, in Burma and Borneo in 1852, and in aid of the Turks at Hodeida in 1856.

[1] 9 Geo. IV, c. 72.

5. RELIGION, EDUCATION, AND SOCIAL REFORM

The charter of 1698 had provided for the maintenance of ministers and schoolmasters in the Company's factories, but the Company's representatives in India were far from anxious for any missionary efforts. In Madras the existence of a strong Roman Catholic element induced a certain rivalry, and German and Danish missionaries received some support from the directors. But the essential attitude of the governments was expressed in Bengal in the regulations of 1793 which gave an assurance of protection of the Indians in the free exercise of their religion, the maintenance of customs and of endowments. In 1798 Wilberforce failed in an attempt to inculcate on the Company the duty of favouring missionary enterprise, and the Vellore mutiny in 1806 apparently frightened the government at Calcutta into hostility to missionary effort.[1] The directors in the dispute between the government and the Serampur missionaries endeavoured to hold the scales even, and feeling in England pressed for more just treatment. In 1813 the Board of Control was made the final authority to grant licences to missionaries to proceed to India, and provision was made for a bishop at Calcutta and three archdeacons. In 1833 licences were dispensed with, and two sees added at Madras and Bombay. The educational work of the missionaries was also acknowledged by the rule in 1854 that their schools might receive grants in aid for purely secular teaching.

But conversion of Indians brought problems, for it entailed loss of property. In 1832 that was abolished for Bengal,[2] and in 1850 Dalhousie's government passed a law[3] rescinding all laws and usages inflicting loss of property rights on renunciation of, or exclusion from, the communion of any religion. This was necessarily a very strong measure, for Hindu law imposes religious duties on family members, but it was persisted in despite loud protests, renewed when in 1856 the remarriage of Hindus' widows was authorized.

There remained the practice under which a pilgrim tax was levied in each province for religious purposes, and religious

[1] In 1819 a converted sepoy was dismissed and the army virtually closed to Christians. Cf. Kaye, *Admin. of E.I. Co.*, pp. 625 ff.

[2] Reg. VII of 1832.

[3] Act XXI of 1850; Morley, *Digest*, i, p. clxxxiv.

funds and buildings were controlled by government servants. The discontinuance of these practices was suggested by the Board of Control in 1833, but it was not until officials and unofficials in Madras with the support of their bishop had protested against firing of salutes and other ceremonials that in 1838 orders were given to discontinue all such signs of homage. It was much less easy to discontinue the care of religious endowments, and it was not until 1863 that public servants were by legislation relieved of all such duties.

Slavery, as has been seen, was attacked definitely by the Charter Act of 1833 and the legal status abolished in 1843, while keeping or trafficking in slaves was included in the crimes punished under the Penal Code of 1860.

While the abolition of slavery raised no serious difficulties of principle, the case was very different with the practice of the burning with a dead husband of his widow or widows. Warren Hastings was not prepared to interfere with a rite approved by some Hindu authority, but the Supreme Court, to its credit, forbade the practice in the limits of its authority. Cornwallis and Shore unfortunately failed to take the opportunity to discourage it officially, though urging dissuasion, and Wellesley left India before he could act on a report of the Nizamat Adalat, which suggested abolition in some districts and limitation in others. This advice was not acted on; instead in 1812–17 a foolish policy was adopted which appeared to give official sanction to the rite if it was in accordance with the religious law. Various civilians protested, the directors in 1828 were definitely uneasy, but it was left to Bentinck in 1829 to prohibit the practice, despite the doubts even of Ram Mohan Roy, who had led an active campaign against the rite, and to make those who assisted it guilty of culpable homicide or murder. Like action was taken in 1830 in Madras and Bombay. The result in Bengal was a petition which was laid before the Privy Council against the regulation, but it was decisively answered by the Company and rejected. No ill effects followed, and it seems clear that it was unwise so long to acquiesce in a stupid barbarity.[1]

[1] E. Thompson, *Suttee*; Peggs, *India's Cries to British Humanity* (1832); Reg. XVII of 1829. The rite still excites admiration in Bengal.

To Wellesley belongs the credit of striking the first blow against infanticide in the form of the sacrifice of children at Sagor island and elsewhere in fulfilment of vows. Other measures from 1795 were directed at infanticide pure and simple, and a prolonged struggle was waged against the practice, which greatly diminished it before the transfer of authority to the Crown. Human sacrifice in Orissa was extirpated in 1837-52; thagi from 1830 to 1837.

In the field of education[1] the essential issue from the constitutional standpoint was the question whether to encourage the classical languages of India, to develop the vernaculars, or to spread the employment of English. To the latter movement Macaulay, who was appointed president of the council of public instruction, contributed very valuable support when he urged on Bentinck the infinite superiority of English over any oriental language. Macaulay was not concerned with the use of English for teaching science or agriculture, holding that these matters could be taught through the vernaculars, but he was convinced of the cultural and religious importance of English, expecting that in thirty years there would not be a single idolater among the respectable classes of Bengal, whence sound principles would filter through to the lower classes. He entirely failed to realize that Hinduism and Muhammadanism had a hold of the people in such a degree that his panacea could have nominal effect. But only in Bengal was the pursuit of Western learning adopted permanently as the end of education, and even there encouragement continued to be given to the maintenance of the classical languages of India. In 1844 Hardinge's government definitely promised preference in the governmental service to candidates who knew English. Only in 1854 did Sir Charles Wood, president of the Board of Control, lay down a generous system which promised encouragement for vernaculars, for classical languages, and for English, and resulted in the founding in 1857 of the Universities of Calcutta, Madras, and Bombay as examining bodies.

Freedom of the Press was established by Metcalfe in 1835.[2] English journals had appeared in Calcutta as early as 1780, and

[1] Arthur Mayhew, *The Education of India*. By resolution of March 7th 1835 English became the official language for India.
[2] Kaye, *Life*, ii, 249 ff; Act XI.

control of the Press had been enforced by Wellesley[1] and Minto, when they found their actions severely and unfairly attacked, in many cases doubtless by dissatisfied civilians. Hastings was willing that the Press should say what it liked and enable India to obtain education. Under Adam, who acted in 1823, Buckingham, the editor of the *Calcutta Journal*, excited his disapproval, and evoked attack by a rival, Bryce, who, however, was held by the Supreme Court to have libelled his critic. Adam then imposed stringent control, revoking Buckingham's licence; he returned home to vex the Company, to obtain a seat in the House of Commons in 1832, and to receive a pension of £200 as compensation from the Company. Elphinstone, Munro, and Malcolm for various reasons disapproved of freedom of the Press, but Metcalfe held that it was indispensable for the education of the Indian people. In 1857 the intemperate attacks of the vernacular Press, which was suspected of having had something to do with the Mutiny, resulted in temporary restrictions being imposed by Canning, but he was opposed to any permanent interference with Press opinion.

[1] Roberts, *India under Wellesley*, pp. 175–7.

CHAPTER VI

THE DIRECT RULE OF THE QUEEN EMPRESS; THE GOLDEN AGE OF BUREAUCRACY

1. THE ASSUMPTION OF GOVERNMENT BY THE CROWN

It cannot be asserted that the Indian Mutiny, a somewhat misleading description of what was mainly the revolt of a single army, was due in any degree to constitutional causes proper. Many factors influenced those who took part in it. Landlords in the North-Western Provinces and Oudh had seen the Government make terms with their tenants as they claimed. Annexations under the doctrine of lapse, the refusal to Nana Sahib of the ex-Peshwa's pension, and the appropriation of Oudh, and, still more, the careless method in which it was carried into effect supplied grounds for indignation. The advent of railways, of telegraphs, even of the Ganges canal, European education, the project to allow remarriage of women, offended Brahman sentiment. The courts and the police, both by their merits and their demerits, raised in some districts bitter feelings of dislike. The fatal defect, however, lay in the existence of a discontented mercenary force, the Bengal army, whose caste restrictions were respected, and whose faith in the Company's star was shaken by the disasters of Afghanistan, while the annexation of Oudh offended their pride and lessened their privileges. The European forces, moreover, were reduced at the critical moment, partly because of the Persian war, while rumours of Crimean defeats lessened their prestige; there were only 42,200 Europeans to 248,000 natives. Moreover, the order that recruits must be willing to serve overseas added to the latent resentment. Wild rumours of endeavours to destroy their caste and the incident of the greased cartridges resulted in an outbreak which, ineffectively handled, resulted in disaster. Of definite conspiracy there seems to have been little that was effective. The proclamation of the titular King at Delhi by Muhammadan zealots was a vain attempt to secure an effective head for a movement which lacked all supreme direction, nor was Nana

Sahib's appeal to the Marathas of more importance. Sikhs, Punjabis, and Gurkhas rendered invaluable aid; the rajas of Patiala, Jhind, and Nabha were of decisive service.

Inevitably the blame for the debacle fell on the Company, and its rule was doomed. It was anomalous in any case, and the Mutiny had stressed the anomaly of two navies and two armies. In vain was a very weighty petition[1] presented asking for delay. Palmerston introduced proposals,[2] but was turned out of office before carrying them. Disraeli[3] urged by Ellenborough, put forward a scheme under which the responsible minister for India would have been advised by a council, part Crown nominees, part elected by men who had served or possessed interests in India, part by the electors of the great commercial cities. This proved unacceptable, and Ellenborough having resigned as the result of his criticism of Canning's proclamation as to Oudh, Stanley carried resolutions which were embodied in the Government of India Act, 1858.[4]

The government of India was transferred to the Crown acting through a secretary of state, who received the powers of the Court of Directors and the Board of Control. He was to be aided by a council of fifteen members, eight appointed by the Crown, seven by the directors. They were to hold office during good behaviour, subject to removal on petition of both houses. The major part of both categories were to be qualified by ten years' residence or service in India, and must not as a rule have left India more than ten years before appointment. In future nine members at least must be so qualified. Vacancies were to be filled by the Crown, and as regards the elected members by the council. The council was to be advisory, without initiative; the secretary of state was to preside with a casting vote, and his written approval was required for any decision taken in his absence. He could normally overrule his council, but not in certain cases, including appropriation of revenues or property, the issuing of securities for money, sale or mortgage of property, contracts, alterations of salaries, furlough rules, etc. It must meet once a week, the quorum being five. All dispatches to India must be communicated to

[1] *Hansard*, 3rd Ser., cxlviii, App.
[2] Ibid., 1276.
[3] Monypenny and Buckle, *Disraeli*, iv, 138, 164 f.
[4] 21 & 22 Vict., c. 106.

it, unless they were too urgent, when this must be notified to the members, or unless they dealt with war or peace or treaties or policy towards any prince or state, when they might be marked secret and withheld from the council. The governor-general and the governors of Madras and Bombay might similarly[1] mark their dispatches, when they could only be seen by the council by express permission of the secretary of state.

The nucleus of the India Office staff was furnished by the establishments of the Board of Control and the Company. The salaries of the secretary of state and of his establishment were charged on Indian revenues. These revenues were also to bear the burden of the debt of the Company and the dividend, and otherwise must be applied only for Indian purposes, and a safeguard against unwise use was provided, as noted above, in requiring the assent of a majority of the council. The property of the Company was vested in the Crown, and the secretary of state in council was rendered able to sue and be sued as the successor of the Company in respect of contracts and such other matters as could have formed the subject of litigation by or against the Company. This necessary innovation was a simple matter of justice.

The Crown was to appoint the governor-general and the law member of his council, the governors and the advocates-general; the members of councils generally were to be selected by the secretary of state in council acting by a majority; lieutenant-governors by the governor-general, subject to approval by the Crown.[2] Appointments made in India were to continue to be made there. In the case of appointments made from home the secretary of state in council with the advice of the Civil Service Commissioners was to make rules for the admission of all natural-born British subjects to competitive examination. Military cadetships were to be shared between the secretary of state and his council.

The naval and military forces of the Company were transferred to the Crown without alteration of their local character. The sending of any order to commence hostilities in India must

[1] They could also mark other dispatches secret, in which case they would if necessary be referred to the council.

[2] Minto was resentful of Morley's initiative in appointing councillors.

be communicated to Parliament within three months. Save to prevent or repel invasion or under other sudden or urgent necessity, the revenues of India were not to be used without parliamentary assent to defray the cost of operations carried on beyond the frontiers by Indian forces.[1]

The form of the council and its powers represented the deliberate decision of the government, and Gladstone[2] for the opposition approved giving weight to the council, though recognizing that the secretary of state must be supreme. The Bill was amended in its passage so as to secure the need of a majority of the council for expenditure, the obvious difficulty that the powers of the secretary of state to send secret orders might involve expenditure which the council could not veto being passed by. It was stressed that government must mainly be carried on in India, but that the supreme direction must be retained in the hands of the ministry and Parliament. The council was a device to secure that so far as possible there should be no rash experiments.[3]

The proclamation of the new régime of November 1st 1858 contained reassurances to the princes that 'all treaties and engagements made with them by or under the authority of the East India Company are by us accepted and will be scrupulously maintained, and we look for the like observance on their part. . . . We shall respect the rights, dignity, and honour of native princes as our own.' The principle of religious toleration was inculcated, differentiation on grounds of race or creed in the public service was disapproved; the ancient rights, usages, and customs of India were to be respected, and due regard to be had to rights in land. An amnesty of a generous character was offered to those who had rebelled.

No change in the royal title accompanied the assumption of direct rule, though Ellenborough had contemplated the transfer to the Queen of the imperial style. In 1876, however, the Royal Titles Act[4] gave power to alter the title in India of the sovereign, and on January 1st 1877 Victoria was proclaimed as Queen Empress, and in 1903 and 1911 similar action was taken as regards Edward VII and George V. The step caused

[1] S. 55.
[2] *Hansard*, 3rd Ser., cli, 470, 757 f.
[3] *Hansard*, 3rd Ser., cli, 1454 f.
[4] 39 & 40 Vict., c. 10.

curious and needless anxiety in England. It was unquestionably a perfectly prudent and justifiable measure, for the Crown possessed unquestioned empire over the peninsula in so marked a degree as to render formal acknowledgment most desirable. The Queen, who since Ellenborough's time had corresponded with the governor-general, took much interest in Indian affairs until pressure of business compelled her to limit herself to great changes and matters affecting the state. Edward VII and George V followed the same tradition, including that of correspondence with the Viceroy, and at the former's bidding Lord Curzon did not press on retirement his grievances.[1]

2. THE HOME GOVERNMENT OF INDIA

The council form of government was unquestionably essential in the initiation of the important measures which accompanied the transfer of authority, including the reorganization of the legislatures, of the courts, and of the armed forces. Sir Charles Wood, secretary of state from 1859 to 1866, bore testimony to its essential value,[2] but its formalism and delays chafed in 1866 the energetic spirit of Lord Cranborne and induced him in 1869[3] to propose to limit the power of the council which, he asserted, claimed the right to control general policy against the secretary of state by its power over expenditure. But the Duke of Argyll insisted that the true view was that the power of the council ceased when the Cabinet had decided on any policy, and this undoubtedly was the accepted position; Lord Salisbury's grievance apparently arose out of commercial proposals to which his council wisely or not demurred. But legislation in 1869[4] strengthened with Salisbury's help the secretary of state's position. It gave to him the filling of vacancies, acting for the Crown, and similarly as regards memberships of the Indian councils, while the term of office of members was reduced normally to ten years. In 1876[5] this rule was modified virtually to secure the services of Sir H. Maine

[1] Ronaldshay, ii, 412.
[2] Cf. Dalhousie, *Private Letters*, pp. 416–22, on councils.
[3] *Hansard*, 3rd Ser., cxciv, 1074; cxcvi, 700.
[4] 32 & 33 Vict., c. 97. [5] 39 & 40 Vict., c. 7.

without limit of time, while in 1889[1] power was given to allow the number of the council to fall to ten. Lord Salisbury when next in office carried his foreign policy, including the occupation of Quetta and the separation of the trans-Indus region from the Punjab, without decided opposition from his council, and his chief conflict of view was with Lord Northbrook. He was desirous in effect of determining Indian policy by private correspondence between himself and the governor-general, disregarding official views, but Northbrook sturdily insisted that Parliament had conferred on his council rights which differentiated it from mere officials. There was great force in this contention. Patently Indian history had given the council at home and those in India a position quite different from the public servants in the office of a secretary of state, and we may agree with Lord Cromer that Salisbury, who was more or less contemptuous of the staff of the Foreign Office when head of it, was always inclined to disregard the opinions of subordinates. Lord George Hamilton[2] and Lord Randolph Churchill, on the other hand, bore enthusiastic testimony to the value of the council, which unquestionably controlled carefully expenditure with a continuity of oversight which afforded a valuable check, while it aided the secretary of state in resisting any reckless efforts to add to Indian burdens. Lord Ripon resented its views on the division of army control, and for its part it failed to warn him of Maine's considered advice against the proposals of the law member in India for extending to Indian judges power of trial of European British subjects. Sir Alfred Lyall's view was that the council served to prevent mischief but could not do much positive good. In fact, of course, the control of government was necessarily restrictive rather than suggestive, and it was not desirable that members of the civil service who had left India should attempt to direct fresh policy from Whitehall. Parliament was content in the main to trust the government of India, and did not press its views on the ministry, even when in 1889 and 1891 resolutions on the opium traffic were disregarded or in 1894 when a Liberal ministry

[1] 52 & 53 Vict., c. 65.

[2] Cf. his defence of it against Lord Curzon; Ronaldshay, ii, 235–8. The Cabinet had to be invoked to overrule his appeal to the King to sanction a promise of remission of taxation at the Durbar of 1903.

after consulting the government of India declined to hold simultaneous examinations in England and India for the Indian Civil Service. But in matters where the ministry felt strongly the council, like the government of India, had to yield, as in the case of the decision in 1879 to exempt cotton goods from the general imposition of a 5 per cent import duty, and that in 1894 to impose a countervailing excise on Indian cotton. Normally, however, the council saw eye to eye with the minister, even when they did not inspire his views; thus they stood behind the secretary of state in his controversy with Lord Curzon,[1] which cost India the prolongation of the latter's services.

The system undoubtedly was cumbrous, inelastic, fruitful of delay, but it served well its purpose of preventing home intervention in any lighthearted spirit in Indian government, and it accorded well with the underlying conservatism of British government up to 1906.

Parliament, not inactive nor uninterested under the old régime with its great periodic reviews of Indian conditions, lost interest under the new conditions, especially as growing complication in Indian government coincided with domestic, Irish and foreign crises of such importance as to render attention to Indian affairs seldom easy. Nor were secretaries of state anxious for interest to be taken, peace in their time sufficed, and the constructive suggestion of Maine in favour of a joint committee of both Houses to study Indian finance and other issues was not taken up. A report on moral and material progress was laid yearly before Parliament as required by the Act of 1858, and the secretary of state once a year laid accounts before Parliament when a perfunctory debate attended by a handful of members with Indian interests convinced resentful Indian visitors to the Commons of the complete indifference of the British people to Indian affairs.

[1] *British Government in India*, ii, 115 ff. In the decision to undo the partition of Bengal and fix the capital at Delhi the councils in England and India were ignored, and under Morley and Minto the plan of substituting private letters and telegrams for official correspondence, condemned justly by the Mesopotamian Commission, ran riot.

3. THE CENTRAL AND PROVINCIAL GOVERNMENTS IN INDIA

(a) THE CENTRAL EXECUTIVE

As a sign of the changed position the governor-general was now styled officially, though not by statute, viceroy also, indicating his position as direct representative of the Crown as well as the authority directed to control, superintend, and direct the civil and military administration of India, with the aid of his council. The latter indeed almost suffered extinction early in Canning's régime, for impatient of restraint he disliked council government and desired to substitute secretaries, whom he might consult collectively at discretion but decide at his own judgment. Happily this innovation, which would have transferred too much authority to the secretary of state's council, was dropped, sufficient improvement being effected by the adoption of the portfolio system, under which the councillors were given powers to deal with minor matters and the council was left to deal with greater general issues or questions of special difficulty.

The situation was regularized by the Councils Act of 1861,[1] which added a fifth member to the council in recognition of the necessity of expert financial advice. A member for public works was added in 1874,[2] and converted under legislation of 1904[3] into a member for commerce and industry. Power was given in 1861 to make rules as to the conduct of business, and acts done under these rules were deemed acts of the governor-general in council. Hence the portfolio system was worked on cabinet lines, and the council as a whole was chiefly concerned with issues which were in dispute between departments, which involved the overruling by a department of a local government, which were of general importance, or on which the governor-general and the member in charge of the department differed. The governor-general had, however, power to overrule the council majority if he held the measure affected essentially the safety, tranquillity or interests of the British possessions in India. Instances of disagreement were rare; Lawrence resented

[1] 24 & 25 Vict., c. 67. [2] 37 & 38 Vict., c. 91. [3] 4 Edw. VII, c. 26.

the control of his council, but he had come to office from freedom in the Punjab, and was a tired man. Very varying types of men such as Northbrook, Ripon,[1] Curzon accepted their councils as of value, and Minto in 1907 insisted that it should not be ignored in the matter of relations with Russia. It was in the legislative activities of executive councillors that the issue became serious, and it will be discussed below.

The governor-general himself held the portfolio of the foreign department, conducting correspondence with foreign powers neighbouring India, advising the British Government on relations with Asiatic powers as affecting India, and supervising the relations of the Crown with the native states; the representatives of the Crown at the courts of these states were agents of the governor-general, not of the governor-general in council. The commander-in-chief was regularly made an extraordinary member of council, side by side with the military member, and controlled preparations for war and promotion, while the military member was responsible for supply and transport, including ordnance, clothing, medical stores, and remounts, military works and military finance, including preparation of the budget, suggestions for which were made by army headquarters, presided over by the commander-in-chief, and criticized by the finance department. If governor-general, military member, and commander-in-chief agreed action could be taken; in event of disagreement the council decided subject to revision by the Home Government. This division of authority was resented by Earl Kitchener,[2] who contended that he should be the sole adviser on military matters and that it was unsound that advice should be tendered by a military member of inferior status and experience. Curzon justly objected on the ground of the excessive authority which would thus be concentrated in one man's hands. He was unwisely induced to accept a compromise which lowered the status of the military member, and was forced to resign; the new military member was dispensed with in 1909 and in 1910 his place was filled by a member for education. But, though both a Conservative and a Liberal government accepted Kitchener's

[1] He overruled it as to the retention of Kandahar; Wolf, *Life*, ii, 164.

[2] Cf. Roberts, *Hist. of India*, pp. 552 ff; Ronaldshay, *Lord Curzon*, ii, 373–414, conclusively vindicates Curzon against Mr. Brodrick and Mr. Balfour.

views, India paid the penalty in the ghastly fiasco of Mesopotamia, due unquestionably in the ultimate issue to the undue burden placed on the commander-in-chief.

The council throughout this period was essentially European in constitution;[1] not until 1909 was an Indian admitted. In one respect it differed fundamentally from a British cabinet, the secretaries of the departments were not treated as merely advisers of the member in charge, and their views were regularly submitted to the governor-general and council, while in practice the secretary normally called the governor-general's attention to all matters of importance in the department. This procedure was all the more useful because only three of the council were necessarily qualified by ten years' service in India, and it would patently have been unwise to trust wholly to the views of a member who might ignore the value of Indian experience. At the close of this period there were nine departments: foreign, home, legislative, finance, revenue and agriculture, public works, commerce and industry, education, and army, divided among the six members of council and the governor-general. During his absence from the capital the governor-general might appoint a member to preside, and be given by himself in council full powers alone to execute the powers of the governor-general in council, an authority which seems little to have been used, Lawrence wisely imitating the rule of taking his council with him to Simla.[2] In the absence of the governor-general from indisposition the senior member presided; on death or incapacity he acted pending the arrival of the senior of the governors of Madras and Bombay. It was forbidden to leave for Europe during tenure of office, an anomaly removed only for governors in 1924.[3]

(*b*) THE CENTRAL LEGISLATURE

Dalhousie[4] had taken no exception to the independence of the legislature acting under the Act of 1853, but Canning and Wood disliked criticism, and doubted whether anything was necessary beyond the executive council. Frere, whose influence

[1] Tenure of office was regularly (since 1801) five years.
[2] Cf. *Life of Maine*, pp. 378 ff. [3] 14 & 15 Geo. V, c. 28.
[4] Lee-Warner, *Life*, ii, 237.

on the governor-general's council was considerable, demurred,[1] and ultimately the legislature was reconstituted.[2] For legislative purposes the council was to be reinforced by not less than six nor more than twelve persons nominated by the governor-general for two years, one-half at least of whom must not hold any governmental office. No legal provision required such persons to be Indian, but an assurance was given in the Commons that Indians would be appointed.

The powers of the legislature were restricted wholly to legislation, including the consideration of motions for leave to introduce a Bill. Moreover, the sanction of the governor-general was required to the introduction of any measures affecting the public revenue or debt, religion, military or naval matters, or the relation of the government with foreign princes or states.[3] The governor-general had the right to assent, reserve, or refuse assent, and a Bill assented to might be disallowed by the Crown, or a reserved Bill assented to, in both cases through the secretary of state in council.

The powers of the new legislature were those granted to that of 1853. But it was forbidden[4] to repeal or amend the Charter Acts of 1833 and 1853, the Government of India Acts, 1858 and 1859, any Act enabling the Home Government to raise funds, the Acts punishing mutiny and desertion in the British and Indian forces, subject to the power to make articles of war under s. 73 of the Act of 1833, the Indian Councils Act, and other Acts of 1861, and subsequent Acts. Moreover, it might not affect the authority of Parliament, the constitution and rights of the East India Company, which survived for business purposes to 1874, or any part of the unwritten laws or constitution of the United Kingdom whereon might depend in any degree the allegiance of any person to the Crown, or the sovereignty or dominion of the Crown over any part of the said territories.

The governor-general personally was given a new power[5] whose absence was felt in 1857–8. He might issue on his own authority ordinances which could remain in operation for six months, unless disallowed or repealed by ordinance or law.

[1] Corr. in *Life of Frere*, i, 336 ff.

[2] Indian Councils Act, 1861 (24 & 25 Vict., c. 67).

[3] S. 19. [4] S. 22. [5] S. 23.

The power was to prove later of great use. It was laid down that the cause of issuing such a measure should at once be notified to the secretary of state.

Further, it was enacted that rules and regulations made before the passing of the Act by the governor-general and certain local authorities for non-regulation provinces should be deemed valid, though not passed in the forms required by the Acts renewing the charter. This validation did not affect the future, and its terms were vague, so that in 1872, for instance, Indian legislation became necessary to declare what measures had been so validated.[1]

In 1865[2] the powers of the legislature were extended to cover British subjects even if not servants of the Crown in native states. It has been suggested that only non-Asiatic subjects are intended, but that is not probable, though in practice legislation in such cases has also been based on the Foreign Jurisdiction Act, 1890. In 1869[3] power was given to legislate for native British subjects in any part of the world.

In 1870[4] an important power of legislation was conferred on the governor-general in council to place on a regular basis the power of dealing with special areas. The preliminary step was taken by the secretary of state in council applying the Act to specified areas; thereupon the local government could submit regulations which if approved by the governor-general in council would have the effect of laws. Many measures were passed under this power, while the Indian legislature by the Scheduled Districts Act, 1874, itself declared that in certain specified districts the normal legislation and jurisdiction were in force only in part or with modifications, and authorized the application with modifications if necessary of any enactments in force at the time in any part of British India. Hence many areas were both 'regulation' and scheduled areas, all the former being scheduled.

In 1884[5] the legislature was given the power to regulate within the former charter limits the Indian Marine Service, which had been created for transport and survey work, and minor duties.

[1] Hunter, *Lord Mayo*, ii, 214 ff. [2] 28 & 29 Vict., c. 17. See Penal Code, s. 4.
[3] 32 & 33 Vict., c. 98. [4] 33 & 34 Vict., c. 3; *Life of Maine*, pp. 360 ff.
[5] 47 & 48 Vict., c. 38.

Of the questions arising from these Acts the most interesting was that in 1870,[1] when Lord Mayo and the Duke of Argyll discussed the extent of the authority of the Indian legislature. For the former it was argued that the power given by Parliament was one to be exercised to the best of their judgment: the Crown could disallow, but it could not enjoin legislation. The Duke very properly insisted that the final control and direction of affairs in India rested with the Home Government, and it made no real difference if its directions related to legislative affairs. This principle was recognized in all governments where power was derived from the Home Government and not from representative legislatures, and the government of India on February 1st 1871 accepted the doctrine. In the same year it was provided explicitly that the power of the governor-general to override his council applied generally, and in 1879 Lord Lytton used his power to exempt from customs duty the coarser cotton cloths imported. In 1894 the dispute was carried to more logical conclusions.[2] The secretary of state pointed out that the cabinet system must be followed; executive councillors must vote for the final decision of the governor-general and the British Government; if they could not do so, they must resign office. The argument was clearly conclusive; there must be homogeneity in the government at Whitehall and at Calcutta.

Democratization of the constitution of the council was long in coming. Political claims in Bengal were furthered by the activities of S. N. Banerjea[3] after his early removal on inadequate grounds from the civil service in 1874, and in 1876 he succeeded in founding an Indian Association, which a year later was given a legitimate grievance in the lowering of the age for entry to the civil service, thus penalizing Indians. Further, the Press legislation in 1878, due to violent attacks on government in the vernacular Press, told against the administration. Lord Ripon repealed the measure and pressed for local government as a prelude to political development, and the political interest of Indians was deeply excited by the withdrawal under reckless

[1] Accounts and Papers, 15, East India, lvi, 6–10.

[2] Cf. Mrs. Hamilton, *Lord Wolverhampton*, pp. 315–17. See 33 & 34 Vict., c. 3, s. 5.

[3] *A Nation in the Making* (1925).

pressure of the indigo- and tea-planters of the Bill to extend the power of Indian magistrates in cases concerning Europeans. In 1883 the political group in Bengal held a conference, which was followed by one in Madras in the next year, attended by theosophists from various parts of India. The result was a National Congress[1] whose first meeting took place in 1885. It demanded *inter alia* the presence of elected members in the councils, the right to discuss the budget and to ask questions, the reference to a standing committee of the House of Commons of issues between the councils and governments, simultaneous examinations at a later age for the civil service, the limitation of military expenditure, and the abolition of the secretary of state's council. Despite the indifference of the Muslims on the instigation of the able Sir Sayyid Ahmad, who recognized that their lack of education would hamper them in politics, the demands were put forward with growing strength. Full concession was impossible, but Dufferin contemplated election at least for the local legislatures, and Bradlaugh introduced a Home Rule Bill for India at the request of Congress. Ultimately the maximum then deemed possible and wise by the government took shape in an Act of 1892,[2] which increased the number of additional members of the Indian legislature to sixteen, and permitted the making of regulations under which indirectly election could be introduced, through the nomination by the governor-general of persons chosen in various ways. Ultimately for the Indian legislature the plan adopted was that five of the ten non-official members were chosen by the non-official members of the legislatures of Madras, Bombay, Bengal, the North-Western Provinces, and Oudh. Moreover, the Act authorized the discussion of the annual budget, thus permitting a critical examination of the financial position, and the asking of questions subject to careful limitations to avoid inconvenience to the government.[3] These additional powers were not very important, but it was advantageous that the principle of representation should be given effect, and in the case of the provinces the gains of the system were more considerable.

The powers of the legislature were treated by the courts with

[1] Lovett, *History of the Indian Nationalist Movement* (1920).
[2] 55 & 56 Vict., c. 14. Maine favoured discussion in 1868: *Life*, pp. 362 ff.
[3] Cf. Parl. Paper, Cd. 9109, pp. 55–62.

generosity. In *The Queen* v. *Burah*[1] the issue was raised of the validity of the grant of power to the lieutenant-governor of Bengal to extend to certain districts the provisions exempting the Garo Hills from the ordinary judicial system and laws. It was argued that the legislature having a delegation of power could not delegate authority to another. The Privy Council ruled that conditional legislation of the type in question was not open to doubt; the legislature, when acting within the limits set by the Act creating it was not in any sense an agent or delegate of the Imperial Parliament, but had 'plenary powers of legislation as large and of the same nature as those of Parliament itself. This places the Indian legislature on the same plane as the colonial and Dominion legislatures, save those which have obtained freedom from the supremacy of their constitutions as have the Parliaments of the Irish Free State, and the Union of South Africa by the Statute of Westminster, 1931.[2]

The restrictions on Indian legislation, however, are neither numerous nor have they been applied in any narrow spirit. It had been ruled under the previous system that as no power existed to affect the prerogative it was illegitimate to attempt to limit appeal to the King in Council.[3] But the Act of 1861[4] expressly gave the Indian legislature power to affect the prerogative, and so it was ruled in 1914[5] that the Indian Limitation Act, 1908, could not be deemed invalid in so far as it affected appeals. In the same spirit the provision forbidding the legislature to affect the unwritten laws or constitution of the United Kingdom whereon allegiance might depend was refused any wide application. In *Ameer Khan's case*[6] in 1870 an effort was made to use this clause, dating from the Act of 1833, to invalidate arbitrary detention under Regulation III of 1818, but the effort failed, though it was ingeniously argued that if the Crown withdrew protection it also affected the allegiance due in return. The same argument was revived in 1909, again vainly, to impugn the validity of the Criminal

[1] (1878), 3 App. Cas. 889.

[2] Keith, *Constitutional Law of the British Dominions*, pp. 24 ff.

[3] *Hormusjee* v. *Cooverbhaee* (1856), 6 Moo. Ind. App. 448.

[4] S. 24.

[5] *Abdullah Hossein Chowdhury* v. *Administrator-General of Bengal*, I.L.R. 42 Cal. 35.

[6] (1870), 6 Ben. L.R. 392.

Procedure Code in providing for cases where British subjects need not be tried by jury,[1] and again in 1920, in the latter case an ordinance of the governor-general being attacked because it deprived subjects of trial in the ordinary course of law by the normal courts. The Privy Council pointed out[2] that the enactment referred not to laws by which the accused might deem his allegiance affected, but to laws transferring or qualifying allegiance or modifying the obligations imposed thereby. Thus viewed, the clause probably coincides in effect with the provision retained in the Government of India Act, 1935,[3] that the legislature may not affect the sovereignty or dominion of the Crown over any part of British India. That provision was held in *Damodhar Gordhan* v. *Deoram Kanji*[4] to invalidate any Act of the legislature purporting to cede territory, while the Privy Council denied that the legislature could by any provision of the Indian Evidence Act prevent the courts inquiring for themselves into the validity of any cession. This of course affects in no way the prerogative right of the Crown to cede territory. But these restrictions negative any legislative effort to alter British sovereignty.

It has also been held[5] that no Indian legislature may impair the right to sue the secretary of state in council in cases where the Company might have been sued, so that the Burma legislature could not bar the civil courts from deciding claims as to land against the government.

It remains to add that it was ruled in *Keyes* v. *Keyes*[6] that the Indian legislature had not power to provide for the grant of divorce by Indian courts to persons whose domicile was in England. The actual decision was clearly sound, namely, that in England a divorce based merely on residence as opposed to domicile was invalid, and it is impossible to hold that the Indian legislature could not validly allow divorce of persons merely resident which would be effective throughout British

[1] *Barindra Kumar Ghose* v. *King Emperor*, 37 Cal. 467.

[2] *Bugga* v. *King Emperor*, L.R. 47 Ind. App. 128.

[3] S. 110 (*b*) (i) extended to 'sovereignty, dominion or suzerainty of the Crown in any part of India'.

[4] (1876), 1 App. Cas. 332.

[5] In 1912 in *Secretary of State for India in Council* v. *Moment*, 40 Ind. App. 48.

[6] [1921] P. 204, followed in (1923) 47 Bom. 843, but not at Lahore (1924), 5 Lah. 147.

India. But the difficulty of the invalidity of such marriages outside India would remain, and the knot was cut by British legislation under which Indian courts act as substitutes for the English and Scottish courts in decreeing divorces of persons resident in England and in Scotland respectively, acting in both cases rather absurdly on the doctrines of English law.[1]

The Act of 1861 gave power to make rules of council procedure, and under them the practice grew up of publishing Bills with a vernacular rendering in the gazettes and also a statement of objects and reasons, like action being taken if important changes were made. Usually after introduction a Bill was sent to a select committee and then considered by council, but it might be circulated before or after introduction for criticisms, or dealt with by the council on due notice. The measure therefore was assured of proper publicity and suggestions of desirable changes.

(c) THE LOCAL GOVERNMENTS

Madras and Bombay under the Crown retained a special position as presidencies. They were governed by governors in council, of two members qualified by twelve years' service under the Crown, to whom was added, until the posts were abolished by an Act of 1893,[2] the local commander-in-chief. On matters not financial they could correspond with the secretary of state, they could appeal to him against any order of the government of India, were free to fill their principal appointments at discretion, and were less strictly subjected to central authority as regards forests and land revenue. They could override the councils in case of necessity, but the additional authority in legislative issues of 1870 did not apply to them until 1915. The post was normally filled from England and the governors naturally relied greatly on their official advisers.[3]

Bengal, Bihar, Orissa, and Assam, the Lower Provinces of Bengal, remained connected under a lieutenant-governor until

[1] See Dicey and Keith, *Conflict of Laws* (ed. 5), pp. 943 ff. At the same time the Indian Divorce Act, 1869, was amended to require domicile (XXV of 1926).

[2] 56 & 57 Vict., c. 62.

[3] Curzon complained of Lord Sandhurst's failure to correspond and suggested reducing the status of the presidencies: Ronaldshay, ii, 58–60. But see Maine's view, *Life*, pp. 372 ff.

1874, when Assam was made a separate province under a chief commissioner. But in 1905 the territories were rearranged as Western Bengal, Bihar, and Orissa, and Eastern Bengal and Assam both under lieutenant-governors, an arrangement whose fate will be described below.

The North-Western Provinces, under a lieutenant-governor, and Oudh, under a chief commissioner, were distinct until 1877, when one officer was appointed to both posts. In 1902 the two territories were styled the United Provinces of Agra and Oudh in order to distinguish them from the North-West Frontier Province. The latter was separated from the rest of the Punjab in 1901[1] and placed under a chief commissioner. The Punjab itself had been converted into a lieutenant-governor's province in 1859. The Central Provinces were created in 1861 by the placing under a chief commissioner of the Sagar and Narbada territories and Nagpur. Berar was placed under the same control when it was leased perpetually in 1902 by the Nizam. Lower Burma was placed in 1862 under a chief commissioner; in 1886 Upper Burma was added to it, and in 1897 it became a lieutenant-governorship.

Coorg was a chief commissionership, an office conjoined with that of resident at Mysore, Ajmer-Merwara in like position since 1871 was administered by the governor-general's agent for Rajputana. British Baluchistan was placed in 1887 under a chief commissioner, who acted as agent in dealing with the neighbouring tribes, and a like system prevailed as regards the chief commissioner of the North-West Frontier Province. The Andaman and Nicobar islands were united in 1872 under a chief commissioner.

In the governments other than Madras and Bombay no provision was made for councils for executive business, the theory being that personal supervision and complete responsibility to the governor-general in council were essential. Lieutenant-governors had to have at least ten years' Indian service, and the governor-general's choice was normally accepted by the Crown.

Power to alter the boundaries of provinces and to create lieutenant-governors and chief commissionerships[2] was vested

[1] Ronaldshay, ii, 131 ff.

[2] 24 & 25 Vict., c. 67, ss. 46–9.

in the governor-general in council by statute, subject to the control of the secrctary of state in council.

(*d*) THE LOCAL LEGISLATURES

The destruction in 1858 of legislative power in the case of Madras and Bombay was remedied in 1861.[1] The governors were instructed to add to their councils for legislative work the advocates-general and from four to eight members, half non-officials, to hold office for two years. Moreover, the Indian government was required to establish a similar council for Bengal, as was done in 1862,[2] and provision was made for establishing lieutenant-governorships with legislative councils. So in 1886 the North-Western Provinces, in 1897 Burma and the Punjab were provided with legislatures. But no such authority was given for the chief commissioners' provinces.

In legislative power the provinces differed from the central legislature in territorial extent of their legislation, which was confined to the province. But in addition the prior consent[3] of the governor-general was required for any legislation affecting the public debt or customs or other taxation imposed by the central legislature; currency; posts and telegraphs; the penal code; religion; naval and military matters; patents and copyright; and relations with foreign states or princes. They could not alter Acts made by the central legislature from 1861,[4] nor affect any Act of Parliament. This category included the Indian High Courts Act, 1861, but it was ruled that this did not affect the right to regulate local courts, though indirectly this might increase or limit the appellate business of the High Court,[5] nor to alter the rights and duties of subjects in Bombay, though not to affect the jurisdiction of the court over such subjects.[6] The right to deal with the prerogative was not wholly clear, for the express grant in the Act of 1861 to the

[1] 24 & 25 Vict., c. 67, ss. 29 ff.
[2] Lawrence actually proposed its abolition in 1868; *Life of Maine*, pp. 364 ff.
[3] Ss. 42, 43, 48.
[4] Limit removed by 55 & 56 Vict., c. 14, s. 5, since otherwise legislation was too restricted.
[5] *Premshankar Raghunathji* v. *Government of Bombay*, 8 Bom. H.C. Rep. O.C. J, 195.
[6] *Collector of Thana* v. *Bhaskar Mahadev* (1884), I.L.R. 8 Bom. 264.

central legislature might be held to exclude any such right in the local legislature.[1] In 1871 full power to enable magistrates to deal with European British subjects was conceded.[2]

The authority of the legislatures was purely legislative as in the case of the central legislature. Like extended authority to discuss the budget and ask questions was accorded by the Act of 1892.[3] That Act also provided for the increase of the size of the legislatures of Madras and Bombay by making the additional members not less than eight nor more than twenty, while the members of the councils of Bengal and the North-Western Provinces might be raised to twenty and fifteen respectively. Nomination was in certain cases based on election by select constituencies. Each of the great capitals had a representative, as also the trading associations and the senates of the Universities. Others were chosen by representatives of the district boards and smaller municipal boards, large land-owners in Bombay, and later in Bengal were given a representative. But, of course, the number was minimal and the only important point was that the principle of election was thus indirectly recognized.

(e) THE RELATION BETWEEN THE CENTRE AND THE PROVINCES

The essential position of the local governments was that of complete subordination in administration and legislation to the centre, which exercised also, as will be noted below, full financial control. As has been seen, the legislative power of the provinces was completely controlled by the requirement of the governor-general's previous consent to the introduction of many kinds of Bill and of his assent to any measure passed, though matters were simplified by allowing as valid any Act once assented[4] to even if not introduced with the requisite consent. More-over, the central legislature maintained the practice of legis-lating on a wide field, including the penal and procedure codes, police, prisons, forests, mines, factories, and public health. In

[1] Held otherwise in *Bell* v. *Municipality of Madras* (1901), 25 Mad. 457, 474.

[2] 34 & 35 Vict., c. 34; passed in view of *R.* v. *Reay*, 7 Bom. Cr. Ca. 6; cf. India Act XXII of 1870.

[3] 55 & 56. Vict., c. 14, s. 2.

[4] 24 & 25 Vict., c. 67, s. 43.

practice the local governments did not attempt legislation without first consulting the government of India, which in its turn was bound to ascertain the views of the India Office. The legislatures in effect were useful instruments for carrying out a centralized policy controlled from home.

No exact delimitation of functions was ever desired or attempted. Some matters the central government necessarily controlled, such as foreign relations, defence, general taxation, debt, currency, tariffs, posts and telegraphs, insurance, patents and copyrights, mining, explosives, railways, accounts and audit. The provinces were concerned with ordinary internal administration, police, civil and criminal justice, prisons, the assessment and collection of the revenue, education, medical and sanitary arrangements, irrigation, buildings and roads, forests and the control over municipal and rural boards. But the centre had an active supervision over provincial subjects. It laid down principles to be followed and examined the reports made to it to ascertain if they were obeyed. It appointed commissions of inquiry on such topics as police, education, famine, irrigation, agricultural and archaeological research and laid down principles to be respected. It undertook the support of central institutions on scientific matters connected with bacteriology or agricultural and veterinary science, since small local institutes obviously were comparatively inefficient. It appointed experts to advise and inspect many provincial matters such as agriculture, forests, irrigation, medical and sanitary matters, education, archaeology,[1] printing and stationery, excise and salt. Of vital importance was the control over the creation of new appointments, the grading of the service, the rules for salaries, pensions, and leave of absence, and such matters as the Public Works and Forest codes were laid down by the central government with the approval of the Home Government. Moreover, the right of appeal from decisions of local governments was widely permitted and utilized. It followed necessarily from the responsibility of the secretary of state to Parliament, and added necessarily to the elaboration of the records kept by the governments, local and central.

[1] Curzon's services were invaluable; Ronaldshay, ii, 211, 212, 333 ff.

It was inevitable that at times disputes should arise regarding the limits of authority on either side. Men of energetic nature such as Frere[1] and Sydenham[2] complained of undue interference, while Curzon[3] deprecated the heptarchical condition of educational policy and would have liked to see Madras and Bombay reduced to lieutenant-governorships so as to be more amenable to his control. But the variety of conditions unquestionably demanded variation of treatment, even if at the close of this period we find Morley[4] and Minto in accord in regarding with some dismay the headstrong character or the weakness of some of their subordinates, who, it may be feared, might with equal justice have been critical of their superiors.

4. INDIAN FINANCE

The transfer of authority to the Crown brought with it essential changes in Indian finance.[5] Final responsibility was now vested in the secretary of state in council, and in lieu of the haphazard control by the governor-general in council over the rest of India, a finance member of council became responsible in 1859 for the preparation of an orderly financial system. The principles of the English budget system were adapted as far as possible to India, the first budget presented being that for 1860–1, the year ending on March 31st as in England. That sound steps were taken was largely due to the debt of £42,000,000 added by the Mutiny, making the total debt £98,000,000, while the year 1859–60 showed a deficit of £7,250,000. James Wilson increased taxation by imposing an income tax and drastically reduced civil and military expenditure, so that in 1864 the deficit was a thing of the past.

The revenue which in 1860 was £48,000,000 was derived primarily, to the extent of 40 per cent in that year, from land revenue, which was reassessed usually at thirty-year intervals.

[1] *Life*, i, 441, 442.
[2] *My Working Life*, pp. 229 ff., 247 (on relations with Morley).
[3] Ronaldshay, *Lord Curzon*, ii, 57 ff., 416. He demanded private correspondence, a bad precedent.
[4] *Recollections*, ii, 263. His view of Minto and the latter's view of him are amusing contrasts.
[5] Strachey and Richard, *Finances and Public Works of India, 1869–81* (1882); P. Banerjea, *Provincial Finance in India* (1929); *History of Indian Taxation* (1930).

The tendency was unquestionably for assessments to fall in comparison with the real value of the land, and at the end of the century only 25 per cent of the revenue came from this source. The opium monopoly on sales to China and elsewhere, local sales being ranked as excise, was important, until in 1907 its gradual extinction was provided for. The most important source of taxation was salt. Full control was long delayed by the necessity of dealing with the rights of native states and only in 1882 was it possible to fix a uniform price of two rupees per maund (82 lb.). The rate was varied from time to time, being increased in emergency but lowered as soon as practicable when finances improved.

Customs duties in 1860 were generally 10 per cent on imports and 4 per cent on many exports. After fluctuations, in 1882 general import duties were abolished, as affording protection against British cotton exports *inter alia*. But, later, duties had to be reimposed. Excise revenue was levied on intoxicating liquors, hemp, drugs, and opium consumed in India. The yield was in 1860 only a million—later it was greatly increased. Stamp duties were represented by stamps on judicial proceedings and on commercial documents.

Governmental policy aimed at keeping as low as possible land and salt revenue, and instead developing the possibilities of more elastic sources, customs, excise, and income tax. The last-named was originally imposed for the war emergency, but from 1886 it became recognized as absolutely indispensable.

At first expenditure was devoted merely to the essentials of government. Only at the close of the Company's existence had roads, public buildings, public utility services, railways, and irrigation come into consideration. Railways from 1853 were at first constructed by British joint-stock companies, which received 5 per cent on the cost and half any surplus profits, a system gradually superseded by direct governmental construction, while the older railways were acquired from time to time under the terms of the original contracts. About 1900 receipts from railways and irrigation began to form a substantial element in the public revenue.

Until 1872–3 currency caused little anxiety, the rupee remaining steady about 2*s*. Thereafter it declined in value owing to world changes involving the demonetization of silver by Germany and the Latin union. Finally in 1893 the free coinage of silver ceased, and a gold standard was introduced, which by 1898 resulted in a stable rupee at 1*s.* 4*d.*

Relations between the centre and the provinces were fixed by the regulations laid down by James Wilson on the basis of meticulous control, necessary at the time, but more and more vexatious as time passed. The local governments had the responsibility of collecting and developing important branches of revenue, but their expenditure was narrowly supervised, and they gained nothing from economy in administration. The competing claims of the provinces were naturally urged with one-sided energy, with the result that the winner of the competition might not be the most deserving claimant. In Mayo's government in 1871 a beginning of a better system was made, and extended in 1877. Certain branches of revenue were treated as wholly central, such as the post office, railways, and tributes from the states. Other sources retained as central to meet its enormous burden of expenditure were customs, salt, and opium. The income from other sources, land revenue, excise, stamps, registration, and forests, was divided in certain proportions between centre and provinces. At first periodic arrangements[1] were made, which had the disadvantage that a province might be discouraged if it managed matters too carefully, and more permanent assignments came to be made. From their shares of revenue the provinces were expected to defray their expenditure for the most part in addition to the cost of collection. The arrangement, however, was purely a business one, without constitutional quality; the central government determined the allocation from time to time at its unfettered discretion, and the whole appeared as one budget, the provincial expenditure making about a third of the imperial. It was only in 1904–5 when definite shares in certain sources of income were awarded to the provinces, that a real beginning was made in the direction of genuine autonomy.[2]

[1] 1882, 1887, 1892, and 1897.

[2] Only in 1912 was the settlement made permanent. Cf. Parl. Paper, Cd. 9109, pp. 89 ff.

5. DEFENCE

The Act of 1858[1] transferred the military and naval forces of the Company *en bloc* to the Crown. The transfer seems for no very adequate reasons to have been resented by officers and men alike, and evoked a minor mutiny, which passed over without serious consequences. But it was decided to abandon the idea of a separate European force for India, once favoured by Canning, and an Act of 1860[2] formally abrogated the Acts permitting the raising of such a force. The officers and men of the existing forces were with a few exceptions merged in the regular army under an Act of 1861,[3] some officers joining instead the native regiments. Thus the artillery and engineers of Bengal, Madras, and Bombay became part of the Royal Artillery and Royal Engineers, and the nine European regiments, including those raised during the Mutiny, became regiments of the line. The Bengal army had to be reconstituted of cavalry and infantry, and it and the armies of Madras and Bombay were reorganized on a new footing, under which native officers commanded troops of cavalry and companies of infantry, while British officers commanded squadrons and wings, i.e. half battalions. British officers served under the Army Act of the United Kingdom, the rest of the Force under Indian legislation, which finally became the Indian Army Act, 1911.

To render service with native regiments attractive officers were treated as staff appointments carrying extra allowances. Addiscombe[4] was closed and appointments made from British regiments. Later, entrants for Sandhurst who desired to serve in India competed for vacancies, being attached for a year to British regiments in India before posting to a native regiment. Promotion in the staff corps was regulated by strict time limits, but officers in civil employment ceased later to be promoted above the rank of lieutenant-colonel.

The whole force as reorganized and reduced was divided between the armies of Bengal, Madras, and Bombay, the Punjab frontier force, the Hyderabad contingent, and local irregular corps, the total being 65,000 British and 140,000

[1] 21 & 22 Vict., c. 106, ss. 56, 57.
[2] 23 & 24 Vict., c. 100.
[3] 24 & 25 Vict., c. 74.
[4] Opened in 1812.

native troops. The danger of Russian aggression after 1885 resulted in the increase of the numbers to 73,500 and 154,000. After Maiwand (1880) the practice of permitting officers seconded for civil employment to return to the regiments was abandoned; though they were allowed to advance to the rank of lieutenant-colonel for pension purposes, they were retired at age fifty-five on pension.

The practice under which each presidency had its distinct army took curiously long to disappear. In 1891 the three staff corps were amalgamated into one, and in 1893[1] Parliament at last swept away the offices of commander-in-chief at Madras and Bombay and the control of the local governments over their armies ceased. A logical conclusion was the renaming of the staff corps as the Indian Army in 1903 at the Coronation Durbar.

In 1895 the old armies became four army commands, Bengal being divided into the Bengal and Punjab commands, and in 1904 the renumbering of the regiments removed one of the last traces of the old régime. In 1903 the new arrangement regarding Berar had rendered it possible to merge the Hyderabad contingent in the regular army.

From experience in 1886 the poor quality of the Madras army was generally recognized; eight regiments therefore were permanently stationed in Burma, and recruited from the north-western areas. In 1895 Telingas ceased to be recruited, and between 1902 and 1904 Moplahs, Gurkhas, and Punjabis replaced local recruits in infantry and cavalry to a large extent.

In 1900 the native infantry was reorganized as four double-company battalions. Native officers remained in charge of each company for internal administration, but British officers commanded on parade and in the field.

Under Lord Curzon[2] important changes were carried out partly prepared before Lord Kitchener's appointment as commander-in-chief, partly the result of his initiative. The moment was favourable, as the cessation of the frontier rising, which had taxed Indian finances and occupied the full attention of the commander-in-chief, had relieved the financial strain

[1] 56 & 57 Vict., c. 62. [2] Ronaldshay, ii, 368–72.

and left funds available for reforms. At the same time the advance of Russian strategic railways and the proof in Manchuria of the carrying capacity of even a single line were a warning of the necessity of greater strength for the field force, while South African experience pointed the way to reform. It was therefore found possible to reduce the garrisons kept for the purpose of securing internal order and to increase to nine divisions the size of the field army, the danger from external aggression now ranking above that from internal disturbances. In 1907 effect was formally given to the changes carried out by transforming the four Army Commands into Army Corps Commands, the northern with divisions at Peshawar, Rawalpindi, and Lahore; the eastern with divisions at Quetta, Mhow, and Poona; the western with divisions at Meerut and Lucknow, while the Secunderabad and Burma divisions remained directly under the commander-in-chief.

In the matter of army control Lord Kitchener's influence proved disastrous. He determined to secure for himself complete authority over military matters, executive and administrative, and for this purpose to reduce to impotence the military member of council whose presence had given the council the benefit of a second informed opinion on military matters and had relieved the commander-in-chief of a vast mass of administrative work. It is clear that in England the exact force of his project was not appreciated by Lord Roberts or Lord Lansdowne, who supported the compromise scheme for a Member for Military Supply decided on by the government.[1] Curzon saw the error made, and resigned on that score; the useless post[2] disappeared in 1909, and his opinion was vindicated at the expense of Indian soldiers and British honour in the Mesopotamian fiasco, when the commander-in-chief lamentably failed to sustain his prime duty of command.

In the second Afghan war the value of the troops offered by the Punjab states was proved, and 1885 evoked fresh offers in case of war with Russia. Hence there arose in 1889 the plan of accepting, where deemed suitable and not too burdensome to

[1] Ronaldshay, ii, 383. Cf. § 3 (*a*) above.

[2] The officer had only minor duties, not two hours' work a day in Curzon's estimate, for Kitchener would not allow him to advise the council on any military matters proper.

state finances, the offer as available for service with the British forces of imperial service troops. These troops are trained and disciplined under the supervision of British inspecting officers appointed by and responsible to the government of India, but they are controlled in time of peace by the state government and are commanded by Indian officers appointed by the state.[1]

The Indian navy was transferred to the Crown under the Act of 1858, but in 1863 it was renamed the Bombay Marine. Its long record of war service was continued in the China war of 1860, but thereafter its employment as a fighting force became minimal.[2] In 1877 it was reorganized as the Indian Marine, with a western division at Bombay and an eastern at Calcutta, and its duties were defined as the transport of troops and stores; the stationing of ships in Burma, the Andamans, Aden, and the Persian Gulf; maintenance of gunboats on the Irawadi and Euphrates, and the building, repairs, etc., of governmental vessels. In 1882 a single director from the Royal Navy was appointed to reside at Bombay. The discipline of the force was, as already mentioned, provided for by the Indian Marine Service Act, 1884.[3] The Admiralty conceded the right to use the blue ensign with the star of India, and in 1891 the title was altered to the Royal Indian Marine, and its officers were given rank immediately after officers of like title in the British Navy.

In 1871 for coast defence there was set up a Naval Defence Squadron which in 1889 consisted of two turret ships and seven torpedo-boats manned by officers and men of the Indian Marine. In 1892 a British naval officer was placed in command, while other officers were chosen from the Royal Navy and the Royal Indian Marine, the crews including British sailors and lascars. In 1903, however, Indian defence was taken over wholly by the Royal Navy and the squadron was abolished.

[1] See, e.g., agreement with Hyderabad, 1900; Mukherji, *Documents*, i, 573.
[2] The Admiralty was to undertake defence from aggression; Wood to Admiralty October 20th 1862.
[3] 47 & 48 Vict., c. 38.

6. FOREIGN AFFAIRS

Prior to the transfer of power to the Crown, circumstances of distance and difficulty of communication had made the government of India largely independent of effective control. But the advent in 1870 of the telegraph and cable curtailed enormously the power of the Indian government and rapidly transferred the effective control of foreign policy to London, with the result that at the close of this period it had become possible to contemplate an *entente* with Russia with little concern for Indian views. Naturally also foreign relations were the point in Indian affairs which could most easily be understood by British politicians.

The Crimean war had destroyed the understanding of 1844 which had checked the Russian advance towards India, but an agreement of 1855 with the Amir of Afghanistan and joint action against Persia in 1857 had placed relations on a footing of mild friendship. Dost Muhammad's death in 1863 led to a disputed succession, and Lawrence refused to countenance any decided policy until 1867, when the Russian command of Bokhara induced a change of attitude and Sher Ali was enabled to establish his authority. In 1869 he met Mayo, but the latter was unable to promise him aid against external and internal enemies, and his request for a definite assurance of aid against external attack in 1873, though favoured by Northbrook, was rejected by the Duke of Argyll, and the Amir could not obtain any promise to recognize as his heir his son Abdulla Jan. He turned then to Russia, and messages were freely exchanged with Kaufmann, governor-general of Turkestan. The British government decided that the Amir must accept a British envoy, and Northbrook resigned office rather than carry out a policy of which he and his government disapproved.[1] Lytton as his successor had to overcome opposition in his council[2] to the new policy, which was accompanied by the much more defensible decision to occupy Quetta by agreement with the khan of Kalat. In 1878 the Amir received a Russian envoy, and in September a British envoy had to turn

[1] Parl. Papers, 1878–9, lvi, 503 ff.
[2] Lady B. Balfour, *Lytton's Indian Administration*, pp. 64 ff.

back. The Cabinet after bitter disputes approved Lytton's plan of insisting on acceptance of the British proposals by an expedition. Sher Ali retired to Russia and the treaty of Gandamak in May 1879 provided for the acceptance of an envoy and of British control of foreign affairs. But the envoy was massacred on September 3rd and a new campaign was necessary. Finally, the new government in London found a solution by accepting as Amir Abdur-Rahman, who agreed to follow British advice in external relations and to agree to the British retention of Sibi and Pishin, while in return he received a subsidy.

Russian movements towards Afghanistan naturally continued. Merv was seized in 1884 and in 1885 Afghan forces were ejected from Panjdeh. After much discussion Salisbury, who succeeded Gladstone in the midst of discussions, accepted delimitation of the boundary to give Russia Panjdeh, while Afghanistan kept Zulfikar. In 1895 a further accord gave Russia some territory north of the Panjah and Afghanistan an area south of the Oxus, and settled the boundary question. But the refusal to permit direct relations with London asked for by Nasr-ullah, the second son of the Amir, when he visited England in 1895 was resented. On the other hand, in 1893 an accord was reached by Sir M. Durand, fixing the boundary between Afghanistan and the British sphere of influence, which gave the Amir an increased subsidy and permission to import munitions of war. On his death in 1901 the Indian government claimed that the treaty was personal, and disputes followed so that Habib-ullah only received a mission in 1904 and not until March 21st 1905 was a treaty accepted renewing the existing arrangements.[1] Habib-ullah next year visited the Viceroy, but gave assurances to Russia that he would not permit British influence in Afghanistan and would expect Russian aid to prevent it.

For other reasons, however, Russia was now seeking an *entente* with the United Kingdom, and dire offence was given to the Amir by the fact that the treaty of 1907, which continued the exclusion of Russian influence from Afghanistan, was concluded behind his back, and very naturally he declined to

[1] For Curzon's disputes with the British Government see Ronaldshay, ii, 261–71, 346–8, 365–8.

take any notice of it. In this matter the governor-general and his council were overridden by the secretary of state, whose attitude was clearly mistaken and unfair.[1]

The same control of the British Government is seen in the treatment of relations with Tibet.[2] That state, nominally a dependency of China, had remained closed even to Indian trade, though in 1890 and 1893 China had agreed to treaties providing for such trade. Under Lord Curzon the matter was complicated by Russian issues. The Dalai Lama, who controlled temporal relations, had succeeded in growing up to exercise his nominal authority, and had the Russian Dorjieff as his adviser. Dorjieff entered into attempts to interest Russia in Tibet, and the Indian government conceived that it should take up the matter and counter Russian intrigue by insistence on its trade rights. The British Government demurred, but an unjustifiable protest against any expedition evoked permission for an advance. This was successful despite Tibetan attacks; and a treaty was signed at Lhasa in 1904 which established trade marts, imposed an indemnity, and claimed the occupation of the Chumbi valley for three years as a pledge. But the British Government felt indisposed to encourage any attempt at political influence. It recognized that to establish British control at Lhasa, when an effort was being made to stabilize relations with Russia, was unjustifiable, and accordingly in 1904 it gave a pledge to Russia not to annex Tibet, assert a protectorate over it, or interfere in its internal affairs if no other power intervened.

Constitutionally for these negotiations with powers outside Indian limits the governor-general was invested on occasion with specific authority from the Crown which enabled him to enter into engagements and to declare war and make peace, following the old tradition of the delegation of sovereign prerogatives to the East India Company.

In the same way the governor-general was maintained as the channel of relations with Burma, though King Mindon (1853–78) sent a mission to the Queen to ask for the right of direct relations, but he accepted from 1862 a British resident, and agreed to further British trade with Burma and through

[1] Cf. Buchan, *Lord Minto*, p. 226.

[2] Parl. Papers, Cd. 1920, 2054, 2370; Ronaldshay, *Lord Curzon*, ii, 204 f., 272 ff., 344; iii, 43.

it with Yunnan. In 1875 he agreed to recognize Karenni as independent, and thus now that state is the only substantial part of Burma which is not also British territory. Unfortunately his death led to anarchy under Thibaw, while France and Britain prevented any of his brothers ousting him by interning them. Finally Thibaw in 1885 entered into negotiations with France, which induced the government of India to take the opportunity of the King's reckless mistreatment of the Bombay Burma Trading Corporation to send him an ultimatum, requiring him to receive without undignified ceremonial a British resident, to accept British control of his foreign relations and the governor-general's arbitration in the dispute with the Company. On the refusal of these terms annexation followed, to be succeeded by a long and tedious process of suppressing the resistance of the disbanded army which took to dacoitry. The annexation as opposed to a protectorate seems not to have been desired by the Indian government, and the imposition of direct administration had the disadvantage of ignoring the native form of government and the legitimate influence of the Buddhist church, which vainly offered its aid in 1887 if the government would confirm its traditional jurisdiction over the clergy.

7. FRONTIER RELATIONS

The annexation of the Punjab brought India into close relation with the Pathan tribes, just as that of Sind made them neighbours of the Baluchis. In the latter area Jacob as agent of the governor-general with the Sind irregular horse succeeded in protecting the border by effective patrols, and in addition to acting as political agent performed the functions of chief of police, magistrate, and revenue officer. In the Punjab, on the other hand, it was necessary to trust largely to managing the tribes, and the task was at first entrusted to the deputy commissioners of the six border districts, which in 1876 were grouped under the commissioners at Peshawar and the Derajat. Political agencies were created first in 1878 for the Khyber, in 1892 for Kurram, and in 1892–5 for Malakand, Tochi, and Wana, the agents save that of Malakand being subject to the Punjab government.

In Baluchistan, relations with the khan of Kalat were regulated by treaties of 1854 and 1876 which subjected his external relations to British control, allowed the occupation of Quetta, and authorized the location of British troops in his territories and the construction of telegraphs and railways. In 1877 this led to the appointment of an agent to the governor-general in Baluchistan, which was induced to peace by subsidies paid on condition that outrages were duly punished by the tribal authorities or jirgas. The agent was entrusted with the control of the Sibi and Pishin areas ceded by Yakub Khan in 1879, which were declared British territory in 1887 and became British Baluchistan; the area includes besides agency territories and the native states of Kalat and Las Bela.

The drawing of the Durand line in 1893 presented a frontier beyond which the Amir was not expected to interfere, but as the boundary does not rest on any natural division it has always been difficult to secure that it should be respected, while the tribes near it have normally shown no desire to accept British rule, an exception being the Kurram valley which was handed over by its people in 1892. Later Chitral became from 1893 to 1895 the source of much anxiety, as its retention involved the making of an effective communication from Peshawar. The Liberal government in 1895 declined to approve this action, but the policy was reversed by the Conservative government. The decision to maintain a garrison in Chitral and other causes, including religious incitement and the dubious attitude of the Amir, resulted in 1897 in widespread risings in the Malakand, Afridi, and Maizar regions which involved much fighting. Curzon's policy[1] withdrew British forces from advanced positions, protected tribal areas by local militia, concentrated British forces behind them in British territory as a support, and improved communications in the rear. Thus Kashmir imperial service troops were used until 1935 to garrison Gilgit, the Khyber Rifles and the Kurram Militia replaced regulars, and the Northern and Southern Waziristan Militia were created. Regulars held Dargai, Malakand, and Chakdarra, where the Swat is bridged, and light

[1] Ronaldshay, ii, 40 ff. A railway to the Khyber was at last opened in 1925.

railways or roads provided the probability of early relief by British mobile columns held in readiness for action.

The political counterpart of this action was the creation (1901) of the North-West Frontier Province, in order that relations with the frontier tribes should be brought under the immediate control of the governor-general, instead of falling to the government of the Punjab. The province was divided into two areas, the settled area of Peshawar, Kohat, Hazara, Bannu and Dera Ismail Khan, and the area between the administrative frontier and the Durand line. In the latter direct government is not attempted. In the area from Chitral to the Kabul river there are chiefs with whom dealings can be carried on, thereafter the tribal jirga, which consist of elders, and often of most members of the clan, is dealt with. In the settled districts power was given under the Frontier Crimes Regulation III of 1901[1] to deal with causes by referring them for the opinion of tribal jirgas.

In one set of cases the Indian government was recognized to have special interests, which have remained unaffected to the present time. The Persian Gulf has in history essentially concerned India and accordingly Aden, occupied in 1839, was placed under the control of the government of Bombay. India also was used as the centre to regulate the officers deputed to manage relations with the chiefs in the gulf. These relations[2] which established British supremacy were the object of serious challenge under Lord Curzon's régime when both France and Russia showed signs of denying the British monopoly. Eventually the British Government, though reluctantly, supported Curzon's policy and a visit backed by a naval force to Maskat, Kuwait, and Bahrein in 1903 marked the re-establishment of British authority.[3] The officers who act as political agents in these territories are in direct relations with the government of India. The trucial chiefs[4] on the Pirate Coast similarly

[1] Amended by VII of 1926. The creation of the Province was marred by Curzon's failure to let the lieutenant-governor express his views; Ronaldshay, ii, 136 ff., 170 f. Since 1924 the state of Swat has been formed in the borderland.

[2] The chiefs undertook not to cede territory to any other power, Bahrein in 1880, Kuwait in 1899 (Ronaldshay, *Lord Curzon*, ii, 50).

[3] Ronaldshay, ii, 305–19. It was reasserted in 1935.

[4] They are bound by treaty of 1892 not to cede territory to any other power. Their disputes are arbitrated for by the resident.

fall in the sphere of the political resident in the Persian Gulf.

8. THE INDIAN SERVICES

The executive and legislative power in India was under the system above described virtually controlled by civil servants, subject to the authority of the Home Government and the personal views of the governor-general. Their training, therefore, and selection have been always a matter of vital interest. The Act of 1858[1] transferred their services to the Crown and gave the governor-general in council with the aid of the Civil Service Commissioners the duty of determining the conditions of admission by competitive examination, and in 1859 the preliminary step was taken of reducing the maximum age of entry to twenty-two and requiring a year's probation in England. In 1861 a more important step was taken in the passing of the Indian Civil Service Act, 1861.[2] It was necessitated by the wholesale neglect which had been shown of the strict rules of the Act of 1793 regulating appointments in India. Contrary to its terms posts had been freely given to military officers, domiciled Europeans, Eurasians, and Indians, and it was realized that the practice was reasonable and must be legalized. But at the same time it was held essential that the civil service should be left definitely attractive to men of high ability. Accordingly, a schedule of posts was prescribed which were to be filled only under normal conditions by members of the service recruited by competition. If, however, the governor-general in council desired to make an exceptional appointment of any person who had resided for at least seven years in India, he might do so, but the final decision lay with the secretary of state acting with a majority of the council. Moreover, officers for the revenue and judicial departments must pass the same examinations as for the covenanted civil servants, whose appellation was due to the continuance of the practice of making a formal agreement with each recruit. Other offices could be filled without regard to the Act of 1793, and the rule of promotion by seniority was banished. In 1876 the schedule was

[1] 21 & 22 Vict., c. 106, s. 32.

[2] 24 & 25 Vict., c. 54. See O'Malley, *The Indian Civil Service* (1931) and Curry, *The Indian Police* (1932).

in effect extended by the addition to the reserved posts by the secretary of state in council of corresponding posts in the non-regulation provinces, the original having been chiefly confined to posts in the regulation provinces.

The age for competition was lowered in 1866 to twenty-one, and two years' probation in England was required. In 1869 three Bengalis were successful, next year one out of seven. But the rate of progress was slow and the Duke of Argyll regarded the position as a virtual failure to honour the pledge of 1833 in favour of equality of opportunity for Indians. In 1870,[1] therefore, authority was given to admit Indians without regard to the existing conditions, but the rules of the government of India must be approved by the secretary of state in council. This condition proved hard to fulfil. Rules approved in 1875 proved unsatisfactory, and in 1879 Lytton set aside one-sixth of the posts available each year for Indians recommended by their local governments and approved by the governor-general in council. Of these statutory civil servants sixty-nine in all were appointed, but their educational deficiencies prevented some at least of them proving adequate to their responsibilities.

The work not appropriated to the covenanted civil service or to military officers was done by the uncovenanted service. Some of its members in non-regulation provinces might hold posts of high importance, but, as we have seen, in 1876 this state of affairs came to an end as regards most of these areas, and it stopped in Sind in 1885, in the Punjab in 1903, and in Assam in 1907. The great majority of this service were natives of India, appointed by the local governments with or without a qualifying examination and probation.

The police force was reorganized generally on the basis of the recommendations of a commission of 1860. The force was under inspectors-general in each province, district-superintendents, and assistant-superintendents, the inspectors and superintendents being usually British. Appointments of these officers at first were made from the military forces; from 1893 they were recruited by competitive examination from age seventeen to nineteen in England for Europeans only; a smaller number of

[1] 33 & 34 Vict., c. 3, s. 6.

appointments was made in India by nomination and examination for which Indians were eligible.

The engineering service was filled after 1871 mainly from men trained at Cooper's Hill, established in 1871 for that purpose, and Indians trained in the Indian engineering colleges at Rurki, Bombay, and Madras, while some recruits came from the Royal Engineers. Other branches of the public works department included state railways and accounts, each with a superior and a subordinate staff.

The finance department was directly under the government of India. It brought to account and audited the expenditure of all the branches of the civil administration, and dealt with questions of currency, coinage, and loan operations. The accountant-general in each province was further required through his staff to audit local governmental accounts and was treasurer of charitable funds. All were subject to the comptroller and auditor-general. The highest officers were taken from the civil service, the lower were appointed, both European and Indian, in India until 1899, when it was found necessary to decide that at least four out of nine should be selected in England. Ten years later it was agreed that half the posts should be reserved for Indians.

The forestry service owes its effective inception to the conquest of Ava, and Dalhousie's recognition of the danger of the destruction of its forests. In 1864 Brandis was appointed inspector-general and next year the first Act was passed for the protection and management of forests. In 1866 the recruitment of officers was arranged for, their training to be carried out on the Continent. From 1885 to 1905 training took place at Cooper's Hill, supplemented by Continental tours. In 1905 competitive examination was replaced by selection by an India Office Committee. The high posts were reserved for Europeans, and the management of forests was assigned to the local governments, subject to the powers of the inspector-general of the Indian government.

The Indian Medical Service was primarily military in purpose, but lent its officers for civil work, such as the administration of hospitals and dispensaries, medico-legal work, attendance on government servants, jails, and public health generally. Each province had an inspector-general of hospitals or surgeon-general, and an inspector-general of jails; below them were civil surgeons with subordinates, usually Indians, who also filled some superior posts. A director-general of the government of India supervised the officers who worked under the local governments.

In the education department of each province from 1865 onwards, officers were either graded as superior and appointed by the secretary of state, or as teachers and inspectors selected by the local governments. A director was at the head of each province, and definite subsidies were awarded by the central government. The governments shared responsibility for higher education with the universities,[1] which were subject to a certain measure of control by the central government in the case of the University of Calcutta, by the presidency in the cases of Madras and Bombay.

In the numerous other services, agricultural, posts and telegraphs, customs, excise, salt, opium, mint, prisons, archaeological, geological, survey, meteorological, and registration, the higher officers were British, the rest of the staffs recruited in India.

Naturally with the passing of time the demand for the admission of Indians to the higher posts increased. The lowering of the examination age to nineteen in 1878 pressed hard on Indians, so that from 1892–1905 it was raised to twenty-one to twenty-three, and from 1906 to twenty-two to twenty-four, and thus assimilated to the examination for the home civil service. The number of Indians who succeeded was low, for example, only two in 1900 when fifty-two vacancies were filled. The Indian National Congress in 1885 and subsequently pressed for simultaneous examinations, but Muhammadan opinion was hostile to a move which must benefit Hindus and Parsees at their expense. A public services commission under Sir C. Aitchison devised a plan which was finally approved in 1889. Under it the number of posts reserved for covenanted civil servants was reduced, and below the Indian Civil Service were created provincial services, below which were subordinate civil services whence the provincial services were in part recruited,

[1] Cf. Ronaldshay, *Lord Curzon*, ii, 184–94.

while other members were chosen for executive work by examination, for judicial by selection from barristers or pleaders. Ninety-three posts were ascribed to the new service to begin with, and one-sixth of the appointments usually given to the Indian civil service were to be filled from the provincial services after the claims of the existing statutory civil servants had been duly met. The results of the reform were unquestionably to improve greatly the services, but Indians remained dissatisfied with the inferior status of the provincial services, especially in the case of the civil service, education, and public works.

In 1893 the House of Commons pressed for simultaneous examinations, with the result that the situation was very carefully reviewed by the Indian governments with a result decidedly unfavourable to the proposal save in the case of Madras.[1] It was pointed out that there were only 781 posts in the general executive and judicial administration of the country reserved for the covenanted service and military officers, the latter especially in the Punjab, Burma, and Assam, and on them rested the welfare of 217,500,000 people. It was undesirable to reduce the European element, and Indians could best be added to the service by promotion after good work in the subordinate services. This decision was adopted by the government. In 1893 the fall in value of the rupee resulted in the grant of exchange compensation allowance, but the pressure of work steadily increased with the expansion of trade and commerce, of education, and of political agitation.

Lord Curzon's régime marked the further perfection of the bureaucracy for its task. His police reforms were significant. The higher posts, down to assistant-superintendent, were ranked as imperial posts, and recruitment was carried out by competitive examination from candidates between nineteen and twenty-one years of age, who were placed on probation for training for two years after arrival. They were reserved for Europeans. The deputy superintendents and those below them were recruited normally from Indians, and for exceptional merit promotion to the imperial service was possible. Pay of all ranks was increased in order to secure better service and to meet

[1] Parl. Papers, 1894, Accounts 10, LX, 1–110.

many of the abuses produced by the wielding of power by underpaid subordinates.

The public works department was reorganized, the creation of a Railway Board being carried out to secure more efficient management but without change in mode of recruitment. The public works department thus fell into two main groups, concerned with irrigation, and roads, buildings, and bridges. In all these services there was the usual division of an imperial and a provincial service. In 1906 Cooper's Hill College was abolished as unnecessary and superior appointments were made by nomination of the secretary of state on the advice of a selection committee from candidates, technically qualified, between ages twenty-one and twenty-three. In 1910 the accounts branch of the public works service was merged with the civil accounts branch of the Indian finance department.

Other services, including the agricultural, received the governor-general's care, but he recognized clearly that the service was overburdened with reports and office work to the sacrifice of personality, initiative, and dispatch, and of personal touch with the people. But he could do nothing to deal with the enormous increase of legal work, the result of the growth of the legal profession, and his enthusiasm for efficiency rendered him a practiser of centralization, provincial autonomy inevitably hampering efficiency.[1]

9. THE JUDICIARY AND THE LEGAL SYSTEM

(a) THE JUDICIARY

One of the essential gains of the new régime was the termination of the duplication of jurisdiction as between the courts of the Company and of the Crown. The Indian High Courts Act, 1861,[2] the third of the great measures marking the reforming spirit of the new régime, authorized the creation by letters patent (December 28th 1865) of high courts at Calcutta, Madras, and Bombay, and on their establishment the Supreme Courts and the Sadr Adalat Courts of the Company were to

[1] Cf. Ronaldshay, *Lord Curzon*, ii, 62 ff.; L. Fraser, *India under Curzon and After* (1911).

[2] 24 & 25 Vict., c. 104.

disappear, their powers and jurisdiction being conferred on the new courts. The result was in a certain degree anomalous, since the jurisdiction of the Supreme Courts had been rather anomalous, but the advantages of the change far outweighed any considerations of symmetry. The courts were to consist of a chief justice and not over fifteen judges; one-third were to be barristers, including the chief justice, one-third members of the covenanted civil service. All were to hold office at the royal pleasure. The way was left open for the appointment to the court of persons who had acted as pleaders before a high court for ten years at least or as subordinate judges or judges of small cause courts for five years. In 1866, under the powers conferred by the Act a new high court was established at Allahabad, with jurisdiction over the North-Western Provinces.

The jurisdiction of the high courts was thus original and appellate, the former being derived from the Supreme Courts, the latter from the Sadr Courts. Their exclusive jurisdiction over European British subjects in the districts in serious criminal cases disappeared in 1861, special provisions for the protection of such persons being made in the Criminal Procedure Code. But the limitations on their original jurisdiction, as provided in 1781 and noted above, were duly retained. No great extension of jurisdiction was either necessary or accorded. Before they came into existence by the Admiralty Jurisdiction (India) Act, 1860,[1] persons charged with offences within the Admiralty jurisdiction and punishable in Indian courts under the Admiralty Offences (Colonial) Act, 1849,[2] which applies[3] to India, were given the right to claim trial by the Supreme Court in certain circumstances. The Courts (Colonial) Jurisdiction Act, 1874,[4] which regulates punishment for Admiralty offences where there is no corresponding colonial offence applies also to India, and so does the Colonial Courts of Admiralty Act, 1890,[5] under which the Indian legislature declared the high courts at Calcutta, Madras, Bombay, and Patna, the Recorder's Court at Rangoon, the court of the resident at Aden, and the district court at Karachi, Courts of Admiralty with the jurisdiction of that Act. The courts have

[1] 23 & 24 Vict., c. 88.
[2] 12 & 13 Vict., c. 96.
[3] 23 & 24 Vict., c. 88, s. 1.
[4] 37 & 38 Vict., c. 27.
[5] 53 & 54 Vict., c. 27; Indian Act XVI of 1891, s. 2.

also jurisdiction under the Merchant Shipping Act, 1894,[1] over British subjects for offences committed on foreign ships to which they do not belong and on British ships in foreign ports, over aliens for offences committed on British ships on the high seas, and over members of ships' crews or ex-members for offences committed anywhere outside the British dominions, and under the Territorial Waters Jurisdiction Act, 1878, over offences committed by aliens on alien ships in territorial waters.[2]

How far the original jurisdiction of high courts in revenue matters is excluded was a matter of dispute. It was ruled in 1873 that the court at Calcutta could not issue a mandamus requiring the Board of Revenue to prescribe rules fixing liquor licence fees,[3] but it was also suggested at Madras that the rule applied only to land revenue. In any case it can be varied by the legislature.[4]

The high courts were invested with administrative superintendence of courts subject to their appellate jurisdiction, and might call for returns, direct the transfer of suits, make general rules for proceedings, prescribe forms, and settle fees, but only with the approval of the government of India in the case of Calcutta, of the local government in other cases. In 1865[5] power was given to the governor-general in council to transfer any area from the jurisdiction of one high court to another, and to authorize any high court to exercise its jurisdiction over

[1] 57 & 58 Vict., c. 60, ss. 686, 687. Where persons subject to the Penal Code are concerned, its terms can be applied; where others are concerned, the true view seems to be that the crime is to be determined by English law, the penalty under the Act of 1874 by local law, as held in *Queen Empress* v. *Barton*, I.L.R. 16 Cal. 238 (1889), and 21 Cal. 782 (1894). Cf. Mayne, *Criminal Law of India*, ch. ii.

[2] 41 & 42 Vict., c. 73, passed to undo the effect of *R.* v. *Keyn*, L.R. 2 Ex. 63; the permission of the governor-general or governor is requisite for prosecution. That territorial waters are subject to jurisdiction was assumed in *R.* v. *Edmonstone* (1870), 7 Bom. Cr. Ca. 109; *R.* v. *Kastya Rama* (1871), 8 Bom. Cr. Ca. 63. The sovereignty and property in the soil up to the three-mile limit and in islands emerging belongs to the Crown: *Secretary of State for India* v. *Chellikani Rama Rao* (1916), 39 Mad. 617.

[3] *Audhur Chundra Shaw, Re*, 11 Beng. L.R. 250. But in *Alcock, Ashdown & Co.* v. *Chief Revenue Authority of Bombay* (1923), 47 Bom. 472, the Privy Council allowed mandamus to the revenue to carry out the procedure of the income tax legislation.

[4] *Collector of Sea Customs* v. *Panniar Cithambaram* (1874), 1 Mad. 89. Its validity in land revenue cases is established by the Privy Council in *Spooner* v. *Juddow* (1850), 4 Moo. Ind. App. 363.

[5] 28 & 29 Vict., c. 15: this power was extended by 1 & 2 Geo. V, c. 18, s. 2.

any Christian[1] subjects of the Crown resident in the Indian states.

The court may sit in divisions according to such rules as it makes. A vacancy in the chief justiceship was filled provisionally by the Indian government in the case of Calcutta, by the local government elsewhere.

While the number of chartered high courts was not altered, courts of like authority came to be established from time to time. Thus in 1866 the Punjab received a chief court, in 1900 Lower Burma was given a like court, between 1861 and 1868 judicial commissioners were set up for Sind, Aden, the Central Provinces, Oudh and Coorg, while in 1890 a judicial commissioner was appointed for Upper Burma. These courts were given the same powers over subordinate courts as the high courts, and their decisions subjected in the same way to appeal to the Privy Council.

In Bengal the subordinate courts remained without substantial change after the magistrate and collector, or district officer, was established in 1859 as the head of his district. The higher criminal and civil jurisdiction was exercised by the district and sessions judge, while minor jurisdiction was added to in 1860 by establishing small cause courts, whose judges were in 1867 amalgamated with the corps of principal sadr amins and munsiffs into a single provincial department of subordinate judges and munsiffs. From 1859 to 1869,[2] cases between landlord and tenant were referred to the revenue courts of the collectors, but then returned to the ordinary courts. For Calcutta stipendiary magistrates were appointed for minor cases and a municipal magistrate for offences against municipal regulations. The general powers of criminal jurisdiction were settled for British India by the Criminal Procedure Code, which, as re-enacted in 1898, recognized sessions judges, and permitted the appointment of additional, joint, and assistant judges. Under it presidency magistrates and those of the first class might pass sentences of imprisonment up to two years, and impose fines up to 1,000 rupees; magistrates of the second

[1] The term 'Christian' was probably used to extend matrimonial and testamentary jurisdiction over Christian native subjects for whose causes provision otherwise would be lacking.

[2] Acts X of 1859; VIII of 1869; VIII of 1885.

class could imprison up to six months and fine up to 200 rupees; those of the third class might fine up to 50 rupees and imprison for a month. But in certain parts of the country first-class magistrates might be empowered to try offences not involving the death penalty and magistrates of the first or second class might impose sentences of whipping.

European British subjects, subjected in 1872 to the jurisdiction of the provincial courts, were prior to 1883 entitled when in the districts to trial by a sessions judge or a justice of the peace of their own race. Sir C. Ilbert's Bill to take away this privilege as obsolete raised a bitter controversy,[1] which no one in India seems to have expected, and Sir H. Maine's warning was not communicated to the governor-general by the council of India. In the end the government yielded to the popular clamour, thus setting an ominous precedent of concession to unregulated violence, and the Act as passed merely conferred jurisdiction on all sessions judges and district magistrates of whatever race, and on justices of the peace being magistrates of the first class and of European race. Moreover, a European British subject,[2] if tried by a district magistrate was authorized to claim trial by a jury, one half of which must be European or American, and, though the power of the district magistrate to inflict punishment was increased, it still remained necessary to commit offenders in more serious cases to the high court.[3]

The code allows appeals freely on fact and law, and provides machinery by which questions of law could be brought under review by the high courts. The jury system, hitherto confined to the presidencies where grand juries were abolished in 1865, was applied tentatively to the districts in such cases as the governments might direct, the alternative being trial by a judge and assessors. The number of the jury in the high court was fixed at nine, in the districts it was decided within the limits of three and nine by the local government. But a judge

[1] Curzon, *British Government in India*, ii, 243; Cowell, *Courts and Legislative Authorities* (1905), pp. 189 ff.

[2] European covers persons born, naturalized, or domiciled in the United Kingdom, the European, American, Australasian, and South African colonies, their children and grandchildren.

[3] The discriminations in substance disappeared under Act XII of 1923 which accorded similar advantages to Indians and provided special rules for all cases involving racial issues.

may refer even a unanimous verdict to the high court which may convict. In the high courts a majority numbering six jurors, and in the districts a majority at the discretion of the judge, may decide. Appeals against acquittals are permitted.

In Madras the introduction of the Penal Code and the Code of Criminal Procedure resulted in the repeal of a mass of legislation and the cessation of the exercise of criminal jurisdiction by the civil courts. In 1873 the civil jurisdiction was reorganized as district and sessions judges, with unlimited civil jurisdiction, subordinate judges (formerly principal sadr amins) with the same civil jurisdiction, and munsiffs with jurisdiction in the districts up to 2,500 rupees. In 1889 the powers of the village civil courts was extended and village benches created.

In Bombay in 1868–9 the civil courts were reorganized in four grades—district judges, assistant judges, first- and second-class subordinate judges, the old titles of sadr amin and munsiff disappearing. The judge of Poona acted also as agent for the sardars in the Deccan and decided disputes between certain noblemen under Regulation XXIX of 1827. The Deccan Agriculturists' Relief Act, 1870, resulted in the appointment of village munsiffs and conciliators with powers to settle petty disputes and to persuade agreement or arbitration in major issues. Small cause courts were also created in Bombay and the smaller towns.

For Sind a separate judicial commissioner was appointed in 1866, and was later recognized as a high court. It acted also as district and sessions court for the Karachi district and as a colonial Court of Admiralty. The resident at Aden was given in 1864 (Act II) rather wider powers than a district and sessions judge, and the collector of West Khandesh acted as the court for the Mewasi chiefs.

In the former non-regulation provinces, the Punjab and the Central Provinces, the system of the Criminal Procedure Code was introduced, and the civil jurisdiction was soon assimilated to that of the regulation provinces, the collector losing his civil jurisdiction except as regards suits between landlord and tenant. As early as 1884 in the Punjab the divisional commissioners handed over their criminal and civil powers to divisional judges, later assimilated in name to the district and session judges to whom they corresponded. The employment of Indians in judicial work was rapidly extended, nearly the whole of the ordinary civil litigation being in their hands by the close of this period.

In Burma in 1862 the chief commissioner was himself the high court; he had three commissioners who were sessions and divisional judges trying murder cases and second civil appeals; below them twelve deputy commissioners and district magistrates and district judges tried cases not requiring more than seven years' imprisonment, major civil causes and first appeals; subordinate officers, mostly native, tried minor criminal causes and most civil causes. In Rangoon (1864–1900) and Moulmein (1864–72) there were recorders subject to the Calcutta High Court. In 1872 a judicial commissioner relieved the chief commissioner of judicial functions; in 1890 a judicial commissioner was appointed for Upper Burma, and in 1900 a Chief Court at Rangoon. A beginning in the separation of judicial and executive functions was made in 1905 in Lower Burma, the commissioners ceasing to deal with judicial work, and the deputy commissioners confining themselves to major criminal causes. In Upper Burma commissioners and deputy commissioners continued to try most criminal and some civil causes. Moreover, in the Shan states, though British territory, the major chiefs were allowed to retain powers of life and death and to administer their customary law, not British code law.

There are in the provinces in greater or less degree areas which, under the imperial legislation of 1870 or the Indian legislation of 1874, are exempt from the ordinary laws and often subject to special judicial arrangements, which are usually based on combining judicial and executive functions. The history of India proves that with primitive peoples any other system is certain to work the greatest injustice. In the North-West Frontier Province, even in the settled districts, some use is made, as noted above, of the tribal jirga or assembly as a means of settling or suggesting settlement of civil and criminal causes, and the system prevails in the unadministered areas beyond the region of settlement.

(*b*) THE LEGAL SYSTEM

The transfer of the government to the Crown was rapidly followed by the settling in final form of the Code of Civil Procedure pending which the establishment of the new high courts had been held up. In 1860 followed the Penal Code, in 1861 that of Criminal Procedure. The Civil Procedure Code did not apply to the Supreme Courts, but was in part adopted in the Letters Patent setting up the high courts. In the presidency towns the English criminal procedure was retained until 1875–7, when it was introduced into the high courts and magistrates' courts. These measures were followed by one on succession in 1865,[1] the work of the commission appointed in 1861, but its other projects failed to receive approval and its members ceased to work in 1870. The work then fell to the legal member of council in India, who produced in 1871–2 a new Limitation Act to replace that of 1859,[2] a second edition of the Criminal Procedure Code,[3] an Evidence Act, and a Contract Act.[4] Later measures included in 1877, a Specific Relief Act and in 1881–2 measures on negotiable instruments, private trusts, transfer of property,[5] and easements. In 1890 a Guardians and Wards Act, and in 1908 a Provincial Insolvency Act, and a Presidency Towns Insolvency Act, 1909, marked the conclusion of this sphere of activity.

Important as these measures of codification are, it must be noted that they leave untouched most of the essentials of private law. Thus the Succession Act was not to apply to any Hindu, Buddhist, or Muhammadan, though by special enactment it has been made applicable in certain cases, and the Contract Act was ruled not to apply between parties if one or more were a Hindu or Muhammadan, in the presidency towns. That regarding negotiable instruments is not made applicable to instruments in Oriental languages.

Hindus retain their family law, regulating marriage, adoption, the joint family, partition, and inheritance. Muhammadans preserve their law of marriage, of testamentary and intestate

[1] Revised in 1925 (XX, XIX) and 1926 (XXXVII and XL).
[2] Now IX of 1908. [3] Now V of 1898.
[4] Sale of goods and partnerships are regulated by Acts III of 1930, IX of 1932.
[5] Amended by XX and XXI of 1929.

succession, and of religious endowments. In the legislation as to rent and land tenure Indian principles are intermingled with English doctrines. The law of torts is practically English law, as pronounced by the judges, an effort to enact as a code having failed to secure sufficient support.

The application of Hindu and Muhammadan law is complicated by the existence of different systems which prevail more or less definitely in different parts of the country. Moreover, in many places local usages differ from any system of either law; in Bombay under Regulation IV of 1827 such usage is given preference over the personal law of the defendant, the normal doctrine applied under legislation, and the same rule was laid down for Oudh in 1876 and by Acts IV of 1872 and XII of 1878 for the Punjab which has peculiar usages of its own accordant neither to Hindu nor to Muhammadan law. Few changes were attempted in the great systems of law, though for certain cases of making wills authority was given by the Hindu Wills Act, 1870, and the Probate and Administration Act, 1881.[1] But on grounds of humanity the Age of Consent Act, 1891, practically forbade consummation of marriage before the age of twelve of the girl.[2] In the Indian Majority Act, 1875, children are protected against the earlier attainment of majority and legal capacity.

Hindu law has naturally been developed considerably by the jurisprudence of the courts, partly in the direction of recognizing more widely the right of the individual to deal otherwise than by gift with his share of property and the right to dispose by will of property independently acquired, in the latter case legislation being involved in order to guide the courts.[3]

The Parsee community has special rules of succession which were codified in an Act of 1865. The native Christians of Coorg preferred to keep their own law of succession as was permitted under the Act of 1865, and some twenty years after the Act had been accepted for the Jews of India in general,

[1] Now XXXIX of 1925.

[2] Ages eighteen and fourteen are prescribed by Act XIX of 1929 for marriage; cf. XXIX of 1925.

[3] See Mayne, *Hindu Law and Usage*, and Trevelyan, *Hindu Law*; for Muhammadan law, see Vesey-Fitzgerald, *Muhammadan Law*; Wilson, *Digest of Muhammadan Law*.

those of Aden obtained sanction for the retention of their own code, the Pentateuch.

Buddhist law, which prevails in Burma, is based on Hindu law, but with various important deviations. It has not shown any special lines of development since annexation. From Hindu law it has departed partly because the idea of the joint family has been gravely weakened, though heirs still have a right of pre-emption, partly because women are recognized as equals, so that marriage creates equal rights in property. The chief authority[1] in existing conditions is the Mànugye Dhammathat, promulgated as authoritative by King Alaungpaya in 1756. Only since 1926 has the legislature started on codification.

The case of Christian natives naturally caused the necessity of special legislation for marriage, the Indian Christian Marriage Act, 1872, while for non-Christians was passed the Special Marriage Act, 1872, which also includes provision for divorce, supplied for Europeans and others, where one party is Christian by the Divorce Act, 1869. That measure was deliberately[2] intended to allow divorce in case of residence, as opposed to domicile; when it appeared that such marriages were invalidly[3] dissolved, it was replaced by legislation based on domicile and supplemented by British legislation. The high courts, of course, recognize and give civil effect to divorces carried out under the personal law of non-Christians.[4]

10. THE INDIAN STATES

(a) ADMINISTRATIVE AND POLITICAL RELATIONS

A vital change in the relations of the government and the Indian states resulted from the transfer of authority to the Crown and the deposition of the last King of Delhi. The

[1] Privy Council judgment (1914), 8 L.B.R. 1; Forchhammer, *Essay on the Sources and Development of Burmese Law* (1885). Cf. *Phan Tiyok* v. *Lim Kyin Kauk* (1930), 8 Ran. 57.

[2] *Life of Maine*, pp. 99 ff. The Special Marriage Act was extended by XXX of 1923 to Hindus, Buddhists, Sikhs, and Jains.

[3] *Keyes* v. *Keyes*, [1921] P. 204. See Dicey and Keith, *Conflict of Laws* (ed. 5), pp. 943 ff.; § 3 (*b*) above.

[4] Remarriage of Christian converts was permitted by Act XXI of 1866; Maine, pp. 130–54. See also *Khambatta* v. *Khambatta* (1935), 59 Bom. 279.

paramount power of the Company had been long undisputed, but the nominal sovereignty of the Emperor had never been renounced by him, and with his passing a new position emerged. The Crown was now in India what the Emperor once had been, a completely sovereign power predominant over all others and claiming allegiance. The tone adopted by Canning is explicable only by his realization that the Crown had succeeded to the whole authority of the Empire, in so far as it chose to exert it, and the Crown, unlike the Emperor, had means fully adequate to make effective use of its power.

Under the Company's régime no meticulous regard had ever been paid to treaties. Many states had none; only some forty states now possess such compacts. Intervention in internal affairs might be excluded specifically or by silence, but it would be exercised if necessary to secure the carrying out of financial obligations or to maintain order. The system was capricious, for Dalhousie,[1] for instance, refused to interfere in Hyderabad, despite wretched misrule. Canning[2] was emphatic on the right to interfere to set right such serious abuses in a native government as might threaten any part of the country with anarchy or disturbance, and to assume temporary charge of a native state in the event of there being sufficient reason for such a step. Elgin[3] equally recognized that the alternative to intervention in case of misrule must be annexation. It is clear, therefore, that both these viceroys placed no literal meaning on the assurances of the maintenance of engagements given in the Act of 1858[4] and the royal proclamation. The treaties were taken over as interpreted in the course of time. What was essentially new was the royal assurance that no extension of territory was desired, which negatived the Company's conviction that no honourable possibility of acquiring territory should be passed over. The policy was implemented by the sanads, or instruments of grant—some 140 in all—of adoption issued in 1860 and later to Hindu princes assuring them that adoptions would be recognized, and to Muhammadan princes stating that

[1] Fraser, *Memoir of J. S. Fraser*, p. 291. Yet from 1811 there had been constant intervention. Cf. Lee-Warner, i, 124 ff.

[2] April 30th 1860; Lee-Warner, *Native States of India*, pp. 164, 165.

[3] Walrond, *Elgin's Letters and Journals*, p. 423.

[4] 21 & 22 Vict., c. 106, s. 67 (now contained in 25 & 26 Geo. V, c. 42, s. 284).

any succession legitimate by Muslim law would be upheld. The princes, who eagerly welcomed the concession, recognized that their security was essentially dependent, as under the Empire in the days of its strength, on the authority of the Empire, and their action was quite inconsistent with any claim to be sovereign independent states on a footing of equality with the Crown. As Canning wrote in 1860,[1] 'There is a reality in the suzerainty of the sovereign of England which has never existed before, and which is not only felt but is eagerly acknowledged by the chiefs.' Loyalty to the British Crown[2] is referred to in the sanads of adoption, and in 1875 the Prince of Wales received every sign of loyal devotion on his visit to India, and at the durbar to proclaim the Queen Empress the leading Maratha prince rose to hail her as Shahin-shah Padshah, the old imperial title. The corollary of loyalty was its reward by titles of honour, such as the princes had been wont to seek at the hands of the Emperor; the Nizam himself was happy to accept (January 1918) the style His Exalted Highness. Moreover, no prince is treated as of royal rank, following the Delhi precedent, and the order of the Star of India is freely granted, since its creation in 1861, to Indian princes.

The external relations of the states had already under the Company been subjected to effective control, and the only important change was the definite assertion of the right in the case of Kashmir.[3] On its creation as an independent state in 1846 the government had required that any disputes with neighbouring states must be submitted to British arbitration, but had not insisted on appointing a resident. In 1878 matters had changed through the advance of Russia to the Pamirs, and Northbrook wished to send a resident but the secretary of state refused to overrule the objections of the maharaja. In 1884, however, the appointment of a resident was insisted upon and made effective on the death of the maharaja. It was claimed for the state that it was independent and outside the Indian political system, but neither claim could possibly be deemed valid. The principality was merely the creation of the Company for reasons of policy at the time, and the suggestion

[1] Lee-Warner, op. cit., p. 317. [2] e.g. to Sindhia, March 11th 1862.
[3] Parl. Papers, 1890, LIV, 231 ff.

that it was independent is hard to take seriously. In 1889 this step was followed by the acceptance of enforced resignation by the maharaja, suspected of treasonable relations with Russia, and the appointment of a council of regency. It is possible that so drastic a step might have been deemed unnecessary but for the importance of Kashmir as a factor in securing India from foreign aggression.

As regards succession to the throne of the state the Company had insisted since 1834 on its approval, and the Crown naturally did the same. The new ruler was formally installed by the British agent, and no person could be regarded as prince without formal recognition.[1] The justification for this principle under the Company's régime may be difficult to find outside the cases in which it acted as successor to the Peshwa. But the Crown clearly could claim the rights of the Emperor, whose approval for successions had been regularly sought and paid for even in the days of his decline, as by the Nizam in 1803.[2] It followed clearly from the right to control successions that the deposition of a ruler could not be carried out without the approval of the Crown. The issue came to the front in the case of Manipur in 1890. The then raja was expelled by his heir-apparent and his leading supporter, a turbulent chief. The government of India, after consideration, decided to recognize the new raja but to expel the chief in question, but the chief commissioner of Assam and four officers sent to carry out this decision were murdered. The retribution taken was firm; the chief and the new raja were executed after trial as murderers, despite the objections of the Queen, and the attempt to claim that they should be treated merely as guilty of acts of war was overruled. The government of India in a notification of August 21st 1891 pointed out that 'the principles of international law have no bearing upon the relations between the government of India as representing the Queen Empress on the one hand, and the native states under the suzerainty of Her Majesty on the other. The paramount supremacy of the former presupposes and implies the subordination of the latter.' It will be remembered that in the case of Coorg in 1834 war was formally declared and

[1] See letter, January 1884 (Kolhapur); Lee-Warner, p. 323.
[2] Cf. the position in 1838; ibid., p. 318.

that Dalhousie had treated relations with Oudh as governed by international law. The disappearance of the Emperor had disposed of any possibility of such a view of relations with the states.

An extension of the same principle led to the rule that in case of misgovernment intervention was necessary, though it might not be consistent with an early treaty. Thus the prohibition of interfering with the prince's country in the treaty of 1803 with Alwar was held to be consistent with the supersession of the ruler in 1870 in favour of a council of regency aided by the British resident. Similarly in 1867 the nawab of Tonk was deposed in favour of his son as punishment for his complicity in the massacre of the supporters of a dependent chief, who was released from the control of the state. Two years earlier the ruler of Jhabua was fined and deprived of his salute for allowing the mutilation of a temple thief. The khan of Kalat in 1892 was deposed for brutal executions and barbarous conduct towards his wazir. But the most striking case was that of the Gaekwad of Baroda (1873–5), who was arrested, and the administration of his state taken over by the government pending investigation by a commission of his alleged attempt to poison the resident, who had been urging on him compliance with the requirements of the government of India for the removal of evils in his administration, determined by an impartial commission. The British commissioners were satisfied of the attempt to poison the resident, but the three Indian members found that the Gaekwad's complicity was not proved. He was, however, deposed on the score of maladministration, not in view of the presumption of his guilt. But the state was continued in being to the satisfaction of the contemporary opinion of the states.[1] In this case, however, unlike the others above mentioned, the treaty of 1802, confirmed in 1805 and 1817, gave the right of intervention should the prince commit anything improper or unjust.

Six years later the Crown gave a further and signal proof of its loyalty to its pledge not to extend its territory. Mysore had been administered since 1831 under British control, and the

[1] Parl. Papers C. 1252, 1271. The form of commission may have been due to the Queen, who had suggested it in 1859.

late ruler had left only an adopted son when he died in 1868. But it was decided to place him on the throne if he grew up worthy to rule, and this was deemed to be so in 1881. At the same time the Crown[1] laid down a set of principles which illustrate the claims which it deemed proper to make from a native state. They summarize what its policy had become in the light of the new conditions of communication by road and rail and telegraph, and of commercial activity in India, which demanded that the states should lend active co-operation in furthering the common interest.

The prince was granted possession and administration, not sovereignty, and his possession was made conditional on his remaining faithful in allegiance and subordination to the Crown. Each succession must be recognized by the governor-general in council. The military forces of the state must not exceed the limit fixed by the same authority and the production of munitions was strictly limited. For the British cantonment in the state exemption was required from customs dues or other control. The laws and the system of administration in force must remain unaltered unless change was approved by the governor-general in council. Land requisite for telegraphs and railways must be granted, telegraphs must be worked as part of the British system and full jurisdiction over railway lands must be ceded. No action must be taken to the injury of the salt and opium monopolies of the Indian government. The doctrines here laid down authoritatively and as of right were followed where possible in regard to other states, by persuasion, by taking advantage of minorities[2] when the Crown claimed the right to secure due safeguarding of the minor and the state alike, and by appeals to the duty of princes to co-operate in the interests of India as a whole. In this way the political department under the viceroy built up more or less of a system which it could appeal to when any issue arose in any state. The treaties admittedly were old and had never been revised. It might have been possible to declare them

[1] March 1st 1881; Lee-Warner, pp. 179 ff. This grant is replaced by a new grant of 1913, and since 1934 the state has been free to legislate without prior permission. But the essential conditions stand, and (s. 21) the right to intervene generally for good government and rights and interests of the British.

[2] Adoption favoured minorities and was preferable to collateral succession on that score; *Life of Maine*, p. 394.

abrogated since circumstances had completely changed since their conclusion. Instead, the milder and less provocative device of constructive interpretation was relied upon to secure like results without raising unpleasant controversies.

The whole tendency of the time was towards the doctrine of Lord Curzon,[1] which demanded that the princes should become essential parts side by side with the governor-general in the working of the scheme of Indian government. In this spirit he treated absence in England or on the Continent for frivolous ends as unworthy and improper, and undoubtedly he tended to strain the prohibition of any prince entering into foreign relations in treating the government as entitled to object to absence of princes overseas.[2] Unquestionably it was putting an extensive interpretation on treaties to demand that princes should be the hardworking servants of the people, and resentment of this attitude was natural, especially as it lowered the prestige of the princes in their states, threatened as it was in any case by Press criticism in British territory over the borders and the growth of a critical spirit among subjects who could see the advantages of British rule.

It is dubious if the princes felt repaid by the insistence of the viceroy that the residents should cease to receive allowances from their revenues and that they should show greater courtesy to them. They resented his assertion that their relationships were neither feudal nor federal but tended to a type not based on treaty.[3] The skill and efficiency with which they were drilled for the durbar for the proclamation of Edward VII reminded them too painfully of their subordination and excited them to efforts at self-assertion at a time when the government of India was beginning under political pressure to contemplate utilizing their services to counter revolution.

There was maintained almost intact through this period the doctrine of isolation of each state from the others. The Company had insisted upon it, and the Crown was little disposed to relax the condition which was normally inserted in every treaty that relations with other states, like those with

[1] Speech at Gwalior, 1899; Raleigh, *Curzon in India*, p. 217.

[2] Ronaldshay, *Lord Curzon*, ii, 91. The right to regulate visits to, and acquisition of property in, British India is clear.

[3] Speech at Bahawalpur, November 12th 1903; Raleigh, p. 226.

external powers, must be conducted through the government of India. Lytton[1] was disposed to reverse this policy, adducing the not very opposite experience of Austria whose failure in her Italian provinces he ascribed to her repression of the native noblesse, though she governed well. He wished, therefore, at the durbar to proclaim the Queen Empress to announce the formation of an Indian Privy Council confined to the great chiefs, who were to confer with the governor-general on topics of common interest. The project was not favoured at home, and dwindled down into the conferring on a few princes of the style of Councillors of the Empress.

On the other hand, there disappeared the distrust of native forces which resulted in the order sent to Sindhia in 1867 to disband his military police and to refrain from massing his troops at his capital. In this it is curious that the foreign department took the lead, at a time when military opinion was adverse, continuing to treat state forces as a possible source of danger. From the offer in 1885 of aid against Russia came the initiation of the imperial service troops already mentioned. They were differentiated from the earlier examples of forces maintained by the states because their raising and maintenance was voluntary, their officers were Indian save in so far as British officers were appointed to train them, and the commander-in-chief had no control over them except in war. Instead of being a burdensome obligation these forces represent the participation by the state on its own volition in the effective security of India as a whole.

One episode of this period was fated to have repercussions later, the agreement reached with the Nizam in 1902 under which Berar was placed permanently under British control. It was later contended that the accord then achieved with the Nizam was virtually procured by undue pressure, and was not morally binding.[2]

The general principles which guided British relations with the states during this period may therefore be summed up as follows:

(1) Their foreign relations were entirely in British hands,

[1] Lady B. Balfour, *Lytton's Indian Administration*, pp. 109 ff.
[2] Parl. Papers, Cmd. 2439, 2621; Ronaldshay, *Lord Curzon*, ii, 214–20.

with the result that it was in the power of the British Government to include the states in treaties affecting India if it felt it necessary to do so. A declaration of war by the United Kingdom involved the states in war and a declaration of neutrality or peace was likewise applicable. It followed that in foreign states the British Government was bound to protect state subjects as British protected persons, and in cases where the Crown exercised jurisdiction in foreign states to exercise jurisdiction over them on that score.[1] Accordingly they were provided for in the Orders in Council regarding jurisdiction in Zanzibar, Maskat, etc., and the Foreign Jurisdiction Act, 1890, lays down the general rule that Orders in Council dealing with persons under the protection of the Crown bind natives of the states. On the other hand, the British Government was responsible to foreign countries for the proper treatment of their nationals in the states, and it was of course equally responsible in a different way to the Dominions.

(2) Partly as a result of the duty owed to foreign states, partly in the interests of India as a whole, and partly in the interest of the welfare of the people of the state, the British Government was bound to take a certain measure of interest in the conduct of the affairs of each state. It was bound to secure proper conditions for British subjects who entered lawfully the states, and for foreigners. It exercised a control over successions, interposed its authority during minorities, could depose a prince whose misgovernment was exciting revolt, but would aid on its own terms[2] a prince against unjust internal agitation.

(3) Each state was definitely bound to facilitate defence by affording to the British Government all necessary facilities in regard to the Indian army. Thus lands must be made available for the maintenance of garrisons if necessary, all facilities for these garrisons must be afforded, and nothing done which might endanger the security of India. Hence careful control was exercised over the production of arms in any state or the maintenance of forces likely to be a danger to the public peace. On this ground also could be justified the demands made from time to time on states to facilitate railway development and

[1] So on the high seas as regards slave trading: 39 & 40 Vict., c. 46.
[2] Lord Harris to nawab of Cambay, October 9th 1890; Lee-Warner, p. 301.

telegraph construction by cessions of land and jurisdiction, and to aid in the construction of military roads.

(4) In a few treaties the rulers had been required definitely to aid economic schemes for the welfare of the country. But the right to make claims on this account was not asserted as necessarily inherent in the relation of the states to the Crown. Rather persuasion and concessions of various kinds were employed to secure co-operation in such matters as the closing of local mints, the surrender of the right to levy customs on seaborne goods, and the placing under governmental control of salt production.

(5) The paramount power of the Crown resulted in the decision resting with it regarding the precedence and salutes due to the states and all matters of ceremonial.

On the other hand the British Government made no effort to alter the constitutions of the states or to enforce the adoption of principles such as the separation of state and personal revenue, the independence of the judiciary, the organization of the civil service on an effective basis free from corruption, the maintenance of the rights of the subjects to liberty and property, and so forth. Gross inhumanity would not be tolerated; very poor government was acquiesced in freely enough.

(b) JUDICIAL RELATIONS

Complex questions necessarily arose regarding jurisdiction in respect of native states. British subjects, European and native, frequently resided in these states, and to a limited extent foreigners might be found there. It was in several cases necessary to have cantonments for troops in strategic situations or in healthy stations. Further, it was requisite that over railways which often must enter states there should be a single system of jurisdiction. A privileged position necessarily attached to the resident who represented the Crown in the larger states, and who necessarily had a considerable body of subordinates and dependants. Hence there developed continuously from the days of the Company several forms of jurisdiction resting on various bases:

(1) The Crown exercises through the governor-general in

council exclusive[1] jurisdiction in every state over European British subjects, requiring them to be tried by British courts established in the native state[2] or by a British court outside the state. It doubtless would exercise a similar right regarding any European foreigner.

(2) It is not customary to claim jurisdiction over native British subjects, but the right to do so doubtless exists and could be asserted in any suitable cases, as is the practice as to servants of the Crown. It is clearly possible that the local law might be such that though the government could not demand its abrogation as regards subjects of the state, it could refuse to allow British subjects to be judged under it.

(3) In certain cases the Crown exercises complete jurisdiction over all kinds of persons on a given territory. Instances are (*a*) the Berars, permanently transferred to British control; (*b*) the residencies, which by custom exercise jurisdiction over an area wider[3] than the mere residency itself, and a few civil stations such as Rajkote; (*c*) the cantonments,[4] which in any case would on the principles of international law be exempt from local jurisdiction; (*d*) railway lands. In their case an occasional cession of territory was obtained; later mere transfer of jurisdiction was required, and it was ruled in 1897[5] by the Privy Council that the jurisdiction must be understood in the case to be restricted to jurisdiction for railway purposes only.

(4) In other cases we find that the jurisdiction of the state is shared with the Crown. Thus in the Kathiawar[6] peninsula the early policy of Bombay had recognized rights of sovereignty in those whom it found in possession of a measure of judicial power. In 1831 the government set up a criminal court presided over by the political agent to assist the durbars of the states to try serious crimes. In 1863 the situation was further developed. The powers of the chiefs were defined, and in each

[1] Insisted on against Bhopal in 1863 (Lee-Warner, pp. 345 ff.).

[2] Travancore was allowed to try by a European magistrate; *Memoir of Sir H. Maine*, p. 400.

[3] e.g., at Indore or Srinagar, recently curtailed; Panikkar, *The Indian States* (2nd ed.), p. 96.

[4] e.g., Secunderabad, Bangalore (*re Hayes* (1888), I.L.R. 12 Mad. 39), Mhow, Sialkot, Bhuj (Panikkar, pp. 74, 75).

[5] *Muhammad Yusuf-ud-din* v. *Queen Empress* (1897), L.R. 24 Ind. App. 137.

[6] Panikkar, op. cit., pp. 179–81.

of the four divisions into which the peninsula was divided for administrative purpose an assistant to the political agent was set up with power to exercise a wide civil and criminal residuary jurisdiction. This slowly developed into a more formal organization with a judicial assistant to the agent who aided him in trying serious criminal cases and heard appeals civil and criminal from the decisions of the political agents of the divisions, who received the aid of assistants for minor jurisdiction.[1] Various other instances of this division of jurisdiction occurred, as in the Bihar and Orissa states, and as regards feudatories in Cutch and Kolhapur, and even where jurisdiction could be exercised, it might be necessary to receive authority from the local political agent for the execution of a sentence of death or imprisonment for life, as is the case with all the chiefs of Central India, and the Simla hill states.

(5) For temporary purposes, as in the case of disturbances in a state or a minority, jurisdiction might be taken into British hands to be restored again when matters had become normal.

The formal authority under which these powers of jurisdiction were exercised was originally the royal prerogative, which authorized the Crown to acquire jurisdiction and to exercise it by such officers as it thought fit. The existence of the power was recognized and its exercise in some measure regulated by the Foreign Jurisdiction and Extradition Act, 1879, of the Indian legislature, which followed in its recitals the doctrines of the British Foreign Jurisdiction Acts. But it was obviously far from clear what right the legislature had to exercise the authority it purported to exert in that Act, and in 1902 the decision was taken to resort to the Foreign Jurisdiction Act, 1890, of the Imperial Parliament. The Indian (Foreign Jurisdiction) Order in Council, 1902, therefore confirms all existing steps taken under the Indian Act and authorizes the governor-general in council to exercise any authority of the Crown or of the governor-general in council existing in parts of India outside British India or elsewhere. The authority may be delegated and provisions made for the law to be followed, the

[1] No appeal lies to the Privy Council from such jurisdiction: *Hemchand Devchand* v. *Azam Sakarlal Chhotamlal*, [1906] A.C. 212; *Taluka of Kotda Sangani* v. *State of Gondal*, ibid.

persons by whom it is to be administered, and also the courts by which jurisdiction ancillary to that in question may be exercised by courts in British India. This last provision obviates the necessity of Indian legislation conferring such duties on the courts of British India.

The powers of the Order are in judicial matters exercised by orders constituting civil and criminal courts and prescribing the law which is to be applied to persons subject to the jurisdiction in question. This, of course, accords legislative power over such persons. The executive power exercised in the states would also be covered by the order, while the Act itself makes the declaration of a secretary of state conclusive evidence of the existence and extent of any jurisdiction which may be claimed in any state. In this way Parliament, which normally does not legislate for the states, secures the effective exercise of legislative authority to such extent as it believes itself to have the right to legislate for persons and places in the states, and the final decision in law of such issues lies with the Crown itself.[1]

Extradition between the states and British India was formerly largely regulated by treaty, but the Indian Extradition Act, 1903, provides a simple procedure which renders treaties unnecessary. The states are bound in any event to surrender fugitive criminals[2] from British India. Where the state seeks extradition of an offender from British India it may proceed under its treaty, but it may simply ask the political agent to issue a warrant, which will be executed by a magistrate in British India subject to the right to appeal to the local government, or to make application to the local government for surrender. European British subjects, of course, are not surrendered under normal conditions, and other subjects need not be, if the agent certifies that the case is suitable for trial in British India, for offences committed by British subjects and servants of the Crown in the states are justiciable under the law of British India.[3]

[1] The Crown can authoritatively decide what is British territory, though the courts may have to consider the issue; *Empress* v. *Keshub Mahajun* (1882), I.L.R. 8 Cal. 985; *Re Bicitramund* (1889), 16 Cal. 667.

[2] Deserters from the Indian army and Indian state forces (Act XVI of 1922) are also handed over.

[3] Penal Code, s. 4; Code of Criminal Procedure, s. 188.

In British India the position of Indian princes is governed by the Code of Civil Procedure,[1] which deals with sovereign princes, ruling chiefs, and ambassadors and envoys of foreign states. Suit is not permitted against such persons unless he (*a*) has instituted a suit against the person desiring to sue him, (*b*) by himself or another trades within the local limits of the jurisdiction of the court, or (*c*) is in possession of immovable property and is to be sued in respect of it or of money charged thereon, when suit lies with the permission of the governor-general in council. But no assent is necessary where the plaintiff sues as tenant. Execution can only issue in case of suit with the assent of the governor-general in council. The protection given is more restricted, for obvious reasons, than that accorded in England.[2]

[1] S. 86. No exemption in case of crime is given by the Penal Code. Cf. *Gaekwar Baroda State Railway* v. *Habib Ullah* (1933), 56 All. 828.

[2] *Statham* v. *Statham and Gaekwar of Baroda*, [1912] P. 92. Taxation is leviable under the Act of 1935 (25 & 26 Geo. V, c. 42, s. 155) on a ruler's private property in British India, and public property used for trade.

CHAPTER VII

POLITICAL UNREST, THE MINTO-MORLEY REFORMS, AND THE NEW DELHI

1. THE DEVELOPMENT OF POLITICAL UNREST

THE Indian National Congress in its earlier efforts was dominated by men trained in British political principles, who demanded the gradual application to India of the doctrines which had triumphed in the United Kingdom. But it was soon to be deeply affected by a very different influence, that of a Hinduism proud of its past and intolerant of all change. In Bengal the passing of the Age of Consent Act, 1891, induced by the scandal of the death of a Hindu child-wife, raised bitter protest, and so vehement were the denunciations of the *Bangabasi* that its editor, manager, and publisher were prosecuted for sedition. The freedom of the Press had been re-established in 1882 by Lord Ripon, but it had degenerated into licence. This was soon shown in Bombay, where, under the aegis of the Sanskrit scholar, Bal Gangadhar Tilak, reactionary Hinduism had made rapid strides. In 1896 to famine was added bubonic plague, and the measures of segregation attempted, in carrying out which British troops were used, gave admirable opportunity to the *Kesari*, his organ, to excite indignation against the barbarians. This took the practical shape of the assassination of two officers and led to Tilak's conviction of exciting disaffection against the government. Tilak's action in encouraging school boys and students to join gymnastic societies with revolutionary ends was imitated in Bengal, and by 1902–3 a definitely revolutionary movement was there in being. Strength was lent to it by Curzon's well-meant schemes of educational reform, which were interpreted as designed to lessen the influence of the Bengali intelligentsia, and by the decision to divide Bengal into two provinces. Justified as this step was by considerations of public interest and sound administration, it evoked much bitterness among the Hindus of Bengal who resented the fact that the new province would be specifically

Muslim, while lawyers were jealous of the establishment of a new High Court at Dacca, ignoring the injustice with which Eastern Bengal had so long been treated. Moreover, the resentment of Curzon's action was increased by his attitude of benevolent despotism and mental superiority, while the prestige of the European race was suffering gravely from Japan's victory over Russia and the economic success of the Japanese was attributed to freedom from British exploitation. Secret societies were speedily formed, arms were collected, funds secured by political dacoities, and the weapon of Press attack and of assassination directed against the lieutenant-governor and leading to the murder of two ladies at Muzaffarpur on April 30th 1908. The weapon of boycott of British goods under cover of promoting the use of local products was employed freely. It was advocated by the Indian National Congress at its session of 1905, and again in 1906. In the Punjab the revolutionary movement waxed strong in 1907, when the Colonization Act of the legislature was deemed to be a breach of faith with the colonists, and when efforts were made to sap the loyalty of the police and the troops alike. But there some relief was attained by the deportation under a regulation of 1818 of Lajpat and Ajit Singh and Minto's disallowance of the Punjab Act, despite his reluctance to encourage agitation by seeming to yield to it.

Congress during this struggle was divided between the moderates or party of constitutional advance and extremists, whose views were represented in London by India House, established by Shyamaji Krishnavarma, which became the headquarters of revolutionary propaganda leading to the murder of Sir W. C. Wyllie and Dr. Lalkaka at the Imperial Institute on July 1st 1909. In 1906 a split in Congress was avoided by the adoption of swaraj, which to the moderates meant parliamentary self-government, to the extremists independence, to English sympathizers self-government of colonial type. In 1907 an effort of the extremists to capture Congress was defeated by the efforts of G. K. Gokhale and Pherozeshah Mehta of Bombay, and of Surendranath Banerjea from Bengal, and not until 1916, after Gokhale's unfortunate death, was the hold of the moderates lost. Tilak, for his part, by his comments on the Muzaffarpur case, brought upon himself a sentence of six years' imprisonment at Mandalay. The prosecution, though deprecated by Gokhale and Morley,[1] was manifestly essential if any regard were to be had to law. The action of the government for the time checked extremist action, and the same result was effected by the Maniktollah conspiracy case, where fifteen of the Bengali agitators were found guilty of conspiracy to wage war. Deportation was also used to remove prominent extremists from Bengal. The extreme violence of the Press was met by the Indian Newspapers (Incitement to Offences) Act, 1908, and when that failed by the Press Act, 1910, which was based on the principle of requiring security which might be forfeited on conviction of the use of the Press to produce seditious matter, while in case of repetition of the offence the Press itself might be confiscated. Legislation was also passed in 1908 to prevent the holding of seditious meetings, to regulate the control of explosives, and to accelerate trials and to suppress associations formed for unlawful acts. These measures were passed with the reluctant assent of Morley, who was exposed to constant criticism in the ranks of the Liberal Party for failure to respect the principle of freedom of the Press and the rule of law, both points on which he was very sensitive.

2. THE MINTO-MORLEY REFORMS

In addition, however, to these methods of assertion of the law the government planned constitutional changes which might secure the support of the Indian moderates and of the aristocracy of India for the government. Congress had in 1904 and 1905 put forward claims for extension of representation in the legislatures and the presence of Indians selected by the elected members of the councils on the executive councils in India and the secretary of state's council in London. Minto and Morley were prepared to meet these suggestions in some measure, but the preparation of proposals was a very lengthy business, partly owing to the very proper desire to consult important bodies and individuals in each province before

[1] Sydenham, *My Working Life*, pp. 224, 225.

taking decisions, and it was only in 1909[1] that legislation became possible. The most important aspect of the measure carried was the increase of the representative element in the legislative councils and the extension of their powers. The additional members of the governor-general's council were increased from 16 to a maximum of 60, those of Madras, Bombay, and Bengal to a maximum of 50, which was assigned also to the United Provinces, and Eastern Bengal, while the Punjab and Burma were to have up to 30. It was decided by Morley that in the provincial councils there was no need to keep an official majority, but that such a majority was essential in the Indian legislature. In the result the immediate increase of members was from 124 to 331, and of elected members from 39 to 135, who were formally elected. The electoral regulations were necessarily very elaborate. They were intended to secure due representation of all important interests. Thus the municipal boards in the larger cities were to select members; in the smaller cities they were to act with district councils, landholders, and chambers of commerce, Indian commercial interests, special interests such as jute and tea-planting, and the universities were to be represented. By a vital decision the demands of the Muhammadans for separate representation by members chosen by themselves only were conceded, and the further concession was made that in assigning representation regard should be had to its political importance and its services to the Empire as well as to its proportionate numerical strength.

In the case of the Indian legislature an important element was to be derived from election by the provincial councils, the non-official members alone voting. As constituted after the changes in 1912, which will be referred to below, it included the six members of council, the commander-in-chief, the head of the province where it happened to sit, 33 nominated members, not more than 28 being officials, 13 members selected by the legislative councils, 6 by landholders, 5 by the Muhammadans of the greater provinces, 1 by Muhammadan landholders, and 2 by chambers of commerce. In Madras and Bombay, in addition to the three members of the council and the advocate-general,

[1] 9 Edw. VII, c. 4; Parl. Papers, Cd. 4425 (1908); 4987 (1910); Morley, *Recollections*; Lady Minto, *Minto and Morley*.

there were 21 nominated members, not more than 16 official, 2 experts, and 21 elected members. Bengal had actually 28 elected members to 20 nominees (16 officials), 2 experts, and 8 councillors. In all cases the elected element was substantial save in Burma, where the Burma chamber of commerce alone elected a member.

The functions of the legislatures were definitely extended so as to cover the serious discussion of the finances. The estimates of the governor-general in council were to be presented to the council,[1] and thereafter it was open to any member to move any resolution relating to alterations in taxation, new loans, or additional grants to local governments mentioned in the financial statement of the explanatory memorandum. After these resolutions had been disposed of, the member in charge explained the statement in detail, and resolutions could be moved on any points. The effect of such resolutions was merely that of recommendations, to which the government gave such effect as seemed wise. The final budget was presented to the council by March 24th, when any changes made were explained. It could be discussed, but no resolutions might be moved. There were excluded from discussion military, political, and provincial affairs, under the heading 'revenue' stamps, customs, assessed taxes, and courts, under the heading 'expenditure' assignments and compensations, interest on debt, ecclesiastical expenditure, and state railways. Moreover, discussion was prohibited on any matter which the governor-general in council might not deal with by any law, any matter affecting relations with foreign powers or Indian states, and any matters under legal adjudication. The president was further authorized to disallow any resolution on the ground that it could not be moved consistently with the public interest or that it should be moved in a provincial council.

The case of the provinces was dealt with as follows. The draft budget after being fixed in discussion with the government of India, which determined the limit of expenditure on new projects costing over 5,000 rupees, was considered by a small committee of the provincial council, at least half of which was elected. It then went to the government of India to be

[1] Rules, November 15th 1909.

incorporated in the general budget and to be discussed as described above. Any changes made were reported to the provinces, where a like procedure was adopted.

A further change of great importance was the authority given for the movement of resolutions on matters of public interest. There were excluded from such discussion in the central legislature any matters excluded from the legislative competence of that legislature, any matters affecting relations with foreign powers or Indian states, and any matters under legal adjudication. The president could disallow any resolution as inconsistent with the public interest or as proper to be moved in a provincial council. Resolutions might be amended, and as passed had merely the force of recommendations. Questions also could be asked excluding matters of foreign relations and relations with the native states, and matters under legal adjudication, and as an innovation supplementary questions were permitted, though the member in charge might decline to answer. The president had the usual power of disallowance. There were analogous rules for the provincial councils, and in addition to his other powers the presiding officer was given a wide authority to control the length and relevancy of debate.

The Act of 1909 contained also a provision permitting the increase of the numbers of the executive councils of Madras and Bombay to a maximum of four, two to be qualified by at least twelve years' service. It was also proposed to enable an executive council to be constituted for any province under a lieutenant-governor, but that proposal was strongly opposed in the House of Lords, and finally the government had to be content with accepting such a council for Bengal, and providing for the possible creation of others subject to the right of either House of Parliament to disallow, a right exercised in respect of the United Provinces in 1915. It was also provided that vice-presidents should be appointed for the several councils.

The Act was accompanied by a declaration of intention to secure the appointment of an Indian to the governor-general's council, a proposal which was not acceptable to the majority of that body, and which was only permitted by the King after learning that the whole of the cabinet favoured the project and asked for its sanction. It was unquestionably of far more importance than the step taken by the secretary of state in 1907 in admitting to his own council[1] two Indians, and it was accompanied by the addition of an Indian to each of the councils of Madras and Bombay. There were, undoubtedly, difficulties in appointing a Hindu to the governor-general's council without adding a Muhammadan at the same time, but the step was a decisive indication of the doctrine of racial equality and a tardy fulfilment of the policy of 1833. The authors of the reform scheme were fully consistent in this action. They absolutely disclaimed the idea of introducing responsible government or parliamentary institutions into India, but they held that they should spare no efforts to rally to the support of the Crown against the growing forces of anarchy the loyalty of the upper classes of India. In this spirit Minto had thought of reviving Lytton's conception of an advisory council wherein would sit great chiefs and substantial landholders, similar bodies with extended representation of interests being appointed for the provinces. The idea was to revive the Indian practice of consultation of interests before legislation, but the chiefs declined to consider sitting with persons not their peers, and the suggestion reduced itself to an imperial council of chiefs which was not at the moment considered worth while pressing forward for acceptance. But the incident is important as marking a definite step towards the ideal of enlisting the chiefs in the struggle against anarchy and even democracy.

3. THE DELHI DURBAR

The reforms of 1909 failed in their object, if that was to check the propaganda for self-government. But they had the merit of securing improvement in legislative measures, not so much through actual proposals by Indian members as through the circulation of Bills for suggestions and the use of committees to examine in detail their proposals. The passing of resolutions was often fruitful; it is reckoned that of 168 resolutions passed to the end of 1917 in the imperial legislature

[1] By 7 Edw. VII, c. 35, the number of the council was fixed at ten to fourteen, the term seven years, appointment not later than five years from office in India, in lieu of ten years in prior legislation.

78 produced definite action, and the provinces showed analogous results. An interesting example of action even in a very highly constitutional issue was that regarding the appointment of an executive council for the United Provinces, in favour of which the local council passed a resolution. It commended itself to Lord Crewe, but the House of Lords negatived the proposal in 1915.

In the meantime, however, the government of India and the Home Government had decided on a far-reaching step, the removal of the capital of India to Delhi.[1] No doubt, if a change were to be made, on geographical, political, and historical grounds Delhi offered the only alternative. The grounds for change were alleged to rest on the essential conditions which must govern future political development in India. The just demand for a larger share in the government of the country must be met by increasing the limits of provincial autonomy and retaining the government of India, with its absolute control of the legislature, as the authority to deal with matters of imperial concern, while empowered to intervene in case of misgovernment. This involved the separation of the central government from close connexion with any province, a step which would encourage the growth of local self-government while it would follow the precedents of the United States, Canada, and Australia. Administrative advantages would also be achieved. The Indian legislature would be relieved from the close pressure of the local opinion of one province which raised jealousies elsewhere, and the government and the legislature alike would be freed from the responsibility which was wont to be attributed, however wrongly, to them for matters really dealt with by the Bengal government. It was impossible indeed to select a capital where the government could be housed all the year, but Delhi could be used from October to April, and its greater proximity to Simla would reduce the cost of transfer thither. It would be more convenient for control of the railways, posts, and telegraphs to be centrally situated, and the commerce and industry department would be in closer touch with Bombay and Karachi, and less open to the influence of Calcutta. It was admitted that the European community

[1] Parl. Paper, Cd. 5979.

of Calcutta would suffer loss, and that the Bengalis might resent the transfer, but other changes would compensate the latter. It was believed that it was desirable to conciliate the Bengali resentment over the partition of Bengal, by reuniting the province, so far as this could be done without leaving, as before the partition, an unmanageable area to govern. The solution must provide convenient administrative areas, must conciliate the Bengalis, must safeguard the interests of the Muhammadans of Eastern Bengal who had been markedly loyal, and generally conciliate Muhammadan sentiment, and must be so clearly based on principles of administrative or political expediency as to negative any presumption that it had been exacted by clamour or agitation. Unfortunately, no amount of words could conceal the plain fact that the partition was reversed under pressure of unlawful agitation, and it is no wonder that there passed round the Muhammadans at Delhi the bitter jest, 'No bombs, no boons.'

The concrete proposals were, therefore, the creation of a province confined to speakers of Bengali, viz. the Presidency, Burdwan, Dacca, Rajshahi, and Chittagong divisions, 70,000 square miles in area with 42,000,000 of a population, to be governed by a governor in council on the same basis as Madras and Bombay. Bihar, Chota Nagpur, and Orissa were to be placed under a lieutenant-governor in council with a legislative council; the area would be 113,000 square miles, but the population only 35,000,000. Assam, with 56,000 square miles and 5,000,000 people would become a chief commissionership once more. The reunion of Bengal could be justified on the plain ground that in the two provinces the Bengalis found themselves outnumbered, in the one by Biharis and Uriyas, in the other by Muhammadans and Assamese. This disadvantage would become increasingly felt with the increase of the importance of the legislatures, and the concession proposed might go far to remove the existing bitterness between Hindu and Muhammadan. The choice of government by governor and council for Bengal was justified on the ground of efficiency and of the satisfaction to Bengali *amour propre*.

The new policy was duly announced by the King at the durbar which marked his visit to India, and unquestionably this mode of procedure was curiously unconstitutional for a Liberal government, since it precluded the exercise by the House of Lords and the opposition in the Commons of the right of criticism of so far-reaching a change in policy. It was made effective by a series of notifications and proclamations resting on miscellaneous earlier power. Thus the creation of the governorship of Bengal by the secretary of state in council was based on the Government of India Act, 1853,[1] the constitution of a new province on the Indian Councils Act, 1861,[2] of the chief commissionership of Assam on the Government of India Act, 1854,[3] while the delimitation of the boundaries of Bengal was carried out under the Indian Councils Act, 1861,[4] and the Government of India Act, 1865.[5] Certain further steps which were necessary were taken by the Government of India Act, 1912.[6] It conferred on the governor of Bengal those powers which since 1833 had been added to the functions of the governors of Madras and Bombay, reserving, however, to the governor-general in council control of the high court. It made the advocate-general's membership of the legislative council optional, as he might not conveniently be available. It provided an executive council forthwith for Bihar and Orissa, and the grant of legislative councils to provinces under chief commissionerships, Assam receiving a council on November 14th 1912 and the Central Provinces on November 10th 1913. Minor enactments included the fixing of the strength of the legislatures of Bengal and Bihar and Orissa and the recognition of the right of the governor of Bengal to succeed equally with those of Madras and Bombay according to seniority to the office of governor-general in the case of a temporary vacancy. It was also made clear that transfer of territory was possible from or to a chief commissionership. A change of wider importance removed the rule of 1793 under which promotion was restricted to officers serving in the same presidency.

The changes of 1912 necessitated consequential alterations in the regulations regarding the constitution of the legislatures under the Act of 1909, and these were duly made in 1912.[7]

[1] 16 & 17 Vict., c. 95, s. 16.
[2] 24 & 25 Vict., c. 67, s. 46.
[3] 17 & 18 Vict., c. 77, s. 3.
[4] s. 47.
[5] 28 & 29 Vict., c. 17, s. 4.
[6] 2 & 3 Geo. V, c. 6.
[7] Parl. Paper, Cd. 6714 (1913); Central Provinces, Cd. 7370 (1914).

Under the authority of the Government of India Act, 1854, there was effected in September 1912 the transfer of Delhi from the lieutenant-governorship of the Punjab to the direct control of the governor-general, to be exercised through a chief commissioner, who exercises the functions of the commissioner of a division, financial commissioner, registrar of births, etc., and of joint-stock companies, inspector-general of registration and of police. Other functions are carried out by Punjab officials. The powers of government are regulated by the Delhi Laws Act XIII of 1912, which allot some functions to the governor-general in council, some to the lieutenant-governor of the Punjab. With an area of 673 square miles, it forms a sort of enclave, similar to the district of Columbia and Washington in the United States.

Finally, there should be mentioned the Indian High Courts Act, 1911,[1] which raised to a maximum of twenty the number of judges of the High Courts, permitted the creation of further such courts—the power accorded in 1861[2] being thought to have been exhausted by the creation of the court at Allahabad—and permitted the appointment for a period not exceeding two years of temporary additional judges to any high court.

[1] 1 & 2 Geo. V, c. 18. High Courts were created at Patna (1916), Lahore (1919), and Burma (1922).

[2] 24 & 25 Vict., c. 104, s. 16.

CHAPTER VIII

THE WAR AND CONSTITUTIONAL REFORM; THE MONTAGU-CHELMSFORD SCHEME

1. THE WAR AND POLITICAL UNREST

THE reforms of 1909–12 were clearly unlikely to satisfy the extremists' demands for self-government, and in fact went but a small way to conciliate the moderates. Inevitably the control of the central government over policy was reinforced by reminding the local governments that their officials must not adopt in the legislatures, central or provincial, any attitude critical of the decisions of the Indian government, a fact which excited resentment through the spectacle of the official bloc in the legislatures voting as a solid unit whenever any government measure was under consideration.[1] Moreover, separate representation for Muslims was soon resented, and a motion was proposed in the imperial legislature on January 24th 1911 asking for the discontinuance of the scheme, an act which greatly increased Muhammadan ill-will to the Hindus. The Muhammadans also were perturbed at the war between Italy and Turkey, and the Balkan wars with their weakening of Muslim power, and they resented the carving out of spheres of influence in Persia by the Anglo-Russian treaty of 1907. Their loyalty to the government was further weakened by the undoing of the partition of Bengal, while the Hindus merely concluded from this act that they could extort further concessions by terrorism, and the state entry into Delhi on December 23rd 1912 was marked by an attempt on Lord Hardinge's life.

India in general was also strongly moved by the increasing realization of the humble status Indians occupied in other parts of the Empire.[2] The growth of anti-Indian feeling had recently manifested itself in South Africa with special vehemence. It was remembered that Mr. Chamberlain had urged the Transvaal

[1] Lord Hardinge (1911), Lord Crewe (1912), Parl. Paper, Cd. 9109, pp. 74–6.

[2] Keith, *Responsible Government in the Dominions*, Part V, ch. iv.

to redress the grievances of British Indians, and that this had been followed under crown colony government by the drastic enforcement of pre-war restrictions and the proposal to impose new disabilities, which the Home Government was unable to sanction. But responsible government for the Transvaal was followed by an Act of 1907 virtually excluding immigration. Natal also was systematically endeavouring to restrict the possibilities of earning a living by Indians after the expiry of their periods of indentured service and by those born in Natal itself.

The British and the Indian governments alike took up the matter energetically. In 1910 further indentured immigration to Natal was forbidden from a year later, and the Union government was urged to modify the terms of its exclusion legislation and to make concessions in respect of the entry into the Union of a wife and children of those lawfully there resident, if in fact monogamously married. An Act of 1913 gave a measure of relief, but not all that had been expected, and much resentment was expressed in the Union at the outspoken protests of Lord Hardinge. Naturally it was easy to make anti-British capital out of these facts. It is important also to note that the weapon used against the Union government by the Indians in the Union inspired by M. K. Gandhi was that of passive resistance, which was fated to play a great part in Indian history. But more immediate harm resulted from the activities of a Punjabi who, after stirring up discontent there, proceeded to organize a mutiny (ghadr) movement in the United States, whence the contagion spread to Canada, where some Sikhs had settled in British Columbia only to find that fear of their competition had resulted in legislation intended to exclude further immigration. A Sikh endeavoured to force the hands of the Dominion government by chartering a ship to carry 373 immigrants to Vancouver, where they were rejected, returning to Calcutta in September in a rebellious spirit which led to a clash with the police and bitter hostility to the government. A rising was planned with Bengali aid for February 1915, but was successfully countered, and an outbreak at Benares was likewise foiled.

Muslims also contributed to the spirit of revolt. The

declaration of war against Turkey led to a khilafat movement based on the view that the Sultan of Turkey was the legitimate khalif, an opinion which men like Sir Sayyid Ahmad had repudiated. Some students entered tribal territory and joined with a German and Turkish mission at Kabul in an absurd plot to overthrow the Indian government. The ghadr party in the United States worked more effectively, through Siam against Burma, having some success in weakening the allegiance of an Indian regiment and of the military police. Germany naturally lent a hand, endeavouring to land arms in the Bay of Bengal or to secure arms from the Far East for the use of the revolutionaries. The Irish rebellion had naturally an exciting effect on Indian aspirations, and Mrs. Besant started a Home Rule League, advocating her doctrines with a certain intemperance and acting in close co-operation with Tilak, who had been released in 1914. The government met some of these attacks by passing the Defence of India Act, 1915, which provided for trial of revolutionary offenders by a strong bench of judges without appeal and the internment of suspects. It also relied on the Press Act, and both these measures were used in the endeavour to restrain Mrs. Besant and her associates from doing serious harm. The value of the latter measure was insisted on by Lord Chelmsford when asked to withdraw it in 1917. Its efficacy was shown in the fact that, while 143 newspapers had once been warned, second warnings were infrequent and forfeiture had been necessary only in 3 cases; of 55 presses warned only 13 had their first security forfeited, and only 1 the second. Nor had the Act checked the rapid growth of newspapers, periodicals, and presses. Of the reality of the revolutionary movement and its extent there can be no doubt in view of the report of Mr. Justice Rowlatt and his colleagues in 1918, and, though two high court judges were detailed in 1918 to examine the cases of over 800 prisoners detained under the legislation of 1918 and the Defence of India Act, only in six cases were they able to recommend release. Unhappily the two Bills which the Rowlatt Committee suggested[1] were proceeded with in 1919, when the end of the war rendered their

[1] Parl. Paper, Cd. 9190. Only the Anarchical and Revolutionary Crimes Act, 1919, was passed.

enactment far less easily acceptable, and they were destined to have a most serious effect on the Indian situation.

At the same time the action of India[1] in the war was creating conditions incompatible with the maintenance of the *status quo*. The government of India, of course, was involved immediately in the war by the royal declaration, and the task to be faced was specially heavy, for the government of India had adopted the doctrine laid down by the Army in India Committee 1913 that she must provide for defence against local aggression and against any attack by a great power pending the arrival of reinforcements, but that she was not called upon to maintain troops to be placed at the disposal of the Home Government for wars outside the Indian sphere. But in fact from the first enormous demands of the type ruled out were made and met. The princes offered their Imperial Service troops with alacrity, Nepal afforded generous aid in Gurkhas, Tibet the prayers of her lamas, and the imperial legislature on unofficial initiative desired to share the costs of war. The loyalty of India allowed the British forces for the moment to fall to 15,000 men; in addition to the western front Indian forces hastened to East Africa, to Egypt, to Mauritius, the Cameroons, Mesopotamia, and the Persian Gulf. Later, Gallipoli, Salonika, Palestine, the Sudan, Aden, Somaliland, North-West Persia, Kurdistan, South Persia, Transcaspia, and North China were the scene of their activities. The troops that could be spared from Britain for the relief of the situation were in the main territorial battalions and field batteries. The numbers raised in addition to the 80,000 British and 230,000 Indian troops in being at the outset amounted to over 800,000 combatants and 400,000 non-combatants. The Punjabi Mussulmans provided 136,000 fighting men, the Sikhs 88,000. India accepted the burden of the normal cost of maintaining her troops now overseas, amounting to between £20,000,000 and £30,000,000, accepted further liabilities in September 1918 which cost her £12,000,000 and gave £100,000,000 as a free gift. Her people raised £75,000,000 in loans, and the Imperial Munitions Board from 1917 assisted in the development of Indian resources to relieve pressure on the allies. Unhappily there can be no doubt that the earlier

[1] *India's Contribution to the Great War* (1923).

stages of the Mesopotamian campaign were beyond the capacity of the Indian administration, weakened as it had been by the unwise concentration of all authority in the hands of the commander-in-chief. It was an error also to refrain from placing the supreme direction of the expedition in the hands of the Army Council instead of acting through the India Office, which manifestly could not deal independently with the matter and did not attempt the impossible. The defects in organization revealed in the Mesopotamian Commission Report were grave, and, though the personal responsibility of the secretary of state[1] was not involved, Mr. A. Chamberlain's resignation was valuable as an admission of failure. Incidentally it had the result of affording Mr. Montagu his historical position as a reformer of Indian government.

The collapse of Russia and the German advance resulted in a war conference at Delhi attended by ruling princes, leading politicians, and governmental representatives, whose efforts resulted in the intensification of war effort, as regards recruiting, communications, production, and war propaganda. The European community with some exceptions put themselves loyally at the disposal of the government, and the establishment of the Indian defence force mobilized the British and Anglo-Indian community for internal security purposes.

The political reactions of the war were momentous. The great majority of Indians had espoused the British cause, and naturally they expected due reward for thus showing their solidarity with the Empire in the vindication of public law and the protection of national rights. Extremists, on the other hand, saw their opportunity in the fratricidal conflicts of the Western powers and found in the grave mismanagement of Mesopotamia a means of exciting dislike as well as contempt. The Muslims resented the downfall of Turkey, ignoring the disgraceful treatment of the troops lost at Kut. Moderates could point out that the country had seen administrative work largely in Indian hands, and that Indians had at last been found worthy of the grant of the King's commission. Moreover, in stress of war it had been found necessary to abandon the unwise

[1] Lord Hardinge was much to blame for ignoring his council; Curzon, *British Government in India*, ii, 118.

policy which excluded India from the Imperial Conference and to admit her to share in the Imperial War Cabinets and conferences of 1917–18. There was every ground therefore for the expectation that India must be granted self-government at no distant date. In 1915, when the Congress met at Bombay and for the first time exchanged visits with the All-India Muslim League, Sir S. P. Sinha asked that the British Government should announce the goal of Indian government. Lord Chelmsford, who succeeded Lord Hardinge as governor-general in 1916, found no difficulty in holding that the endowment of British India as an integral part of the British Empire with self-government was the goal of British rule, but the specific steps presented difficulty. Apparently at this time the government of India[1] was not prepared to go further than the increase in the representative character and powers of the municipal councils and district boards, the increase in the number of Indians in the higher administrative posts, and the paving of the way for the increase in the powers of the legislatures by lowering the qualifications for the franchise and increasing the numbers of the elected members. The latter suggestion did not evoke any hearty approval by Mr. Chamberlain, who criticized the idea of increasing the numbers of elected members while denying them power of control.

On the other hand, far wider plans were proposed by nineteen members of the Indian legislature in October 1916, and in December Congress and the Muslim League formally approved a scheme devised by representatives of the two parties in November. This plan demanded the increase of the numbers of the councils to 150 for that of India, and from 50 to 125, according to the size of the provinces, four-fifths in each case to be elected on a wide franchise. There was to be wide provincial autonomy as suggested by the government of India in 1911, certain heads of income and expenditure were to be imperial, there might be imperial legislation on matters of common interest, and a vague power of superintendence was left to the Indian government, but in the main the provinces were to be free. Each legislature was to elect its own president, supplementary questions were to be freely asked and motions

[1] Ronaldshay, *Lord Curzon*, iii, 165.

for the adjournment permitted as a means of raising discussions. Resolutions passed must bind the government unless vetoed by the governor in council, but would become binding if repassed after a year's interval. But no Bill or clause or resolution might be passed if opposed by three-quarters of the members of any community. The executive government would be conducted by a governor, not chosen from the service, with a council, half of which would be elected by the elective members of the council. Of vital historical importance is the fact that Muslims were to be accorded representation in certain proportions which gave them excess members in provinces where they were a minority chosen by special electorates, but were to be debarred from electing members in other electorates. Thus was perpetuated by deliberate Hindu and Muhammadan agreement the principle of communal electorates which had been accepted by Lord Minto.[1]

2. THE MONTAGU-CHELMSFORD SCHEME

The British Government, anxious to meet Indian aspirations but wholly at a loss how best to proceed, on August 20th 1917 committed itself to a formula, whose final form was due to Lord Curzon:[2] 'The policy of His Majesty's government, with which the government of India are in complete accord, is that of the increasing association of Indians in every branch of the administration and the gradual development of self-governing institutions with a view to the progressive realization of responsible government in India as an integral part of the British Empire.' It was made clear that the ideal could be attained only in successive stages to be controlled by the governments, and that advance must be conditioned by the progress in co-operation received and the confidence inspired. The term 'responsible government' was of course vital. It had a perfectly well-known meaning, as connoting the form of government in the great Dominions, and, if Lord Curzon did not understand that it essentially implied parliamentary government, his ignorance was surprising. At any rate Mr. Montagu,

[1] Keith, *Indian Policy*, ii, 116.

[2] Ronaldshay, iii, 167. Quite unintelligibly Curzon did not realize that responsible government meant Parliamentary democracy (ibid., 168–74).

who was deputed with a small committee to consult the Indian government and politicians, had no doubts on the score. He succeeded in having his own way with the governor-general, Lord Chelmsford, and the report which bears their names is certainly an expression of his personality.[1] It is dominated by a complete belief in the necessity of applying to India the traditions of British democracy, ignoring the fact that India is divided by race, sect, and religion in a manner which has no parallel in those countries, mainly British, in which parliamentary democracy has been effectively worked. The idea that men should, like the average Indian peasant, remain satisfied with material interests and good government was repudiated by Montagu, who was anxious to complete their humanity by stirring them to demand control of their destinies through the ballot-box. It is interesting if vain to conjecture whether he would have held the same views fifteen years later when the failure of European nations to work democratic institutions effectively was becoming a patent fact.

The report[2] rejected the proposals of congress as unsuitable. Without accepting the dogma of the necessity of perpetual British control, it recognized that for the time being the government of India must remain in essence unchanged, better machinery for criticism and expression of public opinion on its actions being supplied. Full provincial autonomy in the same way was premature. The election of half the executive was clumsy, and responsibility to the electorate could be obtained in more orthodox ways. The provincial councils could not be given full control of legislation and finance until it was possible to give full responsible government, and it would result in hopeless confusion to bind any government to act on resolutions. There is in fact no doubt that the congress scheme was unworkable. There remained the possibility, suggested unofficially by both Indian and European authority, of setting up smaller areas than the provinces in which genuine responsible government could be given to administrations and legislatures entrusted with local government, primary education, public works, etc. But this suggestion was necessarily rejected as resulting in constant friction between these new bodies, claiming

[1] *An Indian Diary* (1930). [2] Parl. Paper, Cd. 9109.

to represent the people, and the provincial governments essentially official. Hence the report adopted a compromise. In each province there should be a governor who would be assisted by an executive council of two members, one an Indian, and by one or more ministers responsible to the legislature. There would be distinct spheres of action, subjects reserved and transferred, and in regard to the latter the governor would normally take the advice of a minister, though he would have a real discretion to refuse such advice. He would also encourage joint action as far as possible, especially where action taken in one department might affect that to be taken in another. Subjects to be transferred might include local government, education (except universities), medical and sanitary matters, agriculture, public works (except major irrigation works), excise, and provincial taxation. The legislatures would be largely increased in size, with direct election wherever possible. Communal representation was denounced, with a grudging exception for the Muslims, in view of the existing practice. In proportion as the power of the legislatures to control action by the government was increased, that of the British Parliament must cease to be exercised, and it must be clearly recognized that responsible government was the inevitable outcome of the Minto-Morley reforms, despite the disclaimers of both these officers.

The report when published in July 1918 was not welcomed by official opinion which regarded the form of dyarchy suggested as certain to operate with the maximum friction and inefficiency. But the plan suggested in lieu by five heads of provinces in January 1919[1] was clearly of minor value. It suggested that the executive councils should be constituted in equal numbers of officials and of Indians elected by the elected members of the councils, and that the government should remain unitary, the governor allocating portfolios and exercising the right to decide on his own discretion after hearing advice. Further advance would take the form of increasing the number of Indians in the council, giving them increased functions and surrendering the right of overruling the council. But it must be admitted that this plan had the plain defect that it could

[1] Cf. Parl. Paper, Cd. 123 (1919).

hardly be deemed to lead to responsible government. Hence it is not surprising that the Home Government and the government of India agreed in accepting in principle the Montagu-Chelmsford scheme as preferable. It was supplemented by the inquiries of a committee which visited India to suggest franchises[1] and constituencies on the basis of the suggestions of the local governments, with due regard to the possibility of polling effectively the votes conceded. In rural districts the problem to be solved was to devise means for putting the well-to-do peasants on the register, and, while this proved extremely difficult, it was found impossible to secure effective means of electing representatives of the lower castes in many cases. Then prolonged consideration was also given to the question of the division of functions between centre and provinces and of provincial subjects as reserved and transferred, and the financial relations between centre and provinces received special attention, while a strong committee under Lord Crewe examined the subject of the home administration of Indian affairs.[2] Most important of all was the decision to refer the governmental proposals embodied in a Bill to a joint select committee[3] of the two houses of Parliament. This step was a signal admission of the importance of the House of Lords in this regard from its wealth of men with experience of the government of the United Kingdom and of dependencies. The committee sat from July to October 1919, and examined seventy witnesses, but none who could speak as representatives of the rural or working classes, of the landlords, or the martial elements. Its main conclusion was entirely in keeping with the views of the government; the time had come to give to India a generous grant of self-government, with the opportunity so to exercise it as to indicate to future parliaments the justice of according further liberty. That was, unhappily, a point of view which struck no responsive note in the hearts of Indian politicians who did not realize that they were being presented with an opportunity unique in character of proving their full capacity to exercise power wisely, and could only see the mass of restrictions imposed on the measure of self-government conceded.

[1] Parl. Papers, Cmd. 141, 176.
[2] Parl. Paper, Cmd. 207 of 1919.
[3] H. of C. Paper, 203 of 1919.

8. THE GOVERNMENT OF INDIA ACT 1919

(a) THE PROVINCIAL GOVERNMENTS

The essential novelty of the Act[1] was the provision for rules to classify subjects as central, under the government of India, and provincial, and to divide provincial subjects into 'reserved' and 'transferred', to be dealt with by the governor in council and the governor acting with a minister or ministers respectively. The latter distinction involved the alteration of the form of government of the United Provinces, the Punjab, Bihar and Orissa, the Central Provinces, and Assam, so that each fell under a governor with an executive council.[2] The number of members of such councils remained four, but only one need be a civilian of twelve years' standing, so that it was open to reduce the council to two, one an Indian. The joint committee while insisting that the character of any decision as that of the governor in council or the governor acting with ministers should be made clear urged the adoption of the practice of close consultation between the two sides of the government, whose actions might at any time seriously interact; thus a restrictive excise system such as might be anticipated in certain provinces would clearly impose special duties on the forces of law and order. In debate the committee pointed out members of council and ministers should act together, but no minister or councillor should be required to speak or vote for a policy which he disapproved. This obviously emphasized the differentiation between a unitary government even if composed of diverse elements and the system of dyarchy.

The question of finance presented great difficulties. The existing system under which there was no need for an annual Finance Bill, sources of revenue being relatively stable, did not require immediate variation, but it was obviously imperative to devise some way of deciding as to expenditure. The most logical plan would have been to imitate what had more or less tentatively been done as regards the relations of the centre and the provinces, and to assign certain revenues to the transferred subjects, so that ministers would have been responsible for

[1] 9 & 10 Geo. V, c. 101.
[2] S. 3. Burma was added under s. 15 (1) with effect from January 2nd 1923.

making the best use of the money in the knowledge that they must ask for fresh taxation if expansion of services were desired, which could not be effected by economies. This view had the support of the government of India and of common sense. But the joint report and the select committee decided in favour of annual distribution of revenue by discussion, with power to the governor to allocate if there were division of opinion which could not be overcome. It insisted, however, that the ministers were not to be allowed to use the financial issue as an indirect method of controlling the reserved heads, but of this there could hardly be any direct danger. It left unsolved the clear difficulty that must arise regarding fresh taxation if ministers were disinclined to support it on the score that it was really needed to provide for increased expenditure of which they disapproved on reserved subjects.

It was obviously necessary to provide for the case of the refusal of the legislature to pass measures deemed necessary for reserved subjects, and in this matter the select committee improved on the joint report. The latter had proposed that the governor might certify that a Bill of such a nature was essential to the discharge of his responsibility for the peace or tranquillity of the province or any part thereof or for the discharge of his responsibility for the reserved subjects. The Bill would then be referred to a grand committee of from 40 to 50 per cent of the legislature, with a government majority nominated by the governor, but at least one-third must be non-officials. The plan was singularly unsuitable, and might have resulted in the government being defeated even in grand committee. Lord Carmichael insisted that direct responsibility was wiser, and this accordingly was accepted. The governor may certify that a measure is essential for the discharge of his responsibility, in which case it becomes an Act. But such a measure must be reserved for the signification of the pleasure of the Crown by the governor-general, and be laid before both Houses of Parliament before assent, unless the governor-general held that a state of emergency justified his assent forthwith. But such an Act must be laid before Parliament and might be disallowed by the Crown.[1] No similar power was

[1] S. 13.

granted as regards transferred subjects. In case of emergency the necessary legislation might be passed by the central legislature or enacted as an ordinance by the governor-general.

In the case of finance the provision of funds was safeguarded in the case of reserved subjects by authorizing the government to restore a grant which the council refused to pass or reduced if the governor certified that the expenditure was essential for the discharge of his responsibility for a reserved subject.[1] In the case of transferred subjects no such wide power was given, but the governor was given power in case of emergency to authorize such expenditure as might in his opinion be necessary for the safety or tranquillity of the province or for the carrying on of any department.[2]

Subject to these wide safeguards a genuine effort was made in the Act to afford a measure of responsible government. Ministers[3] were to be selected by the governor and to hold office during his pleasure. This gave them a less secure position than the joint report had contemplated, since under it they were to be appointed for the duration of the council. Moreover, their salaries were left to the discretion of the council, which thus was enabled to destroy the tenure of office of any minister by withholding his pay. Moreover, no minister might hold office for more than six months unless he was or became an elected member of the legislature, a provision imitating certain Dominion usage but without special value, since plainly membership of the council was virtually essential under the plan. The governor was to be guided by the advice of his ministers unless he saw sufficient cause to dissent from their opinion, in which case he might require action to be taken otherwise than in accordance with that advice. Moreover, to meet the case of resignation of a minister and inability at once to replace him, rules might be made for the temporary administration in such an event of the subjects concerned. The governor might also appoint council secretaries from the non-official members of the council to assist the government in such manner as he might direct.

The provincial legislative councils fell to be largely increased in size.[4] Madras was given 127 members, Bombay 111, Bengal

[1] S. 11 (2) (*a*). [2] S. 11 (2) (*b*). [3] S. 4. [4] S. 7 and rules thereunder.

139, United Provinces 123, Punjab 93, Bihar and Orissa 103, Central Provinces 70, and Assam 50. The number of official members was not to exceed 20 per cent, those elected must make 70 per cent at least. It was reluctantly felt necessary to continue communal electorates for Muslims and to grant them to Europeans, to Anglo-Indians, and to Indian Christians where their numbers rendered such action proper; thus Christians were provided for in Madras alone, Anglo-Indians there and in Bengal, Europeans in all provinces save the Punjab. Central Provinces, and Assam. There were also special constituencies for the Universities except in Assam, for landholders, and for commerce and industry including mining and planting. Thus in Madras 13 seats fell to special, 20 to communal electorates, leaving 65 for general constituencies, rural and urban. In Bengal there were 21 for special electorates, 46 communal and 46 general; in the Punjab 7 special, 44 communal, including 12 Sikhs, and only 20 general. The figures show the essential difficulty, the fact that, while in the other provinces Hindus predominated, Muslims were in strong force in Bengal and the Punjab, while the Sikhs were of much greater importance than their numbers suggested as a martial race indispensable to the recruiting of the Indian army. A further complication arose in the necessity of reserving 28 seats for non-brahmans in Madras, in view of the predominance there of the brahmans who, though only 3 per cent of the electorate, had secured practically all the representation in the legislature in the past and held three times as many posts as all the other Hindus. The reservation proved needless. A like difficulty was raised in the case of Marathas in Bombay.

For the franchise certain general principles were laid down for the exclusion of women until decided—as was the case—otherwise by the provinces, the restriction of the vote to persons aged twenty-one or over, the exclusion of persons of unsound mind, and of persons not British subjects or subjects of the Indian states. A property qualification was required based on land revenue where such revenue is periodically revised, on local rates in other cases, on municipal rates in urban areas, and on income tax. But all officers, commissioned and non-commissioned, of the Indian army, retired or pensioned, were given the vote. In the case of membership similar disqualifications were provided to those for the franchise, but in addition a member must be twenty-five years of age, and must not be an undischarged insolvent or a legal practitioner under discharge or suspension, and conviction of crime or of illegal corrupt practices in connexion with an election was in certain conditions a bar.

The duration of the councils was fixed at three years, subject to the power of the governor to dissolve at any time and to extend it for one year in special circumstances.[1] After dissolution a new council must be summoned within six, or with the secretary of state's permission nine, months. The governor was authorized to summon and prorogue the council, while the presiding officer might adjourn it. The presiding officer had only a casting vote. As a sign of the new régime the governor ceased to preside, and for the first four years a president appointed by the governor presided; thereafter the president was elected by the council, which could remove him, in both cases subject to the governor's concurrence.[2]

The powers[3] of the councils extended to legislation for the peace and good government of the territories in the province, including the right to repeal or alter any law made for the province before or after the Act of 1919 by any authority in British India. But this power was subject to the rule that the previous sanction of the governor-general was required before the legislature made or took into consideration any law (*a*) imposing new taxation unless the taxation fell within specified heads; (*b*) affecting the public debt or customs duties or any other tax or duty imposed by the central legislature; (*c*) affecting military, naval, or air forces; (*d*) affecting the relations of the government with foreign princes or states; (*e*) regulating any central subject or any provincial subject declared to be subject to central legislation. Such sanction was also necessary before affecting any power vested in the governor-general in council by any law or altering any law made before the commencement of the Act which was declared by rules to be unalterable without prior sanction or any later central

[1] S. 8. Power was extended by 23 & 24 Geo. V, c. 23, to allow of constitutional changes.

[2] S. 9. This sanction was given in the case of Burma in 1935.

[3] S. 10

legislation forbidding alteration. But the fact that assent was given to a Bill passed without due sanction was to render the omission of no effect. Finally, the council could not make any law affecting any Act of Parliament.

The limitations imposed by earlier legislation on the functions of the councils were swept away, but special rules were laid down for finance.[1] Each year a statement of estimated revenue and expenditure was to be submitted to the council, and the government's proposed expenditure was to be submitted in the form of demands for grants. The council might assent, refuse assent, or reduce the amount asked for either by reducing the total of the grant or by omitting or reducing any of the items. No appropriation could be proposed save on the recommendation of the governor, thus maintaining the principle which forbids members of the legislature to suggest expenditure, since they have no responsibility for the budget. There have been noted above the powers of the government to disregard the refusal of the council to vote items. There were exempted from consideration by the council: (1) contributions payable to the central government; (2) interest and sinking fund on loans; (3) expenditure the amount of which was prescribed by law; (4) salaries and pensions of persons appointed by or with the approval of the Crown or by the secretary of state in council; and (5) salaries of judges of the high court and the advocate-general. The governor was given the power to decide whether any expenditure fell within these categories.

A general power was given to the governor to prevent further proceedings on any Bill, clause, or amendment if he deemed that the safety or tranquillity of the province or any part thereof or of another province was affected. Moreover, rules could be made to regulate the proceedings of the council, and where rules made no provision standing orders might be made with the assent of the governor. In any case there was to be freedom of speech subject to the rules and the standing orders, and no person should be liable to proceedings in any court for any speech or vote in the council.

The governor was given power to assent to a Bill, refuse assent or return for reconsideration with any suggested

[1] S. 11.

amendments or to reserve.[1] He was required[2] to reserve Bills containing provisions not previously sanctioned by the governor-general affecting religion, Universities, making a reserved matter transferred, providing for the construction of light railways or tramways, or affecting land revenue, and might reserve matters affecting any matter with which he was specially charged by his instrument of instructions, or central matters, or the interests of another province. A reserved Bill might with the governor-general's assent be returned to the council for consideration within six months and again presented with or without change to the governor. Or the governor-general might assent within six months; failing such action or the return of the Bill, it was deemed to be dropped. An Act assented to by the governor required the assent of the governor-general to be valid; that assent might be withheld or the Act be reserved by the governor-general when it would take effect only if approved by the Crown in council.[3] Any Act might be disallowed by the same authority.

The provisions of the Act were rendered effective by a mass of regulations made under the Act[4] by the Indian government with the sanction of the secretary of state in council and the approval of both Houses of Parliament. The transferred subjects[5] were declared to be local self-government; medical administration; public health and sanitation and vital statistics; pilgrimages within British India; education other than European and Anglo-Indian education and certain specified institutions, including the Benares Hindu University, the Aligarh Muslim University, chiefs' colleges and institutions for the education of children of governmental servants; public works; agriculture; civil veterinary department; fisheries; co-operative societies; forests in Bombay and Burma; excise; registration of deeds and documents; registration of births, deaths, and marriages; religious and charitable endowments, development of industries, including industrial research and technical education; stores and stationery required for transferred departments; adulteration of foodstuffs and other articles; weights and

[1] S. 12.
[2] Notification No. 313-S., December 16th 1920. In Coorg all Bills must be reserved (January 28th 1924).
[3] S. 43. [4] S. 2. [5] Notification No. 308-S., December 16th 1920.

measures; libraries, museums, and zoological gardens; and in Burma[1] regulation of betting and gambling; prevention of cruelty to animals and the protection of animals and birds; control of dramatic performance and cinematographs, subject to Indian legislation as to exhibition of films; and pounds and the prevention of cattle trespass. There were various limitations even of these powers, but their importance was minimized by the fundamental rule[2] that no Act of a province or of the Indian legislature was to be deemed invalid because it went beyond the sphere of such legislation, and in the same way no governor's Act on a reserved matter was to be deemed invalid because it touched on a transferred matter. This was natural, since the governor-general was made an integral part of the authority of legislation.

The choice of topics was dictated by the consideration of the matters which most easily could be entrusted to ministers and which offered them the greatest scope for social and economic development, the nation-building activities, and the sphere of social reform, the latter a sphere in which British officials could not safely operate. Hence the power of superintendence, direction, and control of the governor-general in council was in respect to transferred subjects to be exercised only (1) to safeguard the administration of central subjects; (2) to decide disputes between two provinces; (3) to safeguard his position in respect of duties regarding the High Commissionership for India, the raising of provincial loans, the civil service, and any rules made with the authority of or by the secretary of state in council.[3] In the same spirit the intervention of the secretary of state in council was limited to the same heads, with the addition of the safeguarding of imperial interests, and the determination of the position of the Government of India in matters arising between India and other parts of the British Empire.[4]

To the official side of the government of the provinces were ascribed matters frequently if inaccurately described as law and order, and a wide control of finance. Thus the reserved subjects included water-supplies, irrigation, and canals; land

[1] Notification No. 519-V, February 2nd 1923.
[2] Act, s. 16 (2).
[3] Devolution Rules, December 16th 1920, s. 49.
[4] Notification No. 835-G, December 14th 1920.

revenue administration; famine relief; land acquisition; administration of justice, including courts, civil and criminal, subject to Indian legislation as to high courts and criminal courts; law reports; the administrator-general and official trustees; non-judicial stamps subject to Indian legislation and judicial stamps subject to such legislation as regards fees in the original jurisdiction of high courts; development of mineral resources; factories, settlement of labour disputes, electricity, boilers, gas, smoke nuisance, and welfare of labour, including provident funds, industrial insurance, and housing subject in most cases to Indian legislation; ports other than major ports; inland navigation subject to Indian legislation; police, betting and gambling, prevention of cruelty to animals, protection of wild birds and animals, control of poisons subject to Indian legislation; control of motor-vehicles on the same condition, and control of cinematographs subject to Indian legislation as to sanction of films; control of newspapers, books, and printing presses, subject to Indian legislation; coroners; excluded areas; criminal tribes; and European vagrancy subject to Indian legislation; prisons and reformatories subject to Indian legislation; pounds and prevention of cattle trespass; treasure-trove; provincial government presses; elections for Indian and provincial legislatures; regulation of professions, subject to Indian legislation; local audit fund; control of government services; sources of revenue not included under other heads; borrowing of money; any matter declared by the governor-general in council to be of a merely local or private nature, e.g. gazetteers, statistics, and ancient manuscripts; and any matters relating to central subjects on which powers were given to local governments by law.

Doubts as to the classification of any subject as provincial were solved by the governor-general in council, as to that of any subject as reserved or transferred by the governor, who when any matter affected both sides of his government was instructed to have it considered jointly, but must finally decide in which department action was to be taken. Officers dealing with transferred subjects were controlled by the governor with a minister, but were safeguarded by requiring the personal concurrence of the governor in matters affecting emoluments or pensions, formal censure or unfavourable replies to memorials, and his assent was necessary also for the posting of All-India service officers. Further, each government was required to employ on such conditions as the secretary of state in council thought fit officers of the Indian Medical Service, a rule inserted to secure due facilities for medical attention to officials in the service.

Elaborate arrangements were provided as to finance.[1] The provinces were granted as sources of revenue (1) balances to their credit at the time of the Act taking effect; (2) receipts from provincial subjects; (3) a share in the growth of revenue from income tax collected in the province so far as the increase was due to an increase in the amount of income assessed; (4) recoveries of loans and advances made by the local government and of interest thereon; (5) payments made by the Indian government or any province for services rendered or otherwise; (6) proceeds of taxes imposed by the province; (7) proceeds of loans; and (8) any other sources assigned by the Indian government. The Berar revenues were given to the Central Provinces, but conditionally on proper sums being expended for its due administration. All government revenue was to be paid into the public account, of which the governor-general in council was custodian, and the latter was authorized to make rules regarding the mode of dealing with the account. Provision was made for annual contributions from the provinces to the centre, but these it became possible to remit in 1927–8. The central government was also authorized to limit the extent to which any province might draw on its balances, but in that case interest had to be paid. Provision was made for the rate of interest on sums due to the centre on provincial loan account of April 1st 1921, and for the liquidation of the sum due in twelve years. Capital expenditure by the centre on irrigation and other works handed over to a province was to be treated as an advance on which interest was to be paid, and the centre might lend sums on agreed terms as to interest and repayment fixed by the centre.

Local governments were also required to make annual payments at specified rates to a famine insurance fund, which

[1] P. Banerjea, *Provincial Finance* (1929).

could be used only for direct relief or construction of protective irrigation or other works for famine relief or on loans to cultivators. Interest was made payable by the centre on the sums to the credit of the province each year, and assignments could be suspended when a sum equal to six times the annual assignment had been accumulated.

Proposals for taxation or borrowing must be considered by the whole government, but the decision must be arrived at by the side of the government which initiated the proposal. For expenditure in the event of dispute the governor could decide by allocating proportions of the revenue and balances; failing agreement or allocation the proportions of the preceding year were made applicable; in fact, agreement was preferred. The local government was authorized to sanction expenditure on transferred subjects up to the amount voted by the legislature, and in the case of non-votable items subject to any consent required from the centre or the Home Government. Control, however, was exercised by the Home Government in the form of forbidding the local government to include certain matters in any demand for grants without the sanction of that government. The items in question were matters affecting any permanent post usually held by members of the All-India service; the creation of a permanent post on pay exceeding 1,200 rupees a month or the extension beyond two years of such a temporary post or the creation of a temporary post with pay exceeding 4,000 rupees a month; the grant of extraordinary pensions or gratuities except in certain specified minor cases; and expenditure irregularly incurred on imported stationery. Request in these matters must be sent through the centre for the sanction of the Home Government.

To secure the effective working of the financial system the creation of a finance department under a member of the executive council was required in every province. Its head was a financial secretary to whom if ministers desired could be added a joint secretary specially concerned with the finance of transferred subjects and proposals for borrowing or taxation made by ministers. It was made responsible for the local loans account, the famine insurance fund, the examination of all proposals for the increase or reduction of taxation, the examination of proposals for borrowing and the raising of loans sanctioned, the laying down of rules for keeping of accounts, and the preparation of the budget and supplementary estimates. It was required to receive reports from the audit officers of unauthorized expenditure, and to require the department concerned either to obtain sanction or to cease, and it prepared and laid before the committee of the legislature on public accounts, which was annually appointed, the audit and appropriation accounts, calling special attention to unauthorized expenditure. The committee normally was constituted to the extent of two-thirds of members chosen by the unofficial members of the council, and its procedure was based on that of the corresponding committee of the British House of Commons.[1] The power of approving transfers within a grant between major, minor, and subordinate heads was given to the department, ministers and members of council being restricted to transfers between subordinate heads. It must be consulted on all proposals affecting establishment charges, on all grants and concessions of land, water-power, mineral, and forest rights; on abandonment of revenue budgeted for and on proposed increases of expenditure. When consulted it was empowered to require that its report should be laid before the governor for the order of the local government, and the governor might direct the laying of the report before the public accounts committee.

As regards borrowing for permanent works, for irrigation, for famine relief, for the provincial loan account and repayment or consolidation of loans the assent of the Indian government was requisite for any loan to be raised in India, that of the Home Government for any loan to be raised outside India, the Indian government being consulted in that case.

As regards expenditure on reserved matters the sanction of the Home Government was required in those cases where it was requisite in respect of transferred subjects, and in addition it was requisite for capital expenditure on various classes of public works where the interests of more than one local government were concerned, where the original estimate

[1] Finance Committees to advise the Finance Department on issues referred were set up at the centre, Bombay, Madras, United Provinces, Punjab, and Burma, and later in Assam; Cmd. 3568, pp. 370, 371.

exceeded fifty lakhs of rupees, where a revised estimate exceeded by more than 15 per cent an approved estimate, where a further revised estimate was proposed; for changes of establishment costing more than five lakhs, or if the legislature had recommended the charges exceeding fifteen lakhs; and for certain expenditure on the governor, his residence, and transport for his or other high officials' use.

The powers of the legislatures to impose fresh taxes[1] were restricted by rules to the case of taxation of betting or gambling; of advertisements; of amusements; on specified luxuries; registration fees and stamp duties other than those of which the amount was fixed by Indian legislation. They could also authorize without previous sanction of the governor-general taxation for local purposes in the form of tolls, taxes on land or land values; buildings, vehicles or boats, animals, menials and domestic servants, octrois, terminal taxes on import or export, taxes on trades, professions and callings, on private markets and in respect of services rendered such as water, lighting, sanitary, drainage and market rates. In other cases prior sanction was necessary and the free activity of the legislatures in general legislation was distinctly reduced by the length of the list of Acts which they might not affect without such sanction, for the rules included in this list most of the important legislation of the Indian legislature.

In finance, therefore, and in legislation the freedom left to the provincial legislatures was very narrowly limited, for the control of the governor-general in council precluded much freedom on the part of the governor, who was thus compelled as well as authorized closely to control the actions of his ministers. Nevertheless it was intended that ministerial control should be preserved whenever possible. While it was recognized that provision must be made for the case where a ministry was vacant for any cause, it was provided that the portfolio should if possible be given temporarily to another minister, and if the governor had to act himself he must report to the governor-general in council that an emergency had arisen, compelling such action, and it was expected that a minister should be appointed so soon as possible.

[1] Notification No. 311-S, December 16th 1920.

In addition to provincial functions proper it was provided that the governor in council might be employed by the Indian government in the performance of central functions, the cost of such action to be defrayed from central funds. Where a department served both central and provincial purposes, and there was divergence of view as to the proportion of cost to be borne by each, the secretary of state in council was given the decision.

(b) THE GOVERNMENT OF INDIA

The joint committee went farther than the report in reconstructing the Indian legislature. The report had contemplated that the second chamber, the Council of State, should be mainly nominee, only 21 out of 250 members being elected, chiefly by the non-official members of the provincial legislatures. It would have occupied a minor position in ordinary legislation, measures passed in the assembly being put before it, a joint session following if the council desired amendments which the Assembly did not wish to accept. The joint committee preferred that the Council should be placed on the footing of an ordinary second chamber, and rejected the idea that it should be elected in part by the provincial legislatures, a decision which was to affect in an important degree the constitution of 1935. Hence the Council was composed[1] of 19 official and 6 unofficial nominated members and 34 elected members, general 20, Muslim 10, Sikh 1, and European 3. The franchise was fixed at a high property qualification. The president was appointed by the governor-general, and nominated as a member of council, an experienced British parliamentarian being selected. The Legislative Assembly was composed of members of whom not less than five-sevenths were elected, while of the rest one-third must be non-officials. The first president was chosen for four years by the governor-general, the office thereafter being filled by election with his approval. There were in the first Assembly[2] 143 members, officials 25, non-officials nominated 15, and elected 103.[3] Of the latter 51 were returned for general

[1] Act of 1919, s. 18, and rules.
[2] S. 19 and rules. [3] In 1934 the figures were 26, 13, and 106; Cmd. 4939.

constituencies, 30 for Muslim constituencies, 2 represented Sikhs, 7 landowners, 9 Europeans, and 4 represented Indian commerce. In the case of the Assembly as of the Council a high franchise was required, though of much more generous type, women being admitted. In 1934 the electorate was 1,415,892, but only 81,602 women.

The duration of the Council was fixed at five, of the Assembly at three years.[1] The governor-general was empowered to dissolve either house separately, and to extend their existence if necessary; thus the Assembly of 1930 was continued to 1934. After dissolution a new chamber must be summoned within six, or, with the secretary of state's approval, nine, months. The governor-general was authorized to summon and prorogue, and the presiding officer to adjourn the chamber; to him was accorded only a casting vote.

As in the case of the provincial councils, no official was permitted to stand for election to the legislature,[2] and any non-official ceased to be a member on appointment to office. An elected member of either chamber ceased to be so on election to the other chamber, and if any person were elected to both, he was required to signify in writing his choice, whereupon his seat in the other chamber became vacant. Every member of the executive council must be nominated to one chamber or other, but had, further, the privilege of attending in and addressing the other chamber, but not of voting therein.

There were similar provisions regarding the making of rules of procedure and of standing orders. The existence of two houses necessitated deadlock provisions, but all that was laid down was that, if either chamber did not within six months accept, with or without agreed amendments, a Bill from the other, the governor-general might at his discretion summon a joint session.[3]

In finance[4] it was required that the estimated annual revenue and expenditure should be laid before the legislature; all initiative of appropriation was reserved to the governor-general, but certain matters were not merely excluded from the vote of the assembly but also from discussion without his

[1] S. 21. [2] S. 22. [3] S. 24. [4] S. 25.

sanction: (1) interest and sinking-fund charges on loans; (2) expenditure the amount of which was prescribed by law; (3) salaries and pensions of persons appointed by the King or the secretary of state in council;[1] (4) salaries of chief commissioners and judicial commissioners; and (5) expenditure classified by the governor-general in council as ecclesiastical, political, and defence. The governor-general was given final power to decide whether any expenditure fell within the categories mentioned.

The governor-general in council's demands might be accepted, refused, or diminished by the Assembly, but he might declare that any demand was essential to the discharge of his responsibilities and act as if assent had been given, and he could further authorize any expenditure necessary in his view for the safety or tranquillity of British India or any part thereof.

In the case of failure by the chambers to pass legislation in the form recommended by the governor-general he might certify that the passage of the Bill was essential for the safety, tranquillity, or interests of British India or some part thereof, in which case the Bill would become law forthwith if already accepted by one house, or on being accepted by the house which had not yet considered it; failing this it would become law on his signature. Such an Act had to be laid before both Houses of Parliament before it could be assented to by the Crown and become operative, but it could be given immediate effect by the governor-general if a state of emergency existed.[2]

To the restrictions already existing on the action of the legislature were added the requirement of prior sanction of the governor-general to the introduction of any Bill dealing with provincial subjects which were not made subject to Indian legislation; repealing or amending any provincial Act; or repealing or amending any Act or ordinance of the governor-general. The governor-general was also given power to prevent proceedings on any Bill or amendment by certifying that it affected the safety or tranquillity of British India or any part thereof.[3]

[1] This provision was expanded by 15 & 16 Geo. V, c. 83, to cover payments made by order of the Government on appeal.

[2] S. 26.

[3] S. 27.

The powers of the legislature were thus largely expanded through the representative character of the Assembly, and it was made a more effective means of criticizing and holding the government within lines of action approved by Indian feeling. The executive, however, remained wholly free from direct authority of the legislature, and the changes[1] made in it were simply intended to strengthen it in order to secure greater efficiency, all the more necessary with a legislature so strengthened. The limit of numbers was removed, and the qualification of the legal member enlarged by permitting the appointment of a pleader of the high court for ten years, the original five years being similarly extended for barristers and advocates. Power[2] was also given to the governor-general to appoint council secretaries who might assist the executive councillors in the legislature, the idea being that thus closer contact might be established between the legislature and the executive. It was understood, though not provided by law, that half of the executive council would normally be Indian.

The subjects which were confided to the central legislative and executive control were as follows:

> 'Defence of India and all matters connected with His Majesty's Naval, Military and Air Forces in India, or with His Majesty's Indian Marine Service, or with any other force raised in India, other than military and armed police wholly maintained by local Governments; naval and military works and cantonments; external relations, including naturalization and aliens, and pilgrimages beyond India; relations with States in India; political charges; communications to the extent described under the following heads, namely—(*a*) railways and extra municipal tramways, in so far as they are not classified as provincial subjects; (*b*) aircraft and all matters connected therewith; and (*c*) inland waterways, to an extent to be declared by rules made by the Governor-General in Council or by or under legislation by the Indian legislature; Shipping and navigation, including shipping and navigation on inland waterways, in so far as declared to be a central subject; light-houses (including their

[1] S. 28. [2] S. 29.

approaches), beacons, lightships and buoys; port quarantine and marine hospitals; ports declared to be major ports by rule made by the Governor-General in Council or by or under legislation by the Indian legislature; posts, telegraphs and telephones, including wireless installations; customs, cotton, excise duties, income-tax, salt and other sources of All-India revenues; currency and coinage; public debt of India; savings Banks; the Indian Audit Department and excluded Audit Departments, as defined in rules framed under section 96D (1) of the Act; civil law, including laws regarding status, property, civil rights and liabilities, and civil procedure; commerce, including banking and insurance; trading companies and other associations; control of production, supply and distribution of any articles in respect of which control by a central authority is declared by rule made by the Governor-General in Council or by or under legislation by the Indian legislature to be essential in the public interest; development of industries, in cases where such development by a central authority is declared by order of the Governor-General in Council, made after consultation with the local Government or local Governments concerned, expedient in the public interest; control of cultivation and manufacture of opium, and sale of opium for export; stores and stationery, both imported and indigenous, required for Imperial Departments; control of petroleum and explosives; geological survey; control of mineral development, in so far as such control is reserved to the Governor-General in Council under rules made or sanctioned by the Secretary of State, and regulation of mines; botanical survey; inventions and designs; copyright; emigration from, and immigration into, British India, and inter-provincial migration; criminal law, including criminal procedure; central police organization; control of arms and ammunition; central agencies and institutions for research (including observatories) and for professional or technical training or promotion of special studies; ecclesiastical administration including European cemeteries; survey of India; archaeology; zoological survey; meteorology; census and statistics; all-India services; legislation in regard to any provincial subject, in so far as such subject is stated to be subject to legislation by the Indian legislature, and any powers relating to such subject reserved by legislation to the Governor-General in Council; territorial changes, other than inter-provincial, and declaration of law in connexion therewith; regulation of ceremonial titles, orders, precedence and civil uniform; immovable property acquired by, and maintained at the cost of, the Governor-General in Council; the Public Service Commission; all matters expressly excepted from inclusion among provincial subjects; all other matters not included among provincial subjects.'

(c) MINOR PROVINCES AND BACKWARD TRACTS

The proposals of the Report left for the direct control of the government of India the frontier provinces, the North-West Frontier Province and Baluchistan, and the smaller tracts of India such as Delhi, Coorg, and Ajmer-Merwara, while Burma was left out of account on the score that the people were in another stage of political development and problems were different. It was suggested that in these areas advisory councils might be associated with the personal administration of the chief commissioner. In addition attention was called to the fact that even in the eight provinces there were certain backward areas, generally the tracts mentioned in the schedules to the Scheduled Districts Act, 1874, which required specific treatment. The Act of 1919[1] therefore authorized the governor-general in council to declare any territory to be a backward tract, and with the sanction of the Home Government to direct that the Government of India Act should apply to the territory subject to such exceptions and modifications as he might prescribe. Thereafter, he might direct that any Act of the India legislature should not apply to the territory, or should apply only subject to such exceptions or modifications as he thought fit and might authorize the governor in council to give similar directions as regards any local Act. These areas, of course, remain subject to the existing powers of the making of regulations by the executive under the powers of the Government of India Act.[2] In accordance with these proposals certain areas,

[1] S. 15 (2). [2] S. 71, derived from the Act of 1870.

including in Madras the Laccadive Islands and Minicoy, in Bengal the Chittagong hill tracts, in the Punjab Spiti, in Burma all the backward tracts[1] and, in Bihar and Orissa, Angul were excluded from the legislative power of the central and the provincial legislatures, though the governor in council might apply provincial Acts subject to modifications; proposals for expenditure need not be submitted to the legislature, nor questions asked, or matters affecting tracts discussed therein. In the case of other tracts legislative power was not excluded, but Acts made were only to come into force to the extent determined by the central or local government. Darjeeling and Lahaul were otherwise totally excluded. In the other areas, including those of Assam, Chota Nagpur, the Santal Parganas, and Sambalpur, ministers were given authority over transferred subjects, subject to the power of the governor to protect backward classes. Some attempts, not very successful, were made to represent the interests of these tracts in the legislatures.

Of the other territories not dealt with by the Act, Burma was soon brought into the provincial system on the wish of her government and legislature.[2] In her case the proportion of elected members was put at 60 per cent, and the maximum number of members at ninety-two. Coorg was offered inclusion in Madras; when this proved unacceptable, there was created under existing authority a legislative council with the former drastically restricted powers as under the Acts of 1892 and 1909, consisting of fifteen elected and five nominated members.[3] The territory of Ajmer-Merwara, under a chief commissioner since 1871, Ajmer having from 1832 been associated with the North-Western Provinces, was held to be too small to allow of a legislature being created, and it remained accordingly subject to the central legislature, with power for the governor-general in council to make regulations under the Government of India Act, and to extend laws of other parts of India to it as a scheduled district under the Act of 1874 of the Indian legislature, which applies to every district placed under the system of regulations. The Andaman and Nicobar Islands were

[1] The governor assumed charge of the Shan states. In 1923 a Federated Council was formed.

[2] Notification 225, October 7th 1921, operative January 2nd 1923.

[3] Notifications F. 248, 22 I, October 30th 1923.

in like case, while Delhi remained under the régime of Act XIII of 1912.

The North-West Frontier Province, after discussion at the Round Table Conference, was given the status of a governor's province in April 1932, with a governor, executive councillor, minister, and a legislature of forty members, twenty-eight elected. A subsidy of a crore of rupees yearly was provided for three years.

Aden became a chief commissionership from April 8th 1932, for civil government, but for military and political affairs there and for the protectorate the chief commissioner was made subject to the British Government;[1] he was aided especially for protectorate business by a political secretary; his judicial assistant was drawn from the Indian Civil Service.

(*d*) THE SECRETARY OF STATE IN COUNCIL

The home administration of Indian affairs was examined by a committee under Lord Crewe, whose recommendations were in part modified by the joint committee. The essential proposal of the former body was the vesting of control of Indian government in the secretary of state alone, thus depriving the council of any controlling power. He would have been able to obtain advice from an advisory council. The joint committee, recognizing that this meant a very important step in relaxation of control was unwilling to go so far, and merely agreed to modifications of detail.[2] Thus the personnel of the council was reduced from ten to fourteen to eight to twelve, one half to be qualified by ten years' residence or service in India, and not merely British India. The term of office was reduced to five years, and payment was provided at £1,200 a year plus £600 for persons of Indian domicile, in order to render it easier to secure well-qualified Indians willing to serve. Weekly meetings gave place to monthly meetings and a wide discretion was given to the secretary of state in council to prescribe matters affecting the form of communications to India and from India. But no concession was made, directly at least, to the secretary of

[1] See 20 & 21 Geo. V, c. 2; Order in Council, August 15th 1929.

[2] Ss. 31, 32, 34. For the writer's views as member of the Crewe Committee see Cmd. 207, pp. 36–60.

state of power to withhold matters at his discretion from his council, as had been proposed in a Bill which Lord Crewe[1] had endeavoured to secure in 1914 but to which the House of Lords was clearly opposed. Nonetheless the position of the council was recognized as clearly subordinate to the secretary of state, with an exception to be noted below.

A change of great constitutional importance was made by providing that the salary of the secretary of state must be and that of his staff might be met from funds voted by Parliament. The principle by which India paid for the India Office was a relic of the days of the Company which had remained operative to save expense to the British treasury; it was disapproved by Lord Crewe's committee and the joint committee heartily concurred.

The secretary of state in council was authorized to restrict by rules[2] the power of superintendence, direction, and control vested in him, and such rules, if dealing with transferred subjects had immediate effect, but must be laid before both Houses of Parliament and rescinded if an address was passed by either House asking for annulment. Other rules were not to be effective until expressly approved after being laid in draft before the Houses. The Crewe committee urged that in any matter legislative or administrative the concurrence of the legislative assembly as regards non-official members and the government of India should carry with it approval of the Home Government unless the secretary of state felt that his responsibility to Parliament for the peace, order, and good government of India or paramount considerations of imperial policy required him to seek reconsideration of the issue by the Assembly. The joint committee favoured the growth of a convention that the secretary of state might consider that only in exceptional circumstances should he intervene in matters of purely Indian interest where the government of India and the legislature were in accord. In the case of tariffs it was suggested that a convention should be allowed to develop under which the government of India and the legislature might impose such duties as they desired without regard to the

[1] *House of Lords Debates*, XIV, 1574 ff.; contrast Curzon, XVI, 484.
[2] S. 33.

interests of British manufacturers, but with due consideration for Indian consumers as well as manufacturers. The concession thus made was very important, for the government of India was naturally more or less indifferent to the interests of British trade, especially as popularity with Indian politicians could easily be obtained, and it was natural that the Indian manufacturers, who had many friends in the legislature, should press for the adoption of a policy of high protection for their products which paid scant attention to the needs of consumers. The principle of acceptance of the combined view of the government and legislature of a province in transferred matters was accepted, and the joint committee recommended its adoption in respect of reserved matters also. It is dubious if in making these recommendations the joint committee intended that India should be at liberty to negative the idea of imperial preference, but the point was not specifically taken and the Indian government showed no desire to make it effective. Yet the joint committee had suggested that that intervention in fiscal matters was justified to safeguard the international obligations of the Empire or any fiscal arrangements within the Empire to which His Majesty's Government was a party, and the principle of imperial preference might well have been regarded as included in the latter head.

The many matters dealt with by rules under the Act were to be effected by rules made by the governor-general in council with the sanction of the secretary of state in council, and such rules were not alterable by any legislature. They must, however, be submitted after enactment to both Houses of Parliament and might be cancelled on the request of either house. In his discretion the secretary of state might present them in draft for approval by both Houses in which case they need not subsequently be laid.[1] In order to secure due consideration of rules laid before the Houses and of enactments similarly laid, the joint committee favoured the appointment of a joint committee of the Houses, and this course was duly adopted.

While the power of advising the disallowance or assent to Acts or Bills remained with the secretary of state in council, it was provided that the formal disallowance or assent should

[1] S. 44.

be expressed by the King in Council.[1] This change, recommended by the Crewe committee, was manifestly proper when the legislatures became representative.

By an important decision recommended by the Crewe committee it was resolved to separate the agency work of the India Office from its political business, and to establish by Order in Council a High Commissioner with such functions as might from time to time be imposed on him.[2] The High Commissioner thus differed in large measure from the officers representing the Dominions in London whose functions tended to increase in political importance.

(c) THE CIVIL SERVICES IN INDIA

Special provisions were felt necessary to regularize the position of the civil services in India, as they had developed in somewhat haphazard manner, and the advent of control by the legislatures even in minor degree rendered it essential to remove all legal doubts and to distribute control for the future.[3] All existing rules by whatever authority made were declared valid, but alterable by the rules to be made in future. The general power of making rules regarding the classification of the civil services in India, the methods of their recruitment and the conditions of their service, pay, and allowances, discipline and conduct, was vested in the secretary of state in council, who might delegate the power to make rules to the governor-general in council or to local governments and might authorize the Indian or local legislatures to regulate the public services, subject to the rule that any civil servant appointed before the commencement of the Act should retain his rights or receive equitable compensation therefor. Pensions similarly could not be varied to the disadvantage of existing rights. The general principle was laid down that every person in the civil service of the Crown held office at pleasure and might be employed in any manner required by a proper authority within the scope of his duty, but no person could be dismissed by an authority inferior to that by which he was appointed, and the secretary of state in council might reinstate any person

[1] S. 43. [2] S. 35. [3] S. 36.

dismissed. Any person appointed by the secretary of state in council was given a right to secure the review by the governor personally of any order by an official superior by which he believed himself to be wronged.

In imitation of the Civil Service Commission in the United Kingdom and like bodies in the Dominions power was given[1] to establish by Order in Council a Public Service Commission of not more than five members, to hold office for five years, but with eligibility for reappointment, and removable only by the secretary of state in council. Its functions were to be prescribed by rules by the secretary of state in council, and might extend not merely to recruitment as in the United Kingdom but to control. The secretary of state in council was also[2] authorized to facilitate the admission of Indians to the Indian Civil Service by making rules respecting the admission of persons domiciled in India. The interests of the services were in all these matters safeguarded in some degree by the rule that the majority of votes in council was required for action, while in the case of rules for admission of domiciled Indians to the service they must be laid before both Houses of Parliament for thirty days before taking effect.

Finally, the diminution in detailed control of finance by the India Office was in part compensated for by the provision that no office might be added to or removed from the civil service, and no remuneration varied, without consultation by the government concerned with a finance authority designated in rules,[3] and the secretary of state in council was authorized to appoint an auditor-general with such functions as might be assigned to him. These rules and all those made regarding the civil services required the assent of a majority of votes at a council meeting, and formed part of the independent functions assigned to the secretary of state in council.[4]

The structure created by Parliament was obviously so complex that revision must be contemplated. It was thought fit to give a breathing space of ten years from the passing of the Act. Thereafter the secretary of state with the concurrence of both Houses of Parliament was to appoint, with the approval of the

[1] S. 38. Commissions were provided for Madras (Act XI of 1929) and the Punjab (Act II of 1932).

[2] S. 37.

[3] S. 39.

[4] S. 40.

Crown, a commission to inquire into the working of the system of government, the growth of education and the development of representative institutions in British India, and the commission was required to report whether and to what extent it was desirable to establish the principle of responsible government or to extend, modify, or restrict the degree of responsible government then existing therein, including the question whether the establishment of second chambers in the provinces was or was not desirable. The Crown might also refer to the commission for report any other matter affecting British India and the provinces.[1]

(*f*) THE INDIAN STATES

The Report recognized to the full the importance of the position of the states and the effect which the reform scheme must have on their interests. It recognized that a certain degree of uncertainty as to their future was being widely felt, and this was attributed to certain causes. The term Native States had been applied to states of very different standing, and the rules applicable to minor rulers might have been applied to major states without sufficient regard for the difference of stature. Further, the treaties had come to be interpreted largely by usage, and there had been derogation, often necessary and proper, from their strict terms. It would be desirable to codify the existing practices with due regard to treaty rights. Further, it was desirable to place on a regular basis the system of consultation with the princes, inaugurated by Lord Hardinge and carried further by Lord Chelmsford, by establishing a Council or Chamber of Princes[2] to meet the viceroy annually for discussion of issues of common interest. A standing committee of that body might be consulted by the political department on issues referred to it. Difficulties between two states or a state and a local government or the government of India might be referred for report by a commission presided over by a judge, and consisting of one nominee of either side. If the viceroy could not accept their finding, he would refer

[1] S. 41.

[2] The minor rulers were not to share in the chamber. See Chapter X, §24, below.

to the secretary of state. Similarly in the case of charges against a ruler investigation might be entrusted to a judge, two ruling princes, and two other persons.[1] It was further proposed to place all important states in direct relations with the viceroy instead of with local governments as was then often the case, and to arrange for some means of consultation between the princes and the representatives of British India.

The vision of the authors was of the provinces as self-governing units under a central government dealing with issues of common concern, defence, tariffs, exchange, opium, salt, railways, posts and telegraphs, all matters interesting the states, whence it followed that an ultimate federation must be the ideal. But they deprecated any efforts to hasten a result, for which natural causes were working.

[1] Resolution 426 R., October 29th 1920, applies the procedure to (1) cases of depriving a ruler of rights or dignities, (2) debarring the heir apparent or other members of the family from succession.

CHAPTER IX

THE OPERATION OF THE REFORMS, THE REPORT OF THE SIMON COMMISSION, AND THE ROUND TABLE CONFERENCE

1. THE OPERATION OF THE REFORMS

BEFORE the Act of 1919 could be passed into law, matters in India had assumed an aspect unfavourable to the atmosphere of good will indispensable for working so complex a machine, for which the King in his proclamation of December 23rd and the Duke of Connaught in opening the Indian legislature made earnest appeal. The post-war conditions of India were as unsatisfactory as those of Europe in general. Large fortunes had been made in which the workers and peasants did not share, the influenza epidemic had killed thirteen millions and left others debilitated, and politicians soon concluded that there was no serious intention to make good the hopes excited in 1917. Unfortunately, among those who formed this conclusion was a man of remarkable character, M. K. Gandhi, whose appeal to his countrymen was due to many causes, his approximation in outlook and practices to the Hindu ascetic ideal, his humble bania caste which won him wide sympathies among men of substance, his knowledge of industrial issues, his readiness to take up the cause of the depressed classes, the mill-workers, and the Indians overseas, where he had won honourable renown for his championship of the Indians in South Africa. He had practised with success in South Africa the doctrine of passive resistance and had proved the merits of the tactics of driving the government to repression measures which attracted sympathy to those against whom they were directed. He had the advantage that his idealism had won him high repute overseas, especially in America, and that through him there was a growing tendency outside the United Kingdom for the giving of sympathy to any cause he advocated, while in the United Kingdom he was certain of appealing strongly to Liberal and Labour idealism.

An opportunity to attack the government on favourable ground was soon presented by the Bills introduced to carry out the recommendation of the Rowlatt Committee regarding the control of the Press, and the trial of political offenders by judges without juries, and the internment of persons suspected of subversive aims. Violent protests were directed at projects of no great importance, and Gandhi put in operation his doctrine of passive resistance under which the law was defied on the plea of adherence to the ideal (satyagraha) but without resistance (ahimsa). The old Indian plan of a hartal, or day of fasting and abstention from business, was revived with spectacular effect. In March and April 1919 disturbances were not rare in the Punjab and the west of India; the pressure of the war-period recruiting had been grave in the former, and the west had been distinguished by scandalous profiteering, none of the profits being expended on the proper and necessary improvement of the conditions of the overcrowded and badly paid workers. Unhappily the outbreaks coincided with strained relations with Afghanistan, which resulted in Afghan attack and defeat in May[1] and led to the declaration of martial law in the Punjab on April 15th.[2] This followed on rioting on the 10th when several Europeans were disgracefully murdered, and on the 13th the episode of the Jallianwalla Bagh, when, on the defiance of General Dyer's orders forbidding meetings, a meeting was held, and dispersed by his orders with the loss of 379 killed and over 1,208 wounded. The general appears not to have realized that the space was enclosed so that dispersal was impossible, but his official defence, probably owing to second thoughts, insisted that the firing was carried out to produce such a moral effect as would secure order in the Punjab. At the time his action was approved by the local government and under martial law which lasted until June 9th a good many indignities were imposed on Indians in areas believed to be disaffected. Unquestionably the episode should forthwith have been inquired into in fairness to all concerned. Only in October was a committee under Lord Hunter[3] appointed to investigate, and it condemned General Dyer's action on the irrefutable ground that the duty of the military in such cases

[1] Parl. Paper, Cmd. 324. [2] Cmd. 534 (1920). [3] Cmd. 681.

is to take such action only as is essential to prevent loss of life and destruction of property by the rioters, and that ulterior views such as that of striking terror into the rest of the province must be disregarded. General Dyer's action was also disapproved by the secretary of state[1] and the Army Council, but it found defenders in the Press, the House of Lords, and years later in the considered opinion of Mr. Justice McCardie in a case in which the officer who had been lieutenant-governor of the Punjab at the time successfully defended his conduct on that occasion. The episode unhappily cast a dark shadow over the inception of the reforms and brought racial feeling out far more bitterly than at any time since the Mutiny. Lord Hunter's committee unfortunately divided on racial lines on the questions of the effort of the war administration of the province and the necessity of enforcing martial law. Here again the delay in the investigation tended to unsatisfactory results, for by the time it was held the menace from Afghanistan had passed away in the defeat of the Afghan forces by the resources of aircraft, high explosives, and wireless telegraphy, now for the first time employed to full advantage in frontier war, and it was easy to overlook the fact that at the time the situation was one of great danger. Even when peace was signed, the government of India recognizing the Amir as independent, dropping the former subsidies and closing the frontier to transit of arms, it remained to subdue the Mahsuds and Waziris, whose enmity was rendered serious by the enormous mass of modern rifles which had passed into the country.[2] After investigation by a committee in 1921 the plan of opening up the Mahsud and Waziri country by providing roads and raising local levies, backed by regular forces at Rasmak and Manzai, was adopted. But the risk from the frontier remained operative, though Amanulla gradually became more friendly, his propensities for modernization leading to his overthrow in 1928 and the advent to the throne of Nadir Shah, whose assassination in 1933 did not alter the friendly relations he had established with the Crown.

A further cause of estrangement between Indians and British affected the Muslims in the first instance. The attitude

[1] Cmd. 705.

[2] Parl. Papers, Cmd. 310, 398 (1919).

of the British Government towards Turkey, as seen in the treaty of Sèvres, was deeply resented, and unhappily Mr. Montagu, by publishing in 1922 the views of the government of India on the course of relations[1] offended against a fundamental principle of cabinet solidarity and was forced to resign, thus giving India the impression that its friend had been forced out of office by intransigent Conservatism. With their inevitable skill in fishing in troubled waters, the Moplahs, part Arab Muslims in Malabar, broke into revolt which took the form of forcible conversion of many unfortunate Hindus and massacre. This fact weakened the affection of political Hinduism for the khilafat movement, which further suffered from the decision of the Angora Assembly in 1924 to abolish the office and exile the last holder of it. But it had sent thousands of devout Muslims on a fruitless mission to Afghanistan and very naturally, if illogically, the blame for their sufferings fell on the British Government when the disappointed emigrants returned disillusionized home.

It was under these unhappy circumstances that the reform elections were held in October 1920. The Congress party boycotted them, but about a third of the electorate of six millions went to the polls which was no mean result in view of the boycott, the vast extent of the constituencies, the absence of any immediate issues, and the painfully high proportion of illiterates among the voters. It was found fairly easy to secure ministries in the provinces, but the ministers had to be chosen from a variety of political and communal groups, and it early appeared that collective responsibility would be impossible to secure. Ministers could not be, and were not, chosen because they had a common policy, but because they were leading men of groups strong enough to insist on representation in the ministry. There was, however, an exception in Madras, where the non-brahmans had secured unexpectedly a large number of seats and the ministry could be selected so as to present their views. In that case Lord Willingdon contrived to secure something reasonably approaching a British cabinet through the co-operation of both sides of his government.[2]

[1] Ronaldshay, *Lord Curzon*, ii, 285, 286; Keith, *Governments of the British Empire*, p. 277.

[2] On the working of dyarchy, see Parl. Paper, Cmd. 3568, pp. 203 ff. In Bengal

Unfortunately ministers fell on evil days in the matter of finance. The contributions to be required from them were fixed by the Meston Committee at rates which were certainly high, but which had to be enforced, because the campaign against Afghanistan, the partial failure of the monsoon in 1920, and world conditions all contributed to confusion in Indian economics and finances, the rupee falling in no great period of time from three shillings to half that amount in value. At the same time the bad harvest and the increased cost of anti-revolutionary measures affected provincial finances. There was small scope for expenditure on nation building in any form, and ministers soon realized that, when challenged on issues of efficiency, they were able to meet criticisms and add to their popularity by disclaiming responsibility on the score that finance was in the hands of the official government which required so much for reserved subjects as to leave wholly inadequate sums available for the ministry. The difficulties of the financial system thus manifested themselves in their most complete form, and proved the essential unreality of talking of responsible government when ministers were not effectively in control of any side of finance. Yet another obvious disadvantage lay in the fact that the ministers had only a limited control over their officials; in fact they received in the main willing and effective service, but it was always possible for a minister to suggest that his work was hampered by the fact that officials could defy him. The rule under which the permanent heads of the departments were required to bring to the notice of the governor matters of importance affecting his responsibilities, and had direct access to him, unquestionably secured efficiency in large measure, but it did obscure the responsibility of ministers. But even more destructive of true responsibility was the need as a normal rule of winning the support of the official bloc. A ministry which was on good terms with the official side of the government possessed a sound basis of support which rendered it possible to hold office although the parties represented by ministers were weaker than

also when ministries could be formed they acted with the executive council, but transferred subjects had to be taken over for a time in 1925; cf. Banerjea, *A Nation in Making*, pp. 333–91. The Central Provinces had a like experience. See also Paper 70–230 (1928).

their opponents. A healthy development on normal party lines, which is requisite for the working of responsible government as understood in the United Kingdom, was impossible when each council was composed of so many sectional interests, and though in different circumstances the system developed rather in the direction of ministers supported precariously by combinations of groups based on agreements to further sectional ends rather than on any wide divergence of policy. Nor could the enormous influence of the governor as an expert be ignored; it tended to weaken ministers' importance and initiative and to reduce them to the advisers of a more or less independent governor. But that did not prevent much good work being accomplished in education, in sanitation, in local government. The chief errors in these fields lay in the reluctance of the ministers to impose adequate control or when imposed to exercise it, and it was to this factor that there was due some of the deterioration of the effectiveness of the administrative machine which marks this period, side by side with a genuine desire to effect important reforms. In 1920 a very striking example was given of the desire of the government to make the share of Indians in government real, when Lord Sinha was made governor of Bihar and Orissa.

The legislative assembly during this period showed its real importance and value as a critic of the government; naturally its interests were focused on the issues which had so often been dealt with by the National Congress, finance and army expenditure. Substantial victories were achieved on every side, though their importance was underrated by men who had demanded responsible government at the centre and disliked everything done by an official government. The old dispute over tariffs was largely ended. The Indian government without much regard for British interests set about evolving a system of protection for Indian industry, in which the interests of the consumer as usual went to the wall. A Tariff Commission, the precursor of the Tariff Board, was set up to report on projects of protection and soon the principle was in full force, suggestions of British preference being greeted with much coldness.

Currency and loan issues evoked deep interest, and censure was freely lavished, not perhaps without cause, at the raising in 1921 of a loan at 7 per cent, while all manner of criticism was addressed against the mode in which the secretary of state managed financial relations between India and the United Kingdom; always a delicate operation, it had become more and more complex with the breakdown of the normal exchange system. The complaints led to the appointment of the Currency Commission and to an understanding that India should have a larger say in regard to the flotation of loans. The same spirit of criticism was addressed to the budget, and when Sir B. Blackett in 1923 determined to end the period of deficits by doubling the salt tax, the opportunity of winning popularity as protectors of the poor was eagerly seized by the legislators, whose intransigence forced the governor-general to certify the measure rather than remain in deficit. Yet, in the main the legislature was not disposed needlessly to oppose the government. The process of certifying Bills was avoided; feeling, however, against the princes ran sufficiently strong in 1922 to compel the certification of a measure intended to protect the princes from attacks on them in British India calculated to bring them into disrepute in their states. There was distinct need for the measure in theory, but it proved in practice difficult to operate and the certification was rather unfortunate.

In the field of defence great strides were made, though scant recognition was accorded to this fact. The war had had the essential result of rendering in 1917–18 Indians eligible for the King's commission as opposed to that of the governor-general, and a small number of such appointments had been made. But it left India with an army whose cost in 1921 was eighty-two crores of rupees as against a pre-war average of thirty crores, a burden of the most severe character. No wonder that it was easy and popular to denounce the cost of the army, to assert that it was largely due to the heavy charges involved in employing British troops, and to denounce the government for failing to build up an Indian army manned and officered by Indians. Unfortunately the politicians were presented with a genuine grievance in the report issued in October 1920, of the Esher Committee,[1] for that document

[1] Cmd. 943; see Sir Sivaswamy Aiyer, *Indian Constitutional Problems*, pp. 111 ff., 176 ff. for a strong criticism.

unquestionably could be understood to advocate treating the Indian army as maintained as part of the scheme of imperial defence, a conception not adopted in pre-war days. It was of course in the light of war experience easy to feel that the earlier policy had from a military standpoint been mistaken, but it was not realized that the vital political changes rendered it impossible to decide army policy in India without regard to Indian national feeling. Fortunately in the commander-in-chief, Lord Rawlinson, Indian politicians found an authority who sympathized with their aspirations while conscious of the essential dangers of the position in a manner which was foreign to his critics. He explained authoritatively in 1921 the essential functions of the army, the field army for foreign service, the covering troops to hold the frontier, and the internal security forces, to preserve security at home, and the mode of application of these doctrines in India. He spared no effort to secure efficiency at less cost, and in four years the expenditure fell to fifty-six crores, the British troops being brought down from 75,000 to 57,000, and the Indian from 159,000 to 140,000. The foundation of a territorial force purely Indian in 1923 opened up the army to middle-class Indians in a manner similar to that in which the formation of the auxiliary force had opened it to Europeans and Anglo-Indians. But of vital importance was the question of Indianizing the command of Indian regiments, and for this purpose in 1923, eight units[1] were marked out that arrangements might be made to render them in the rather distant future completely Indian in personnel. This necessitated, of course, opening training at Sandhurst to Indians specially selected, and this naturally led much later (1928) to their admission to Woolwich and Cranwell also, but for the time being the establishment of an Indian counterpart to Sandhurst[2] was naturally deemed premature. It must be remembered that even thus early the difficulty of securing suitable Indian candidates for the army had presented

[1] Five infantry battalions, two cavalry regiments, and a pioneer unit only. No commissions in artillery, engineers, etc., were then contemplated. Cf. Maurice, *Lord Rawlinson*, pp. 284–6. In 1922 a complete technical reorganization was carried out.

[2] Recommended by the Indian Sandhurst Committee under Sir A. Skeen (1926). It disapproved the eight-unit plan, but its views on that point were rejected. Parl. Paper, Cmd. 3568, pp. 98 ff.

itself. The elements in India whence officers could be expected to come were limited, for the prospects of civil service or law or commerce rendered able youths singularly unwilling to seek commissions. But this fact was deliberately and not very candidly ignored by the critics of the government, who were naturally appalled to find how long it must be before there would exist Indian units under Indian control, forgetting that the process of evolving a capable commander is necessarily slow.

Much useful legislation was passed both by the Indian and by the provincial legislatures. The former amended the Factories Act, passed a Mines Act and provided for workmen's compensation, while the latter made serious contributions in provisions for local government, education, and health.

At the same time steps were taken by the British Government to enhance in the eyes of the world the new position of India. Despite the admitted domination of Indian foreign policy by the British Government, India was treated as on a footing of equality with the Dominions in the issues which arose from the treaties of peace, and these treaties were duly signed specially for India, as they were for the Dominions. Of essential importance was the grant to India of a place in the League of Nations on a footing of equality with the Dominions, and India was not merely included in the Labour Organization under the League Covenant, but received in the former the recognition due to her position as one of the chief industrial countries of the world. Moreover, the policy of treating India as on the same footing as the Dominions was shown by her representation at the Imperial Conference of 1921 and 1923, where the Indian representatives manfully struggled to secure practical recognition of the admitted anomaly of the position of India as an equal member of the Empire and the existence of disabilities upon British Indians lawfully domiciled in other parts of the Empire. All these matters, however, failed to secure appreciation of the British attitude. It was felt merely that the Indian delegates to the League and the Imperial Conference were no more than mere spokesmen of the British Government and that India was not accepted in either body as really of Dominion status. The result was disappointing, as it might have been hoped that consciousness of national status would have reconciled politicians to acceptance of necessary delay in evolving responsible government. But Gandhi and Congress with him had definitely declined any programme of moderation. He had secured control over Congress in 1920 by preaching the doctrine of swaraj to be conceded within a year, and his failure, together with the Moplah rebellion (August 1921) and the riots induced by his non-co-operation policy when the Prince of Wales visited India (November 1921), discredited him and his principles,[1] and these adverse factors were followed by the ghastly murder of twenty-one police-officers by his National Volunteers at Chauri Chaura in February 1922. It elicited from Gandhi a declaration of horror at the outcome of his teaching, and, luckily enough for him in his distracted condition of mind, the government acted, and on its charges he was convicted and sentenced to six years' imprisonment, later reduced to two.

This eclipse of the advocate of non-co-operation led to the control of Congress by Mr. C. R. Das and Pandit Motilal Nehru, who preferred to enter the legislatures and obstruct the government from that vantage-point. Common sense of course would have induced from the first entry into the legislatures and effective working of the machinery of government with a view to obtaining control of it. But the new policy at least was better than mere negation; as such it was widely approved and the elections for the provinces and the assembly showed substantial success for the policy, the Congress men carrying two provinces and providing the central legislature with a solid bloc of forty-five members. Their position negated, inevitably, the possibility of the gradual evolution of dyarchy into full responsible government. The Congress was determined to destroy the constitution, and naturally enough was concerned not with the morality but the efficacy of the means which it employed for this end. Moreover, their hopes were encouraged by the advent to office of the Labour government in the United Kingdom, as the Prime Minister with wonted lack of balanced judgment had pronounced himself in earlier days in

[1] Congress at Ahmadabad (December 1921) authorized mass civil disobedience and gave Mr. Gandhi dictatorial powers to challenge the government.

favour of great concessions to Indian sentiment, and Congress did not realize how much a politician may change his views when he is in a position where he may carry them into effect. Disillusionment increased bitterness, and led to the deliberate destruction by the Congress majority of the working of dyarchy in Bengal and the Central Provinces, compelling the governors to take administration into their own hands. In the central legislature, where the government was safe from attack, the Swaraj party in 1925 walked out from the legislature in a body and remained outside, declaring that in their absence the legislature had no right to continue functioning.

It was under this feeling of captious criticism that the report of the Lee Commission,[1] appointed by Lord Peel in 1923, was received. The report in fact went very far in urging the acceleration of the Indianization of the services, suggesting that two-fifths of the annual requirement of new members for the Indian Civil Service should be selected in India, two-fifths in England, and one-fifth promoted from the provincial service. It was also willing to provide for the steady equalization of numbers in the Indian police, and the government accepted its suggestions, with the result that from 922 Europeans in the Indian Civil Service in 1928 there was a decline by January 1932 to 843, and for the police the figures were 569 and 528 respectively. Moreover, the Commission recognized that save in these two services and in such technical work as irrigation engineering the process of Indianization had definitely taken root, and the elimination of Europeans was merely a matter of time. It might have been expected that the sincerity of the government's policy in this regard was proved, but in fact the chief attitude was complaint at the slowness of progress.

Play was also made with considerable success with the Asiatic grievance regarding the anti-Asiatic attitude of the Dominions,[2] and the fact that the government of India could do little to secure just treatment of Indians overseas was naturally made the occasion for propaganda to secure the separation of India from an Empire which could not treat

[1] Parl. Paper, Cmd. 2128 (1924).

[2] Keith, *The Governments of the British Empire* (1935), pp. 195 ff.

Indians abroad with decency. General Smuts, in 1923, in fear of a general election, was peculiarly intransigent, declining Sir Tej Bahadur Sapru's suggestion of the appointment of a Committee of Inquiry to visit the Union. Naturally General Hertzog was still less favourable to Indians, and pushed forward proposals which would have further and most seriously restricted the rights of Indians to live and trade in areas where as petty traders they could earn profits. Fortunately it was found possible at last to establish personal touch, and an accord was reached in the Union in 1927. But this agreement, though it bound the Union government to seek to aid domiciled Indians to attain a European standard of life as the condition of their permanent settlement in the Union, was essentially intended to secure Indian governmental co-operation in repatriating Indians, on the score that they formed an unassimilable element in the population, and added seriously to the complexities of a difficult situation as between Europeans and natives and coloured persons. Even more harm was done by the discussions over Kenya, for which the imperial government was responsible. At one time (1922) it seemed as if racial discrimination would be dropped, but Conservative dislike of recognizing the equality of native races prevailed, and the result was in 1923 the acceptance of communal electorates which gave the European population an unfair share of the seats available. Segregation, which had been proposed was stopped, largely because it proved impracticable, and immigration was not absolutely barred. But unquestionably the position presented a serious grievance, for the reservation of the highlands for European settlement only was racialism undisguised, and the hectoring attitude adopted by the European settlers towards the government of the colony and the reluctance of the Colonial Secretary to assert his authority encouraged Congress in the belief that justice was unobtainable by peaceful persuasion, and that the British Government could yield to force what it denied to reason. The very justifiable feeling that neither there nor in any other part of the Empire were Indians heartily welcome went far to embitter resentment and to encourage propaganda in favour of independence.

High hopes were in some quarters entertained when in 1924

a committee under Sir A. Muddiman[1] was set up to examine the working of the system, but these were overthrown when the report was actually presented to Lord Birkenhead in the following year. It turned out that the majority of three British and two Indian members held their function to be restricted to the making of suggestions for the better working of dyarchy, while the minority of four Indian members including Sir Tej Sapru held that dyarchy was unworkable and possessed inherent demerits explaining the difficulties enumerated in its operation by the provincial governments. This denunciation of dyarchy was readily taken up in India by politicians generally, and Lord Birkenhead welcomed it on July 7th 1925 on behalf of the orthodox Conservatives, holding that dyarchy was a pedantic arrangement unsuited to Anglo-Saxons and therefore to those whose political ideas were based on Anglo-Saxon ideas. Congress for its part sponsored a National Demand movement for a Round Table Conference whose business it would be to draw up a constitution according India full Dominion status. Some members indeed showed a more realistic attitude. Mr. V. J. Patel consented to become President of the Assembly on the expiry of the four years for which the first President had been appointed, and Mr. C. R. Das before his untimely death (June 16th 1925) entered into communications with Lord Birkenhead which suggested that, had he lived, he might have sought to guide Indian politicians along the path of fruitful co-operation,[2] based on the value to India of the imperial connexion and on recognition of the difficulty inherent in establishing self-government in a country permeated with communal spirit, excited to fresh manifestations by the prospect of the passing away of British control. Unhappily with him perished the best chance of the evolution of a party of responsive co-operation.

Another unhappy feature of the operation of the reforms was the inevitable impetus given to sectarian strife. It was obvious to Hindus and Muslims alike that the change in the form of government meant the possibility of securing effective domination by legal means; especially in the case of Bengal and the

[1] Parl. Papers, Cmd. 2360, and 2 vols. of evidence; Pole, *India in Transition*, pp. 58 ff.; Sir Sivaswamy Aiyer, *Indian Constitutional Reform*, pp. 59 ff.
[2] Bose, *The Indian Struggle*, pp. 123–32.

Punjab, where numbers are fairly balanced, was this effect seen in operation. Hindu-Muslim[1] tension showed itself fiercer and fiercer with the passage of the years, and confusion was increased by the efforts made on either side at conversions. It must be remembered that perhaps five-sixths of the Muslims of India are the descendants of converted Hindus. It was natural that the Arya Samaj should seek to proselytize the poorer Muhammadans, while the lower-caste Hindus offered a fertile field of missionary enterprise for the Muslims. A further complication was produced by the movement patronized by Gandhi to improve the status of lower castes and outcastes in the Hindu community. Reform movements appeared among the Sikhs, which had grave political consequences; the Akalis, in their zeal for purity of religion, fell foul of the vested interests which opposed reform; a ghastly massacre perpetrated (1921) by Pathans employed by the Mahant of Nankana Saheb proved the necessity of government intervention and of legislation[2] for the due management of the holy shrines, but not until grave unrest had been caused between the rulers of Nabha and Patiala. It was one of the minor disadvantages of the new state of affairs that communal tension spread to the Indian states, since it was obvious that the Crown must interfere to maintain order in case of grave unrest. Among the Muslims also there was propagated a wild but not negligible scheme for the creation of a Muslim state based on Afghanistan and embracing all those north-western areas where the faith is strong. Such a state inevitably would form a permanent source of danger to India.

It was manifest that no solution of the difficulties of the position lay in dyarchy, which had never operated in any effective sense and in which no one, European or Indian, had any real belief. But the policy of 1919 had a definite effect in diminishing the driving power of the Indian Civil Service, whose members realized that the old possibilities of high office and power were vanishing and that they would be well to seek some other career for their sons, even if they cared to stay to the

[1] The census of 1931 gives 177·2 million Hindus, 66·5 million Muslims, 3·2 million Sikhs, 3·6 million Christians.

[2] Punjab Act VIII of 1925 (superseding an Act of 1922); Indian Act XXIV of 1925, as to appeals, these being beyond provincial power.

end of their normal years of service, instead of accepting the possibility of retirement on a proportionate pension. It was therefore of real importance that Lord Reading's successor as governor-general, Lord Irwin, came to his task in 1926 with the constructive ideal of achieving harmony in India between Hindu and Muslim, and co-operation with the British elements in securing the political advance of India. He found Hindu-Muslim bitterness at its height, and one of his first efforts was by means of conferences at Calcutta and Delhi to bring the leaders of the two religions into agreement, though without much success. Moreover, at this critical period a new reinforcement was gained by the cause of Congress. The Currency Commission[1] recommended that the rupee should be stabilized at 1*s*. 6*d*., while Sir Purshotamdas Thakurdas in a dissenting report urged the adoption of 1*s*. 4*d*. This plan naturally appealed to the cotton manufacturers of western India, who argued that they were speaking also in the interests of the agriculturists, and Congress now received the influential support of the representatives of Indian commerce. They had long been jealous of the position of British commercial interests, and American agents had been quick to assure them that British industry and finance were declining fast, and that it was wholly to the disadvantage of India to remain tied to the British system. They added to the strength of Congress and impressed on its policy a definite tone of hostility to British trade which was to affect substantially the future constitution.

2. THE SIMON COMMISSION REPORT

It was in these difficult conditions, aggravated by the cleverness of the Congress in sponsoring at the suggestion of Jawaharlal Nehru and Subash Chandra Bose a youth movement which appealed to the excitable and half-educated young men with irresistible force, that the British Government decided to obtain the sanction of Parliament[2] for the acceleration of the appointment of the Commission of Inquiry provided for after the lapse of ten years by the Act of 1919. The matter was

[1] Parl. Paper, Cmd. 2687 (1926).

[2] 17 & 18 Geo. V, c. 24. The commission of seven included two Labour members and one Liberal, Sir J. Simon.

mismanaged from the first,[1] and Indian moderates were induced to share the Congress attitude of unreasoning hostility. The seven members first selected were all British, and it was only later that it was laid down that they were to co-operate with the elected members of the Indian legislature, who were to report simultaneously but not jointly with the British members. The necessity for information was clear, but shortsighted agitation resulted in the great parties and the Central Assembly boycotting the Commission, though the provincial councils as a rule took a much more sensible view and enabled the Commission to acquire much essential information. What was worse, local branches of Congress openly condoned the campaign of political assassination which broke out in Bengal and the Punjab and spread to the rest of India. Violence also marked the strikes which cost the country thirty million working days in 1927–8, and which in some degree were prompted by communist propaganda,[2] working on the perfectly intolerable conditions under which Indian labourers were employed in the textile factories.

In response to the challenge of the Commission a party truce was arranged, and in 1928 an All Parties' Conference drafted a constitution of an interesting kind, resting essentially on the doctrines of full responsible government, though some effort was made to safeguard the question of defence preparations. But the report contemplated the system of joint electorates with reserved seats for minorities only[3] and for ten years as the manner in which effect should be given to the guarantee of Muslim rights, and this introduced a serious element of discord between the Muslim and Hindu members of the Congress. At its Lucknow session Maulana Shaukat Ali attacked the proposals, and the result of the project was the revival of the Muslim League as the outcome of the belief that agreement with the Hindus would not accord the safeguards for Muslim interests necessary. On the other hand, the importance of the backing of the Congress programme by the industrialists was

[1] Pole, *India in Transition*, pp. 72 ff.

[2] In December 1927 Communist strength was seen at the All-India Trade Union Congress.

[3] This denied the Muslim demand for reservation of a majority of seats in Bengal and the Punjab. The Sikhs also refused to accept the proposals.

seen in the support given by Muslims and Hindus alike to the proposals of Mr. S. N. Haji's Bill to regulate the coasting trade by the process of reserving the right to participate in it to Indians. It was of course impossible to secure the passing of so confiscatory a measure, but it afforded a warning of the hostility to be shown to British trade and the necessity of anxious safeguarding. Further, the strength of Congress was focused and strengthened by the decision at the meeting of Congress at Calcutta in December 1928 to welcome Gandhi as leader, for he was able to consolidate the alliance of the industrialists with political extremists and to secure the necessary funds for the payment of volunteers to carry out the policy of Congress, and his popularity in the United States was deemed an asset in the campaign to eliminate British influence. Moreover, his connexion with South Africa was taken advantage of to determine on the taluka of Bardoli in the Surat district as the scene of a no-tax agitation, because many of the ryots there were emigrants who had returned from South Africa. On the other hand, the general belief that concessions must be made by the British Government was strengthened by the Labour victory of 1929, for the new Prime Minister was judged by his ideals for India expressed in the irresponsibility of opposition by a politician whose talent was chiefly journalistic, and the anticipation resulted in renewed efforts of groups of interests to perfect their organization. Hence the Hindu Mahasabha stressed orthodox Hinduism, and the depressed classes began to organize under the leadership of Dr. Ambedkar, and Rao Bahadur M. C. Rajah.

For the moment the government of India was content to urge the passing of the Public Safety and the Trade Disputes Bills,[1] justifying these unpopular measures by allegations of serious communist conspiracy, and fortifying their arguments by instituting proceedings against three British and twenty-six Indian industrial agitators. The proceedings were deliberately protracted by the defence, showing clearly the defects of the judicial system when the accused desire to exploit them, but the prosecution was doubtless badly planned, for when it was

[1] Act VII of 1929. It adopts part of the Trade Disputes and Trade Unions Act, 1927.

at last after five years concluded, the sentences imposed were drastically reduced on appeal and some convictions were not upheld. The court unquestionably did its best, but it was easy to misrepresent its proceedings. Moreover, the government was harassed in the Assembly by the quite unfair tactics of the Speaker, who instead of confining his activities to the control of debates lent his energies to endeavouring to frustrate the plans of the government and so bring it into contempt,[1] just as his brother was attempting to do as leader of the agitation at Bardoli. It must be admitted that the futility of the session was not without importance in moulding policy. It seems to have led to the decision of Lord Irwin to impress by a personal visit to England on the new ministry the impossibility of working a government which was purely official, when exposed to irresponsible criticism by an Assembly whose members were not restrained by the knowledge that, if they defeated governmental projects, they must be prepared to take office and themselves become the object of attack. The fruits of this visit were momentous, for the governor-general came back with authority to ask representatives of Indian opinion to meet in conference British representatives, and on October 31st it was intimated that Dominion status was the natural issue of the constitutional progress of India. The statement was far-reaching in its consequences, and strengthened the claim that India should deal on a footing of equality with Britain. Mr. MacDonald at the British Commonwealth Labour Conference on July 2nd 1928 had welcomed the idea of seeing within a few months a new Dominion added to the Commonwealth as an equal, and Indian politicians might be excused if they assumed that he meant what he said, and that the Round Table Conference contemplated was intended to settle the basis of a constitution of Dominion type based on equality as proclaimed by the Imperial Conference of 1926. But neither the Conservatives nor the Liberals were prepared to accept so radical an idea, and the result was seen when Gandhi was received by Lord Irwin, a few hours after an attempt (December 23rd 1929) to assassinate him. The demand that the Conference should

[1] As he improperly refused to allow discussion of the Public Safety Bill, it was passed as an Ordinance.

draw up a scheme for full Dominion status to operate forthwith was necessarily denied, and Congress at Lahore retaliated by demanding complete independence.

In striking contrast to the ideals of Congress stood the views of the Simon Commission which were issued in May 1930. The report[1] received little of the sympathy which was its due, and its merits were such as to render it unpopular throughout India. It emphasized in a perfectly fair manner the fundamental difficulties of the Indian situation, the racial and communal dissensions, the problem of defence and its bearing on British control, and the necessity of considering the position of the states in any constitutional reconstruction. These matters essentially demanded candid reflection in India, and it was imperative to make them clear to British politicians. The state question had been long allowed to remain in abeyance. British Indian politicians seem to have contented themselves with the view that, when responsible government was attained, as it must be in due course, the government of India would continue to exercise the powers which it then possessed as regards the states. But such a view was naturally wholly repugnant to the minds of the rulers, who had taken advantage of the changed attitude towards them of the paramount power since Minto to develop claims for full consideration of their views before any fundamental change was made in the Indian constitution. They had become increasingly conscious of the fact that with the new policy of high protection their subjects were being affected by increased cost of imported goods, with results unfavourable to the state revenue. They strongly disliked the idea of Indian defence and other questions being settled by a responsible government in India in which they had no part, and they were quite determined to refuse to accept the dictation of a responsible ministry in India. They were, on the contrary, most anxious as against the Crown itself to secure a definition in the narrowest terms of paramount power and to reverse the process of encroachment on their rights.

In pursuit of these views the princes secured a legal opinion by eminent counsel which exhibits unhappily singularly little

[1] Parl. Paper, Cmd. 3568, 3569; cf. 3700, 3712.

sense of constitutional law.[1] It was perfectly easy to prove that the terms of the treaties with the states had been often disregarded and were probably in no case fully respected. But to ignore the course of usage was absurd. The rulers had accepted the invasions on their technical rights as the condition of continued existence as independent entities, and to repudiate the means by which they had been able to live was inadmissible. The hollowness of the arguments used by the advisers of the princes was easily exposed by the Indian States Committee, but the unfortunate result of the advice given was seen in the demands which the princes were shortly to make as the price of their co-operation.

The actual recommendations of the Commission, which was not authorized to investigate the issue of the states as a factor in a possible federation, were treated at the time with complete dissatisfaction by Indian politicians and with little respect by the British Government. Moderate and prudent, they failed to please extremists and offended Conservative opinion in the United Kingdom as dangerously generous. Their solid value is proved by the fact that, though the report seemed to be discarded with indifference, much of its substance is embodied in the reform scheme. It was recommended that responsible government should be made real in the provinces. Dyarchy had not worked, and should be definitely laid aside. The matters generally comprised in the popular phrase 'law and order' should be placed under control of ministers. In a carefully reasoned argument it was shown that to deny these matters to the ministry was to negate responsible government and to perpetuate the worst features of dyarchy. Safeguards were no doubt necessary, but they must be supplied in part by the grant of special powers to the governor, in part by the maintenance of complete control of the Indian government. The existence of dyarchy in the central administration was absolutely negatived; there must be unity and freedom from domination by the legislature. The Commission, however, did not regard this position as intended to last indefinitely. It looked forward to the possibility of a federation[2] to include the states which would render it possible to reconsider the issue of

[1] Parl. Paper, Cmd. 3302, pp. 59–73. [2] Cmd. 3569, pp. 193 ff.

responsibility, provided that arrangements could be made for defence which would facilitate transfer of authority. In sympathy with Indian ideals it suggested that the protection of India from external attack might be taken over by the British Government,[1] leaving to India the far less formidable, if difficult, task of maintaining forces sufficient to secure internal order. It was hoped that in this way a considerable reduction of cost might ensue, which would enable India to spend more on nation-building services. The suggestion, naturally, was open to many difficulties and was hastily ignored both in the United Kingdom and in India.

It was probably foolish of Indian opinion to repudiate the report out and out. If it had been accepted, the British Government could hardly have failed to work on it, and responsible government in the provinces would have been achieved much earlier than it could be under any later scheme. Moreover, the pressure of such governments on the centre would doubtless have operated strongly in the direction of inducing the British Government to aim at federation and the states to come to terms with Indian political leaders. It is noteworthy that the Commission endeavoured to suggest that responsible government in India need not follow rigidly existing models, a fact which at once rendered it suspect in the eyes of Indian politicians, whose views on these topics have throughout shown a remarkable lack of ingenuity and a determination slavishly to copy Western models hardly compatible with the national spirit by which they are animated.

3. THE ROUND TABLE CONFERENCE

(a) THE MOTIVES AND ASPIRATIONS OF THE PARTIES TO THE CONFERENCE

As against the calm wisdom of the Commission's report must be set the revolutionary violence by which the Congress under the scheme of civil disobedience endeavoured to destroy the prestige and power of the government of India. The movement for the manufacture of salt in defiance of the government

[1] Comd. 3569, pp. 173 ff. For the Government of India's criticism, see Cmd. 3700, pp. 130 ff.

monopoly was skilful, for the monopoly was unpopular, and it was easy to insist that the unhappy peasants were compelled to pay an unjust tax on a prime necessity of life. But the government failed to take the matter sufficiently seriously and this attitude evoked violent attacks on governmental and other property and the assassination of officers, both British and Indian. A commercial boycott was called into being, and popular feeling was excited to picket liquor shops, with the inevitable result of struggles with the police. Agrarian unrest was excited in the United Provinces, disaffection on the frontier encouraged as well as rebellion in Burma. A most daring raid against the armoury at Chittagong secured arms for the malcontents, while towns like Peshawar and Sholapur for a time fell under the control of the mob. An ominous feature was the appearance in the North-West Frontier Province of a 'red shirt' movement under Abdul Ghafur Khan which claimed to support Congress views, but was also marked by a strong pan-Islamic feeling. The value of the aid of the Indian business world was soon seen. Their contributions enabled the payment of volunteers for the cause, their technical knowledge guided the boycott of banks and insurance, and terrified the British commercial community into willingness to make terms with Indian aspirations. Moreover, the boycott showed by its success that successful appeal was being made to the lower classes of the people who were losing respect for a government which failed lamentably to counter the movement in its inception.

Fortunately the widespread character of the disorder roused the government to assert its strength. The power of the governor-general to issue ordinances was invoked, and drastic measures[1] passed to counter the different features of the boycott. Many supporters of Congress including Mr. Gandhi were arrested, troops were placed in the more disturbed areas, and martial law applied locally.[2] The results were considerable. The prevalent idea that the government had abdicated its functions received a useful check, and the strength of the administration when it chose to exert it was revealed.

[1] The Press law was revived; the property of associations declared unlawful could be seized; intimidation by pickets, boycotting of public servants, and incitement to pay no rent or taxes became illegal; see Ordinance 10.

[2] Ordinances 4 and 8 (Sholapur and Peshawar).

But mere repression was no part of the governmental programme, for it set great store by the Conference which it had authorized the governor-general to invite to meet at London. The personnel collected was remarkable for the strength of the spokesmen of the states, who included Sir Akbar Hydari for Hyderabad and Sir Mirza Ismail from Mysore as well as the Maharaja of Bikaner. But every great interest in India save Congress was represented, and much unanimity prevailed on vital principles. The states were prepared for federation provided the federation was independent of British control, though for a transition period that independence might be modified by the existence of limitations. The motives for this attitude have been indicated above. It was felt that by such an attitude it would be possible to secure in framing the constitution a much stronger position for the states than mere numbers would give them, and that at the same time they would be able in non-federal matters to secure freedom from intervention by the Crown except on definite and agreed grounds. It was argued that British interference in the name of better government and satisfaction of the growing demand for some degree of control on the part of the people would become more and more insistent unless bounds could be set to paramountcy, which had been declared by Lord Reading to depend on the will of the Crown when the Nizam of Hyderabad had endeavoured to reopen the assignment of Berar by his father on the score that his consent had been virtually due to unfair pressure. The British Government was clearly being impelled towards responsible government in the provinces; it could not safely concede that if the central government remained autocratic, since the result would be a constant assault on the centre by the provinces relying on their position as exponents of the will of the people. It must therefore build up a Conservative central authority, and the states could serve that purpose and achieve their own ends, for the British Government would be prepared to pay a price. Hence throughout the long period of negotiation the states stood out clearly as seeking to attain the maximum advantage for themselves, and above all security from intervention in their domestic affairs by the federation or the Crown. No doubt many princes were also moved by the ideal of a united India soon free from British dominion, and there is no ground to suppose that any of them were prepared for such an end to sacrifice anything of their internal autocracy. They naturally believed in that system of rule; not even the Gaekwad of Baroda claimed to accept democracy in India as wise, and that being so their attitude was inevitable; it was their duty to their country and themselves to entrench as far as possible the principle of autocracy.

British Indian politicians welcomed at first with enthusiasm the idea of making with the princes a common stand against British control. Many of the leaders were decidedly oligarchic or aristocratic and Conservative in their views, and they saw no objection to having in the representatives of the princes an assured strength of Conservatism to prevent any risk of democratic encroachments. It was only gradually that it came to be realized by the more advanced of moderate politicians that the princes were engaged essentially in the business of securing a definite position whence they could defy the introduction of any form of democracy in their dominions, and that they would act rather as a support for British control than as furthering Indian autonomy. Moreover, a further difficulty presented itself. The princes in the main were Hindu and their presence in the federation might well strengthen the Hindu as opposed to the Muslim element. From another point of view the objection was taken that Muslim rulers like the Nizam might well select Muslims as his spokesmen, so that Hindus would be misrepresented by Muslim nominees. Others again took exception to the status of representatives of the states, as bound to vote according to the dictates of the rulers as opposed to the representatives of provincial electorates. But the original feeling was one of readiness to co-operate as a means of replacing British control.

The British commercial community also favoured federation. Their motives were largely enlightened self-interest. They realized that concession to Indian demands for responsible government was inevitable in view of the attitude adopted by the Labour party, and they concluded that the best way in which to secure such safeguards as might be possible lay in co-operating with moderate Indian opinion. They were therefore not concerned with the wider question of the proper form of government for India, a subject on which they were not well qualified to judge, since they had little contact with the issue of government outside the commercial centres. But they did realize that the Congress movement was backed by a strong nationalist economic policy on the part of Indian manufacturers and merchants, and they knew that a mere attitude of opposition would merely result in the utter disregard of their interests. Nor, it must be remembered, were they necessarily interested in the development of the control of British manufactures; they were in part interested in other countries' export trade, and this fact explains the comparative indifference shown by them to all attempts to secure opportunities for British exports. Moreover, they had been convinced by experience of the danger of the boycott, and they believed, whether rightly or wrongly, that it was less likely to be used as a weapon if they appeared in Indian eyes as favouring reform.

The Labour government in the United Kingdom was in control during the early stages of the Conference, and unquestionably it was largely affected by the doctrine that democracy was essentially justifiable and could not properly be withheld from the Indian people. The rank and file of the party were also under the impression that the reforms contemplated conferring on the workers of India control of the government, and thus would replace capitalism by workers' control. Only gradually did it come to be realized that the proposals which would emerge from any Conference could never be successful in according any control to workers, and that any scheme must place the power in the hands of a middle-class intelligentsia and the Conservative retainers of the Indian princes. It was then impossible for the party to do more than reiterate its conviction that India should have a constitution far more generous in concession than that proposed. But throughout every effort was made to ignore the salient fact that the project meant sacrificing any power that still existed of preserving the interests of the lower classes. Occasional use was made of the argument that the grant of responsible government opened the way for the masses of India to secure power of controlling their own destinies. But it was ignored that the structure of the constitution presented no means by which the classes whom it enfranchised, and the intelligentsia to which it accorded power, could be forced to surrender any share of authority to the lower orders of the people, and that, on the contrary, it entrenched them in an unassailable position fortified by the knowledge that any revolutionary efforts to overthrow their rule, should such happen, would be destroyed by the British forces.

The Conservative opposition[1] to the proposals was open to attack on many specious grounds. It was urged that it was based on old-fashioned ideals of domination, expressed by retired officers who could see no good in change. This view was reinforced by insistence on the fact that the reforms were accepted by the heads of the provincial governments and members of the governor-general's council, a contention which deliberately ignored the obvious fact that after 1919 it would have been absurd for the British Government to entrust high office to men who were not genuinely in favour of the reform movement. That such men should remain adherents to it was only to be expected; critics naturally either retired prematurely or on completion of service without achieving the highest offices. Again the opposition was charged with the desire to exploit India for the benefit of British trade, and no credence was accorded to their contention that extreme protection in India was working hardship on the consumer, a fact which was candidly admitted in 1935 by the member of council in charge of finance, though he confessed that revenue considerations precluded the serious reduction of tariff rates. The opposition stressed also, quite fairly, the fact that India owed much to British protection, and that some favour in trade would have been not inconsistent with imperial history. Canada when she gave her early preferences recognized that in this way she was paying her debt for British defence. It pointed out also the grave danger of the removal of British control over sectarian vehemence, a view sadly strengthened by the deplorable bitterness which was to be shown at Cawnpore and Karachi between Hindus and Muslims, now actuated by the

[1] Cf. Sir R. Craddock, *Asiatic Review*, 1935, pp. 217 ff.

hope or fear of political domination. It contended that the vast mass of the people of India was wholly unused to democratic ideas and only desired effective and impartial government, which would disappear in the introduction of responsible government under the quite unsuitable conditions of India. In the course of the discussions the failure of democracy in most lands was naturally stressed as an argument against its extension to India, and great importance was attached to the attitude of Congress which asserted the right of India to full independence, while even more moderate men spoke of drastic revision of the burden of the Indian debt and the transfer of such part of it as represented wars of aggression to British shoulders. The utter inconsistency of yoking British India with the autocracy of the states was adduced, and great stress came to be placed on the danger of anarchy, once the police force fell under ministerial control, with the resulting danger that it would fail to act impartially as between Hindu and Muslim. To this argument stress was lent by the constant manifestation of anarchic movements in Bengal, which proved extremely difficult to counter, and which showed in what constant danger lived the men who were engaged in combating this menace.[1] It was not very difficult to adduce evidence of deterioration of public services under ministerial control; in fact, the desire to give local government institutions free room to develop had resulted in an unwise relaxation of central control, and in inefficiency and increased cost.

At the first session of the conference it was clear that, while the general principle of federation was accepted, there would be grave difficulty in arranging the details, for each great interest was determined to secure the maximum of concessions as the price of co-operation. The principle of democracy as understood in the Dominions, the rule of the majority, could not be accepted by the Muslims nor any other of the great minorities represented at the Conference. Nor were the Hindus themselves united in demanding orthodox democracy, for the depressed classes among them felt much apprehension lest the new constitution should place them helplessly in the hands of

[1] See Bengal Administration Report, 1933–4, p. xxxii; H.C. Paper 5 of 1933–4, ii, 391 ff.

the brahmans and other higher castes. In addition to safeguards for minorities, it was necessary to provide safeguards to ensure India against external and internal instability. The most enthusiastic Indian politician in his moments of cool reflection was bound to admit that his country was not yet prepared to maintain itself against external attack, and that apart from danger from a great power, the masses of tribesmen on the north-west frontier and the possibility of Afghan co-operation rendered a powerful defence force essential. To make that force Indian would be a long business, and politicians could not overlook the danger that the force once created might use its strength to establish the control of those classes who belong to martial races and enlist in and become officers of the Indian Army. There was also deep anxiety regarding the maintenance of internal order, for the time being secured by the use of British troops completely free from any racial or communal bias. But the maintenance of British forces must mean the reduction of the measure of responsible government, for the British Government plainly could not surrender to an Indian legislature and a ministry dependent upon it the control over the British troops. This position involved at once financial consequences of the gravest kind, for the cost of the army[1] was bound to absorb the major portion of the available revenue, and the necessity of providing funds to meet it must mean the direction along certain lines of both taxation and currency policies. Not less important was the question of security for loans. These had been regularly raised in England by the secretary of state in council, and nothing had been done, as was done in the case of Dominion loans,[2] to make it clear to lenders that they must look to Indian revenues alone for reimbursement. After all, in the days of the Company, lenders of money had looked to reimbursement by the Company without thinking of the source of its revenues, and naturally it was assumed by lenders that the British Government must so order Indian policy that there could be no chance of default. Moreover, apart from this strong moral argument, there was the fact that it would be disastrous to British credit in general if

[1] 46·20 crores in 1933–4 out of 77·91 crores, the revenue being 78·16.
[2] Keith, *Letters on Imperial Relations*, 1916–35, pp. 227, 228.

any part of the Empire were allowed to default. It was remembered that pressure had been successfully brought to bear on the Commonwealth of Australia to undo the damage done by the default of New South Wales, and this precedent was strengthened in 1934 by the terms given to Newfoundland[1] rather than risk the effects of a default there. Plainly it would be necessary to control finance to such an extent as to secure payment of the army and of the interest on the public debt.

Protection was also necessary for British commercial interests, whether those of manufacturers who had found entry into India for their goods hampered by high tariffs and more gravely still by boycott, or those of the British mercantile community and financial interests. They had reaped large profits from India, but they had also conferred upon it great benefits, and had inspired Indian firms to rivalry and the desire to make use of political power to make good their handicaps in the competition for business. It was essential also to safeguard the position of civil servants. The lower posts had already largely passed into Indian hands, the education service had been Indianized perhaps too completely and hastily for its own good, and there remain mainly the Indian Civil Service, the Indian Police, and the civil side of the Indian Medical Service, with irrigation engineering as open to systematic European recruitment side by side with Indian. The members of these services must be protected in the enjoyment of their rights, but it was also necessary to secure the continuance of the British recruitment for the services for the period of transition.

Hindu-Muslim rivalry added enormously to the difficulties of the situation, for the Muslims were not willing to contemplate the creation of the strong central government desired by the Hindus, to exercise financial and general control over the provinces, since it was clear that in the centre there must be a Hindu majority. Moreover, the Muslims realized and freely used the tactical advantage to be derived from refusing to take any serious part in discussing the powers to be accorded the central government until they had secured a decision in their favour on the question of the composition of the legislatures.

[1] Keith, *Journ. Comp. Leg.*, xvi, 25 ff.

They had early seen the advantage which would accrue if they could have in as many provinces as possible Muslim majorities, so that in the other provinces anti-Muslim propaganda might be held in check by fear of reprisals. It was a rather ingenious plan, and resulted in the steady pressure put on the government to concede the erection of the North-West Frontier Province into the status of a governor's province with the usual legislature and dyarchy, a result achieved in 1932, and to create a new predominantly Muslim province by separating Sind from Bombay, a connexion admittedly historical and artificial, though it was defended on the score that Sind gained greatly from expenditure on it at the expense of Bombay.

(b) THE FIRST SESSION OF THE CONFERENCE

The result of the first session of the Conference[1] established the exemption from ministerial control of the issues of external relations and defence. The latter issue necessarily evoked serious reserves from Indian delegates, and various plans were mooted by which the governor-general might be brought into close touch with Indian opinion in his conduct of defence policy. It was suggested, for instance, that his adviser for defence should always be an Indian chosen from the elected members of the Assembly. It was common ground that every effort must be made to interest Indian legislators in defence matters and to obtain helpful co-operation in the difficult task of preserving the security of India while training an Indian army. It followed therefore that the governor-general must have a special responsibility for financial stability, seeing that he was responsible for defence which controlled the financial position, but that the governors need not be required to act in this sense. It was also agreed that governor-general and governors must co-operate in protecting minorities, and that the position of the civil service must be safeguarded. On commercial discrimination a way out seemed possible on the basis of an agreement between India and the United Kingdom on a basis of reciprocity;[2] as the United Kingdom was wont to

[1] Parl. Papers, Cmd. 3778, 3972.

[2] For a draft see Keith, *Letters on Imperial Relations*, 1916–35, pp. 234–44.

accord complete equality of treatment to Indians, the same treatment might properly be granted in return. Further, it was agreed that the governor-general and governor must be given the widest power of independent action in case of emergency and to prevent the breakdown of government. It was endeavoured on the part of the British delegates to make out that such safeguards were part of every British constitution, but this clearly was an over-statement and it had little effect beyond confusing the issue, and also commentators on it. The obvious truth was that India presented problems *sui generis* and that the safeguards were novel, because they were planned to meet new conditions and must stand or fall on their own merit.

Burma, it was agreed, might well be severed from India, as advised on geographical, ethical, religious, and social grounds by the Simon Commission.

The accord achieved, defective as it was, represented the consensus only of a minority of politically minded Indians, for Congress was hostile and derided the claims of the Indian delegates to bind India. Hence Lord Irwin decided to seek accommodation with Mr. Gandhi as the dominating figure in Congress. The civil disobedience movement was ruining the trade of the towns, it pressed heavily on finance, and it strained the police organization and the jails to the utmost, besides adding gravely to the almost intolerable burden of civil administration. On the other hand, Mr. Gandhi probably felt that an opportunity was at last afforded to strike an effective blow for his side in a positive effort at construction. At any rate, the accord of March 1931 put an end to civil disobedience, though it permitted peaceful picketing in support of a campaign in favour of purchase of Indian products, and released those political prisoners who had not been found guilty of violent crimes. The temporary ordinances most objected to were to be recalled, and in return Congress was to take part in the next session of the Conference. It must be admitted that the pact was a distinct triumph for the governor-general, though it might also be held to be a signal tribute to the power of an Indian leader to secure a formal agreement with a government as to its political conduct. But the fatal mistake was made of sending Mr. Gandhi as the solitary spokesman of Congress to

England, for he obviously represented only one of its many aspects and in social and economic views he differed very seriously from many of his ardent followers on political issues.[1] Moreover, the Congress meeting at Karachi was agitated by frutless efforts to save from execution the Sikh Bhagat Singh condemned to death for the murder of Mr. Saunders, and the efforts of Congress volunteers to enforce a hartal on Muslim shopkeepers resulted in a disgraceful massacre at Cawnpore[2] which was terminated only by military efforts.

(c) THE SECOND SESSION OF THE CONFERENCE

The proceedings (September 7th–December 1st 1931) of the second session of the Conference were unhappily rendered from the start unfructuous by the attitude adopted by Mr. Gandhi in claiming that he spoke for the people of India as a whole and in denying the representative character of the spokesmen of the minorities.[3] In any case the Conference was held under conditions unfavourable to dispassionate consideration of Indian issues. The financial and economic crisis of 1931 had driven the Prime Minister to secure retention of office at the expense of a coalition which resulted in the definite repudiation of their leader by the vast majority of Labour politicians and most of the Labour electorate. Naturally it was widely thought that the change of government might induce a change of view on the part of the ministry. But Mr. MacDonald was able to secure from the rejection of his cherished tenets certain principles, including the continuation of his Indian policy without much change. An effort was made to suggest that it might be well to consider provincial autonomy apart from the creation of the federal structure, but this was unanimously repudiated by the Indian delegates and the suggestion was not pressed. There were hopes that it might be possible to secure through Mr. Gandhi accord on the vexed question of communal representation, but here again failure was recorded, for Mr. Gandhi probably realized that his popularity was on the wane

[1] Bose, *The Indian Struggle*, pp. 247–61.

[2] Parl. Paper, Cmd. 3891.

[3] Parl. Paper, Cmd. 3997; British India had sixty-five representatives, the states twenty-two, the British parties twenty. For Burma a separate Conference sat from November 27th 1931 to January 12th 1932, Cmd. 4004.

and that any concession made by him would be resented by his followers in India. On the other hand, the minority representatives got together and planned a scheme of safeguards for themselves which went a good deal beyond anything reasonably likely to be accepted. Ultimately it became patent that nothing could be expected from agreement in the way of the disposal of the communal issue, and that if progress was to be made the British Government must act.

The chief result of the change of government was probably the complete change of attitude on the part of the government of India under Lord Willingdon. The return of Mr. Gandhi found just cause for action afforded to the government by the action of Abdul Ghafur Khan and his followers in the North-West Frontier Province, and the decision was taken to strike at the activities of Congress by declaring its operations illegal, while Mr. Gandhi was again imprisoned. The weapons of preventive arrest and sequestration of property of any illegal organization were resorted to, and met with much success. It was natural that the propaganda of Congress could not be kept up indefinitely. The hartals ceased to be exciting and shopkeepers began to count the cost in loss of trade; the no-rent campaigns among the peasantry ceased to satisfy when their political purpose was realized by the peasants, who saw little prospect of gaining anything. Indian industrialists were not willing to risk further sums on an illegal organization, and the minorities could not forgive Mr. Gandhi for his effort to speak for them in London. Moreover, within the party there were serious difficulties due in part to rivalries such as that of Mr. Subash Chandra Bose and Mr. Sen Gupta in Bengal, and in part to the growth within the party of a wing which was decidedly communistic in outlook and had little sympathy with the Mahatma's muddled idealism. The result was that the restoration of the effective authority of the government was rapid. The fact that interned persons could safely be released was shown by the decline in the number of those detained for civil disobedience from 34,458 in April 1932 to 4,683 in July 1933. The reassertion of governmental authority[1] was plainly

[1] For measures in Bengal against terrorism cf. Bose, *The Indian Struggle*, pp. 334–40.

a necessary preliminary to any effective progress with the difficult work of reform. At the same time the ground for advance was thoroughly explored by a committee which investigated on the spot the crucial issue of the franchise, while another committee devoted its attention to the financial claims of the Indian states. The report of the franchise committee was followed by the announcement of the government's decision of the communal issue.[1] It was naturally based on the large measure of agreement already achieved, which explains why it proved difficult to induce general resistance to its terms. But Mr. Gandhi was deeply moved at the idea that the depressed classes should be treated as distinct for voting purposes instead of being included in the general constituencies. The result was that he forced the hands of the leaders of these classes, Dr. Ambedkar in particular, and secured a pact[2] which was of manifest material advantage to the depressed classes, and doubtless of spiritual advantage to Mr. Gandhi. The number of seats allocated to these classes was to be increased at the expense of the general body of Hindus, but the depressed classes were to vote in general constituencies. But they were separately to select four times as many candidates as there were seats to be filled by representatives of these classes, so that no person might be chosen to fill one of these seats who was not acceptable to the classes concerned. The net result unquestionably has been to penalize the higher-caste Hindus, who had allowed themselves to be outmanœuvred and who had thrown overboard the principle of due regard to numbers in allocating seats by their support for tactical reasons of the demands of the Sikhs of the Punjab for recognition far beyond their numerical rights. The other point of chief interest in the franchise proposals of the committee was their failure to find any workable form of direct election which would enable villagers to have a say. The administrative difficulties were found to be too great, and eventually the committee had to be content with enfranchising as they judged about 27 per cent of the people for provincial elections, while for elections to the federal Assembly some seven or eight million voters might be provided.[3]

[1] Parl. Paper, Cmd. 4147 (August 4th 1932).

[2] Poona Pact, September 24th 1932.

[3] Parl. Paper, Cmd. 4238, pp. 25, 26.

(d) THE THIRD SESSION OF THE CONFERENCE

There followed a third session[1] of the Conference (November 17th–December 24th 1932), which was convened rather reluctantly by the British Government, for it had hoped that all that remained to be done in the way of consultation might be carried out in India. The character of this session was marked by the cessation of Labour co-operation in the Conference, thus introducing a definitely party element into the proceedings, and by the absence of any spokesman of Congress, a fact which helped to accelerate the proceedings. It now remained for the government to accept responsibility for definite proposals to effect the carrying into law of the measure of accord achieved by the Conference, together with such further issues as must be decided to complete the scheme. This took the form in March 1933[2] of a set of proposals for reform which were to be submitted to a joint select committee of Parliament for examination and report. The White Paper was on the whole a very fair reproduction of the results achieved, but it is quite fair to say that it was rather definitely drawn up in order to placate the volume of Conservative criticism which had been steadily growing ever since the conclusion of the first session of the Conference. General approval of the policy then arrived at had been accorded by the Liberal and the Conservative parties, but on this head Mr. Churchill had separated himself in 1931 from the group of ex-ministers who formed Mr. Baldwin's shadow cabinet, and ever since then had led the revolt against concessions.

(e) THE REPORT OF THE JOINT SELECT COMMITTEE

The proceedings of the Joint Select Committee[3] suffered from the limitation of its membership. It was contended by the opponents of the scheme, with some degree of justification, that the constitution of the committee was too definitely marked by

[1] Parl. Paper, Cmd. 4238.

[2] Parl. Paper, Cmd. 4268. Despite the indecisive result of the Burmese election of 1932 on the issue of separation, its advantages clearly outweighed the objections in the view of the government.

[3] H.C. Paper 5 of 1933–4; H.C. 112 of 1933.

approval of the governmental policy and that a more impartial body should have been set up. As a result Mr. Churchill and Lord Lloyd declined to serve upon it and thus allowed their chance of improving the proposals to go by default. The committee, however, had a measure of assistance from a select body of Indian representatives, who took part in its proceedings somewhat in the attitude of assessors, and who presented to it an expression of their views on the position. The most interesting feature of the proceedings was the attitude adopted on several points by the Labour members of the committee. They accepted as inevitable the main outlines of the scheme, and regretfully confessed that there was no real chance of the workers, agrarian or industrial, controlling for a prolonged period the legislatures, though they would have widened the franchise substantially. But they objected to the proposal to constitute the federal legislature of two houses, on the ground *inter alia* that the legislature was in any case too large for all the work it could have to do, and that there was much danger of its seeking to interfere in issues which were really provincial. Exception was also taken to the reservation of foreign affairs in the hands of the governor-general. It was held to be only fair that India should be entitled to define her own attitude on external issues, especially as that attitude would largely determine the cost of defence. Further, it was urged that Indianization of the forces should be arranged for at a definite date, on the ground that the military authorities if given this task would succeed in bringing it to a satisfactory conclusion, but that, if the matter were left undefined, there might be serious delay in its accomplishment. It was also argued that control over finance should be left to the Indian government, which could not be free without such control; responsibility could be learned only by exercising it. Safeguards in general were deprecated with an exception for such only as Indians demanded through distrust of one another. Commercial safeguards in special were perfectly futile, for India was thoroughly conversant with the art of political boycott. Even in the case of defence there should be a statutory committee of the legislature which from the first should be kept in touch with defence problems.

In essence the majority of the committee accepted the governmental proposals, but emphasized still more the necessity of safeguards as a result of the evidence given to them on behalf of the civil service and the police, and perhaps still more because of the facts laid before them by the government itself regarding the prevalence of anarchical conspiracy in Bengal which had distinguished itself by political assassination, young women being dragged into the contest. None the less the committee rejected suggestions of reserving law and order, and accepted the contentions of the Simon Commission on this head. The fundamental argument was simply that the sense of responsibility must be destroyed by the functioning of government in watertight compartments separated under the constitution, and that friction between the parts of a government so divided was inevitable. On a like ground the committee rejected the view that there could be an irresponsible federal government side by side with responsible ministries in the provinces. Provincial ministers would constantly be able to disclaim responsibility on the score that the economic policy and the finance of the central government precluded their carrying out their programmes of social betterment. It was naturally admitted that the reservation of foreign affairs and defence did create dyarchy within the central government, but it was pointed out that these departments had normally few points of contact with other fields of central administration under the new constitution. It was necessarily admitted that control over the army involved a certain measure of control over railway and road communication, but the importance of that might be minimized. Perhaps insufficient attention was paid to the fundamental fact that the demands of defence on revenue really must determine the economic and financial policy of any government in very large measure, and that to assert that a responsible government was possible when it must devote most of the revenue it raised to purposes over which it had no control was to treat responsible government in a rather curious manner. Nor was sufficient stress laid on the fact that the federal legislature must tend to devote its attention to securing control over issues which so deeply affected its powers as those of defence and external relations. The decisive factor, however, was the absolute determination of the princes not to accept federation without responsibility. The difficulty caused by the inability of the princes to accept the full list of subjects which could be made central as federal raised much discussion. It was felt to be impossible to surrender the chance of legislating for all the provinces in certain important issues, and the best conclusion that could be arrived at was that a convention might suitably be developed under which the representatives of the states would not vote on central questions, though the possibility of providing for this by any legal provision was ruled out.

(*f*) THE GOVERNMENT OF INDIA BILL IN PARLIAMENT

The passage of the Bill through the House of Commons resulted in certain changes of considerable, though not primary, importance. The position of the states raised serious objections on the part of the princes, who were most anxious to maintain that their acceptance of federation must not be treated as if they were subject to the legislative authority of Parliament.[1] The sixth clause of the Bill as introduced provided that a ruler must accept the Act as applicable to himself and his subjects, specifying in his instrument of accession the subjects on which the federation was to have power to legislate for the state and specifying any condition to which his accession was to be subject. The princes seem to have desired to establish the point that the Act should be in force in each state solely by authority of the instrument of accession. Obviously, if there were any substance in the view of the princes, it was impossible to give effect to it, and the position was dealt with merely by verbal changes, and the clause as altered provides that a ruler 'accedes to the federation as established by this Act' instead of accepting the Act. It may be doubted if the position of the princes is in any way improved by the change of phrase. In a number of other points of minor importance concessions were made as regards wording, and in one major provision. The original proposal regarding the possibility of a breakdown of the constitution had provided for the indefinite

[1] Parl. Papers, Cmd. 4843, 4903 (1935).

suspension of the constitution by the authority of the British Government. It was now made clear that any suspension could not last beyond three years without parliamentary legislation being undertaken. On the other hand, the government declined to accept the suggestion that in the case of suspension any state should have the right to secede from the federation, and it equally declined to undertake to define and limit its paramount powers as an inducement to the states to accept federation. Such inducements as are offered therefore are chiefly financial, and the possible grant of full control over such civil stations as Bangalore in the case of Mysore. It was, however, made clear in the case of Tangasseri that no transfer to Travancore could be carried out against the wishes of the people.

As regards the federal executive the chief change made was in respect of the special responsibilities of the government generally towards the services. These were made to extend to persons who had been in the government service and to the dependents of officials and ex-officials, thus placing beyond doubt the position of the governor-general in respect of pensions and family pensions. For the purpose of further assurance of rights in these matters the obligation of the central and provincial governments to provide the secretary of state with sufficient funds to meet liabilities due was extended to include specifically pension liabilities. The responsibility of the secretary of state for the payment of pensions due outside India was explicitly recognized, and the right to sue the secretary of state in respect of pension liabilities was preserved. It was claimed on behalf of the pensioners that express power to pay out of British funds should be included in the Act, but this was refused, as was also the much more reasonable claim for a formal guarantee. The arguments of the government were far from happy; it was contended that a guarantee was unnecessary, but clearly if it removed anxieties it would have served a useful purpose. It was further urged that it was undesirable as it would enable an Indian government to use a refusal to pay pensions as a means of pressure on the British Government in the knowledge that the pensioners would not suffer. It is ludicrous to suppose that such knowledge would affect in any way the action of an Indian government, and the doubts of pensioners were not wholly removed by the argument that it would be the duty of the secretary of state to instruct the governor-general to raise necessary funds by taxation or to issue a loan in order to pay pensions.[1] The difficulty obviously is that Indian finance may be so disintegrated that pensions cannot be paid without taking away funds necessary for current business, and in such an event the fate of pensions is obvious. Clearly the new security is much inferior to the old, and attempts to hold that under the former régime the British Government was not ultimately bound to obtain funds from Parliament if need be to meet pensions were wholly unconvincing.

The essential provisions regarding the federal legislature passed without substantial change. The Liberal opposition contended strongly, in harmony with the views of the government of India[2] and of Indian politicians, in favour of the direct election of members by the Assembly by territorial constituencies. The chief arguments against this project were based on the impossibility of any real contact between the electorate and the member when constituencies must be so large, and the advantage to be derived from securing close contact between those responsible for provincial legislation and the federal Parliament.

The provincial executive was accepted by the Commons without serious change. The chief anxiety expressed by the opposition turned on the control of terrorism, of communism, of the no-rent campaign, and of civil disobedience; but the government insisted that the provisions inserted in the Bill which added to the special responsibilities of the governor the duty of supervision of police regulations, and of combating attempts to overthrow the government were adequate for the ends desired. One substantial change only was made and that affected the provincial legislatures. Assam was given a second chamber as a further concession to the conservative character of the whole scheme. The franchise for the lower chambers was definitely made part of the Bill by being embodied in a schedule, and it is a sign of the care with which the Act was

[1] Lord Zetland to Lord Rankeillour, July 16th 1935.
[2] Cf. Parl. Paper, Cmd. 3700, pp. 114 ff.

passed that the terms of the schedule were carefully scrutinized in committee. Efforts were made by the Labour party to extend the franchise, but the government naturally enough resisted firmly this project, on the score that the report of the franchise committee showed the administrative impossibility of any wider franchise. Only minor amendments thus could be made, including the grant of the vote to retired officers and men of the Indian police on the same conditions as to officers and men of the army. The electorate was calculated at 35,000,000, 14 per cent of the population, 27 per cent of the male population, and 43 per cent of the adult male population. In the case of females the Commons adopted the changes proposed by the joint select committee. The proposals of the franchise committee were estimated to enfranchise women in the proportion of 1 : 4½ to men. The White Paper reduced that to 1 : 7 by requiring women who were qualified in respect of their husbands' property holdings to claim registration and by imposing a higher educational test. The select committee recommended that the necessity of application might be removed in certain provinces and areas, and that in certain provinces the educational test should be lower, thus increasing the proportion to 1 · 5, subject to reduction if the requirement of application, where retained, proved to discourage enrolments. These views were given effect in the Commons, and the government there promised to provide facilities in the Bill for the removal before the second election of the application test in those cases where it was retained at first, except where social conditions would make such rapid progress dangerous.

A further concession to women was made in the undertaking to reserve for them six seats on the Council of State, to which they might otherwise never attain entry, and in the declaration that a person shall not be disqualified by sex from being appointed by the Crown to any civil post under the Crown in India, but with due power to the secretary of state, the governor-general, and the governors to make exceptions to this principle.

The question of legislative power in the federation and the provinces resulted in no serious change. The provisions regarding the prevention of discrimination against British trade were much debated, but it was accepted that legislative discrimination must be directly prohibited in the constitution by enactment, thus accepting the plan which the British community had proposed without acceptance to the Simon Commission. But at the same time the compromise of the select committee was included, under which the restrictive clauses of the constitution may be held in abeyance by Order in Council if a convention covering the issues is successfully negotiated with the new Indian government. The wording of the restrictive clauses was made more extensive, but was not extended to executive discrimination, which was left a special responsibility of governor-general and governors. Moreover, the government definitely refused to accept the proposal to forbid the imposition of penal duties on United Kingdom exports, insisting that this would needlessly limit Indian authority.

The government made further concessions in the matter of excluded and partially excluded areas, which it had proposed to define in a brief schedule. It was pointed out that the issue was one of great importance in the interests of the backward tribes. Excluded areas would be administered at the governor's discretion, in partially excluded areas he would be responsible for protecting the interests of the aborigines, and it was therefore desirable, especially as the Act had provision only for transforming an excluded into a partially excluded area and for merging a partially excluded area into a province, to mark out as many areas as possible for such protection. The weight of the contention was serious, and the governmental argument that it was difficult to delimit areas owing to the scattered condition of the aboriginal tribes, and that assimilation was to be aimed at, failed to carry much conviction. Finally it was decided to accept neither the government's brief schedule nor the longer one proposed in lieu, but to determine the areas by Order in Council based on a White Paper, giving the relevant facts, to be laid before the Houses.

A rather bitter controversy was waged over the question of the desire of the Labour and Liberal parties to include in the Bill a definite reference to Dominion status as the goal of Indian government. The government adopted a curious attitude. It definitely accepted the pledge contained in the preamble of the Act of 1919 of the gradual development of self-governing institutions with a view to the progressive realization of responsible government in British India as an integral part of the Empire, and the interpretation put thereon by the governor-general in 1929 with the authority of the government of the day: 'The natural issue of India's progress as there contemplated is the attainment of Dominion status.' But it refused to put anything of this kind in a preamble, and instead insisted on preserving the preamble to the Act of 1919, when repealing that measure under the new Act. The preservation of the smile of the Cheshire cat after its disappearance was justly adduced by critics as the best parallel to this legislative monstrosity, and the omission of any reference to Dominion status, following on the complete silence of the joint committee, inevitably caused a painful feeling in India, and annoyance to those supporters of the ministry who realized that its action was certain to be interpreted in India as in some way seeking to evade frank acceptance of Dominion status as the final goal.

In the House of Lords the reception accorded to the Bill was naturally even more conservative than in the Commons, though the principle of the measure was definitely homologated and any idea of serious change was ruled out. But only one vital change was made with the assent of the government. The election of the British Indian members of the Council of State was transferred from the upper chambers of the provinces, where these existed, and special electoral bodies to be created, to the direct election in electorates with a high franchise to be delimited subsequent to the passing of the Act and approved by Order in Council submitted to Parliament.[1] It was difficult to find any logical justification for the change, and in the Commons Sir A. Chamberlain justly criticized the plan by which an Upper House was given a direct connexion with the people denied to the Lower House, and made indissoluble. The only excuse that could be adduced for the change was that it in a faint manner served to conciliate the Liberal opposition, which pressed for the adoption of direct election to the Assembly, and in fact it was accepted by that section of opinion, presumably

[1] 25 & 26 Geo. V, c. 42, s. 18 and Sched. 1.

because it must involve at no distant date direct election for the Assembly in order to remove an absurd anomaly. By an unkind fate the under-secretary who a short time before had proved unexceptionably that direct election for the Council was out of the question had to prove equally effectively that it was desirable. Unfortunately less than thirty private members took the trouble to attend the debate on this issue, perhaps because it was felt difficult to defend the *volte-face*, and Lord Eustace Percy could only plead that anomalies were an inevitable part of the new framework.

Other amendments were of minor importance. The governor-general and the governors were specifically encouraged to send messages to the legislatures to indicate their views on pending Bills[1] affecting their responsibilities. The previous sanction of the governor-general was made necessary for the introduction of any Bill varying the Indian side of the arrangement regarding relief from double income tax. The power of the Indian legislature was restricted by forbidding it to affect the right of the Crown in Council to grant special leave to hear appeals from the decision of courts in India except as specially authorized in the Act, thus extending a clause originally referring to criminal appeals. The rights of the Anglo-Indian community in respect of appointments in the post and telegraphs and railways departments were specifically recognized, and in the Commons the customs department was added to those specified. The necessity of the approval of the governor acting in his discretion or the governor-general to the leave of absence as well as the promotion of any officer appointed by the secretary of state was laid down.

It was decided that the secretary of state, the governor-general, and the governors should be given complete immunity from the jurisdiction of Indian courts during their term of office, including any process such as summons as a witness. When no longer in office the same immunity will apply as regards official acts save by special permission of the King in Council. But proceedings in England are not affected. It was also provided that during the transitional period before federation certain powers of the governor-general should be available.

[1] Ss. 20 (2), 63 (2).

On one point the government found the House of Lords especially anxious. The proposal to refuse power to the Indian legislature to penalize British imports was renewed, and ultimately a clause was moved to secure for British imports most favoured nation treatment. A very strong case could be made out for this concession, Canada having just reaffirmed her belief in this principle by extending not only to the United Kingdom but to South Africa, Australia, and New Zealand the benefit of her latest concessions to foreign powers. But the government refused to alter its standpoint that compulsion was inadmissible and was sustained by a small majority. Lord Derby voting in the minority, despite a faithful support of the Bill, which had led to his using his influence to secure the withdrawal of certain evidence originally proposed to be placed before the joint committee on behalf of the cotton industry, a procedure ultimately producing a change of standing orders as to witnesses destined to prevent a repetition of similar action.[1]

For convenience the Act was directed by the Government of India (Reprinting) Act, passed on December 20th 1935 to be reissued as the Government of India Act, 1935, and the Government of Burma Act, 1935.

[1] H.C. Paper 84 of 1934–5, May 9th 1935.

CHAPTER X

FEDERALISM AND RESPONSIBLE GOVERNMENT UNDER THE GOVERNMENT OF INDIA ACT 1935

1. THE SALIENT CHARACTERISTICS OF THE FEDERATION

MUCH learning was displayed in the course of the discussion of the federation in the adduction of suggestions for guidance from other federal constitutions, but the essential principles of the new federation were obviously derived from those in operation in Canada and Australia, both of which Dominions owed much to federalism in the United States. Continental models furnished little that could be adopted, for the problem was new. None of the units to be federated had international status of any kind *inter se*, but on the one hand the provinces had been under the strict control of the central government and were now to be accorded a wider autonomy, while on the other the states had definitely to accept the restrictions of a federal system in place of a vague and varying measure of control by the Crown.

The federation exhibits all the normal characteristics of federal government.[1] There is a rigid constitution, with a very elaborate distinction of federal and local powers, and a federal court whose duty it is to secure the due observance of the limits placed on the centre and the local governments and legislatures. The constitution is written, and amendment is definitely and narrowly restricted. But the special circumstances of India result in many variations between the Indian constitution and those of Canada and Australia. On the other hand, it is truly federal, and therefore it differs essentially from the constitution of the Union of South Africa, which, under a semblance of federalism due to historical causes, is essentially unitary.

In Canada and in Australia federation was formed by the

[1] Keith, *Responsible Government in the Dominions* (1928), Pt. IV; *The Constitutional Law of the British Dominions* (1933).

agreement of colonies, each self-governing, to unite for certain purposes of common interest, while retaining in less degree in Canada, in greater in Australia, their original authority in matters not given to the federation. In India the provinces were not self-governing, and were already united under the control of a central government with plenary powers, the provinces thus being in law wholly subordinate divisions of a unitary state. The federation in their case confers on them an autonomy which they never before possessed, and gives it a legal basis. The provinces at the same time suffer diminution of functions and power in certain respects, for federal matters are now separated from provincial questions and taken away from provincial authority, which was unnecessary under the earlier régime when central control rendered provincial action with central approval legitimate in any field. A second element of the federation is afforded by the states, which do surrender definitely a considerable measure of their former authority, and thus conform closely to the normal federal type. This combination of wholly disparate elements gives a unique character to the federation and produces certain abnormal features. Thus, while the provinces are subject to a single system applicable to all, the states are definitely exempt from the application of a number of federal powers of legislation, unless they expressly accept them, which is not expected to be the case. In the same way the executive authority of the federation is uniform in regard to the provinces, but it may vary as regards the states. Moreover, both as regards federal legislative and executive authority, there may be variations between states, though naturally a certain uniformity is intended. The states again differ from the provinces in the essential fact that in each case adhesion is voluntary, while the provinces have federation imposed from above.

The division of powers in Canada rests on the assignment to federation and provinces of defined spheres, the very limited grant of concurrent powers on agriculture and immigration to both, federal legislation being paramount, and the grant of all residuary power to the federation. In course of legal interpretation the sphere of provincial power has been extended beyond the intentions of the fathers of federation, and the importance of the residuary power was until recently minimized by the courts. In Australia the federation has a few exclusive powers, and a large number of concurrent but paramount powers, while all power not expressly or by necessary implication made federal exclusively can be exercised by the states, subject to being overridden by federal legislation. In India the attempt has been made very elaborately to assign power to the federation and to the units by enumeration of subjects, while a wide sphere may be regulated by both. In the latter case the units are permitted with the assent of the governor-general to legislate in such a manner as to override prior federal Acts on the same topic,[1] and the governor-general has the unusual power[2] of assigning to federation or units at his discretion heads of legislation or finance not allocated by the Act.

In Canada the heads of the provincial governments are appointed by the federal government and may be removed from office by that government, but this power has ceased to be used in any substantial manner to effect federal ends, the lieutenant-governors having been in practice assimilated in functions to constitutional sovereigns. In Australia the appointment and removal of governors of the states rests with the British Government, and the federal government has no influence whatever in the matter. In India the governors of the provinces are subject to the control of the governor-general, subject to the approval of the secretary of state, in all matters in which they are required to act at their discretion or in their individual judgment.[3] In Canada and Australia the governor-general is a constitutional monarch as regards his ministers; in India he is subject to the secretary of state[4] in matters of his discretion or individual judgment.

In Canada provincial legislation may be disallowed by the federal government, but this power is now largely if not entirely disused as a method of enforcing federal authority, Acts of dubious validity being left to the courts to declare invalid. In Australia no power of disallowance exists on the part of the Commonwealth, and in practice the power of the British Government to secure disallowance is almost obsolete;

[1] 25 & 26 Geo. V, c. 42, s. 107 (2). [2] S. 104. [3] S. 54. [4] S. 14.

in any event it would never be used to affect matters which could be determined by the courts in respect of state versus federal power.

In both federations enjoying Dominion status the units and the federal government are in possession of full responsible government, which is denied in India, in greater measure in the federation, for defence and foreign relations are administered by the governor-general in his discretion, subject to the control of the Home Government. In the same way the constitutions of Canada and Australia can be amended only at the will of their governments, and Parliaments, with in the case of Australia a popular referendum. The Canadian constitution can be changed only by the British Parliament which would act only on a definite request from both houses of the Dominion Parliament, and such a request would normally be based on agreement with the provinces. In the case of India the power to alter the constitution is entirely vested in the British Government and Parliament.[1]

The judicial control in Canada is exercised primarily by the provincial courts, which are organized by the provinces, but whose judges are appointed by the federal government, and on appeal by the Supreme Court, with a final appeal to the Privy Council, or by the Privy Council. In Australia the final control of constitutional issues respecting the relations *inter se* of the federation and state rests with the high court, which may, but in fact does not, allow appeal to the Privy Council in such causes. In India constitutional issues will be dealt with partly by the high courts, partly by the federal court, but the final interpretation of the constitution will rest always with the Privy Council, from which appeals cannot be shut out by any Indian legislation.[2]

2. THE CROWN AND ITS REPRESENTATIVES

The authority of the Crown over India, which was formerly exercised through the East India Company and which was declared directly exercisable by the Government of India Act, 1858, is declared[3] to be exercisable by His Majesty except in so

[1] S. 308. [2] S. 110 (*b*) (iii). [3] S. 2.

far as may otherwise be provided by or under the Act, or as directed by His Majesty. This declaration extends to (1) the rights, authority, and jurisdiction of the King Emperor over the territories in India vested in him, and (2) those exercisable by him in or in relation to any other territories in India, and includes all powers hitherto exercised by the secretary of state with or without his council, the governor-general with or without his council, any governor or local government.

The territories vested in the King are made up of the governors' provinces and the chief commissioners' provinces, which make up British India.[1] India includes British India, all territories of any Indian ruler under the suzerainty of His Majesty, all territories under the suzerainty of such a ruler, the tribal areas, and any other territories which His Majesty in Council, after ascertaining the views of the federal government and legislature, may declare to be part of India. The tribal areas include the frontier lands of India and Baluchistan which are not parts of British India, or Burma, or any Indian or foreign state. The definition shows how anomalous is their position, but internationally they must be recognized as part of India. The Crown has asserted protection over the areas without necessarily securing the assent to the tribes to such a position, and by treaty[2] the intervention of Afghanistan in regard to these areas has been excluded.

The difference between the relation of the Crown to these areas and territories is reflected in the form of its representation in India.[3] The governor-general of India is appointed by commission under the sign manual[4] to perform the powers and duties imposed on him by or under the Act, and such other powers, not being powers connected with the exercise of the functions of the Crown in its relations to the Indian states, as His Majesty may be pleased to assign to him. The excepted functions fall to the representative of the Crown as regards relations with Indian states in so far as they are assigned to him by His Majesty. Moreover, it is under his authority that powers in this regard can be exercised by any other officers. It was

[1] S. 311 (1); contrast 52 & 53 Vict., c. 63, s. 18.

[2] Cf. Parl. Paper, Cmd. 324 (1919), 4701 (February 3rd 1934).

[3] S. 3.

[4] The Instructions under the sign manual and signet require an oath on assumption of office, so since 1918; Curzon, *British Government in India*, ii, 187.

suggested by the Round Table Conference[1] that this vital distinction of representation might be emphasized by styling the officer charged with relations with the states Viceroy, but there were obvious objections to this plan which were duly recognized by the joint committee. The term could not well be denied to the governor-general in his position as head of the federation; it therefore will remain ceremonial, and the two aspects of the Crown will not thus formally be distinguished. But, though the two positions may be held by the same person, this is not necessarily the case, and they may be separated should in practice it prove difficult for the governor-general to exercise both sets of functions without inconvenience. Normally, it is suggested, the governor-general, as responsible for the welfare ot British India, may be inclined to exercise his functions with some measure of predisposition in favour of his main charge.

The Act clearly recognizes that its terms do not exhaust the powers of the Crown, which can exercise in respect of India all prerogative powers in respect of oversea territories save in so far as they are regulated by the Act.[2] Thus the Act leaves untouched the vital prerogatives of the control of foreign affairs, including the right to cede territory,[3] and of making war or peace or declaring neutrality. It recognizes and saves the right of the Crown or by delegation the governor-general to grant pardons, reprieves, respites or remissions of punishment.[4] It recognizes again the supreme ownership of all land[5] in British India by the Crown, and the resulting doctrine of escheat, and the doctrine under which *bona vacantia* fall to the Crown,[6] but it regulates in both cases[7] the exercise of the prerogative by assigning the property in question to the Crown for the purposes of the province in which the property is situate. This distinction of the character of prerogative

[1] Cf. the Indian Government, Parl. Paper, Cmd. 3700, p. 192.

[2] *Att.-Gen.* v. *De Keyser's Royal Hotel*, [1920] A.C. 508.

[3] The legislature is forbidden to act by s. 110 (*b*) (i). See § 16, below.

[4] S. 295 (2). The prerogative was delegated for the first time in the Royal Warrant of Appointment in 1916.

[5] Cf. *Transfer of Natural Resources to Province of Saskatchewan*, [1932] A.C. 28.

[6] Cf. *Att.-Gen. of Ontario* v. *Mercer* (1883), 8 App. Cas. 767; *Collector of Masulipatam* v. *Cavaly Vencata Narrainapah* (1860), 8 Moo. Ind. App. 500.

[7] S. 174.

authority is necessary since the unity of the authority of the Crown is necessarily broken by the creation of the federal system. In the same way, while under the existing régime it lay with the Crown to allocate executive authority so far as it was not dealt with by statute between the governor-general and the governors or lieutenant-governors of the provinces, its freedom of action is limited by the distinction of federal and provincial spheres. It may be assumed on the analogy of Canadian law that the prerogative right over gold and silver mines[1] attaches to the Crown in respect of the province where such mines are situated, and the waste lands in the provinces are duly vested in the Crown in right of the province, while those in any territory under the federation directly would be federal.

The Crown again enjoys apart from statute immunity from suit for itself, and its property, including its ships.[2] This immunity has been modified in the case of India,[3] as in the case of Canada and Australia in diverse ways by statute, and direct suit against the federation and provinces and in certain cases against the secretary of state is conceded.

There remain reserved to the Crown, free from statutory control, the grant of honours of all kinds[4] whether in British India or to rulers and subjects of the states, and the regulation of precedence whether in British India[5] or as between the rulers. In the case of British India these are prerogative rights of the ordinary kind; in that of the states they flow from the special position of the Crown as demanding and receiving the allegiance of the rulers. Acceptance of foreign orders is also regulated by the Crown.

The prerogative of annexation of territory remains unaffected. But to add territory to British India requires the inclusion of such territory in a province, and the inclusion must take place in a specified manner with the consultation of the government and legislatures of India and the province concerned.[6] But territory could be annexed and included in India with due consultation with the federal authorities only.[7]

[1] *Hudson's Bay Co.* v. *Att.-Gen. for Canada*, [1929] A.C. 285.
[2] *Young* v. *S.S. Scotia*, [1903] A.C. 501.
[3] S. 176.
[4] Star of India (1861), Indian Empire (1877).
[5] Warrant, April 9th 1930.
[6] S. 290.
[7] S. 311 (i).

In general the Crown enjoys in British India all the privileges it has under the prerogative in the case of England save in so far as these are limited by statute. Thus it is entitled to the benefit of the rule that no statute is deemed to bind the Crown unless this is specifically mentioned or is essentially implied by the measure.[1] It enjoys similarly priority in respect of debts[2] due to the Crown unless precluded by statute.

Further, however, the rights of the Crown in India may exceed apart from statute those of the Crown in England, for it succeeds to all the rights of the East India Company, and that body had by virtue of the acquisition from earlier sovereignties of territory the same rights over these territories as their late sovereigns had.[3] This is of importance in certain cases regarding lands and minerals where the Crown has more extensive powers than under English common law.

3. THE UNITS OF THE FEDERATION

The federation is made up of governors' provinces, chief commissioners' provinces, and federated states.[4] The relation of the federal executive and legislature to these three elements differs in essentials. It is far extending with regard to chief commissioners' provinces, which are subject to the control of the governor-general in executive matters and for which the federal legislature can pass laws, but it is definitely restricted on federal principles for the governors' provinces and the federated states.

The governors' provinces are, under the powers of the Act, increased by the addition of Orissa, which is extended in area by joining to it areas in Madras and the Central Provinces occupied by Oriya people, and of Sind, separated from Bombay.[5] They thus number eleven, Madras, Bombay, Bengal, the United Provinces, the Punjab, Bihar separated from Orissa,

[1] *Secretary of State for India* v. *Bombay Landing and Shipping Co.* (1868), 5 Bom. H.C.R., O.C.J. 23; *Ganpat Pataya* v. *Collector of Canara*, I.L.R. 1 Bom. 7, *per* West, J.; *Secretary of State for India* v. *Matthurabhai* (1889), 14 Bom. 213; *Bell* v. *Municipal Commissioners for Madras* (1901), 25 Mad. 457.

[2] *Ganpat Pataya's case, u.s.*

[3] *Rana Ubhee Singh Raja* v. *Collector of Broach* (1821), 2 Borr. 44; *Salaman* v. *Secretary of State for India in Council*, [1906] 1 K.B. 613; *Bapoojee Rughoonath* v. *Sinwar Kana* (1822), 2 Borr. 342.

[4] S. 311 (2).

[5] S. 289.

Central Provinces and Berar, Assam, North-West Frontier Province, Orissa, Sind, and such other provinces as may be created under the Act, which authorizes such creation by Order in Council after consultation of the federal executive and legislature and the authorities of any province affected.[1] The boundaries of provinces can be varied in like manner. Berar,[2] though still under the sovereignty of the Nizam is to be administered with the Central Provinces as one province, but, should the agreement for administration cease, the Crown in Council may make any necessary adjustments affecting the provisions of the Act dealing with the Central Provinces. For the purposes of the Act, therefore, British India includes Berar and save as regards any oath of allegiance Berari subjects rank as British subjects.

The chief commissioners' provinces[3] are British Baluchistan, Delhi, Ajmer-Merwara, Coorg, the Andaman and Nicobar Islands, and the area of Panth Piploda, now given that status, together with such other provinces as may be created under the Act. Aden, on the other hand, ceases to be a part of India, and is to be governed as directed by Order in Council, without prejudice to the power of the Crown in Council to legislate for the territory. But appeal is to lie to an Indian Court, doubtless the High Court of Bombay, whence a further appeal may be brought to the Crown in Council.

Inclusion in the federation is for the provinces of both kinds automatic, but in the case of the states accession is voluntary, and the date of the proclamation of federation is made to depend on action by the King when an address is presented by both houses of Parliament, and such action is conditional on the accession to the federation of rulers entitled to fill not less than half the 104 seats of the Council of State and having as subjects not less 89,490,956 persons.[4] Accession is effected by the King's acceptance of an instrument of accession executed by the ruler personally, whereby he for himself, his heirs and successors, declares that he accedes to the federation with the intent that the King, the governor-general, the federal legislature, the federal court, and any other federal authority shall by virtue of his instrument of accession, but

[1] S. 290. [2] S. 47. [3] S. 94. [4] S. 6.

subject always to the terms thereof and for the purposes only of the federation, exercise in relation to his state such functions as may be vested in them by or under the Act, and assumes the obligation that due effect is given within his state to the provisions of the Act, so far as applicable under the instrument. The terms, it will be seen, are carefully chosen to make it clear that the Act asserts no authority over the state save such as follows from his freely executed instrument, which will, of course, permanently and irrevocably limit his sovereignty. The accession, however, can be executed conditionally on the attainment of federation before a prescribed date, thus simplifying the difficult business of securing the necessary accessions by removing the possibility of long delay.

The instrument[1] must specify the matters on which the federation is to have power to legislate for the state, and any limitations of that legislative power and of the federal executive power. The extent of federal power may be enlarged, but not diminished, by a subsequent instrument duly accepted. The federal legislature is given no power over accessions for twenty years after federation is established. Thereafter any request for acceptance of accession must not only be sent through the governor-general, but no request may be transmitted unless both chambers of the legislature have addressed the King asking that the state may be admitted to the federation. The period is somewhat long, but no doubt any later accessions may be weighed by the Crown in the light of feeling in the legislature, though it has no formal *locus standi*. Any instrument must be laid after acceptance before both Houses of Parliament, and it and the acceptance must be judicially noticed by all courts.

Each instrument of accession must provide that a number of provisions of the Act in Schedule II may be amended without affecting the accession of the state, but no such amendment, unless accepted by a supplementary instrument, may extend the functions exercisable by any authority in respect of the state. In view of the improbability of any early amendment of the exempted portions by Parliament, the provision is probably of no immediate importance, but it may well prove to raise

[1] Draft in Parl. Paper, Cmd. 4843, pp. 43, 44.

very difficult questions, should it later be desired to alter the provisions excepted from the general rule. Thus apparently any change as regards the position of the governor-general towards the issues of external affairs and defence would not be consistent with the position of the states. The Act is silent as to the position in such an event; it would certainly be open to any state to argue that such action was equivalent to a breach of the instrument of accession but there is no legal means provided under which the state could attain redress. On the other hand, from the point of view of British India it may seem that a complete bar to full responsibility is presented.

The King is not obliged to accept any instrument, and his discretion is made absolute in this regard. Further, he may not accept any accession whose terms are inconsistent with the scheme of federation embodied in the Act. The latter provision binds the Crown in principle not to accept for the federation any state which is unwilling to accept the greater portion of the subjects in the federal list. Exceptions or reservations to this list ought in the opinion of the joint select committee,[1] to be justified by any ruler on the score of special conditions affecting his state. There are cases of existing treaty rights or usage in matters affecting the postal service, coinage and currency which may justify exemption from the normal rule of federal control; but it is clear that no state could be allowed to claim entry on the score of being willing to accept a select list of topics. Further, the committee stressed the advantages of securing that instruments shall be as far as possible in common form as regards terminology. The interpretation of federal rights in a state may well turn on wording, and it would embarrass the courts if they had to construe instruments differing verbally. A draft form of instrument accordingly has been prepared.

Apart from the control given to the federation by the instrument of accession, the rights and obligations of the Crown in respect of the Indian states remain unaffected by the Act, and a state which does not accede is in theory unaffected by the federation. Indirectly, of course, federation must affect deeply every state. The grant of responsible government to adjacent

[1] Report, i, 87.

provinces must stimulate ambitions in the states; the governor-general is the head of the federal government, and, though directly ministers will have no power over the state relations with the Crown, it is significant that in the case of the Union of South Africa it was felt desirable in 1930 to separate the offices of Governor-General of the Union and High Commissioner in control of Basutoland, the Bechuanaland Protectorate, and Swaziland.[1] There is therefore every motive for states to accept federation and thus exert authority from within the federal structure, a position in entire harmony with accepted Indian ideals of polity. In specific cases there is added the possibility of remission of tribute[2] or like payments and in one or two that of retrocession of territory or control thereof, as in the case of the rendition of Bangalore to Mysore.

As the King's representative will not control any forces, if he needs the aid of such forces to carry out his duties towards the states he is to be entitled to requisition forces from the governor-general, any extra expense involved being ranked as expenses of the Crown in relation to the states. In this respect, it is clear that special importance attaches to the combination of the offices of representative and governor-general, for, if the two posts were in different hands, there might be grave possibilities of friction, the governor-general doubting if his federal responsibilities were consistent with the proposed use of the forces. As it is, the combination of offices must be deemed sufficient to ensure that policies shall be made consistent with the double form of obligation on either side. It may be noted that the commander-in-chief is commander-in-chief in India, not in British India only.[3]

The representative of the Crown is authorized to make arrangements with the governors of the provinces for the discharge by the latter and their officers of functions appertaining to the representative. This renders possible the continued employment of local governments for relations with states where this course is recommended by considerations of usage or convenience.

The special case of the jurisdiction already enjoyed by the

[1] Cf. Keith, *Letters on Imperial Relations*, 1916–35, p. 203.
[2] Parl. Paper, Cmd. 4103. The total may be £750,000 a year.
[3] S. 4.

Crown in certain areas in the states, e.g. at Secunderabad and Bangalore, is provided for by the rule[1] that the Crown may in signifiying acceptance of any accession declare that the federal authority shall not apply, due notice of course being given to the ruler that the acceptance will contain such a declaration. By agreement between the Crown and the ruler the federal authority may later be extended on such terms as may be specified in a supplementary instrument of accession. But no notice can be given in respect of any area which is under the Crown's jurisdiction solely in connexion with a railway. Subject to the above rule, on federation any authority of the Crown under the Foreign Jurisdiction Act, 1890,[2] or otherwise, shall become exercisable by the federal authorities, including the railway authority, except in so far as any agreement may be made under Part VI of the Act for administration of federal legislation by the ruler. The law in the matters concerned in force in the state is to be deemed to be a federal law in so far as the federation under the instrument of accession could re-enact it, but shall cease to have effect after five years if not so enacted, or amended, or repealed. In all other cases the powers of the Crown in a state shall remain unaffected, without prejudice to its power to relinguish such authority, and the Order in Council of 1902 is reaffirmed as valid. It is also provided that an Order under the Act of 1890 may validly authorize judicial or administrative authorities to act in respect of a state though situated outside the state, and that appellate jurisdiction from British courts in Indian states may validly be conferred on the federal court. Moreover, nothing in the Act is to limit the power of the Crown to determine by what courts British subjects and subjects of foreign countries shall be tried in respect of offences committed in Indian states.

4. DYARCHY IN THE FEDERATION

Dyarchy, rejected by the Simon Commission, is deliberately installed in the federation. The governor-general[3] is granted the executive power of the King, no provision for personal exercise by His Majesty being contemplated. That power[4] extends to

[1] S. 294. [2] 53 & 54 Vict., c. 37. [3] S. 7. [4] S. 8.

all matters in respect of which the federal legislature can make laws, the raising of defence forces for the Crown in British India, and the governance of the forces of the Crown borne on the Indian establishment, and the exercise of rights possessed by treaty, grant, usage, sufferance, or other lawful means in respect of the tribal areas. But in the federated states it extends only to matters over which the federation has legislative power in so far as such executive authority is not reserved in whole or part to the state, and state authority remains unless expressly excluded.

For the administration of federal subjects there shall be a council of ministers[1] chosen and sworn by the governor-general who hold office at his pleasure and may be dismissed by him, acting in his discretion, which means that he need not consult any one as to his action. He fixes their salaries, until settled by the legislature; they may not be varied while in office. Ministers cease to hold office if for any period of six consecutive months they are not members of one of the chambers; this legislative enactment of what is better left a constitutional rule follows the Act of 1919. In the same meticulous spirit it is expressly provided that no court may inquire into the advice given by ministers, and it rests with the governor-general in every case to decide whether or not he is required to act in his discretion or to exercise his individual judgment. He is required to exercise his individual judgment in respect of matters in which he has a special responsibility;[2] his ministers will advise, but the decision rests with him. These issues are: (*a*) the prevention of any grave menace to the peace or tranquillity of India or any part thereof; (*b*) the safeguarding of the financial stability and credit of the federal government; (*c*) the safeguarding of the legitimate interests of minorities; (*d*) the securing to, and to the dependents of, persons who are or have been members of the public services of any rights provided or preserved for them by or under this Act and the safeguarding of their legitimate interests; (*e*) the securing in the sphere of executive action of the purposes which the provisions of Chapter III of Part V of the Act (dealing with prevention of commercial discrimination) are designed to secure in relation to legislation; (*f*) the

[1] Ss. 9, 10. [2] S. 12.

prevention of action which would subject goods of United Kingdom or Burmese origin imported into India to discriminatory or penal treatment; (*g*) the protection of the rights of any Indian state and the rights and dignity of the ruler thereof; and (*h*) the securing that the due discharge of his functions with respect to matters with respect to which he is required to act in his discretion, or to exercise his individual judgment, is not prejudiced or impeded by any course of action taken with respect to any other matter.

The wide terms of these responsibilities must, of course, be considered in relation to the discussions on which they are based. Minorities to be protected are not political or parliamentary minorities, but well-known classes of the population, and the rights to be protected must be legitimate; minorities cannot claim to block all social or economic progress. The rights of Indian states so far as they are subject to federal control need not be conserved by the governor-general; his responsibility refers to federal, not provincial, action inimical to a state or states, and to the rulers he owes the obligation of securing that due regard be paid to the personal status which they have hitherto enjoyed in British India. He will be bound[1] to secure to the several communities a due share in public appointments. He may not hamper the power of the government and legislature to develop a distinctive fiscal and economic policy, including the making of agreements with the United Kingdom and other countries, and his interference should be limited to prevent action intended to injure the interests of the United Kingdom rather than to further the economic interests of India. But he must oppose indirect as well as direct discrimination or penalization. The task set, of course, is very serious, for it must always be possible to argue that a measure is intended to further Indian economic interests even if it injures British interests. He is also bound to secure that no budgetary or borrowing policy is adopted which would prejudice Indian credit in the world money markets, or affect the capacity of the federation duly to perform its financial obligations. To aid him in his duty and to provide an officer capable of giving financial advice to the government if asked, he is authorized to appoint

[1] Instrument of Instructions in Parl. Paper, Cmd. 4805.

a financial adviser[1] whose conditions of service and whose staff he shall determine. But before any appointment but the first is made, ministers shall be consulted as to the person to be chosen. In safeguarding public officers he is to prevent inequitable treatment, and in dealing with commercial discrimination he is to prevent action which though itself apparently not in conflict with any specific provision of the Act would in practice result in discrimination. To enable him to secure that none of his responsibilities are overlooked, he may after consulting ministers make in his discretion rules as to the information to be given to him, and requiring not only ministers but secretaries to bring to his notice any matter likely to involve a responsibility.[2] The provision also derives from the Act of 1919, and involves the grave inconvenience of placing the secretaries of departments in the position of compelling ministers to submit to the governor-general issues which the minister may regard as within his sphere.

Too narrowly interpreted the responsibilities might destroy the possibility of responsibility. But the Instructions contemplate as far as possible collective responsibility. The governor-general is to select the council of ministers in the mode usual in choosing a cabinet, that is in consultation with the person most likely to secure a stable majority in the legislature, and, though he is to endeavour to include representatives of the states and minorities, he is to remember the need of collective confidence in the legislature and the fostering of a sense of joint responsibility. Presumably it is accepted that the lower house must determine the tenure of office of the ministry. Ministers will differ in one respect from British ministers; their salaries fixed by the governor-general or the legislature shall not be diminished while in office, a device intended to secure that the government may not be forced to do without ministers through refusal to vote adequate salaries. The advice of ministers is to be followed unless in the governor-general's opinion a special responsibility or some function in which individual judgment is prescribed compels him to act otherwise; curiously enough, no mention is made of the normal case of refusing advice, when the ministry no longer represents the will of the majority of the

[1] S. 15. [2] S. 17 (4).

legislature or in some cases of the people.[1] It may be taken, therefore, that it is not expected that the governor-general shall feel it right to determine all matters of special responsibility in accordance with his personal preference; that would impose on him too great a burden, and interfere too seriously with ministerial authority. But the responsibilities mark out a sphere in which refusal to accept the advice of ministers and decision to order otherwise will be constitutional.

If in exercise of his rights in these matters the governor-general refuses advice, what is the position of ministers? The answer clearly is that, having accepted office under the constitution which gives such powers, they should remain in office, when the governor-general acts according to his plain duty under the constitution. They have the safeguard against error on the part of the governor-general that in action under the Act in his discretion or individual judgment he is subject to the instructions of the secretary of state,[2] provided that he satisfies himself that any direction he may wish to give is not inconsistent with the Instructions. Relief can therefore be obtained, if the governor-general is in error by an appeal, as in the classical case in 1892[3] in New Zealand when ministers remained in office on the refusal of the governor to add members to the Upper Chamber, until the governor was advised by the Colonial Secretary to accept their advice. They can, of course, resign office, but it would be difficult to justify such action in view of their having taken office in full knowledge of the restrictions on their powers.

In certain fields the governor-general has wider powers, and may act at his discretion.[4] These cover defence, ecclesiastical affairs (relating in effect to the provision of ministrations to British forces and servants), and external affairs except relations between India and any part of the King's dominions. He exercises also discretion in regard to the tribal areas. In these issues he will be aided by three counsellors appointed by himself, whose conditions of service are determined by the King in Council. But it is not intended that ministers should be ignored; joint consultation is recommended, especially in the

[1] See Keith, *Letters on Imperial Relations*, 1916–35, pp. 210, 347, 348.
[2] S. 14. [3] Keith, *Responsible Government in the Dominions*, i, 219 ff.
[4] S. 11.

administration of the department of defence, and the views of ministers are to be obtained in matters affecting the appointment of Indian officers to Indian forces or the employment of such forces outside India. The ministry, and in special the minister of finance, are to be consulted before the defence estimates are settled and laid before the legislature. At the same time the commander-in chief's views are to be obtained on any question of defence and communicated to the secretary of state if he so desires. It will be seen that the way is open to relieve the commander-in-chief of the excessive burden of taking part in the work of the executive council.

The Act leaves vague the delicate question of the use of Indian troops outside India. It provides,[1] however, that no burden shall be imposed on the revenue of the federation or the provinces except for the purposes of India, so that the governor-general could not provide Indian forces at Indian cost unless he was satisfied that their dispatch served the purposes of India. Nor clearly could he provide forces unless he was satisfied that India could spare them. Clearly if he held that the dispatch of forces did not serve the purpose of Indian defence, though troops were available, he could hardly act without the support of the federal ministry, and in that event the necessary funds would have to be provided by the legislature or the British Government. It is, however, no longer necessary for the British Parliament to approve payment by India for troops employed outside India; that restriction of the earlier régime is swept away.

Control of defence inevitably must involve control in matters ancillary thereto of other departments under ministers and also of the provinces. For both[2] needs the Act makes full provision. The governor-general therefore may require the minister charged with communications and the railway board to afford facilities for movements of troops, and may order the governors to give the necessary directions in regard to the control of lands, buildings, and other requirements for the forces, facilities for manœuvres, the safeguarding of the health and security of defence units stationed in the provinces, and if necessary the guarding of roads, bridges, canals, etc. In all

[1] S. 150. [2] Ss. 12 (*h*), 126.

these powers, of course, he is subject to the secretary of state, whose orders he must obey. Where responsibility does not rest with the Indian legislature, it must rest with the British Parliament acting through the secretary of state. This responsibility of Parliament is in the case of India formally expressed, for the Act[1] provides that the original Instrument of Instructions and any later amendment or revocation shall be laid before Parliament and to have effect must receive the approval of both houses. But action may not be questioned on the score of disregard of the Instructions. Though approved by Parliament, the Instructions remain a prerogative instrument, and, if responsible government develops, it will do so under their terms. For instance, it would be possible to instruct the governor-general to consult ministers before acting in his discretion in matters of defence and external relations. This, however, is as far as the power extends. It is clear that, if an attempt were made to require him to act in these matters on ministerial advice, it would contravene the spirit of the Act, which expressly imposes on the governor-general the duty of acting in his discretion, and provides that that part of the measure may not be altered without affecting the adhesion of the states.

The duties of the governor-general involve the appointment by him of an advocate-general,[2] to perform such functions of advising the federal government and other legal duties as may be assigned to him. He has audience in all British Indian Courts and in federal issues in federated state courts. The governor-general decides his remuneration, and as to appointment and dismissal acts in his individual judgment.

The governor-general is required to make rules of business after consulting ministers,[3] and he is instructed to provide that the finance minister shall be consulted on proposals affecting finance, and also on re-appropriation of sums within grants; if there is difference of opinion in a matter of this kind, the council of ministers must decide. This involves assimilation of Indian practice to British Treasury control.

The executive action of the federation is taken in the name of

[1] S. 13. This is a marked innovation on Dominion usage.

[2] S. 16. He corresponds to the Attorney-General in England; 53 Geo. III, c. 155, s. 111; 21 & 22 Vict., c. 106, s. 29.

[3] S. 17 (3).

the governor-general, and orders authenticated under rules made by him may not be questioned on the ground that they are not his acts.[1]

The difficulties of dyarchy were clearly exposed in the provinces under the Act of 1919, and there is no reason to suppose that they will not be repeated in the federation. As will be seen, the composition of the legislature is adapted to render it very difficult to secure the basis of an effective ministry, and that may assist the governor-general to secure the assertion of the great authority vested in him. The position of the ministry is deeply affected by the exclusion from its control of the most important expenditure, that on defence, and it may well prove that through this limitation of power responsibility cannot be established effectively.

5. THE FEDERAL LEGISLATURE

The legislature consists of the King, represented by the Governor-General, the Council of State, and the House of Assembly or Federal Assembly.[2] The Council of State is a permanent body, members retiring to the extent of a third every three years, the Assembly has a maximum duration of five years, the period now normal in Canada and the United Kingdom. Annual sessions are provided for, and the governor-general may in his discretion summon either chamber or both, prorogue the chambers, or dissolve the Assembly.[3] He may address either chamber and send messages on pending Bills or other matters. Ministers, counsellors, and the advocate-general may speak in either chamber, but may only vote if elected, or nominated a member.[4] Each chamber selects a President (Speaker) and deputy, who may be removed only by a vote of the majority of all the members passed on fourteen days' notice.[5] Approval by the governor-general is not requisite in either case. The speaker holds office on a dissolution until immediately before the meeting of the new Assembly. The presiding officer has a casting vote only. Proceedings in the legislature are to be valid, though later it appears that some unqualified person has sat and voted.[6] This resolves the doubt

[1] S. 17 (2). [2] S. 18. [3] S. 19. [4] Ss. 20, 21. [5] S. 22. [6] S. 23 (2).

debated in *Strickland* v. *Grima*,[1] but not passed on by the Privy Council, whether an Act is invalid because it was passed by persons not duly elected. It is made the duty of the presiding officer to adjourn or suspend a sitting if less than one-sixth of the members are present; what the legal effect of omission to act would be is conjectural.[2]

The composition[3] of the Council of State is 156 members for British India and up to 104 for the states. The number in the case of the states depends on the number of states acceding to the federation; so long as a tenth of the possible seats is vacant, the members appointed to the seats filled may choose up to half the number of seats unfilled, but this power shall not last for more than twenty years after federation. The provision is intended to secure that states may be induced to enter early, without undue fear of being swamped by British Indian representatives. It is obviously open to objection, and indeed the whole purpose of federation can be fulfilled only by general accession of the states.

The British Indian members are to be directly elected, for reasons given above, with the exception of six, to be nominated by the governor-general so as to secure due representation for the scheduled classes, i.e. the depressed classes, and women and minority communities. There are 75 general seats, 6 for scheduled castes, 4 in the Punjab for Sikhs, 49 Muhammadans, and 6 for women. Seats for Europeans (7), Indian Christians (2), and for an Anglo-Indian are to be filled indirectly by members of electoral colleges composed of such members of the chamber or chambers of the provincial legislatures. The territorial seats are allocated to the governors' provinces at the rate of 20 for Madras, Bengal, and the United Provinces, 16 for Bombay, Punjab, Bihar, 8 for Central Provinces, down to 5 apiece for the four smallest provinces, with one each for Delhi, Ajmer-Merwara, Coorg, and British Baluchistan. Allocation of seats among the states proved of the utmost difficulty, but finally, having regard to the dynastic salute, as opposed to personal salutes and other factors, it was decided to grant 5 seats to Hyderabad, 3 each to Mysore, Kashmir, Gwalior, and Baroda, and less numbers to smaller states, or groups of states,

[1] [1930] A.C. 285. [2] S. 23 (3). [3] S. 18 and Sched. 1.

whose rulers would then choose jointly or in rotation. The rules are complex. Necessarily for the first Council it has to be arranged that certain members shall sit only for brief periods, so that the system of the triennial retirement of one-third of the members may be worked. The state representatives are appointed by the rulers, and, though appointed for definite periods of time, the power of resignation could no doubt be insisted on by any ruler who desired to change his nominee. The result in any case is that the members of the Council are essentially of two kinds—members who speak for a limited electorate, and members for expressing the views of an autocratic prince.[1]

In the Assembly there are 250 representatives of British India and 125 as a maximum for the states, with a limited power to fill vacancies due to non-accession of states as in the case of the Council. The joint committee decided on indirect election on the ground that contact between member and electorate was vital and could not be achieved under direct election except by making the constituencies hopelessly unwieldy or increasing to absurd proportions the size of the Assembly. Hence the Hindu, Sikh, and Muhammadan members of the provincial Assemblies are to select members of these communities; in the case of the Hindu or general seats a certain number are allocated to the scheduled castes; for them the persons selected as eligible candidates at the primary elections for the provincial Assemblies choose four times the number of vacant seats, to be voted on by the general electorate. The system of proportional representation with the single transferable vote is adopted. Similar voting in electoral colleges made up of the members of each community in the Assemblies is to supply the European, Anglo-Indian, and Indian Christian members, and the seats reserved for women are to be filled by the women members of the Assemblies. Seats for commerce and industry fall to be filled by chambers of commerce and like bodies, for landholders by landholders, for labour by labour organizations. There are four non-provincial seats, filled by the Federated Chambers of Commerce, the

[1] S. 18 (2) and Sched. 1. Madras, Bengal, United Provinces, 37 seats; Bombay, Punjab, Bihar, 30; Central Provinces, 15; Assam, 10; N.W.F.P., Orissa, Sind, 5; Delhi, 2; British Baluchistan, Ajmer-Merwara, Coorg, 1 each.

Associated Chambers of Commerce, commercial bodies in Northern India, and labour organizations respectively.

In the case of the states regard is had *inter alia* to population. Thus Hyderabad with 14,436,148 population has sixteen seats, Mysore with 6,557,302 has seven, Travancore with 5,095,973 five.

No person may be a member of the legislature unless he is a British subject or the ruler or subject of a federated state, and for the Council he must be thirty, for the Assembly twenty-five, years of age, but this restriction is waived in the case of an acting ruler. No member may sit without taking an oath or affirmation in lieu.[1] A British subject swears to be faithful and bear true allegiance, a ruler to do so in his capacity as member of the chamber, a subject of a ruler saves his faith and allegiance to his ruler. A ruler, of course, owes general allegiance, but the specification of the capacity in which he swears derogates in no way from the direct obligation.

Membership[2] may be resigned, and either chamber may declare vacant the seat of any member absent without permission for sixty days, while a seat is vacated on the occurrence of any disqualification. Disqualifications include the holding of office under the Crown, not being ministerial office or membership of a service of the Crown retained while serving in a state; unsoundness of mind declared by a competent court; insolvency not discharged; offences in connexion with elections declared by Order in Council or federal Act to disqualify; conviction in British India or a federated state of an offence, punished by transportation or imprisonment of not less than two years, unless five years have elapsed since release, or a less period fixed in his discretion by the governor-general; and failure in certain cases to return electoral expenses. No person serving a sentence of imprisonment may be chosen. The penalty for sitting or voting when disqualified is 500 rupees a day recoverable as a debt to the federation.

The privileges[3] of members are specifically limited. Freedom of speech in the legislature is assured, subject to the limits of discussion which may be set by the governor-general, as described below, and to the standing orders, and there can be no proceedings in respect of papers published by order of either chamber.

[1] S. 24. [2] Ss. 25–7. [3] S. 28.

Other privileges[1] enjoyed by the former legislature are continued, and may be added to, but no Act may confer on either chamber or any officer the status of a court or any punitive power other than that of removing persons infringing the rules or standing orders or otherwise behaving in a disorderly manner. The power of committing for contempt persons who refuse to give evidence or produce documents before committees of the chamber is thus denied, and it was only under pressure in Parliament that the Act was amended to authorize legislation to inflict penalties on conviction by a court of persons refusing to give evidence or produce papers, and the governor-general in his individual judgment is to make rules safeguarding confidential matters from disclosure and regulating the attendance of persons who are or have been civil servants. This power is doubtless necessary; it represents, of course, the limits observed in practice in these matters in the British Parliament. Freedom of speech, of course, does not include the right to publish a speech which is libellous,[2] apart from publication ordered by either chamber.

Members are to receive such salaries as the legislature may determine; pending action, they are to be paid on the same scale as in the Indian legislature.[3]

All proceedings in the federal legislature shall be in the English language, but the rules of procedure must permit persons insufficiently or wholly unacquainted with English to use another language.[4]

The rules of procedure[5] are to be made by either chamber, but the governor-general after consulting the president and speaker shall make rules regulating the procedure in matters affecting functions to be discharged at his discretion or individual judgment; securing the timely completion of financial business; forbidding the discussion of or questions on any matter connected with a state outside the federal sphere, unless he considers that it affects federal interests or a British subject and consents to discussion or questions thereon; prohibiting save with his permission discussion or questions in respect of (*a*) the relations of the Crown or the governor-general and any

[1] See Act XXIII of 1925: freedom from service as juror or assessor, and civil inprisonment or arrest during session.

[2] *R.* v. *Creevey* (1813), 1 M. & S. 273.   [3] S. 29.   [4] S. 39.   [5] S. 38.

foreign prince or state, (*b*) matters connected with the tribal areas (save in relation to estimates of expenditure) or any excluded areas; (*c*) his action in his discretion in relation to provincial affairs; and (*d*) the personal conduct of the ruler of a state or of a member of his family. The last restriction imposes a serious limitation on the possibilities of exposing scandals, but is part of the price paid for securing state accessions, the rulers being justly resentful of candid criticisms of their medieval methods. The governor-general also makes rules for joint sittings of the chambers. A further grave responsibility[1] to prevent freedom of discussion is given to the governor-general. If he thinks that the discussion of any Bill or clause thereof or amendment would affect the discharge of his responsibility for prevention of any grave menace to the peace or tranquillity of India or any part thereof, he may negative further proceedings thereon. Further, no discussion is permitted of the conduct of a judge of the federal court or of any high court, including states courts of that status, in the discharge of his duties.[2] This drastic limitation of power is deemed necessary to preserve the independence of the judiciary; in fact, in the British Parliament criticism of judges is drastically limited by convention. Finally, the intervention of the courts is excluded in matters affecting regularity of procedure and the actions of officers in carrying out the procedure of the chambers.[3] This affirms a constitutional principle observed in regard to the Imperial Parliament, but whose application to the Dominions is less clearly established.

Legislative procedure[4] requires that a Bill should normally require the assent of both chambers to become law, It may, save if it is concerned with finance, originate in either house. A dissolution of the Assembly causes the lapse of any Bill passed by it if pending in the Council of State, but does not affect a Council of State Bill. If a Bill is passed by one chamber and rejected by the other, or the chambers disagree as to amendments, or it is not presented for assent with six months after its reception by the other chamber (excluding any period of

[1] S. 40 (2). [2] S. 40 (1).
[3] S. 41. In 1924 the High Court of Calcutta was prepared to forbid putting of a motion; 51 Cal. 874 (1924).
[4] Ss. 30, 31.

prorogation or adjournment over four days), the governor-general may notify his intention to call a joint sitting. Such action would normally be taken on ministerial advice, but in his discretion he may summon a joint sitting if the measure relates to finance, or to a question affecting his duty of discretion or exercise of judgment, and he need not wait for rejection or disagreement or the six-month period. The joint session in normal cases takes place in the next session of the legislature after the expiration of six months from the date of notification, but when he acts in his discretion it may take place in the same session. In any event the holding of a session is not affected by the dissolution of the Assembly. At the session questions are determined by a majority of the members voting, and such amendments only may be made as are necessary by lapse of time or arise out of amendments, if any, proposed by one house but rejected by the other.

When a Bill has been passed, it must be presented for assent, refusal of assent, or reservation in the discretion of the governor-general.[1] No delay in such presentation would be constitutional. The governor-general may return the Bill for consideration in whole or part and may suggest amendments and the chambers must take his suggestions into consideration. A reserved Bill drops unless within twelve months from presentation the governor-general notifies the royal assent. A Bill may be disallowed within twelve months from assent, whereupon the governor-general must forthwith notify disallowance, the Act becoming void from the date of notification. Such disallowance, of course, does not invalidate action taken while the Act was in being. Assent to a reserved Bill and disallowance are expressed by Order in Council.

In financial matters,[2] the governor-general is required to lay before the legislature a financial statement of estimated receipts and expenditure, showing the sums which are charged on the revenues of the federation and those which are required to meet other expenditure which it is desired to charge on the revenues. Sums on revenue account are to be distinguished from other expenditure and note must be made of those amounts which are included because they affect the special responsibilities

[1] S. 32. [2] Ss. 33–7.

of the governor-general. There are charged on the federal revenues, and therefore exempt from the vote of the legislature, (*a*) the salary, allowances, etc., of the governor-general; (*b*) debt charges, including interest, sinking fund, redemption, and cost of raising loans; (*c*) salaries and allowances of ministers, counsellors, chief commissioners, the financial adviser and his staff, and the advocate-general; (*d*) salaries, allowances, and pensions of judges of the federal court, and pensions of high court judges; (*e*) expenditure on defence and external affairs—so far as the governor-general is required to act in his discretion, tribal areas, and other territories, and up to forty-two lakhs, exclusive of pensions, on ecclesiastical affairs; (*f*) sums payable in respect of the functions of the Crown in respect of the states; (*g*) grants for excluded provincial areas; (*h*) sums required to meet any judgment decree or award of any court or arbitral tribunal; and (*i*) any other expenditure charged by the Act or any federal Act on Indian revenues. The decision of the governor-general in his discretion determines the classification of any items. It is open to either chamber to discuss, though not to vote on, the excluded items save those affecting the governor-general and expenditure in respect of the states. This makes it clear that discussion of defence expenditure will be allowable.

Other expenditure must be submitted in the form of demands for grants recommended by the governor-general, the government thus controlling the maximum sums desired, private members having no power to propose or increase expenditure, a legal assertion of the British principle. Either chamber may refuse or diminish a proposed grant, the Assembly being first consulted; if it refuses or diminishes a grant the governor-general may direct that the full grant or some other less amount may be submitted to the Council of State; otherwise the demand is dropped or the diminished sum asked from the Council. In case of disagreement on grants a joint sitting decides.

After discussion the governor-general authenticates a schedule specifying the grants made by the chambers, to which he may add sums not exceeding the amount originally asked for, when the chambers have refused or reduced a grant which he considers necessary in respect of his special responsibilities, and the sums charged on the revenues under the Act. The authenticated schedule must be laid before the chambers but may not be discussed by them, and it affords the sole authority for expenditure, unless supplementary grants become necessary, when a supplementary statement of expenditure must be laid and subjected to the same procedure as the original statement. Under this procedure the legislature controls expenditure, unless it falls within the reserved heads or affects the special responsibilities of the governor-general. This affords a certain amount of authority to the legislature, but its extent is greatly diminished by the comparatively limited amount of the revenue[1] which remains over after the fixed charges are defrayed.

The initiative of the legislature is denied in the case of a Bill imposing or increasing taxation, regulating the borrowing of money, giving a guarantee or affecting financial obligations of the federation, or charging expenditure on federal revenues; the governor-general must recommend any such Bill, and it may not be introduced in the Council of State. More generally no Bill may be considered which, if enacted, would impose expenditure, without the governor-general's recommendation. It is, however, as usual provided that a Bill is not to be deemed to impose expenditure if it imposes fines or pecuniary penalties, or authorizes fees for licences or for services rendered. Similar exemptions are common in Dominion constitutions and rest on the practice of the House of Commons as regards House of Lords Bills.

As regards legislation certain emergency powers are given to the governor-general.[2] When the legislature is not in session ministers may advise that circumstances have arisen to require immediate action, and in that case he may issue an ordinance. But he must exercise his judgment as to doing so if the measure is one which could only have been introduced into the legislature with his previous sanction, and he may not promulgate without the King's instructions any ordinance which he would have been bound to reserve, had it been a Bill; this rule covers measures inconsistent with Acts of Parliament, derogating

[1] In 1933–4 debt took 15·86 crores, defence 46·20 crores, pensions 3·02, grant to North-West Frontier Province 1 crore, 66·08 crores out of 78·16 crores revenue.

[2] Ss. 42–4.

from the powers of high courts in a substantial degree, or likely to violate the rules against discrimination.[1] Such ordinances must forthwith be laid before the legislature when it meets and last only for six weeks unless sooner disapproved by resolutions of both chambers; they may be disallowed by the Crown and withdrawn at any time by the governor-general.

Where the exercise of discretion or individual judgment is involved, the governor-general may issue an ordinance, whose duration may not exceed six months but which may be extended by a later ordinance for another six months. Any such ordinance may be withdrawn by him at any time or disallowed by the Crown, and any ordinance extending the period must be laid before both Houses of Parliament.

In addition he may enact forthwith permanent legislation in such matters, explaining his action to the chambers by message, or he may send the chambers a draft of his proposed Act, enacting it after a month's delay and after taking into consideration any resolution passed. Such an Act may be disallowed and must be laid before both Houses of Parliament. Whether ordinance or Act is passed, it is, of course, void unless it is within the ambit of federal power.

Further authority[2] is given to him in the case of failure of the constitutional machinery. If he is satisfied that the government of the federation cannot be carried on under the Act, he may issue a proclamation declaring that his functions to such extent as is mentioned shall be carried on at his discretion, and assuming any powers exercisable by any federal authority other than the federal court. He may modify the Act for this purpose so far as it affects any federal authority other than the court. Any proclamation may be modified or revoked by a subsequent proclamation; it must be laid before both Houses of Parliament and ceases to operate six months later, unless both Houses of Parliament approve its continuance, when it shall remain in force for a further twelve months. But, if the government of the federation has been carried on for three years under a proclamation (presumably a fresh proclamation issued after the expiry of an earlier proclamation is included) the government must be resumed under the terms of the Act subject to any

[1] Instructions, clause XXVII. [2] S. 45.

amendment made by Parliament, which must be subject to the restriction of schedule 2 as regards changes which may be made without affecting the accession of the states. Any law made by the governor-general while a proclamation is in force shall last for two years after the expiry of the proclamation, unless sooner repealed or re-enacted by the Indian legislature, or, where the enactment belongs to the field open to the provinces as well as the federation, by a provincial legislature.

The terms of this power clearly place on the Imperial Parliament the onus of determining how far it will permit suspension of the constitution to operate. The limit of three years was inserted to meet the objections of the states to indefinite suspension, while they are further safeguarded by the restriction on Parliamentary amendment to matters consistent with the general scheme of federation.

6. RESPONSIBLE GOVERNMENT IN THE PROVINCES

As in the case of the federation, the executive government of the province is vested in the King and is exercised by his representative, in this case the governor appointed under the sign manual, his salary being fixed by the Act.[1] His position is largely modelled on that of the governor-general, from whom, however, he differs in the fact that there are no important departments of government which are reserved from the control of ministers. Moreover, he is relieved of any responsibility for the financial stability of his province, though the governor-general may require him to act so as to safeguard the stability of federal finance, and he is not concerned to prevent the discriminatory treatment of United Kingdom or Burmese imports, an issue which falls outside the provincial sphere proper. The executive power of the province extends to all matters on which it may legislate, and in its exercise the governor has the advice of the council of ministers,[2] appointed and dismissed by him in his discretion; he fixed their salaries until determined by the legislature, and these salaries cannot be varied while ministers are in office.

The governor's responsibilities[3] thus extend to (*a*) the

[1] Ss. 48, 49. [2] Ss. 50, 51. [3] S. 52.

prevention of menace to the peace or tranquillity of his province or any part thereof; (*b*) the safeguarding of the legitimate interests of minorities; (*c*) the safeguarding of the rights of civil servants past and present and their dependants; (*d*) the securing in the executive sphere of protection against discrimination; (*e*) the securing of the peace and good government of areas declared to be partially excluded areas; (*f*) the safeguarding of the rights of states and the rights and dignity of any ruler; and (*g*) the securing of the execution of orders given to him under Part VI of the Act (dealing with administrative relations) by the governor-general in his discretion. The governor of the Central Provinces and Berar is required to see that a due proportion of revenue is spent on Berar; the governors of provinces in which there are excluded areas are to secure that no action of theirs in respect of such an area is prejudiced by other action; any governor who is acting as agent for the governor-general, as in the case of the tribal areas connected with the North-West Frontier Province, must see that no action is taken inconsistent with his agency responsibilities, and the governor of Sind is responsible for the Lloyd Barrage and Canals Scheme. In such cases he must after hearing ministers' advice act in his individual judgment, and in so acting he is subject to the directions of the secretary of state.[1] His mode of exercise of his functions is further explained in an instrument under the sign manual and signet,[2] which explains his specific responsibilities much as in the case of the governor-general. He is to encourage all classes of the population to take their proper place in the public life and government of the province, to secure minorities a due share of appointments, to protect civil servants from inequitable treatment, to prevent measures which would discriminate though not in form discriminatory, and to avoid interference with rights of the states; in the event of doubt as to the existence of rights he is to refer to the governor-general, who as representative of the Crown in relation to the states will determine the extent of such alleged rights. The governor of the Central Provinces is to have due regard in the administration of Berar to the commercial and economic interests of Hyderabad. Care

[1] S. 54. [2] S. 53, and draft in Parl. Paper, Cmd. 4805.

is to be taken to keep the governor-general informed of the state of matters affecting irrigation in view of the power of the secretary of state to require the employment of officers appointed by himself. Instructions require the approval of both Houses of Parliament. It is to be presumed that he has the right to change a ministry to keep it in touch with the Assembly. He must, it is clear, correspond with the governor-general on all issues affecting the federation, but the Act does not exclude direct relations with the secretary of state as in the case of Australia.

In matters of law and order[1] the governor has special powers. He appoints an advocate-general whose position in the province is similar to that of the advocate-general of the federation. He must exercise his judgment as to the making or amendment of any rules affecting police, civil or military, unless they do not affect organization or discipline. He may also, if he thinks that the peace or tranquillity of the province is menaced by persons meditating crimes of violence for the overthrow of the government, declare that any of his functions shall be exercised at his discretion; he may then authorize some official to speak in the legislature on these issues. He may also in his discretion make rules providing that information in relation to the sources from which information has been obtained regarding such criminal intentions shall not be divulged by any police force member to another member except with the authority of the Inspector-General or Commissioner of Police, or to any other person except on his direction, or by any other person in the service of the Crown to any other person save on his direction. These clauses are intended to provide such security as is possible against any failure in the effort to stamp out terrorism, which in Bengal has prevailed for years, and in 1935 was stated by the governor still to cause grave danger. The necessity of giving authority to the governor is proved by the refusal of the Indian legislature in September 1935 to give permanent force to the legislation necessary to combat terrorism.

The governor after consultation with ministers makes rules of business,[2] and his instructions require him to secure due

[1] Ss. 55–8. [2] S. 59 (3).

consultation of the finance minister on all financial matters, while reappropriation of sums within grants must be made with his consent or that of the council of ministers, as in the case of the federation. He is required to encourage joint responsibility and to avoid any action which permits ministers to evade their own responsibilities by placing the onus on him. In view of the wide sphere of ministerial action, from which practically only the excluded areas in any province are removed, there is every possibility of the development of true responsible government in those provinces where there is the possibility of a stable majority in the legislature, permitting the formation of effective governments. The same result may be possible also in cases where, as in the Punjab and Bengal, one community possesses a slight majority, which, however, will be united by communal feeling.

The governors, like the governor-general, have the assistance of secretarial staffs, appointed at their discretion, whose emoluments they fix.[1] They enjoy also with the secretary of state immunity while in office from any proceedings in Indian courts, and no process may issue from such courts (e.g., to act as witnesses) against them, whether in a personal capacity or otherwise, and except with the sanction of the King in Council no proceedings may be brought in any Indian court against any person who has filled these offices in respect of any official act or omission. The clause[2] is rather obscurely drafted, but it can be interpreted to mean that even in respect of personal actions, unconnected with official duties, e.g., a private debt or assault, these officers are exempt from liability to proceedings while in office. If so the exemption is probably greater than that enjoyed even by the Lord Lieutenant of Ireland. These officials, however, remain liable to proceedings in English courts so far as these can be brought under English law,[3] whether for private debts or for official misdemeanours. Moreover, as the clauses of the Government of India Act dealing with misconduct of officials in India will disappear under the new constitution, these officials may be punished for criminal action in India by the Court of King's Bench under the

[1] S. 305.

[2] S. 306. The Bill was clearer.

[3] Cf. *Mostyn* v. *Fabrigas* (1774), 1 Cowp. 161; *Phillips* v. *Eyre* (1870), L.R. 6 Q.B. 1; *R.* v. *Eyre* (1868), L.R. 3 Q.B. 487.

Governors' Act, 1699,[1] as extended in 1802, or for murder or manslaughter under the Offences against the Person Act, 1861. Though efforts have at times been made to proceed in England against governors, there is no recent example of successful action.

7. THE PROVINCIAL LEGISLATURES

The King represented by the Governor is associated in each province with one or two chambers; in the Punjab, the Central Provinces, the North-West Frontier Province, Sind, and Orissa there is a single Legislative Assembly; Madras, Bombay, Bengal, the United Provinces, Bihar, and Assam have two chambers. The Legislative Councils represent a concession to conservative feeling in India and the United Kingdom, and prime importance attaches to the Assemblies, there being no state interests as in the federation to confer a high importance on the upper chamber. In the federation the states would gladly have seen the upper chamber made of full equality of powers even in finance with the lower, but in deference to precedent certain concessions, as seen above, had to be made in that regard, though otherwise equality of powers was established, subject to the greater numerical strength of the lower chamber in the event of the decision of differences of view by a joint session.

The Council is a permanent body, one-third of the members retiring each three years, the Assembly, unless sooner dissolved, lasts for five. The governor's powers, to summon, prorogue, and dissolve, to address and send messages, the right of ministers and the advocate-general to speak, the election of President and Speaker, the rules as to quorum and the non-effect of irregular membership on proceedings are as in the federation, except that in the case of the councils ten members form the minimum permitted to act.

The membership of the Assemblies was an issue bitterly contested, and as we have seen finally settled by the British Government's communal award of August 4th 1932, as modified by the creation of Orissa as a distinct province, and the Poona

[1] 11 & 12 Will. III, c. 12; 42 Geo. III, c. 85; Keith, *Responsible Government in the Dominions*, i, 97 f.

Pact of September 25th 1932 regarding the treatment of general, i.e. Hindu, constituencies. Under the pact a substantial proportion of the general seats are assigned to the depressed classes—officially the scheduled castes. The members of these bodies in the registered electorate meet in primary elections and choose four candidates for each vacancy reserved for them, and the candidate who is given first place in voting by the general electorate is awarded the seat. This secures the unity of the Hindu community together with protection for the depressed classes. Seats are also provided for Muhammadans, Sikhs in the Punjab and the North-West Frontier Province, Europeans, Anglo-Indians, Indian Christians, representatives of commerce, industry, mining and planting, landholders, and labour. Women have general seats in all save the North-West Frontier Province; there are Muhammadan seats in most provinces, an Anglo-Indian in Bengal, a Sikh in the Punjab, and a Christian in Madras. The size of the houses varies from 250 for Bengal, 228 United Provinces, 215 Madras, 175 Bombay and Punjab, 152 Bihar, 112 Central Provinces and Berar, 108 Assam, to 60 for Sind and Orissa and 50 for the North-West Frontier Province. A small Muhammadan majority is assured in Bengal, where Muhammadans have 117 seats assigned and will have a few others under different heads, in the Punjab where they have 84, and the Sikhs 31, the North-West Frontier Province and Sind with 36 and 33 seats respectively: in the others Hindus predominate, though not very markedly in Assam.

The constitution of the Legislative Councils varies. In Bengal the maximum number is 65, the minimum 63; there are 10 general, 17 Muhammadan, and 3 European seats, 27 selected by the Assembly by proportional representation with the single transferable vote, and from 6 to 8 nominated by the governor to secure due representation in special of the depressed classes and women. In Bihar the corresponding figures are 30, 9, 4, 1, 12, and 3 or 4. The other provinces have no members chosen by the Assemblies, but general, Muhammadan, and European seats, with 3 Indian Christian seats in Madras where the maximum is 56. Bombay has a maximum of 30, the United Provinces 60, Assam 22.

Members[1] must be British subjects or rulers or subjects of federated states or such other states as may be prescribed. They must take an oath before sitting, and their disqualifications are as in the federation. No persons may be a member of the federal and a provincial legislature; the provincial seat becomes vacant after a period prescribed by the governor if the seat in the federal legislature is not resigned. No person may be a member of both chambers; members may resign or be removed for absence. Their privileges are precisely as in the federation; where not defined they are those of the former provincial councils, and their salaries until fixed by the legislature are as under the former régime.

Proceedings[2] in the legislatures shall be in English[3] but with permission to persons insufficiently acquainted therewith to use another language. Rules of procedure may be made by either chamber, and the governor has similar powers to those of the governor-general to make rules regulating discussion, with the necessary exceptions arising from the limitation of his authority to his province. Curiously enough he may not deal with discussions of, or questions on, matters in which he has been instructed by the governor-general to act. He has power to prevent discussion of any Bill or clause or amendment which is likely to affect his responsibility for tranquillity. The discussion of the judicial conduct of any federal judge or high court judge is forbidden, and no irregularity of procedure nor action by officers of the legislature may be called in question in any court.

Procedure in legislation is based on the federal model, but with some distinctions. Thus[4] where two chambers exist, the governor may call a joint sitting only if a Bill is not presented for assent within twelve months after it has been sent by one chamber to another, though the period may be shortened if the Bill relates to finance or a matter of special responsibility. When passed a Bill may be assented to, refused assent, or reserved for the consideration of the governor-general. The Instructions require that any Bill shall be reserved if it is repugnant to an Imperial Act, seriously derogates from the position of the high court, affects the permanent settlement, or

[1] Ss. 67–71. [2] Ss. 84–7. [3] S. 85. [4] Ss. 73–7.

appears to provide for discrimination. In the case of the Central Provinces and Berar reference must be made in assent to the agreement with the Nizam for legislation and administration. The governor may send back a Bill for reconsideration with amendments, and the governor-general may assent to a reserved Bill—with similar reference in the case of a Bill affecting Berar, or refuse assent, or reserve for the King's pleasure, or direct that the Bill be sent back for consideration with a message. A Bill reserved may be assented to and an Act assented to disallowed by the King in Council as in the case of the federation.

In financial matters[1] procedure is analogous to that in the federation. The sums charged on the revenues, and therefore not votable, are the governors' salary; debt charges; charges for salaries of ministers and the advocate-general, and judges; expenditure for excluded areas; sums to meet judgments or awards of court; and any other sums charged by the Act or any provincial Act. The sums for the governor's salary is exempt from discussion; other items may be discussed. Expenditure not thus charged must be presented to the Assembly only in the form of demands for grants; it may refuse or reduce. The governor authenticates a schedule of grants made, to which he may add grants refused or reduced where his responsibilities are concerned, and sums charged; this forms the authority for expenditure subject to his power to submit a supplementary estimate. Financial bills fall under the same principles as in the federation, the councils being permitted a voice but no initiative. A special security is provided for the expenditure on European and Anglo-Indian education. If provision for these purposes has been made in the last complete year before the new system comes into force, then, unless the Assembly by a majority of three-fourths at least of its members otherwise resolves, provision must be included to the extent of the average expenditure for the ten years ended March 31st 1933 unless the total educational expenditure is reduced below that average, when a proportionate reduction is permitted. This legislative safeguard does not lessen the duty of the governor to safeguard minorities.

[1] Ss. 78–83.

The governor[1] may at the instance of ministers when the legislature is not in session issue ordinances, which must be laid before the legislature when it meets and fall under the same rules as governor-general's ordinances. In their case, however, the governor must use his judgment if the ordinance covers a matter which could have been dealt with by Bill only with his or the governor-general's prior sanction, and must not without the governor-general's sanction promulgate an ordinance which could, if a Bill, only have been introduced with the latter's sanction or which must have been reserved. He may also in matter involving his discretion or individual judgment issue ordinance with six months' maximum duration, but capable of being extended for a further six months; this power is directly based on the similar federal power, and except in emergency must be used only with the concurrence of the governor-general; if issued without concurrence, the governor-general may direct withdrawal. An ordinance duly issued has the effect of an Act reserved and assented to by the governor-general in that it can repeal or alter a federal Act operative in the sphere of legislation open to federation and provinces.

With the governor-general's concurrence the governor may also issue permanent Acts either forthwith or after consideration of the views of the legislature. With like concurrence the governor may by proclamation[2] exercise in case of a breakdown of the constitution in the province like functions to those of the governor-general, subject to the same control by Parliament and a maximum duration of three years. Laws made under the proclamation have a duration of two years after its expiry subject to repeal or re-enactment by the appropriate legislature.

The governor[3] is given also a special position as regards excluded or partially excluded areas. These areas are defined by Order in Council, and thereafter the King in Council may direct that the whole or part of an excluded area shall become or be made part of a partially excluded area; that the whole or part of a partially excluded area shall cease to be excluded; alter by way of rectification boundaries of any area; and on the creation of a new province or alteration of boundaries declare

[1] Ss. 88–90. [2] S. 93. [3] Ss. 91, 92.

any area not previously included in the province to be excluded or partially excluded. It will be seen that original exclusion after the first Order in Council is prohibited. In regards to these areas no federal or provincial Act may apply save under notification by the governor, who may provide for its modification or exceptions in its application. Moreover, with the subsequent assent of the governor-general in his discretion, he may make regulations for the peace and good government of any area and repeal or modify any federal provincial or other law applicable thereto. Such regulations may be disallowed by the Crown.

The executive power of the province extends to such areas, but in the case of excluded areas must be exercised by the governor in his discretion.

8. THE FEDERAL AND PROVINCIAL FRANCHISES

The arrangements for the franchise in India rest essentially on the findings of the Franchise Committee[1] appointed after the second session of the Round Table Conference, charged with the duty of recommending a franchise which would give the vote to not less than 10 per cent of the total population as recommended by the Simon Commission, nor more than the 25 per cent favoured by the Round Table Conference. Either figure meant a great advance on the 8,744,000 voters—not more than 398,000 being women—under the Act of 1919. As originally indirect election was proposed for both federal houses, no special federal franchise was necessary, but the decision to provide direct election for the Council of State necessitated a special franchise for that chamber. It was decided to base that on the franchise for the old Council of State, broadening it to give about 100,000 voters, and bringing it into close connexion with the franchise for upper chambers in the provinces.

For the provincial assemblies[2] provision was in part made in

[1] Report and 4 vols. of evidence, etc. (1932); Cmd. 4086. For the electorate for the Council of State, Provincial Councils, and Chief Commissioners' Provinces for the federal legislature, see Cmd. 4998.

[2] S. 291 gives a general power to delimit constituencies, decide franchise qualifications, and deal with the conduct of elections to the King in Council.

the Act, in part left to be made by the King in Council, the provincial legislature, or the governor. As far as practicable territorial constituencies are provided for, certain numbers being allocated as general seats, Muhammadan, Anglo-Indian, European, and Indian Christian. An electoral roll is to be prepared for each constituency, and the persons belonging to the specified classes are to be enrolled in them and excluded from the general constituency. A European is any person whose father or other male progenitor in the male line was a European and who is not a native of India; an Anglo-Indian is a European in this sense who is a native of India; and a native of India is any person born and domiciled within the dominions of His Majesty in India and Burma of parents habitually resident in India or Burma and not established there for temporary purposes only. No person may vote at a general election in more than one territorial constituency, but an exception is made in favour of women where special territorial constituencies for them exist, as they may vote therein and in one other. Territorial constituencies on like bases are provided for the councils, but for general, Muhammadans, Europeans, and in Madras only Christians.

Assignment to a territorial constituency is based on residence, but that varies. Madras demands 120 days in the previous financial year, but residence is not rigorous and may be maintained by occasional sleeping in a house, if there is the possibility of user. Bombay requires 180 days' residence in the constituency or a contiguous area, variously defined. In Bengal the requirements for a Calcutta constituency are fulfilled by residence in Calcutta and a place of business in the constituency, while a European may be enrolled in the European constituency if employed anywhere in Bengal, though on leave of absence.

Universal suffrage being utterly impossible, or indirect voting to give the lower classes representation being ruled out as impracticable on various grounds, the qualification for the franchise in territorial constituencies is necessarily based on property, which may be gauged by land revenue, by various conditions of agricultural tenancy, by assessment to income tax, and in the case of the towns by the amount of rent paid.

These varied conditions, which have had to be adapted to each province so that as far as possible the same types of persons may be given the vote in each, are supplemented by qualification by an educational requirement, also varied, and, in addition, there are special qualifications intended to secure an adequate representation of women and the depressed classes, of whom it is hoped to enfranchise 10 per cent. The task is necessarily one of great complexity. There are also to be prescribed the qualifications for the non-territorial constituencies, such as commerce, industry, landholders, and labour. Moreover, all officers, non-commissioned officers, and men of the Indian forces and the police forces are given the vote if on pension or retired. In the case of labour constituencies there have to be disposed of the contending claims of trade unions and labour constituencies.

In the case of women special provisions had necessarily to be made, because the Hindu social system in the great majority of cases does not permit a woman to possess in her own right property which would entitle her to the vote. Accordingly, in general, women are enfranchised who have the property qualification in their own right, or are wives or widows of men so qualified, or are wives of men with a service qualification, or are pensioned widows or mothers of members of the military or police forces, or who possess a literary qualification. It is, however, required that, where the qualification is not held in the woman's own right, she must make application for enrolment, a condition which may seriously reduce in some cases the numbers enrolled. But this application qualification is waived in the case of Bengal, Bihar, Orissa, the Central Provinces, and the urban areas of the United Provinces. It is hoped thereby to give the vote to more than 6 million women as opposed to 28 or 29 million men, a striking improvement on the 815,000 under the Act of 1919.[1]

In the view of the joint committee the proposals accepted remedy in some degree the balance between town and country,

[1] A committee was appointed (August 1st 1935) to delimit provincial and federal constituencies, one-member constituencies to be preferred, manageable in area in number of voters, and in physical characteristics; in two-member constituencies the single non-transferable vote may be adopted. Only when these preliminaries are over can rolls be prepared and the constitution inaugurated in the provinces.

and provide the vote for the majority of the small landholders, the small cultivators, urban ratepayers, and a substantial section of the poorer classes, beside providing for women, the depressed classes, and industrial labour. No important section of the community should lack means of expressing its wishes, and the general mass of the people is represented fairly.

9. THE CHIEF COMMISSIONERS' PROVINCES

The Chief Commissioners' Provinces, British Baluchistan, Delhi, Ajmer-Merwara, Coorg, the Andaman and Nicobar Islands, and Panth Piploda, fall directly under the administration of the governor-general acting through a chief commissioner appointed at his discretion.[1] Normally the federal legislatures has full legislative authority over them.[2]

For British Baluchistan the governor-general shall act at his discretion, but the executive authority of the federation applies to the territory and to the other provinces. No federal Act, however, applies to the territory unless applied with or without modifications by the governor-general, who may also, subject to disallowance by the Crown, make regulations for the territory which may supersede any federal Act or other law applicable thereto.[3] He possesses like authority to make regulations for the Andaman and Nicobar Islands.[4] In the case of Coorg the existing legislature and financial arrangements stand until altered.[5]

The rules applicable in the provinces to police regulations, the prevention of crimes of violence, and the restrictions on disclosure of documents are applied to the relation of the governor-general to the federal chambers.[6]

Otherwise the rules in force as to these territories remain unaltered. Power exists under the Act to confer on them provincial status.[7]

Aden ceases to be part of British India, and its government may be regulated by Order in Council. In accordance with colonial usage such Order may delegate legislative power to any person or persons in Aden, but without impairing the power

[1] S. 94. [2] S. 110 (4). [3] S. 95. [4] S. 96.
[5] S. 97. [6] S. 98. [7] S. 290.

of the Crown in Council to legislate. The Order must provide for appeal from the Aden court to an Indian court (no doubt Bombay), and such expenses for this service as the King in Council may determine shall be paid; it shall also regulate the appeal to the Privy Council from the Indian court in Aden appeals. Moreover, the government of Aden is to be made liable to suit in cases where it would have lain against the secretary of state in council, and property held for the government of Aden is vested in the Crown for the purposes of that territory.[1]

10. THE DIVISION OF LEGISLATIVE POWER

As is inevitable in a federation there is distinction of legislative authority both as regards ambit and subject-matter. The power[2] of the federal legislature extends to making laws for any part of British India and any federated state, that of the provincial legislatures to making laws for the province or any part thereof. Federal Acts may have extra-territorial operation in regard to (1) British subjects or servants of the Crown in any part of India; (2) to British subjects domiciled in any part of India wherever they may be; (3) to, or to persons on, ships and aircraft registered in any part of British India or a federated state wherever they may be; (4) in the case of matters on which the federation may legislate for a state to state subjects wherever thay may be; and (5) in the case of a law for the regulation or discipline of any naval, military, or air force raised in British India, to members of and persons attached to the force wherever they may be. The definition of power is important and valuable; the failure in Dominion legislation to define the precise extent of authority claimed is extremely confusing. The province, on the other hand, is given no extension of power; it resembles the provinces of Canada which are restricted deliberately to legislation in the province.

As regards subject-matter, as already noted, the constitution provides three lists,[3] the federal legislative list, the provincial

[1] S. 289. Transfer was protested against by the Assembly, September 16th 1933.
[2] S. 99. Cf. Keith, *Journ. Comp. Leg.*, 1935, p. 278. [3] S. 100 and Sched.7.

legislative list, and the concurrent legislative list. A rigid distinction of power thus first appears in Indian legislation, for under even the constitution of 1919 a province might for that area vary central legislation if the governor-general gave previous sanction, and even if sanction were not obtained, a provincial Act assented to by the governor-general could repeal a prior central Act. But the inconvenience of this principle, which renders void any law passed by a legislature outside its sphere, is minimized by the existence of the list of concurrent subjects, which includes most of the matters on which federal legislation may be desirable for international conventions or to preserve uniformity, to give a lead to the provinces as in the case of labour legislation, or to regulate matters extending beyond one province as in the case of diseases of animals. In the concurrent sphere the doctrine[1] that a federal Act supersedes a provincial Act, which is in force in Canada and Australia, cannot be given effect in full, for there would be danger of the federation unduly tying the hands of the provinces and preventing for instance the variation of legislation on crime necessary to meet a provincial need. Hence, while normally a federal Act or a central Act on a concurrent subject overrides a provincial Act, if such an Act has been assented to after reservation by the governor-general, it prevails over prior legislation.[2] The federal legislature may vary such an Act, but the prior sanction at discretion of the governor-general is required for the introduction of such a Bill into the legislature.

The federal legislature may also regulate any provincial subject for two or more provinces at the request of the chambers of these provinces, but any such Act may be varied or repealed by the provincial legislatures.[3]

The governor-general in his discretion may also assign to the federation or the province power to make a law or impose a tax on any subject-matter not included in either list, and the executive power of the federation or province shall also apply.[4] Before making such an assignment, the governor-general necessarily must satisfy himself that there is no provision assigning the matter to one side or the other; in doing so he would presumably consult the federal court.

[1] S. 107 (1). [2] S. 107 (2). [3] S. 103. [4] S. 104.

The Instructions[1] in accordance with the view of the joint committee recognize that in regard to concurrent topics there is real risk of difficulty. The governor-general should take into consideration the question of the burden to be placed on provincial resources, and in cases where his previous sanction to proposed legislation in the concurrent sphere is requisite, because it proposed to give directions for execution of such a law to the province, he is bound to satisfy himself that the provinces have been consulted. In the same way, while he is to consider seriously provincial desires to vary the main codes, he must also bear in mind the advantages of uniformity in such matters.

In regard to the implementing of treaties and agreements with other countries federal power is limited, for it extends only when the governor of the province affected and the ruler of any state affected has given prior assent.[2] An Act so passed may be repealed by the federation, and if the treaty ceases to be operative by the province or state. This limitation, of course, applies only where the subject-matter is not otherwise within federal authority paramount as sole or concurrent, but the limitation may prove inconvenient. In Canada[3] the extent of power to legislate on provincial topics on this ground is still disputed. In Australia it has never been decided that under the authority as to external affairs the federation may invade the field reserved to the states.

The federal legislature may apply the Naval Discipline Act to Indian naval forces, subject to such modifications as may be made by Indian Act to adapt the requirements of the Act to Indian circumstances, and to such changes as may be made by the King in Council to regulate the relations of the British forces and ships to those of India. If, however, the Indian forces and ships are placed at the disposal of the Admiralty, the Naval Discipline Act shall apply without modification.[4]

Invasion of the provincial sphere by the federal legislature may be authorized in his discretion by the governor-general if

[1] Clause XXV, XXVI.

[2] S. 106; Keith, *Journ. Comp. Leg.*, 1935, p. 277.

[3] Keith, *Constitutional Law of the British Dominions*, pp. 324, 332, 333.

[4] S. 105. This corresponds with the position of the Dominions under the Naval Discipline (Dominion Naval Forces) Act, 1911 (Keith, *Responsible Government in the Dominions*, ii, 1009 ff.)

in his opinion a grave emergency exists, whereby the security of India is threatened whether by war or internal disturbance. The governor-general's previous sanction of the proposed legislation is necessary, and he must satisfy himself that the provision proposed is proper. Such legislation during its operation is paramount over provincial legislation, prior or subsequent. But the proclamation of emergency which is the prelude to legislation by the federation may be revoked by the governor-general. It must also be laid before the two Houses of Parliament, and it falls to the ground unless within six months both Houses by resolution approve it. Any federal law thus made expires six months after the expiry of the proclamation of emergency.[1] For this power there is no parallel in Canada or Australia, save to the very limited extent that grave emergency, such as war conditions, has been held sufficient in both Dominions to justify the passing of legislation controlling domestic issues, which in peace the federation could not deal with.[2]

As regards the states the federation may legislate only in respect of matters accepted by the instrument of Accession of the state concerned. The state may legislate, but its legislation is void in so far as it conflicts with a valid federal Act.[3]

The federation has unfettered power of legislation as regards matters in the provincial list except in the case of a province or the parts thereof.[4] This means that it may legislate for any territory not included in the governors' provinces, and may, unlike Canada, legislate, under its extra-territorial power, on provincial matters.

The federation, of course, retains the legislative powers conferred on India by such Acts as the Extradition Act, 1870, the Slave Trade Act, 1876, the Fugitive Offenders Act, 1881, the Colonial Courts of Admiralty Act, 1890, the Merchant Shipping Act, 1894, and other general empowering Acts, but its specific powers render these unimportant in the main. Imperial legislation for India is rare: the Official Secrets Acts are suspended while the Indian Act XIX of 1923 is operative. The provision in the Whaling Industry (Regulation) Act, 1934,[5] giving extra-territorial validity to Indian legislation, is motived by doubts

[1] S. 102. [2] Keith, op. cit., p. 327. [3] S. 107 (3). [4] S. 100 (4).
[5] 24 & 25 Geo. V, c. 49, s. 15 (1).

of the extent of Indian power prior to the new Act of 1935. It is to be noted that nearly all British Acts which apply to India may now be varied or repealed by the Indian legislatures, subject to the prior sanction of the governor-general.[1] This matter might be of substantial importance in the case of merchant shipping, as the present system of control rests on the supremacy of British legislation. It must be remembered that India was proposed as a signatory to the agreement of 1931 regarding merchant shipping.[2] Safeguards on this head, however, are provided in the spirit of that agreement in the present Act.[3]

The Legislative Lists are as follows:[4]

List 1

Federal Legislative List

1. His Majesty's naval, military and air forces borne on the Indian establishment and any other armed force raised in India by the Crown, not being forces raised for employment in Indian States or military or armed police maintained by Provincial Governments; any armed forces which are not forces of His Majesty, but are attached to or operating with any of His Majesty's naval, military or air forces borne on the Indian establishment; central intelligence bureau; preventive detention in British India for reasons of State connected with defence, external affairs, or the discharge of the functions of the Crown in its relations with Indian States.

2. Naval, military and air force works; local self-government in cantonment areas (not being cantonment areas of Indian State troops),[5] the regulation of house accommodation in such areas, and, within British India, the delimitation of such areas.

3. External affairs; the implementing of treaties and agreements with other countries; extradition, including the surrender of criminals and accused persons to parts of His Majesty's dominions outside India.

4. Ecclesiastical affairs, including European cemeteries.

5. Currency, coinage and legal tender.

[1] See § 11 below.
[2] Keith, *Speeches and Documents on the British Dominions, 1918–1931*, pp. 222–30.
[3] S. 115. See § 11 below. [4] Sched. 5. [5] These fall under the state's control.

6. Public debt of the Federation.

7. Posts and telegraphs, including telephones, wireless, broadcasting and other like forms of communication; Post Office Savings Bank.

8. Federal Public Services and Federal Public Service Commission.

9. Federal pensions, that is to say, pensions payable by the Federation or out of Federal revenues.

10. Works, lands and buildings vested in, or in the possession of His Majesty for the purposes of the Federation (not being naval, military or air force works), but, as regards property situate in a Province, subject always to Provincial legislation, save in so far as Federal law otherwise provides, and, as regards property in a Federated State held by virtue of any lease or agreement with that State, subject to the terms of that lease or agreement.

11. The Imperial Library, the Indian Museum, the Imperial War Museum, the Victoria Memorial, and any similar institution controlled or financed by the Federation.

12. Federal agencies and institutes for the following purposes, that is to say, for research, for professional or technical training, or for the promotion of special studies.

13. The Benares Hindu University and the Aligarh Muslim University.

14. The Survey of India, the Geological, Botanical and Zoological Surveys of India; Federal meteorological organizations.

15. Ancient and historical monuments; archaeological sites and remains.

16. Census.

17. Admission into, and emigration and expulsion from, India, including in relation thereto the regulation of the movements in India of persons who are not British subjects domiciled in India, subjects of any Federated State, or British subjects domiciled in the United Kingdom;[1] pilgrimages to places beyond India.

18. Port quarantine; seamen's and marine hospitals, and hospitals connected with port quarantine.

[1] This leaves immigration of Dominion British subjects to federal control.

19. Import and export across customs frontiers as defined by the Federal Government.

20. Federal railways; the regulation of all railways other than minor railways in respect of safety, maximum and minimum rates and fares, station and service terminal charges, interchange of traffic and the responsibility of railway administrations as carriers of goods and passengers; the regulation of minor railways in respect of safety and the responsibility of the administrations of such railways as carriers of goods and passengers.

21. Maritime shipping and navigation, including shipping and navigation on tidal waters; Admiralty jurisdiction.

22. Major ports, that is to say the declaration and delimitation of such ports, and the constitution and powers of Port Authorities therein.

23. Fishing and fisheries beyond territorial waters.

24. Aircraft and air navigation; the provision of aerodromes; regulation and organization of air traffic and of aerodromes.

25. Lighthouses, including lightships, beacons and other provisions for the safety of shipping and aircraft.

26. Carriage of passengers and goods by sea or by air.

27. Copyright, inventions, designs, trademarks and merchandise marks.

28. Cheques, bills of exchange, promissory notes and other like instruments.

29. Arms; firearms; ammunition.

30. Explosives.

31. Opium, so far as regards cultivation and manufacture, or sale for export.

32. Petroleum and other liquids and substances declared by Federal law to be dangerously inflammable, so far as regards possession, storage and transport.

33. Corporations, that is to say, the incorporation, regulation and winding-up of trading corporations, including banking, insurance and financial corporations, but not including corporations owned or controlled by a Federated State and carrying on business only within that State or co-operative societies, and

of corporations, whether trading or not, with objects not confined to one unit.[1]

34. Development of industries, where development under Federal control is declared by Federal law to be expedient in the public interest.

35. Regulation of labour and safety in mines and oil-fields.

36. Regulation of mines and oilfields and mineral development to the extent to which such regulation and development under Federal control is declared by Federal law to be expedient in the public interest.

37. The law of insurance, except as respects insurance undertaken by a Federated State, and the regulation of the conduct of insurance business, except as respects business undertaken by a Federated State; Government insurance, except so far as undertaken by a Federated State, or, by virtue of any entry in the Provincial Legislative List or the Concurrent Legislative List, by a Province.

38. Banking, that is to say, the conduct of banking business by corporations other than corporations owned or controlled by a Federated State and carrying on business only within that State.

39. Extension of the powers and jurisdiction of members of a police force belonging to any part of British India to any area in another Governor's Province or Chief Commissioner's Province, but not so as to enable the police of one part to exercise powers and jurisdiction elsewhere without the consent of the Government of the Province or the Chief Commissioner, as the case may be; extension of the powers and jurisdiction of members of a police force belonging to any unit to railway areas outside that unit.

40. Elections to the Federal Legislature, subject to the provisions of this Act and of any Order in Council made thereunder.

41. The salaries of the Federal Ministers, of the President and Vice-President of the Council of State and of the Speaker and Deputy Speaker of the Federal Assembly; the salaries,

[1] This provision is so vague that the confusion of power seen in Canada is likely to be repeated, Keith, *Responsible Government in the Dominions*, i, 547–9. See List II, no. 33.

allowances and privileges of the members of the Federal Legislature; and, to such extent as is expressly authorized by Part II of this Act, the punishment of persons who refuse to give evidence or produce documents before Committees of the Legislature.

42. Offences against laws with respect to any of the matters in this list.

43. Inquiries and statistics for the purpose of any of the matters in this list.

44. Duties of customs, including export duties.

45. Duties of excise on tobacco and other goods manufactured or produced in India except—

(*a*) alcoholic liquors for human consumption;

(*b*) opium, Indian hemp and other narcotic drugs and narcotics; non-narcotic drugs;

(*c*) medicinal and toilet preparations containing alcohol, or any substance included in sub-paragraph (*b*) of this entry.

46. Corporation tax.

47. Salt.

48. State lotteries.

49. Naturalization.

50. Migration within India from or into a Governor's Province or a Chief Commissioner's Province.[1]

51. Establishment of standards of weight.

52. Ranchi European Mental Hospital.

53. Jurisdiction and powers of all courts, except the Federal Court, with respect to any of the matters in this list and, to such extent as is expressly authorized by Part IX of this Act, the enlargement of the appellate jurisdiction of the Federal Court, and the conferring thereon of supplemental powers.

54. Taxes on income other than agricultural income.

55. Taxes on the capital value of the assets, exclusive of agricultural land, of individuals and companies; taxes on the capital of companies.

56. Duties in respect of succession to property other than agricultural land.

57. The rates of stamp duty in respect of bills of exchange,

[1] Contrast the freedom of migration in Canada and Australia.

cheques, promissory notes, bills of lading, letters of credit, policies of insurance, proxies and receipts.

58. Terminal taxes on goods or passengers carried by railway or air; taxes on railway fares and freights.

59. Fees in respect of any of the matters in this list, but not including fees taken in any Court.

List II

Provincial Legislative List

1. Public order (but not including the use of His Majesty's naval, military or air forces in aid of the civil power); the administration of justice; constitution and organization of all courts, except the Federal Court, and fees taken therein; preventive detention for reasons connected with the maintenance of public order; persons subjected to such detention.

2. Jurisdiction and powers of all courts[1] except the Federal Court, with respect to any of the matters in this list; procedure in Rent and Revenue Courts.

3. Police, including railway and village police.

4. Prisons, reformatories, Borstal institutions and other institutions of a like nature, and persons detained therein; arrangements with other units for the use of prisons and other institutions.

5. Public debt of the Province.

6. Provincial Public Services and Provincial Public Service Commissions.

7. Provincial pensions, that is to say, pensions payable by the Province or out of Provincial revenues.

8. Works, lands and buildings vested in or in the possession of His Majesty for the purposes of the Province.

9. Compulsory acquisition of land.

10. Libraries, museums and other similar institutions controlled or financed by the Province.

11. Elections to the Provincial Legislature, subject to the provisions of this Act and of any Order in Council made thereunder.

[1] This will obviate constant legislation by the Indian legislature to allow appeal to the High Courts under provincial Acts, e.g. Act XXIV of 1932.

12. The salaries of the Provincial Ministers, of the Speaker and Deputy Speaker of the Legislative Assembly, and, if there is a Legislative Council, of the President and Deputy President thereof; the salaries, allowances and privileges of the members of the Provincial Legislature; and, to such extent as is expressly authorized by Part III of this Act, the punishment of persons who refuse to give evidence or produce documents before Committees of the Provincial Legislature.

13. Local government, that is to say, the constitution and powers of municipal corporations, improvement trusts, district boards, mining settlement authorities and other local authorities for the purpose of local self-government or village administration.

14. Public health and sanitation; hospitals and dispensaries; registration of births and deaths.

15. Pilgrimages, other than pilgrimages to places beyond India.

16. Burial and burial-grounds.

17. Education.

18. Communications, that is to say, roads, bridges, ferries, and other means of communication not specified in List I; minor railways subject to the provisions of List I with respect to such railways; municipal tramways; ropeways; inland waterways and traffic thereon subject to the provisions of List III with regard to such waterways; ports, subject to the provisions in List I with regard to major ports; vehicles other than mechanically propelled vehicles.

19. Water, that is to say, water-supplies, irrigation and canals, drainage and embankments, water-storage and water-power.

20. Agriculture, including agricultural education and research, protection against pests and prevention of plant diseases; improvement of stock and prevention of animal diseases; veterinary training and practice; pounds and the prevention of cattle trespass.

21. Land, that is to say, rights in or over land, land tenures, including the relation of landlord and tenant, and the collection of rents; transfer, alienation and devolution of agricultural land; land improvement and agricultural loans; colonization;

Courts of Wards; encumbered and attached estates; treasure trove.[1]

22. Forests.

23. Regulation of mines and oilfields and mineral development subject to the Provisions of List I with respect to regulation and development under Federal control.

24. Fisheries.

25. Protection of wild birds and wild animals.

26. Gas and gasworks.

27. Trade and commerce within the Province; markets and fairs; money-lending and money-lenders.

28. Inns and innkeepers.

29. Production, supply and distribution of goods; development of industries, subject to the provisions in List I with respect to the development of certain industries under Federal control.

30. Adulteration of foodstuffs and other goods; weights and measures.

31. Intoxicating liquors and narcotic drugs, that is to say, the production, manufacture, possession, transport, purchase and sale of intoxicating liquors, opium and other narcotic drugs, but subject, as respects opium, to the provisions of List I and, as respects poisons and dangerous drugs, to the provisions of List III.

32. Relief of the poor; unemployment.

33. The incorporation, regulation, and winding-up of corporations, other than corporations specified in List I; unincorporated trading, literary, scientific, religious and other societies and associations; co-operative societies.

34. Charities and charitable institutions; charitable and religious endowments.

35. Theatres, dramatic performances and cinemas, but not including the sanction of cinematograph films for exhibition.

36. Betting and gambling.

37. Offences against laws with respect of any of the matters in this list.

38. Inquiries and statistics for the purpose of any of the matters in this list.

[1] Cf. S. 174.

39. Land revenue, including the assessment and collection of revenue, the maintenance of land records, survey for revenue purposes and records of rights, and alienation of revenue.

40. Duties of excise on the following goods manufactured or produced in the Province and countervailing duties at the same or lower rates on similar goods manufactured or produced elsewhere in India—

(*a*) alcoholic liquors for human consumption;

(*b*) opium, Indian hemp and other narcotic drugs and narcotics; non-narcotic drugs.

(*c*) medicinal and toilet preparations containing alcohol or any substance included in sub-paragraph (*b*) of this entry.

41. Taxes on agricultural income.

42. Taxes on lands and buildings, hearths and windows.

43. Duties in respect of succession to agricultural land.

44. Taxes on mineral rights, subject to any limitations imposed by any Act of the Federal Legislature relating to mineral development.

45. Capitation taxes.

46. Taxes on professions, trades, callings and employments.

47. Taxes on animals and boats.

48. Taxes on the sale of goods and on advertisements.

49. Cesses on the entry of goods into a local area for consumption, use or sale therein.

50. Taxes on luxuries, including taxes on entertainments, amusements, betting and gambling.

51. The rates of stamp duty in respect of documents other than those specified in the provisions of List I with regard to rates of stamp duty.

52. Dues on passengers and goods carried on inland waterways.

53. Tolls.

54. Fees in respect of any of the matters in this list, but not including fees taken in any Court.

LIST III

Concurrent Legislative List

PART I

1. Criminal law, including all matters included in the Indian Penal Code at the date of the passing of this Act, but excluding offences against laws with respect to any of the matters specified in List I or List II and excluding the use of His Majesty's naval, military and air forces in aid of the civil power.

2. Criminal Procedure, including all matters included in the Code of Criminal Procedure at the date of the passing of this Act.

3. Removal of prisoners and accused persons from one unit to another unit.

4. Civil Procedure, including the law of Limitation and all matters included in the Code of Civil Procedure at the date of the passing of this Act; the recovery in a Governor's Province or a Chief Commissioner's Province of claims in respect of taxes and other public demands, including arrears of land revenue and sums recoverable as such, arising outside that Province.

5. Evidence and oaths; recognition of laws, public acts and records and judicial proceedings.

6. Marriage and divorce; infants and minors; adoption.

7. Wills, intestacy, and succession, save as regards agricultural land.

8. Transfer of property other than agricultural land; registration of deeds and documents.

9. Trusts and trustees.

10. Contracts, including partnership, agency, contracts of carriage, and other special forms of contract, but not including contracts relating to agricultural land.

11. Arbitration.

12. Bankruptcy and insolvency; administrators-general and official trustees.

13. Stamp duties other than duties or fees collected by means of judicial stamps, but not including rates of stamp duty.

14. Actionable wrongs, save in so far as included in laws with respect to any of the matters specified in List I or List II.

15. Jurisdiction and powers of all courts, except the Federal Court, with respect to any of the matters in this list.

16. Legal, medical and other professions.

17. Newspapers, books and printing presses.

18. Lunacy and mental deficiency, including places for the reception or treatment of lunatics and mental deficients.

19. Poisons and dangerous drugs.

20. Mechanically propelled vehicles.

21. Boilers.

22. Prevention of cruelty to animals.

23. European vagrancy; criminal tribes.

24. Inquiries and statistics for the purpose of any of the matters in this Part of this List.

25. Fees in respect of any of the matters in this Part of this List, but not including fees taken in any Court.

PART II[1]

26. Factories.

27. Welfare of labour; conditions of labour; provident funds; employers' liability and workmen's compensation; health insurance, including invalidity pensions; old age pensions.

28. Unemployment insurance.

29. Trade unions; industrial and labour disputes.

30. The prevention of the extension from one unit to another of infectious or contagious diseases or pests affecting men, animals or plants.

31. Electricity.

32. Shipping and navigation on inland waterways as regards mechanically propelled vessels, and the rule of the road on such waterways; carriage of passengers and goods on inland waterways.

33. The sanctioning of cinematograph films for exhibition.

34. Persons subjected to preventive detention under Federal authority.

[1] This list includes matters on which a Federal Act, with prior consent of the governor-general, may confer the power to give directions to a province; s. 126 (2). See § 12 below.

35. Inquiries and statistics for the purpose of any of the matters in this Part of this List.

36. Fees in respect of any of the matters in this Part of this List, but not including fees taken in any Court.

11. THE RESTRICTIONS ON LEGISLATIVE POWER

In the Dominions the powers of those Dominions which are bound by the provisions of the Statute of Westminster, as are Canada, the Union of South Africa, and the Irish Free State, are free from any restriction, save such as are due in the case of Canada to the federal character of her constitution. Australia and New Zealand remain still, unless and until they adopt the Statute, subject to the restriction of the Colonial Laws Validity Act, 1865, under which their Acts, if repugnant to imperial legislation applying to them are to that extent void, and to the much more vague restriction of territorial limitation so that, for instance, it was necessary for express power to legislate with extra-territorial force to be given for the enforcement of the whaling convention of 1931.[1] In the case of India there are certain further limitations of an absolute character, and in certain other cases, in complete deviation from Dominion practice but in accord with Indian precedent, legislation is forbidden without the previous sanction given in the discretion of the governor-general or governor.

The supremacy of Parliament over British India and its power to legislate therefor or any part thereof are reasserted in the Act,[2] in accordance with precedent, and it is expressly provided that no legislature, provincial or federal, may make any law affecting the sovereign or the royal family, or the succession to the Crown, or the sovereignty, dominion, or suzerainty of the Crown in any part of India, or the law of British nationality, or the Army Act, the Air Force Act, or the Naval Discipline Act, or the law of prize or prize courts. All these matters are issues definitely connected with sovereignty, which naturally may not be altered by a legislature definitely subordinate. In the same way the legislatures may not alter, except as specifically provided, the Act itself, or any Order in

[1] Whaling Industry (Regulation) Act, 1934.

[2] S. 110.

Council under it, or any rules made under it by the secretary of state, the governor-general, or a governor in his discretion or in his individual judgment. Further, except as provided in the Act no legislature may derogate from the prerogative right of His Majesty to grant special leave to appeal from any Court.

Any Act which may be passed repugnant to these rules is, of course, *pro tanto* invalid. In other cases Acts may be passed, provided prior sanction is given by the governor-general in his discretion. These include any Bill or amendment which (*a*) repeals, amends, or is repugnant to any provisions of any Act of Parliament which extends to British India; (*b*) repeals, amends, or is repugnant to any governor-general's or governor's Act, or any ordinance promulgated in his discretion by the governor-general or a governor; (*c*) affects matters as respects which the governor-general is required to exercise his discretion; (*d*) repeals, affects, or amends any Act relating to any police force; (*e*) affects the procedure for criminal proceedings in which European British subjects are concerned; (*f*) subjects persons not resident in British India to greater taxation than persons resident in British India, or subjects companies not wholly controlled or managed in British India to greater taxation than companies wholly controlled and managed therein; or (*g*) affects the grant of relief from any federal tax on income in respect of income taxed or taxable in the United Kingdom. Further, the governor-general's sanction is requisite for the introduction into a provincial legislature of legislation of the kind indicated in sections (*a*), (*c*), and (*e*) above, and of legislation affecting any of his Acts or ordinances, while the governor's assent is requisite for legislation affecting his Acts or ordinances or the police force.[1] In addition to these general provisions in certain other cases prior sanction is requisite. Thus the governor-general or the governor must sanction the introduction of financial Bills;[2] the former must sanction the introduction of any Bill in the concurrent sphere which provides for the giving of directions to the provincial governments,[3] or any Bill which affects taxation in which the provinces are interested.[4]

[1] S. 108. [2] Ss. 37, 82. [3] S. 126 (2).
[4] S. 141. See also ss. 153, 166 (3), 182 (2), 226 (2), 267 (*a*), 271, 299 (3).

These restrictions, it will be seen, are in part directed at preventing the passing of legislation which is intended to or would discriminate against British commercial interests in India. These are reinforced by the special responsibility above noted of the governor-general to prevent action subjecting to discriminatory action goods of British or Burmese origin imported into India which is intended not to enable him to dictate Indian fiscal policy, but to interfere in matters where injury to British, not gain to Indian trade, is the chief aim. Further protection is accorded in a series of elaborate clauses against discrimination.[1] A British subject domiciled in the United Kingdom is exempt from the operation of any federal or provincial law[2] which (*a*) imposes any restriction on the right of entry into British India; or (*b*) imposes by reference to place of birth, race, descent, language, religion, domicile, residence or duration of residence, any disability, liability, restriction, or condition in regard to travel, residence, the acquisition, holding, or disposal of property, the holding of public office, or the carrying on of any occupation, trade, business, or profession. But the exemption is conditioned by its suspension in so far as a British subject of Indian domicile is subject to any disability in regard to the same matter imposed on the same ground under the law of the United Kingdom. But the imposition of quarantine regulations and the exclusion or deportation of persons deemed undesirable is not to be deemed a restriction on entry. This provision is so widely worded that it might be misused to provide for the exclusion of almost any person; thus Canada and the Union regard Indians as undesirable citizens on economic grounds. But the governor-general or governor in his discretion in view of grave menace to tranquillity or to combat crimes of violence may suspend the operation of the law for such time as he thinks fit. This, of course, would enable entry to be barred to British communists who might seek to enter India to stir up communal strife.

Discrimination in taxation against British subjects domiciled in the United Kingdom or Burma and against companies incorporated under the laws of the United Kingdom or Burma

[1] Ss. 111–16.

[2] Including by-laws, etc., issued after the Act.

is forbidden, and it constitutes discrimination if the law would result in heavier payments by persons or companies than if they had been domiciled or incorporated in British India. Registration in Burma under Indian legislation prior to federation is to be deemed incorporation under Burmese law. Companies incorporated in the United Kingdom, their directors, members, shareholders, officers, etc., are to be deemed to comply with any federal or provincial requirements as to place of incorporation, situation of its registered office, or the currency in which its capital is expressed or place of birth, etc., of directors, shareholders, officers, etc. Similarly they are to be entitled to preferential treatment in respect of taxation, but in every case the right is lost if reciprocity is not given in the United Kingdom. Again a British subject domiciled in the United Kingdom is deemed to comply with any conditions as to place of birth, etc., in respect of companies incorporated in India so as to be eligible as director, shareholder, officer, etc., again on condition of reciprocity. British companies are to be entitled to equality of treatment, on the basis of reciprocity, in respect of any grants or subsidies provided by the federation or provinces, but there is an important exception in the case of companies which are not engaged in a branch of trade in India when the system of assistance is started. In these cases the legislature may require that the company be incorporated in British India or a federated state, that not exceeding one-half of the directors are British subjects domiciled in British India or a federated state, and that reasonable facilities are given for the training of British subjects domiciled in India or a federated state.

It is further provided that British ships registered in the United Kingdom shall not be subjected to any discriminatory treatment in respect of the ship, master, officers, crew, passengers, or cargo as compared with ships registered in British India, unless there is like discrimination in any matter against ships registered in British India under the law of the United Kingdom. The same rule applies to aircraft.

These provisions, it will be seen, are complex,[1] and are

[1] Yet obviously imperfect. They do not forbid discrimination by caste or colour; duration of residence is provided for, but not continuity. Cf. Keith, *Letters on Imperial Relations*, 1916–1935, pp. 219 ff.

certainly liable to be regarded as oppressive and unfair restrictions. That it would have been much wiser to regulate the matter by convention was recognized by the Round Table Conference at its first session, and Parliament admitted the force of this view by providing that the operations of the law may be suspended by Order in Council if a convention on a basis of reciprocity is achieved and legislation passed in the United Kingdom and India to give effect to it.

The difficult issue of professional qualifications is dealt with by the rule of the necessity of prior sanction of the governor-general or governor to federal or provincial legislation providing for the laying down of professional or technical qualifications for the exercise of any profession, occupation, trade, or business or the holding of any office in British India. Sanction may not be given unless provision is made to save the rights of any person lawfully engaged in any profession, etc., at the time, unless it is necessary in the public interest to prevent continuance on his part. Moreover, all regulations made under federal or provincial legislation must be published four months before they take effect; representations against them may be made by persons affected within two months, and the governor-general or governor in his individual judgment may disallow the regulations in whole or part. The governor-general may apply this principle to regulations made under any Indian law existing before the new Act takes effect.[1]

The position of medical practitioners required careful regulation, because it was essential that the European community should have access to European practitioners if they so desired, and the latter therefore must be assured fair treatment. The British system provides that British subjects of Indian domicile may be registered as qualified practitioners if they hold diplomas granted in India after examination, unless the diploma does not furnish sufficient guarantee of knowledge of and skill for the practice of medicine, surgery, and midwifery, and it is left to the Privy Council to decide any issue as to the value of the diploma. It is therefore provided that, so long as this is the state of affairs in the United Kingdom, British practitioners duly qualified in the United Kingdom shall not be

[1] S. 119.

excluded from practice or registration in British India except on the ground that the diploma held is not adequate proof of knowledge and capacity. Exclusion on such a ground can only be effected if twelve months' notice is given to the governor-general and the authority issuing the diploma, and the Privy Council, if appealed to, holds that the diploma is insufficient evidence. Persons entitled to practise in either country under recognized diplomas must not be differentially treated; this is an enactment for the United Kingdom as well as for India. Provision is made for safeguarding persons domiciled in Burma and entitled to practise in the United Kingdom under British or Burmese qualifications.[1] Finally, any officer on the active list of the Indian Medical Service or any other branch of the forces is *ipso facto* entitled to practise in British India, thus securing their right to attend the civil population.

The legal safeguards are added to by the special responsibility of the governor-general and the governors to prevent in the executive sphere discrimination and by the instructions given to them in case of doubt to reserve Bills which may be discriminatory, though not so in form.

With reference to all these matters of prior sanction it must be noted that the grant of such sanction in no wise fetters the freedom of the governor-general or governor to refuse assent or reserve any Bill, and on the other hand the omission of sanction does not invalidate the Bill if it has duly received the assent, in the case where the governor's sanction was necessary, of the governor, the governor-general, or the Crown, and in the case where the governor-general's sanction was requisite it has received his assent or that of the Crown. The provision is of great importance, since it is clear that it would be vexatious if a measure which had been deliberately assented to were to be ruled invalid on the ground of a technical omission.[2]

Finally, there must be noted certain miscellaneous restrictions on legislative and executive power. No provincial legislature or government may by reason of its power as to trade and commerce within the province and the production, supply and distribution of commodities prohibit or restrict the entry into

[1] S. 120. See Indian Medical Council Act, 1933, Joint Committee Report, i, 212 ff.

[2] S. 109.

or export from the province of goods of any description.[1] This is a very far-reaching prohibition and may be compared with the requirement of free trade between the states in the Commonwealth constitution, which has given rise to difficult issues, still unsettled; for instance, how far may the entry of diseased or suspect cattle from another state be checked? Nor may there be discrimination by toll, cess, tax. or due between goods manufactured in or the produce of the province and other goods or between goods manufactured or produced outside the province according to locality.

Further,[2] no subject of His Majesty domiciled in India shall on grounds only of religion, place of birth, descent, colour or any of them be ineligible for office under the Crown in India, or be prohibited on any such grounds from acquiring, holding, or disposing of property or carrying on any occupation, trade, business or profession in British India. But this prohibition is not to exclude legislation restricting the transfer of agricultural land from a member of an agricultural class to a non-member, or to interfere with rights of members of a community due to personal law, nor does it diminish the obligations of the governor-general or governors with regard to the protection of minorities.

No person[3] may be deprived of his property in British India save by authority of law. Laws providing for the acquisition for public purpose of land or any commercial or industrial undertaking or interest therein must specify the compensation or the mode in which it is to be assessed. Prior sanction of the governor-general or governor is requisite to any federal or provincial Bill transferring to public ownership land or modifying rights therein, including revenue rights. In the same spirit[4] privileges in respect of land granted before January 1st 1870 or for services thereafter and pensions may be taken away or varied only with the assent of the governor-general or governor in his individual judgment. This provision, of course, does not affect the right to forfeit any grant for breach of its conditions, but it is intended to safeguard holders of government grants or pensions against any possibility of vindictive treatment based

[1] S. 297.
[2] The grounds are limited as compared with s. 111. See s. 298.
[3] S. 299. [4] S. 300.

on their former services to government. No doubt it is justified *ex majore cautela*. The series of prohibitions take the place of the declaration of fundamental rights for which many Indians asked and which was discussed at the Round Table Conference.

12. THE ADMINISTRATIVE RELATIONS BETWEEN THE FEDERATION AND THE UNITS

The introduction of federation replaces the complete control of the centre over the provinces by a division of authority, and introduces into the federated states the operation of federal executive authority. It is, therefore, expressly provided that the executive authority of the provinces and states and that of the federation shall be exercised so as to secure due respect for the laws of the federation and the interests of the province or state respectively.[1]

The governor-general may direct any governor to act as his agent in the province in respect of defence, foreign affairs, or ecclesiastical affairs or of the tribal areas, and in so acting the governor acts in his discretion subject to his instructions.[2]

Generally[3] the governor-general may agree with a provincial government or the ruler of a federated state for the carrying out conditionally or unconditionally of any federal executive function. Moreover, an Act of the federation may impose duties and confer powers on a province or its officers or authorities whether in federal or concurrent subjects, and may similarly impose duties and confer rights on a ruler or officers designated by him in respect of federal matters. In such cases the costs of administration must be paid by the federation, the sum being fixed in default of agreement by an arbitrator named by the Chief Justice of India.

An agreement[4] may also be made with any state, and must be made if the Instrument of Accession so stipulates, for the administration of a federal law by the ruler, but the governor-general must be empowered, by inspection or otherwise, to satisfy himself that the administration conforms with the federal policy and to give directions to the ruler in case of dissatisfaction. Such agreements must receive judicial notice.

[1] S. 122, Part VI. [2] S. 123. [3] S. 124. [4] S. 125.

Provincial executive authority must be so used as not to interfere with federal authority, and federal authority extends to giving directions to a province to ensure that end.[1] This is a very striking derogation from provincial autonomy, and as the judge of the necessity of directions is the federation, conflict may result. It is more reasonable that the federation should be authorized to give instructions on matters of the execution of federal laws on certain concurrent issues; as noted above, the previous sanction of the governor-general in his discretion is necessary for legislation to authorize the federation to give such directions. In such cases consultation with the province is obviously desirable, and also in deciding issues as to which legislature should handle concurrent subjects. The federation may also give directions to the province for the construction and maintenance of means of communication of military importance, though it may, of course, itself construct and maintain such communications under its defence power. If the province fails to carry out federal directions a means of compulsion is provided, for the governor-general in his discretion may issue instructions to the governor, who under his special responsibility must then give effect to his orders even against ministers' wishes. But the governor-general, of course, need not give exactly the same directions as the federation proposed, and may use his influence to secure modification. Finally, he has unfettered discretion to give the governor any orders in regard to the maintenance of peace and tranquillity, a power which might be so exercised as to have far-reaching effects on provincial autonomy.

The federation, if it requires land for federal purposes may require the province to acquire the land at federal expense or to transfer government land, the value being fixed in default of agreement by arbitration.[2]

In the case of the states,[3] the executive authority of the state must be so exercised as not to impede the exercise of federal authority under any law, the question of the existence of such authority to be settled on the motion of the federation or the ruler by the federal court. The governor-general after hearing the views of the ruler may issue any directions he thinks

[1] S. 126. See § 10 above. [2] S. 127. [3] S. 128.

fit in his discretion, if not satisfied with the executive action of the state. In this case also he is not bound by advice of ministers, but as in the case of directions to the provinces is bound to act on his unbiased opinion. Fortunately the earlier proposal under which in such cases the authority of the representative of the Crown in relation to the states would have been invoked has been dropped in favour of direct action by the governor-general.

The case of broadcasting[1] requires special treatment. Federal control would have been, as in Canada,[2] desirable, but it was felt that it could not be insisted upon, and the federation may not unreasonably refuse to allow a province or state to construct or use transmitters, or impose fees for their use or the use of receiving apparatus, but it does not concede any power to regulate use of apparatus provided or authorized by the federal government. Functions may be conferred conditionally, including terms of finance, but the matter broadcast by a province or state government may not be subjected to conditions save in so far as they appear to be necessary to enable the governor-general to discharge functions in his discretion or individual judgment, or in respect of peace and tranquillity. Moreover, any issue as to the grant of functions or conditions imposed falls to be decided in his discretion by the governor-general and not by the courts.

In connexion with water-supplies[3] the governor-general is given new functions. Under the Act of 1919 water-supplies fell to the province, but the centre had authority in respect of matters affecting the relations of the provinces or of a province and other territory, and any disputes between units on water-supplies were ultimately determined by the secretary of state. Now, if a province or state complains that it is prejudiced by the executive or legislative action or inaction of another unit, it may complain to the governor-general who, if he regards the complaint as serious, shall appoint a commission of experts in irrigation, engineering, administration, finance, and law which shall report. The governor-general then shall decide, unless the province or the state asks for a decision by the King in

[1] S. 129. [2] *Radio Communication in Canada, In re*, [1932] A.C. 304.
[3] Ss. 130–4, Joint Committee's Report, i, 124, 125.

Council. The decision of either authority shall override any federal, provincial, or state Act. Such a decision may be varied on further application in like manner, and no intervention by the courts is permitted. The governor-general may act similarly in the case of a difficulty affecting a chief commissioner's province. This authority of the government generally may specifically be excluded by any state on accession.

It is contemplated[1] that apart from the federation there may be advantages in inter-provincial and even state co-operation, just as in Canada and Australia alike the provinces and states confer together on issues of common non-federal concern. Power, therefore, is given to the King in Council to set up an Inter-Provincial Council charged with the duty of inquiring into and advising as to inter-provincial disputes; investigating subjects interesting one or more provinces and the federation and one or more provinces, and making recommendations in particular for the better co-ordination of policy and action on any such subject. Representatives of the states may be associated in such a Council.

18. FEDERAL AND PROVINCIAL FINANCIAL RELATIONS

(a) FINANCE

The problem of finance was found of special difficulty by the framers of federation. The government announced that the new system must depend for the period of its inauguration on the fulfilment of conditions making for financial stability, the creation and operation of a Reserve Bank, the balancing of the budget, the provision of reserves, and the attainment of a trade balance.[2] The joint committee[3] was impressed by the difficulty of assigning revenues. It felt that certain provinces were so situated that the sources of revenue available were never likely

[1] S. 135. The governor-general is to be instructed to further federal, state, and provincial co-operation, and the support by the provinces and states of federal agencies.

[2] Cf. Parl. Paper, Cmd. 4268, p. 17.

[3] Report, i, 160–72. See also Report of Federal Finance Committee, March 28th 1932, Cmd. 4069. A commissioner was appointed after the passing of the Act to report on the initiation of federation.

to suffice for a proper scale of expenditure, while the centre was in possession of those sources of revenue which were most apt to expand with the improvement of economic conditions. Inevitably industrialized provinces, Bengal in special, pressed for a further share in the proceeds of income tax. The states raised further difficulties; they had pressed for a share in the steady increase of receipts from customs duties which their subjects had to pay; this could be met by federation which would give them a constitutional voice in fixing charges. But it raised the issue of equality of sacrifice as regards direct taxation, since the states would be opposed to any imposition of such a tax by the federation. They argued that they ought to be exempt from bearing much of the expenditure of the federation—for instance, all that incurred in respect of subsidies to such provinces as might be in deficit. They contended further that the service of the pre-federation debt should be borne by British India, a contention later invalidated by the discovery that the federation would have assets more than equal to its liabilities.[1] They also pointed out that they had special defence burdens in certain cases which the provinces did not share, and that many subjects paid income tax on government securities or as shareholders in companies duly taxed. But, on the other hand, in many cases the states were to continue to draw sums of considerable amount from internal customs duties, levied at the frontier on goods imported from other parts of India, such duties being somewhat akin in many cases to octroi or terminal duties. These were in principle opposed to inter-state free trade as was desirable in a federation, but it was impossible, until new sources of revenue could be found, to deprive the states of this source. There were also in several cases minor sources of revenue which the states intended to retain but which offended against the federal principle.

From the point of view of expenditure, it was argued before the committee that there was much exaggeration in the assertions that federation would greatly add to cost. It was instead estimated that the actual increase would be about one and a half crores attributable in equal proportions to the establishment of provincial autonomy and the federation, in respect of the

[1] Cmd. 4069, p. 20.

increased size of the legislatures and elaboration of machinery of government. This optimistic view was, however, qualified by other considerations. The centre would have to grant substantial subventions to deficit provinces to give them a fair start in autonomy, Burma was to be separated at a loss which might equal three crores minus such duties as might be levied on imports into India thence. When to these duties were added the necessity of increasing the elasticity of provincial finance, it was clear that central resources would be seriously affected. The net result is that the constitution (Part VII) leaves much for later adjustment, but draws the main outlines of a very complex scheme.

I. Duties in respect of succession to property other than agricultural land; stamp duties included in the federal legislative list (on bills of exchange, cheques, promissory notes, bills of lading, letters of credit, insurance policies, proxies and receipts); terminal taxes on goods or passengers carried by railway or air, and taxes on railway fares and freights are levied and collected by the federation. But the net proceeds (except those attributable to chief commissioners' provinces) are distributable among the provinces and federated states in such manner as federal Act prescribes. The federation, however, may impose and retain the proceeds of a surcharge for federal purposes.[1]

II. Income tax[2] (not including in this term corporation tax) is levied and collected by the federation. But a proportion of the net yield (exclusive of sums attributable to chief commissioners' provinces or paid on federal emoluments) fixed by the King in Council is payable to the provinces and states, if any, in which the tax is leviable in manner prescribed by the King in Council. But the federation is safeguarded by the rule that the original proportion cannot be increased. Further, the federation may impose and retain the whole of the proceeds of a surcharge. Moreover, as the financial state is unlikely to permit of the effective operation of this system forthwith, the federation may retain each year for a prescribed period a prescribed amount of the sums payable to the provinces and states; and for a further prescribed period a sum less than that

[1] S. 137. [2] S. 138.

retained in the preceding year by an amount so calculated that the sums to be retained in the last year of the period should be equal to the amount annually deducted. It is forbidden to shorten either of the prescribed periods, and the governor-general in any year of the second period may maintain the sum deducted at the same rate as in the year before, lengthening the period accordingly, but must consult the federation, provinces, and states before action, which is only justified if necessary for financial stability. When a surcharge is contemplated, the governor-general is bound before giving sanction to the introduction of the Bill to satisfy himself that it is imperative, having regard to possible economies and other sources of revenue, including retention of sums normally payable to the provinces.

The duration of the periods and the amount primarily to be assigned to the provinces and states was much discussed. The White Paper contemplated the initial fixing of from 50 to 75 per cent and three years and seven years as the periods prescribed; the joint committee recognized that 50 per cent would be the maximum probable, and that it should be left open to decide the periods and amount later, as is provided in the Act.

When a surcharge is imposed, the Act must impose on federated states which do not pay income tax a charge of such amount as may be prescribed so as to represent as nearly as possible the net proceeds of such surcharge if it were levied. The risk of a surcharge inevitably will make state representatives in the legislature use their full influence to secure that funds shall be found in other ways.

III. The federation levies and retains corporation tax,[1] which is a tax on such part of the income of companies (not being agricultural income) which is not subject to the application of legislation authorizing deduction of the tax from payments of interest or dividends or representing a distribution of profits. But it may not be levied in a state until ten years from federation, and a ruler may demand that instead of levying the tax a contribution shall be payable equivalent to the net proceeds which such a tax would yield. The auditor-general must be supplied with information necessary for him to

[1] S. 139.

calculate the tax, and the federal court is given final authority, without appeal, to determine in any year claims by rulers that the sum fixed is excessive.

IV. Salt duties, federal excise duties, and export duties fall to be levied and collected by the federation. But the whole or part of the proceeds may be distributed to the provinces and states under federal Act. In the case, however, of export duties on jute half of the net proceeds, or a larger proportion as directed by the King in Council, is assigned to the provinces exporting jute in proportion to the amounts grown therein.[1]

To safeguard the provinces and states the prior sanction of the governor-general in his discretion is required for the introduction of all Bills varying any tax or duty in which the provinces are interested, or the meaning of agricultural income as defined in the income tax Acts, or affecting the principle on which moneys are distributed to the provinces or states, or imposing federal surcharges.[2]

V. As regards other sources of taxation no conditions are imposed by law. The federation can impose, in addition to the taxes above mentioned, customs duties, taxes on the capital value of the assets, exclusive of agricultural land, of individuals and companies, and taxes on the capital of companies.

The provincial sources of revenue[3] in addition to grants from federal taxation include taxes raised by them on land, as land revenue; taxes on land and buildings, hearths and windows; taxes on agricultural income and duties in respect of succession to agricultural land, duties of excise on goods manufactured or produced in the province and countervailing duties on goods produced or manufactured elsewhere in India, being alcoholic liquors for human consumption; opium, Indian hemp, and other narcotic drugs and narcotics; non-narcotic drugs; medicinal and toilet preparations, containing alcohol or any of the above substances, other excises being federal; taxes on mineral rights subject to any federal restrictions imposed in respect of mineral development; capitation taxes; taxes on professions, trades, callings, and employments; taxes on animals, boats, the sale of goods, advertisements, on luxuries including entertainments, amusements, betting and gambling;

[1] S. 140. [2] S. 141. [3] Sched. 7, List 2.

cesses on the entry of goods into a local area; dues on passengers and goods carried on inland waterways; tolls; stamp duties in respect of documents not included in the federal list, as enumerated above.

In addition, grants shall be made as determined by the King in Council to such provinces as may be held to be in need of assistance, but such grants cannot, save in the case of the North-West Frontier Province, be increased unless increase is asked for by addresses from both chambers of the legislature. Moreover,[1] any taxes, duties, cesses or fees levied by a province or local authority on January 1st 1935, though included in the federal list, remain to the levying authority until provision to the contrary is made by federal Act.

In the case of the states, in order to secure adhesion to the federation rather generous provision is made. The federation[2] will receive all payments, whether cash contributions or in respect of loans or otherwise, due from the states, and will provide the representative of the Crown with any sums he deems necessary for the performance of his duties towards the states.[3] For states that accept federation[4] the Crown may remit over a period not exceeding twenty years cash contributions payable, and may direct the payment to any state of such sums as it thinks fit if the state has in the past ceded territory in return for the discharge of the state from obligation to render specified military assistance, or for specific military guarantees, provided that the state waives these guarantees. But neither remission nor payment may begin before the provinces have begun to receive payments out of federal income-tax receipts, and the remission shall be complete before the expiration of twenty years from the state's accession to the federation, or the expiry of the second prescribed period in regard to income tax, whichever first occurs. Moreover, account must be taken in fixing the amount to be remitted or paid of any privilege or immunity enjoyed by the state. Where the state has compounded for contributions, the capital sum shall be repaid in instalments as may be directed. The cash contributions to be remitted are (*a*) periodical contributions in recognition of the suzerainty of the Crown, including payments

[1] S. 143. [2] S. 146. [3] S. 145. [4] S. 147; Parl. Paper, Cmd. 4103.

for aid from the Crown, or in commutation of the obligation to provide military assistance, or in respect of the maintenance by the Crown of a special force for service in connexion with a state, or in connexion with the maintenance of local military forces or police, or in respect of the expenses of an agent; (*b*) periodical contributions on the creation or re-grant of a state or on a re-grant or increase of territory; and (*c*) periodical contributions formerly payable to another state but now payable to the Crown by conquest, assignment or lapse. The privileges and immunities to be reckoned on the other side include (*a*) those in respect of the levying of sea customs or the production and sale of untaxed salt; (*b*) sums payable in respect of the surrender of the right to levy internal customs duties, or produce salt or tax salt or other commodities or goods in transit, or sums receivable in lieu of grants of untaxed salt; (*c*) the annual value of any privilege or territory granted in respect of the abandonment of such rights; (*d*) privileges in respect of free service stamps or free carriage of government mails; (*e*) the privilege of entry free from customs duties of goods imported by sea and transported in bond to the state concerned; and (*f*) the right to issue currency notes. But no regard is to be had to such privileges or immunities if they are to be surrendered on accession, or in the opinion of the Crown should not be regarded. Every Instrument of Accession must contain the necessary particulars to enable the Crown to determine such issues. Any payments to be made under these provisions or any payments hitherto made by the centre or a province are to be charged to the federation or the corresponding province, which in case of doubt is fixed by the governor-general.

The property of the federation is exempted from any provincial or state taxation, except in so far as it is subject thereto on federation, when it remains subject until otherwise provided by the federation, which may also subject other of its property to taxation.[1] Provincial governments and rulers of states shall not be liable to federal taxation in respect of lands or buildings in British India or income accruing or received there, but the exemption does not apply to the personal property or income of a ruler nor to any business carried on by

[1] S. 154.

a ruler in British India or by a provincial government outside the province.[1]

Both federation and provinces must keep the secretary of state in funds to meet any payments due to be made in respect of federation or province, and in special the secretary of state and the High Commissioner must be enabled to pay pensions.[2]

Neither federation nor province may place burdens on their revenues except for the purposes of India or some part thereof,[3] but neither is restricted to grants in respect only of such matters as fall within their legislative competence.

In order to maintain financial stability it was from the first recognized that provision must be made to ensure that the control of currency and credit, including the issue of bank-notes and the maintenance of reserves, must be entrusted to a non-political authority. There were objections to this in India, but in 1934 the Reserve Bank of India Act was duly passed, and the bank started operations in 1935. The capital of the bank is fixed at five crores of rupees in a hundred rupee shares with registers at Bombay, Calcutta, Delhi, Madras, and Rangoon. The Central Board of Directors is composed of the governor and two deputy governors appointed by the governor-general in council, four directors nominated by the same authority, eight elected directors and a government official nominated by the government. Under the constitution[4] the governor-general is to exercise in his discretion the appointment and removal of the governor and deputy governors, the fixing of their salaries and terms of office; the appointment of an officiating governor or deputy; the supersession of the Central Board and action consequent thereon; and the liquidation of the bank. In nominating directors he is to act in his individual judgment. Moreover,[5] no Bill affecting currency or coinage or the constitution or functions of the Reserve Bank may be introduced save with his sanction in his discretion.

The separation of Burma necessitated the grant of power to the Crown[6] in Council to make arrangements to regulate the monetary system as a result of separation, to give relief on federal taxation in respect of income taxable in Burma, and

[1] S. 155. [2] S. 157. [3] S. 150. [4] S. 152. [5] S. 153.
[6] Ss. 158, 159; Parl. Papers, Cmd. 4901, 4902.

to regulate in the period immediately following separation the duties to be placed on goods imported into or exported from India or Burma.[1] To these powers by agreement between the governments effect will in due course be given.

Borrowing[2] is permissible both by the federation and the provinces, the amounts to be fixed by Act. The federation may make loans to the provinces or guarantee their loans. Moreover, no province may borrow outside India without federal assent, and such assent is also requisite for borrowing if there is outstanding any part of a central or federal loan or loan guaranteed by the centre or federation, and assent may be made on conditions. But the refusal of assent to borrowing, or to make a loan or guarantee a loan or the reasonableness of conditions imposed in any of these cases falls in case of dispute to be determined by the governor-general in his discretion. His Instructions[3] require him to bear in mind the general financial policy of the federation, but also the importance of arranging a temporary loan in case of emergency. Federal stock[4] is given the advantage of the terms of the Colonial Stock Acts and the Treasury conditions under that of 1900 for admission to trustee status are to be deemed to be satisfied until Parliament otherwise directs. These provisions assure the federation and the provinces of reasonable security against disturbance of the money market or injury to the federation from uncontrolled appeals to the market by provinces.

(b) ACCOUNT AND AUDIT

The governor-general and the governors are[5] given power to make rules in their individual judgment to secure the due payment to the federal or provincial accounts of all receipts, their custody and withdrawal, thus securing the power of personal intervention to assure regularity of accounting. The King[6] is authorized to appoint an auditor-general, whose status is that of a federal judge as regards security of tenure, and whose conditions of appointment may not be varied while he

[1] S. 160; Parl. Paper, Cmd. 4985. [2] Ss. 162, 163, 164.
[3] Clause XXIV. [4] S. 165. [5] S. 151. [6] Ss. 166, 167.

is in office; he is debarred from further office under the Crown in India, so as to secure impartiality. His duties are prescribed by Order in Council or Act, but the previous sanction of the governor-general in his discretion is requisite for the introduction of such an Act. He may act for the provinces, but a provincial legislature not earlier than two years from federation may provide for the appointment on analogous terms of a provincial auditor-general, but the post must not be filled for at least three years after the date of the Act. The auditor-general may give directions as to the mode of keeping accounts; his reports shall be laid before the federal and provincial legislatures as the case may be.[1] For the home accounts[2] of the federation, the railway authority or any province there shall be appointed with like security of tenure an auditor of home accounts, who shall report to the auditor-general or provincial auditor-general if there is one. The auditor of home accounts may be required to act for Burma, in which case Burma will contribute to his salary which, like that of the auditor-general, is charged on the federal revenue, whence also will be paid the cost of his staff.

Payments in respect of the relations of the Crown and the states will be audited by the auditor-general and the auditor of home accounts, the report being made to the secretary of state.[3]

(c) PROPERTY

Provision[4] is made for the vesting in the Crown for the purposes of a province of property therein used for provincial purposes, and in the Crown for federal purposes or for the exercise of its functions in relation to the states of property which was used—otherwise than under a tenancy agreement with the province for these purposes respectively, while property outside India vests in the Crown for the federation or in His Majesty's government if used by the secretary of state in council. The latter property falls under the control of the Commissioners of Works, but their disposal is subject to the assent of the governor-general. All other property shall similarly vest according to its use in the Crown for the federation, in respect of state relations, or for the provinces,

[1] Ss. 168, 169. [2] S. 170. [3] S. 171. [4] Ss. 172, 173.

while arrears of taxes may be recovered by the authority to which the tax is assigned. Property which escheats or lapses or is *bona vacantia* in a province will fall to the province, otherwise to the federation, but property in possession of government will go according to its use at the time it accrued.[1]

The executive authority[2] of federation and province extends to the sale, grant, disposition or mortgage of property and its acquisition and the making of contracts, which are made in the name of the heads of the governments, but no personal liability attaches to them or to the secretary of state in respect thereof nor to any officer executing instruments on behalf of any of them.

(*d*) SUITS BY AND AGAINST THE CROWN

The federation or province may sue *eo nomine*,[3] and be sued in the same cases in which suit was possible against the secretary of state in council, and where claims rise in the United Kingdom service may be effected on the High Commissioner or other representative of the federation, railway board, or province as may be provided by rules of court. Existing contracts are to be deemed made with the federation or province as the subject-matter may be. Liabilities of the secretary of state in council in respect of loans, guarantees, and other financial obligations may be enforced against the secretary of state; they become liabilities of the federation and are charged on the revenues of the federation and provinces alike. Existing or contingent liabilities before federation may be enforced against federation or province as the case may be as well as against the secretary of state; if the latter contracts for federation or province after federation, he may agree that any proceedings may be brought against him. In any case he decides whether federation or province pays, and no imperial liability is accepted. The secretary of state becomes responsible in the same way in respect of contracts in respect of the relations of the Crown with the states, and any sums payable or due fall to be credited to or defrayed by the federation.[4]

Liability to suit therefore depends in essence in cases not

[1] S. 174. [2] S. 175. [3] Ss. 176–9. [4] S. 180.

in contract on the previous liability of the secretary of state in council, and that again is determined by that of the East India Company.[1] Liability in their case rested either on the liability which would have fallen on trading corporations generally or under statute, and did not lie in respect of acts of sovereign authority. Thus it has repeatedly been ruled that acts of state involved in the seizure of territory and of property as matters of sovereign authority could not be dealt with by the courts.

14. THE FEDERAL RAILWAY AUTHORITY

The joint committee[2] recommended that the work of the federal government should not include the direct control of railways. The grounds for this view are obvious. Recent experience in Canada had shown the appalling dangers to governmental finance, apart from the risk of corruption, involved in direct governmental authority, and in the Union of South Africa an effort had been made to relieve the government of immediate control. The Act[3] accordingly gives the duty of regulation, construction, maintenance and operation of railways, including the organization of undertakings ancillary thereto, to the federal railway authority. But the federation remains responsible for securing the safety of members of the public and the operatives, including the holding of inquiries into the causes of accidents to such extent as it thinks it desirable that these functions should be performed by persons independent of the authority.

The tribunal[4] as to at least three-sevenths of its members and its President is appointed by the governor-general in his discretion. Its members hold office normally for five years, and may be reappointed for like periods, and the governor-general controls their conditions of service and tenure of office. No Bill to vary the provisions of Schedule 8 of the Act in this regard may be introduced without the prior sanction in his discretion of the governor-general. The authority[5] must act on business principles, with due regard to the interests of

[1] See § 19 below. [2] Report, i, 280–5. [3] S. 181, Part VIII.
[4] S. 182. [5] S. 183.

agriculture, industry, commerce, and the public, and must take care to meet out of revenue the expenditure charged thereon. Directions on policy may be given by the federation; if there is dispute as to what is policy, the governor-general in his discretion decides. He personally has the right to give directions to the authority on matters affecting his special responsibilities, or matters in which he has to act in his discretion or individual judgment. He may make rules respecting relations between the government and the authority so as to secure that any matter affecting his responsibilities is brought to his notice.[1]

The authority may not acquire or dispose of land except in accordance with federal regulations, and land to be acquired compulsorily shall be acquired by the government.[2] It is a body corporate and can sue and be sued as such in lieu of the government in respect of its contracts and can enter into agreements with state or other owners of railways in or without India as to terms of operation. Provision is made for a railway fund[3] to which receipts are to be paid, and for the meeting thence of expenditure of various kinds, any surplus to be shared with the government on the existing basis, or according to a scheme to be prepared. The authority is to be debited on capital account with the total of capital expenditure and to pay interest thereon as well as to repay capital. Its accounts shall be audited by the auditor-general of India.

A railway rates committee[4] may be appointed to advise the governor-general in case of complaint by users against the rates fixed by the authority, and his recommendation is necessary for any Bill regarding rates which it is desired to propose.

The federation and federated states are bound to afford reasonable facilities for through traffic on the railways for which they are responsible, and no system is to receive unfair discrimination by undue preference or otherwise, and unfair or uneconomic competition is forbidden.[5] Complaints by the authority or a state fall to be decided by the railway tribunal. To it also shall be referred any complaint by a state against a direction by the authority under federal authority as to

[1] S. 184. [2] S. 185. [3] Ss. 186–90. [4] Ss. 191, 192. [5] Ss. 193–6.

interchange of traffic, rates, or terminal charges, on the ground that it involves discrimination or imposes an undue burden, and any dispute regarding the desire of the authority or a state to construct a new railway where it is alleged that unfair or uneconomic competition will result. The tribunal is presided over by a judge of the federal court chosen after consulting the chief justice, and holding office for five years, and is completed by two members, chosen by the governor-general in each case from a panel of eight appointed by him being persons of administrative railway or business experience. The tribunal alone has jurisdiction in such cases, and is subject on a point of law only to appeal to the federal court, whence no appeal lies.

Railway companies[1] which have agreements with the secretary of state in council under which arbitration may be claimed will be entitled to be allowed such arbitration as against the secretary of state. Any award will be payable by the federation and due to it by the authority. The authority also may be required to act for the Crown in relation to railway matters in non-federated states, and the powers of the secretary of state in council to appoint directors and deputy directors of companies will vest in the governor-general acting in his discretion after consultation with the authority.

15. DEFENCE

The Act makes no substantial change in matters affecting the vital issue of defence, and most of its provisions affecting that question have already been noted in other connexions. It is a reserved issue, full control over it is given to the governor-general, subject to the secretary of state and the Home Government; and subject to the existence of the commander-in-chief, whose position and emoluments are regulated by the King in Council. The costs of defence, including pay, allowances, pensions, etc., of personnel are charged on the revenues of India, and controlled by the governor-general in his discretion, though he is desired to associate as far as possible the legislature and ministers with him in dealing with defence requirements,

[1] Ss. 197–9.

and the legislature may discuss, though not vote on, his estimates for defence. Reference has also been made above to the powers which the governor-general may exercise in civil matters ancillary to defence, whether as regards the federation or through the governors the provinces. There exists, therefore, the necessary legal power to secure aid in movements of troops in any contingency and their maintenance at any place.[1]

The use of military forces for civil needs is controlled by the governor-general in the ultimate resort. The authority in this regard is purely federal, the subject being excluded specifically from provincial authority. It rests with the governor-general also to secure through the commander-in-chief the due maintenance of the forces' obligations under the civil law and the bringing before civil courts, as in September 1935, for punishment of men guilty of attacks, whether provoked or not, on civilians, a duty stressed by Lord Curzon, who incurred unfair criticism.[2]

It rests as noted above with the governor-general to decide as to the use of Indian troops outside India, when their employment is desired by the British Government. Payment therefore from Indian revenues can be justified only if the work on which they are employed is for the service of India; otherwise payment must be made by the United Kingdom or other part of the Empire which needs their services. A difficult problem arises as to the validity of the employment of such forces outside India without express parliamentary sanction. But outside the United Kingdom no difficulty would seem to exist regarding their employment as in the past, while it is improbable that their employment within the United Kingdom should occur in such a form as to raise any constitutional issue. The presence of small bodies on ceremonial occasions has raised no discussion As the commander-in-chief explained on September 17th 1935, it would normally be possible in case of a request for aid from Britain to consult the Assembly before proceeding, since it was desired to carry India with Britain

[1] See § 4 above.

[2] For the Rangoon episode (1899), see Ronaldshay, ii, 71–3, and that of 1902, 247–9. Under modern conditions of communications the commander-in-chief is far less subordinate to the governor-general than in Dalhousie's time, when obedience was enforced strictly; see *British Government in India*, ii, 205–8; Lee-Warner, i, 193 ff., 211 ff., 328 ff.

in any action, but it might be necessary to act rapidly to safeguard Aden or the oil reserves in Persia. The occasion of this declaration was the dispatch of a small force for the protection of the legation at Addis Ababa in view of the strained relations between Ethiopia and Italy.

The executive authority of the federation extends to the raising of forces naval, military, and air, and the governance of those of His Majesty's forces borne on the Indian establishment.[1] But no person may be enlisted in forces raised in India unless he is a British subject, a native of India, or a native of the territories thereto adjacent, including naturally the vital case of Nepal. Commissions in these forces shall be granted by the Crown except in so far as the power may be delegated to some other person; such commissions may be granted to any person who might be or has been lawfully enrolled therein.[2] In addition to the post of commander-in-chief, the Crown in Council may require the reservation to himself or some other authority of appointments in the defence forces.[3]

The secretary of state, with the concurrence of his advisers, may decide what rules affecting the Indian forces as regards conditions of service shall be made only with his approval.[4] He is bound to hear any appeal which prior to the Act lay to the secretary of state or the secretary of state in council. These provisions apply also to persons not members of the forces but connected with their equipment, administration or otherwise. There is preserved also the rule that in appointments to the British Army regard shall be had as formerly to the selection of sons of military or civil servants of the Crown in India.

Indianization is not mentioned in the Act, but the joint committee and the Instructions[5] on their advice recognize that the defence of India must to an increasing extent be the concern of the Indian people, and require the governor-general to have regard to this consideration in his administration of defence, and to ascertain the views of ministers on the question of appointing Indian officers to the army and its employment outside India, while in finance the finance minister is to be kept in touch with the control of defence expenditure. The commander-in-chief

[1] S. 8 (1) (*b*) and provisos (iii) and (iv). [2] S. 234. [3] S. 233. [4] Ss. 235–9.
[5] Clause XVII; Report, i, 100–2.

on February 25th 1935 expressly denied that the strength of the forces in India, the purpose for which it was maintained, or the scale of equipment were dictated by the British Government in imperial interests. Conditions both as regards internal and external dangers were not comparable with those of any Dominion. To reduce as suggested the British element by half, or to regard its number as reducible in view of the increased air strength, was undesirable; other powers found it necessary to maintain ground troops in the same strength as before the war. The successes of Indian troops had been achieved under British officers, and the proportion of troops—three to one in brigades in war conditions—had recently been determined by the British and Indian governments in accord. Indianization had been extended under him from five to fifteen units; when the young Indian officers had had fourteen years' service it would be time to decide if the speed of Indianization could be increased. Defence expenditure had fallen from 55 crores when he took office in four years to 46 crores. In the United Kingdom defence cost 30 rupees per head, in the Dominions from 3½ rupees to 8 rupees, in the United States 18½ rupees, in Japan 6½ rupees, in India 1½ rupees. Later, the Army Secretary pointed out that Indianization of a division would be complete by 1952; that the forces did not include any imperial reserve, and in case of foreign aggression by a great power help would be necessary from England. It was intended gradually to replace British by Indian units, but undue acceleration would involve internal and external danger. The total cost had fallen to 26 per cent of Indian revenues as opposed to 34 per cent before the war. Nevertheless the legislative Assembly by 79 votes to 48 declined to approve the grant under Army Department, which is submitted in order to afford a convenient opportunity of discussion of the cost of defence.

The position of the cadets who come from the Indian Military Academy at Dehra Dun[1] and of entrants to the Indian Air Force[2] was laid down by the Indian Army (Amendment)

[1] Admission to the British Colleges was at the same time closed in order to secure the best material for Indian service. But good candidates are still hard to find; Sir P. Chetwode, Council of State, September 24th 1935.

[2] Indian Air Force Act, 1932; the force was constituted on October 8th 1932. Cadets were trained at Cranwell from 1928.

Act 1934. The determination was taken to differentiate between these officers and the British officers serving in the Indian forces by giving the former commissions based on the Canadian model. It was pointed out that only thus would it be possible to create an Indian force subject to an Indian Army Act which could be altered at will by an Indian legislature. It was objected[1] that the Indian commissioned officers would be in a position of inferiority to British officers, since they would not be entitled to take automatically command over units of the British Army in India. But it was pointed out that rules would be made giving the commander-in-chief power to arrange for command in cases of mixed formations and that in the case of the Dominions their commissions gave no automatic right to command British units, the forces being separate and distinct. Some regret was also expressed at the intention that the new Indian officers should supersede for their units the Viceroy's commissioned officers under the old system. But it was pointed out that these officers belonged essentially to the order of things in which no Indian could attain commissioned rank in the British sense, and that when this was possible the maintenance of the Viceroy's commission became illogical.

The age of entry to the Indian Military Academy at Dehra Dun, which was opened in 1932, as the result of the recommendation of the Round Table Conference of 1931 is eighteen to twenty years; the course of instruction is two and a half years. Sixty vacancies are offered each year; of the thirty available each half-year fifteen are given by open competition, while fifteen are awarded to aspirants from the ranks of the Indian army; ten vacancies are also open to the Indian State Forces for the training of officers for these bodies, a plan devised to secure that there shall be uniformity as far as possible in the training of the state and the regular forces.

The strength of the Indian army in 1935 was relatively small, 60,000 British troops, 150,000 Indian army, with 42,500 reserve, enlistment being for five years at least with the colours, and fifteen years combined colours and reserve service; the Indian Territorial Force, of about 19,000 to serve as a second

[1] Debates in Assembly, August 14th–28th; Council of State, September 4th–8th 1934.

line to, and a source of reinforcement of, the regular army; the Auxiliary Force, some 33,000 intended to assist in home defence, and consisting of Europeans; and the Indian State Forces, about 44,000 when these are placed at the disposal of the Indian government.[1] It is organized in three groups; internal security troops to ensure tranquillity within India during the absence of the field army; covering troops to secure that the concentration and mobilization of the field army is carried out undisturbed, and the field army whose size is limited for financial reasons by the number of troops required for security services. In order to render mobilization possible at short notice and to facilitate the maintenance of the field force, the army service corps has been reorganized, and mechanical transport introduced as widely as possible. Moreover, the manufacture of munitions of war has been encouraged in order to make India self-supporting. That these forces are far from excessive seems conclusively shown by the fact that in September 1935 the hostility of the frontier tribes rendered it necessary to concentrate on the frontier no less than 30,000 men; the necessity of securing the lines of communication in such operations precludes the use of smaller numbers, and the employment of air forces in these cases, however valuable as an auxiliary, is insufficient to secure lasting results.

The position of the Indian navy is not altered in substance by the Act. Its present position was due to the Government of India (Indian Navy) Act, 1927,[2] which enabled the legislature to place the Indian Marine if it so desired on the same footing towards the British Navy as is a Dominion navy, subject to the power of the governor-general in council, if the former declared that a state of emergency existed, to place at the disposal of the Admiralty any Indian naval forces. It was, however, made clear that, if any forces were placed under Admiralty control, the revenues of India should not, without the consent of both Houses of Parliament, be applicable to defraying the cost, if and so long as they were not employed in

[1] Now organized as Class A troops trained on post-war Indian lines, B on pre-war lines, C a militia. The Territorial Force consists of provincial battalions affiliated to regular regiments, liable for general service in emergency, even outside the frontier, urban battalions liable for service in the province, and University training corps.

[2] 17 & 18 Geo. V, c. 8.

Indian naval defence. It was only in 1934 that the necessary action was taken by the legislature in the Indian Navy Discipline Act to apply the Naval Discipline Act to the Indian naval forces; action had been delayed by the mistaken supposition[1] that an effort was being made to augment the British force at the cost of India and that the terms of the Washington or London treaties on naval limitation might be evaded. The latter supposition ignored the fact that in these compacts, as in the naval accord with Germany of 1935,[2] the ratio fixed affects the naval forces of the British Commonwealth. In fact the scheme merely enhances the status of the small naval force[3] and ranks it with those of the Dominions. The Act of 1927 is repealed by that of 1935, but its essential provision of legislative power to India is, as has been seen,[4] retained, and the limitation on the use of Indian revenues remains.[5] On the other hand, the governor-general may at his discretion[6] transfer the force to the control of the Admiralty as was done with the Indian Marine in 1914;[7] in this event Indian funds can be used only if the defence of India is involved, and normally no doubt if time permits the legislature will be consulted as in the case of use of the army or air force.

The prerogative to declare war rests with the Crown, though of course the governor-general may be used as the instrument for the expression of the royal prerogative as contemplated in the Act.[8] It rests with the Crown on the outbreak of war to regulate trading with the enemy and to permit to such extent as it thinks fit acts of trade. Thus by proclamation of December 14th 1914 certain transactions which were contrary to the royal proclamation of September 9th 1914, republished

[1] Legislative Assembly, August 7th 1934. [2] June 18th; Cmd. 4953.

[3] Reorganized in 1928; it carries the white ensign; its strength is five sloops, two patrol boats, a survey ship, commanded by an admiral of the Royal Navy; there are sixty-nine executive, forty-nine engineer officers; one Indian to two British officers was the proportion proposed in 1927–8.

[4] See § 10 above.

[5] S. 150 (1). But the absence of British Parliamentary control is unfortunate.

[6] S. 11 (1).

[7] Under 47 & 48 Vict., c. 38, s. 6; S.R. & O. 1914, i, 676–81; 1917, p. 384.

[8] S. 3 (1) (*b*). For the states he would act under s. 3 (2). The Government of India Act, s. 15, required notification of orders for hostilities to Parliament, and s. 44 restricted the governor-general in council to purely defensive operations against Indian states (as in the Act of 1784). Lord Curzon was repeatedly warned not to take military action unsanctioned; Ronaldshay, ii, 196, 267, 268.

in India on October 31st, replacing the proclamation of August 5th 1914, republished in India on August 7th, were notified. Power to make such exceptions had been delegated to the governor-general by proclamation of October 8th. Such action was supplemented by Indian legislation by ordinance[1] and Acts, including the Defence of India (Criminal Law Amendment) Act, 1915. All action taken in India was validated by the Imperial Indemnity Act, 1920,[2] which incidentally overrode the provision of the Government of India Act, 1915,[3] authorizing suit against the secretary of state in council in such cases as it would have lain against the Company.

The regulation of prize law and prize courts is one of the few matters which is removed from the competence of the legislatures in India.[4]

The United Kingdom accepts full responsibility for the security of India from foreign aggression by land or sea. India pays £100,000 a year as a slight token of appreciation of naval defence. As regards the army and air force a plea was raised by India before the tribunal appointed to investigate the sums payable from Indian revenues in respect of home charges for British troops in India in favour of a large contribution based on the theory that the army in India was maintained in the interests of the whole Empire and should be paid for in part by the United Kingdom and the Dominions. The tribunal rejected this contention, but on its advice the British Government agreed to pay £1,500,000 a year as a contribution, based on the facts that the army in India was kept ready for war and that it was a source whence forces could be detached for foreign employment (e.g. China and Ethiopia) on short notice, and that India was a training-ground for active service such as could not be found elsewhere in the Empire. The decision was

[1] Ordinance 6 of 1914; Acts I and XIV of 1915, XVI of 1916.

[2] 10 & 11 Geo. V, c. 48.

[3] S. 32 (2). Such action presumably would not have lain for sovereign Acts (see § 19 (*e*) below).

[4] S. 110 (*b*) (i). Any Colonial Court of Admiralty (a term which covers certain Indian courts) may be given authority to sit as a prize court, as was done in the war of 1914–19. See the Prize Courts Act, 1894; the Naval Prize Act, 1864; the Prize Courts (Procedure) Act, 1915, and amendments; *The Chile*, [1914] P. 212. The governor-general is ex officio 'Vice-Admiral'.

regarded as wholly unsatisfactory by Indian opinion, and criticized by Mr. Churchill as an unjustifiable sacrifice of British interests to conciliate Indian politicians.[1]

16. EXTERNAL AFFAIRS

The control of external affairs rests, as has been seen,[2] with the governor-general acting in his discretion, but from this field is excluded the relations of the federation and the Dominions. The exclusion was necessary, for the treatment of Indian subjects of the Crown in the Dominions had aroused strong feeling in India and the British Government was presented with the alternative of contending with the Dominions on behalf of India, which had involved it in difficulties with the Dominions without much good accruing to India, or allowing India to stand out as an autonomous unit of the Commonwealth in this regard. The fact that by direct negotiation with the Union of South Africa some advantages had been secured for India was an encouragement to adopt this principle. Nevertheless it was proposed in the White Paper[3] to preclude India from differential treatment of Dominion British subjects, except in the matter of immigration. This negation of authority fortunately disappeared in the passage of the scheme through Parliament. It is therefore open to India to deal as an equal with the Dominions. In the case of the colonies not enjoying Dominion status the attitude of India is also unfettered by claim of British control. But the British Government as the authority responsible for the colonies and other parts of the Empire has to decide its attitude towards Indian demands, and the Indian government had in 1935 to criticize action taken in Zanzibar with British approval which was regarded as prejudicing the position of Indian merchants therein, and the position in Kenya has not satisfied the Indian government.

In external affairs connected with foreign countries, other than those in immediate proximity to India, the governor-general is subject to the necessity of acting under the directions of the British Government and through its agencies, and Indian

[1] House of Commons, March 6th 1934.

[2] See § 4 above.

[3] Parl. Paper, Cmd. 4268, p. 70. Cf. Keith, *Letters on Imperial Relations*, 1916–35 pp. 179, 226.

policy is necessarily but a part of the wider British policy.[1] But in the case of territories in immediate proximity to India, though relations are formally in the hands of the Foreign Office, as is now the case with Afghanistan and Nepal, and India has no power to appoint diplomatic agents to them, the interests of India are naturally of high importance and British policy is largely based on Indian advice. So the representatives of the British Crown in Afghanistan, in Nepal and Tibet and the consuls in Afghanistan, Persia, Arabia, and Kashgar are normally chosen from the Indian foreign and political department. In general communications even with the League of Nations and the International Labour Organization pass through the India Office, except those on routine matters or relating to the supply of information. Communications regarding the signature or ratification of or adhesion to international conventions are not sent direct. But the governor-general has authority over the British representatives in the Persian Gulf.[2]

The Crown retains control of the highest prerogatives regarding external affairs, though it may delegate their exercise under the Act[3] to the governor-general. Thus the proclamation of neutrality in the case of war emanates from the Crown, as when neutrality was declared in 1911 in the war between Turkey and Italy and in 1912 in the war between Turkey and Greece. The rules observed in India were those prescribed by His Majesty's orders, issued through the Secretary of State for Foreign Affairs to the Secretary of State for India.[4]

The power to annex territory or to cede territory rests with the Crown subject to any imperial legislation, for it appears that the Act of 1935 perpetuates the restriction of earlier legislation regarding laws affecting the sovereignty of the Crown over any part of British India; the Privy Council seems to have held that the cession of territory by an Act of the Indian legislature would be invalid.[5]

[1] This appears clearly in the Russian accord of 1907, the abortive Persian treaty of 1919, disapproved by Mr. Montagu, and the Turkish issues of 1922, which led to his disappearance from the Cabinet; Ronaldshay, *Lord Curzon*, iii, 215–17, 285.

[2] e.g., Kuwait Order in Council, 1935.

[3] S. 3 (1) (*b*). For the states he acts as representative of the Crown under s. 3 (2).

[4] Government of India Notification 1884 G, October 6th 1911; 18, October 25th 1912.

[5] *Damodhar Gordhan* v. *Deoram Kanji* (1876), 1 App. Cas. 332. See s. 110 (*b*) (i).

The power to make peace similarly is a prerogative power, which, in the case of the settlement of the war of 1914–19, was accompanied by imperial legislation[1] in 1919–24 giving power to the Crown to enforce the terms of the treaties. An Order in Council was duly issued for India in respect of each treaty, and local legislation to give effect to the requirements of the treaties regarding ex-enemy property was also passed.[2] In the case of a frontier war the Indian government may be authorized to act, as in its various Afghanistan settlements.[3]

Since the admission of India to the League of Nations she has been treated in respect of all the great international conventions on the same basis as Canada and the other Dominions and all general treaties therefore are signed separately for India.[4] India is subject to the same rules as the other Dominions of communication of its purpose of carrying on negotiations of any kind with foreign states.[5] When the United States Government proposed to the British Government the conclusion of the pact for the renunciation of war as an instrument of international policy, the British Government insisted that India should be connected with the pact in the same manner as the Dominions,[6] and it was signed duly for India by Lord Cushendun, who was also a British plenipotentiary. India therefore has been regarded for formal purposes as in the same position as the Dominions, and it is noteworthy that in the Locarno Pact, 1925, India was exempted like the Dominions from liability unless expressly accepted by the government.[7] The grant of responsibility to the government as opposed to Parliament in the abortive treaty with the United States and France of 1919 for the protection of France was

[1] 9 & 10 Geo. V, c. 33; 10 & 11 Geo. V, c. 6; 11 & 12 Geo. V, c. 11; 14 & 15 Geo. V, c. 7.

[2] Ordinances 1 and 4 of 1920; 1 of 1921. See, e.g., India Treaty of Peace Order, 1920.

[3] Parl. Paper, Cmd. 324 (1919).

[4] e.g., the London treaty of 1930 for naval limitation. The agreement of June 18th 1935 with Germany applies to India and the other Dominions, which assented to signature by the Foreign Secretary. India shared the conference of 1935–6.

[5] Keith, *Speeches and Documents on the British Dominions, 1918–1931*, p. 427.

[6] Ibid., p. 406. It was separately ratified for India.

[7] Keith, op. cit., pp. xxiv, 356, 366; *Constitutional Law of the British Dominions*, pp. 406, 409. India in the treaties for naval disarmament is treated like the Dominions; Keith, *Speeches and Documents on the British Dominions*, pp. 67 ff., 418 ff. It legislates similarly, Acts VII of 1923, VIII of 1931.

doubtless due to the desire to avoid the necessity of obtaining the approval of the Indian legislature, and a proposal therein to discuss the agreement and its acceptance by India was negatived by the governor-general.

The representation of India at the League of Nations Assembly has regularly been carried out by members chosen by the Crown[1] to represent both British India and the Indian states.

As regards treaty negotiation, the existing practice[2] is that while the treaty may be negotiated in India between representatives of the Indian government and those of a foreign power, signature is effected by representatives of His Majesty's government and not by the governor-general, as in the case of the Commercial Agreement with Japan of July 12th 1934.[3] The joint committee[4] contemplates that on the analogy of the procedure in the United Kingdom, where agreements are negotiated through the Foreign Office which consults the Board of Trade, agreements in India should be made by the governor-general, even though as regards the merits of any commercial issue he acts on the advice of a minister. This suggests that it is contemplated that the governor-general should be given power to enter into agreements with foreign countries. Presumably he would act under full powers granted by the King and of course under the complete control in all matters of procedure of the Foreign and India Offices.

As noted above, treaties made on behalf of the federation are subject to limitation by the fact that the federation has no power to legislate on subjects included in the provincial list without the prior assent of the governor of the province, or in

[1] Council of State, March 8th 1929; the final control is British, though as often as possible the specific Indian point of view is presented, as on September 13th 1935 by the Aga Khan as regards the failures of the League.

[2] Sir J. Bhore (Legislative Assembly, January 25th 1934) insisted that India could not enter into a treaty with a foreign power and a treaty could not be signed in India. This is clearly unsound in legal theory: all treaties are entered into by the Crown, which can act through the governor-general, as well as through the Foreign and Indian Secretaries of State. The treaty includes the states so far as desired by the Crown.

[3] Parl. Paper, Cmd. 4735. The Burma-Yunnan agreement, April 9th 1935, is made for His Majesty's Government in the United Kingdom and the Government of India.

[4] Report, i, 102. Legislation, of course, is necessary for all treaties affecting the existing law, giving tariff concessions, etc.

like matters for the states without the assent of their rulers. It is of course clear that the Crown can give to the governor-general full power to make any treaty whatever, but no doubt by constitutional practice the exercise of that power will be restricted to cases within federal power or cases in which the provinces or states are either willing to extend federal legislative authority or are themselves prepared to pass any necessary legislation.

In respect of conventions arrived at under the procedure of the International Labour Conference it was explained by the secretary of state to the Labour Office on September 28th 1927[1] that it was impracticable to ratify conventions if they were to be regarded as binding the Indian states. The Indian legislature had no power to legislate for Indian states, and it would be impracticable to follow the form of procedure laid down in Article 405 in the treaty of Versailles, 1919. This position has been acquiesced in by the International Labour Conference, but the power of India to apply such conventions more widely will of course arise from the operation of federation. As in the case of the Dominions ratifications of such conventions are expressed by the governor-general in council and not by the Crown.[2]

While it is apparently not contemplated that the states should be pressed to keep abreast of India in such matters as factory legislation,[3] in some matters the necessity of common action is rendered necessary by international considerations. Thus the Convention on the Regulation of Aerial Navigation of October 13th 1919 was signed for the whole of India. To implement it required state action, and the Standing Committee of the Chamber of Princes discussed the issue from 1923 to 1931, when agreement was reached. The sovereignty of the states over the air is admitted, but they agreed to the government of India registering aircraft and pilots, investigating accidents, and inspecting aerodromes and factories. The states may declare prohibited areas after consulting the government

[1] *Labour Office Official Gazette*, November 15th 1927.

[2] Many proposals have been rejected by Government and legislature as impossible in Indian conditions, e.g., age of employment of children, invalidity, old age, and widows' and orphans' insurance.

[3] The Factories Act, 1934, is far in advance of the states; cf. Assembly debates, July 19th 1934.

of India, and establish customs aerodromes, and reserve local traffic to national aircraft.[1] Hence it has been possible to pass the Indian Aircraft Act, 1934, and to legislate to enable British India to accede to the Convention of October 19th 1929 for the unification of certain rules relating to carriage by air.

India, like the Dominions,[2] has the power to conclude governmental accords, not in the name of the King, which are not treaties proper. Such accords deal normally with commercial matters or finance, and this form of agreement may be used for matters affecting the French or Portuguese territories in India,[3] and of course with other parts of the Commonwealth.[4]

The relations of the federation with the United Kingdom are in part controlled by the British Government directly through the governor-general by reason of his special responsibilities. In matters of fiscal concern they rest on the other hand normally on the free agreement of the legislature with the executive government. Thus the Ottawa agreement of 1932 was accepted by the decision of the legislature, but that of 1935[5] was rejected by the assembly.

The governor-general is aided in the performance of his duties by the foreign and political department, which is composed of officers partly selected from the Indian Civil Service, partly from the military forces, and which also advises and aids him in his functions towards the states. This department remains unaltered under the reform scheme.[6]

Since 1927 the Indian government has maintained at Durban an agent-general accredited to the government of the Union of South Africa. He serves to secure co-operation with that government in the policy agreed upon in 1932 in seeking to promote the settlement in some country outside the Union, other than India, of those Indians who desire to leave the Union in deference to the anxiety of the Union to rid herself of any Indians who do not aim at attaining Western standards of life—indeed of all Indians. Moreover, his presence is

[1] Assembly debates, August 7th 1934.
[2] Imperial Conference, 1923; Keith, *Speeches and Documents on the British Dominions, 1918–1931*, pp. 320 ff.
[3] e.g., as to Balasore, L. N. Réc. Traités, xxv (1924), pp. 382 f.
[4] e.g., with the Union of South Africa, 1927 and 1932.
[5] Parl. Paper, Cmd. 4779.
[6] S. 257.

valuable as enabling Indians to secure his legitimate support in any representations which they may desire to offer to the Union government. The position is of special interest, because it forms a precedent for admitting that the government of one unit of the Commonwealth may properly be represented in another unit for the purpose of defending the interests of those racially connected with it, though they may be born in the Union. Agents are maintained also in Ceylon and Malaya, whither Indian emigration is allowed.

17. ECCLESIASTICAL AFFAIRS

The position of the Church of England in India was vitally changed by the passing of the Indian Church Act, 1927,[1] in order to permit of the separation of the Church of England in India from the English Church of which it had so far been an integral unit. This was supplemented by the Indian Church Measure, 1927, and the Indian Church Statutory Rules, 1929, made by the governor-general in council with the sanction of the secretary of state in council and the concurrence of the bishop of Calcutta. The two churches became distinct from March 1st 1930. Arrangements were made by these measures for the taking over by the new church of property held by the old, and for the possibility of action by the governor-general in the eventuality of the churches ceasing to be in communion. But it is sufficient to note that in all these matters the new Act leaves the governor-general in full authority, in view of his special responsibility for ecclesiastical affairs.

The Act[2] contemplates the continuance of the system by which a staff of chaplains is maintained for ministrations to Christians of the Churches of England and Scotland in India. Under the new régime chaplains of the former communion must obtain a licence from the bishop of the diocese in which they are to be employed, and must make the declarations required by the Canons and Rules of the Church of India, Burma, and Ceylon. Nominations are made by the secretary of state on the advice of an Indian Chaplaincies Board of the Church of

[1] 17 & 18 Geo. V, c. 40. There are seven bishoprics. See Chatterton, *History of the Church of England in India* (1924).

[2] Government of India Act, 1935, s. 269.

England. In the case of Scotland the Act provides that, so long as establishments are maintained in Bengal, Madras, and Bombay, two chaplains at least must be appointed of the Church of Scotland. They are nominated by the secretary of state on the recommendation of the General Assembly's Committee on Indian Churches, and must be inducted by the Presbytery of Edinburgh, to whose control they remain subject, subject to the usual appeal to the Provincial Synod of Lothian and Teviotdale and to the General Assembly.

Expenditure on ecclesiastical services is subject to a limit of forty-two lakhs a year, exclusive of pensions.[1]

18. THE SERVICES OF THE CROWN

(a) THE RECRUITMENT AND TENURE OF OFFICE OF THE CIVIL SERVICES

The Act provides elaborate safeguards to secure in part that existing civil servants shall not suffer through the political changes more than is inevitable, and in part that future servants shall be recruited under conditions which will as far as possible maintain sound traditions. It provides for the general principle that servants hold at the pleasure of the Crown,[2] but it safeguards the application of that principle, and it specifically permits for new entrants the inclusion in their contracts of service of provision for compensation in the event of premature abolition of office or retirement not due to misconduct, if the governor-general or governor thinks such a clause necessary to secure a person with special qualifications. It is therefore clear that Parliament has approved the view that relations with civil servants in India can be governed by contract.

A second principle[3] enunciated is that no person may be dismissed or reduced in rank unless he is given an opportunity of showing cause against the action proposed, unless he has been convicted of a criminal offence or it is not reasonably practicable to afford such an opportunity. Moreover, dismissal

[1] Legislation on these issues is federal; List I, no. 4; for finance see s. 33 (3) (*e*).

[2] S. 240 (1), Part. X; *Denning* v, *Secretary of State* (1920), 37 T.L.R. 139, proves that a contract cannot override the rule.

[3] S. 240 (2) (3).

is forbidden by an authority inferior to the appointing authority.

In general[1] the governor-general or some person authorized by him appoints and makes rules for the conduct of servants in the federal sphere, the governors or persons authorized by them in the case of provincial posts. The legislatures may also regulate conditions of service. But, apart from special safeguards for officers serving before the commencement of Part III of the Act, conferring provincial autonomy, the principle is laid down that from any order of punishment or formal censure, interpreting to his detriment any rule of the service, or terminating prematurely his service, an officer must have at least one appeal unless the order be that of the head of the government. Moreover, no rule or Act may deprive the head of the government of the right to deal in the manner which seems to him just and equitable with the case of any person serving in a civil capacity. In the case of the railway services[2] the federal railway authority is given the powers of the governor-general. In recruitment of higher personnel it must consult the public service commission as to the rules to govern its action, but otherwise it is unfettered save that it is bound to bear in mind the claims of the Anglo-Indian community and to obey directions of the governor-general as to proportionate recruitment from the several communities. The claims of Anglo-Indians are also to be considered in framing regulations for the customs, postal, and telegraph services.[3] The conditions of the police services are to be regulated by special Acts.

The secretary of state[4] is to continue to recruit to the Indian Civil Service, the Indian Medical Service (Civil), and the Indian Police, and to any service which he thinks it necessary to establish to aid in carrying out the functions to be performed in his discretion by the governor-general. Particulars of appointment must be laid annually before Parliament. The numbers are determined by the secretary of state. The governor-general must report on the operation of the system and may suggest modification. The secretary of state may also fill posts connected with irrigation if he thinks it necessary.

[1] S. 241.

[2] S. 242.

[3] Government of India Notification, July 6th 1934, indicates the proportions proposed.

[4] Ss. 244, 245.

He[1] must make rules determining what posts are to be filled by persons so appointed, and appointments to these reserved posts are to be made in his judgment by the governor-general or governor as the case may be. The conditions[2] of service of such persons are regulated by the secretary of state so far as he thinks fit; promotions, leave, and suspension require the action of the head of the government in his individual judgment; pay and pensions are charged on the revenues of India, and the secretary of state and the head of the government are given full discretion to deal equitably with any officer. They are permitted to address complaints to the head of the government, and to appeal to the secretary of state against any order of punishment, censure or alteration of conditions of service. The secretary of state may also award compensation to any persons appointed by him whose position is unfavourably affected by the new régime or for any other cause, without prejudice to the right of the head of the government to award compensation in any other cases. These privileges are extended or continued to officers appointed before the new system by the secretary of state in council.[3] There are also special provisions protecting from abolition of office members of Central Services I and II, Railway Services I and II, and Provincial Services without assent of the head of the government in his individual judgment, and these officers alone can affect pay or pensions of officers of Central Service I, Railway Service I, or a Provincial Service serving before the Act began.[4]

Normally only a British subject may serve the Crown in India save temporarily in the individual judgment of the head of the government, but the head of the government may open specified posts to rulers or subjects of states or natives of tribal areas or territories adjacent to India, the secretary of state may open posts in his gift to named natives of such areas or territories or subjects of states. Moreover, a ruler or a subject of a federated state is eligible for federal office.[5] Women are generally eligible, but subject to exclusion of offices by the governor-general, governor, or secretary of state.[6]

As a safeguard[7] the powers of the secretary of state in these

[1] S. 246. [2] Ss. 247–9. [3] S. 250. [4] S. 258.
[5] S. 262. [6] S. 275. [7] S. 261.

matters are to be exercised with the concurrence of his advisers. Though the services of the staff of the High Commissioner for India and of auditor of Indian home accounts are rendered in England, they are to be deemed services rendered in India, and full protection is given to existing members.[1]

(b) THE PUBLIC SERVICE COMMISSIONS

Provision[2] is made for the establishment of a federal public service commission and for provincial commissions, but two or more provinces may agree that one commission shall serve a group or that all the provinces shall use one commission. By agreement of the governor and the governor-general the federal commission may act for a province. The members are appointed by the head of the government in his discretion, and he determines their tenure of office, and conditions of service and provides for their staff, the cost being charged on the federal or provincial revenues. To ensure impartiality the chairman of the federal commission is debarred from further appointment in India, the chairman of a provincial commission may only act in a like capacity or as head of the federal commission, and any other member can only be appointed to another post with the assent of the head of the government.

The commissions[3] shall conduct examinations for appointments to the services, and if asked by two or more provinces the federal commission must aid in the choosing of candidates with special qualifications as for the forest service. Normally they must be consulted on all matters relating to methods of recruitment; on the methods to be followed in making appointments, promotions, and transfers, and on the suitability of applicants; on disciplinary matters affecting any person in a civil capacity; on claims by such a person for payment of costs incurred in defending legal proceedings and for compensation for injuries incurred on duty and the amount of such pension. Exceptions may be made in their discretion by the secretary of state and the governor-general and governors, and no reference need be made on the issue of the award of numbers of posts to different communities, or on questions affecting subordinate

[1] Ss. 251, 252. [2] Ss. 264, 265, 268. [3] S. 266.

police officers other than claims for payment of costs or pensions for injuries.

Further functions[1] may be assigned to a commission by Act with the prior sanction of the head of the government, but such powers may not be exercised as regards officers appointed by the secretary of state, military officers, or officers in reserved posts without the consent of the secretary of state, and in the case of a provincial Act affecting persons not members of the provincial services without the assent of the governor-general.

(c) THE PROTECTION OF OFFICERS

In order to prevent unfair pressure on officers, especially those engaged in anti-terrorist work, the permission in his discretion of the head of the government is required before civil or criminal proceedings are taken against any officer in respect of official acts done before the commencement of federation or provincial autonomy as the case may be. Moreover, any case instituted must be dismissed unless the court is satisfied that the acts were not done in good faith, and in that case the federation or province must pay any costs not recovered from the plaintiff.[2]

In general, officers are to continue to enjoy the protection of s. 197 of the Code of Criminal Procedure and ss. 80–2 of the Code of Civil Procedure, and any authority for prosecutions under the former must be given by the head of the relevant government in his individual judgment. Any Bill to vary the protection given requires the prior sanction of the head of the government. In the case of civil proceedings the head of the government may order that any costs incurred or damages or costs awarded against an officer shall be charged on the relevant revenues.[3]

(d) PENSIONS

Pensions are secured by being charged on Indian revenues, and, as mentioned above, the governor-general has not only the responsibility but the power to secure payment, if necessary

[1] S. 267. [2] S. 270. See § 19 (e) below. [3] S. 271.

by borrowing in the United Kingdom on the security of Indian revenues. Moreover, in addition to persons already in the service of India under the governor-general in council, those who serve in appointments made by the Crown or the secretary of state or serve in reserved posts or in military posts are assured freedom from Indian taxation on pensions if permanently resident outside India.[1]

The case of the Indian Military Widows and Orphans Fund, the Superior Services (India) Family Pension Fund, and funds to be formed out of contributions under the Indian Military Service Family Pension Regulations and the Indian Civil Service Family Pension Rules is dealt with by authorizing the King in Council to appoint commissioners to hold and administer these funds.[2] Pensions thereafter will be payable by the commissioners, to whom the sums to the credit of the funds will be transferred, normally in three years. But any contributor or beneficiary can object, in which case his interest will fall to be treated as part of the revenues of India, and such pensions shall be paid therefrom as the secretary of state directs. No death duty will be payable in respect of any pension derived from the fund.

19. THE JUDICATURE

(a) THE FEDERAL COURT

The system of federation clearly demanded the creation of a federal court which would have jurisdiction over the states as well as the provinces. It was natural to suggest that the opportunity should be taken to create at the same time a court of appeal from all the provinces, whose sole point of unity of control was the distant Privy Council. But there were serious objections to combining the two functions, and the White Paper[3] suggested that there should be a Supreme Court to hear appeals beside the federal court. The objections to this proposal were felt by the joint committee,[4] which pointed out that there might well arise disputes between two distinct courts owing to the difficulty in determining in particular case

[1] S. 272.
[2] S. 273.
[3] Cmd. 4268, pp. 33, 77–80.
[4] Report, i, 195, 196.

whether a constitutional point was involved or not. It recommended therefore that power should be taken to confer such jurisdiction on the federal court, which would no doubt be divided into two divisions to hear federal issues and appeals. This plan was followed in the Act.

The Act, therefore, provides for the constitution of a federal court to consist of a chief justice of India and such puisne judges as His Majesty thinks necessary, the number not to exceed six until an address is presented by the legislature asking for an increase.[1] Judges are appointed by the Crown and hold office until age sixty-five. A judge may resign or be removed on the ground of misbehaviour or of mental or bodily infirmity if the Privy Council on reference by the Crown so recommends. No power is given of suspension by the governor-general or of removal on the address of the chambers, and the discussion of a judge's judicial conduct by the chambers is forbidden. A judge must have been for at least five years a judge of a high court in British India or a federated state; a barrister or advocate of ten years' standing, or a pleader in a high court or courts of like standing. The chief justice must have fifteen instead of ten years' qualification and must be a barrister, advocate, or pleader or have been one when first appointed a judge. These provisions are intended to exclude members of the Indian Civil Service normally from the highest post, but any judge of the court may be appointed to act during a vacancy of any kind in the office. Judges must take the judicial oath, and their salaries, allowances, leave, and pensions are determined by the King in Council, and (except as regards allowances) may not be varied after appointment to their disadvantage. The court shall sit at Delhi or at such other places as the chief justice with the approval of the governor-general may appoint.

The jurisdiction of the federal court is original and appellate.

I. The court has exclusive original jurisdiction in any dispute between any of the federation, the provinces, and the federated states which involves any question of law or fact on which the existence or extent of a legal right depends. But if a state is a party, the dispute must concern the interpretation of the Act or Order in Council thereunder or the extent of the

[1] Ss. 200-3.

legislative or executive authority vested in the federation by the Instrument of Accession; or arise under an agreement under Part VI of the Act for the administration of a federal law in the state, or otherwise concern some matter in which the federal legislature has power to legislate for the state; or arise under an agreement made after federation with the approval of the representative of the Crown between the state and the federation or a province, and including provision for such jurisdiction. Moreover, no dispute is justiciable if it arises under an agreement expressly excluding such jurisdiction.

In any such case the court shall deliver only a declaratory judgment. But it is, of course, the duty of the parties to conform themselves to such judgment.[1]

II. In proceedings in any high court in British India it shall be the duty of the court to give of its own motion a certificate that the case involves a substantial question of law as to the interpretation of the Act or Order in Council thereunder. If this is done, then any party may appeal to the federal court on the ground that the point was wrongly decided, and on any other point on which appeal would have lain without special leave to the Privy Council, and with the leave of the federal court on any other point. In such cases no appeal lies direct to the Privy Council with or without special leave.[2] The meaning of 'substantial' is presumably that the matter is of considerable public interest or private importance.[3]

With the previous sanction of the governor-general in his discretion the legislature may provide for appeals from high courts without certificate, but the amount at issue must be 50,000 rupees or such sum not under 15,000 rupees as the Act specifies or the decree must concern property of like value, unless the federal court gives special leave to appeal. It is unfortunate that the high court is not permitted to give such leave. If such provision is made, provision may also be made to cut off direct appeals from high courts to the Privy Council with or without special leave.[4]

III. In the case of state courts, appeal may be brought on the question of the interpretation of the Act or Order in Council

[1] S. 204.
[2] S.205.
[3] Cf. *Hanuman Prasad* v. *Bhagwati Prasad* (1902), I.L.R. 24 All. 236.
[4] S. 206.

thereunder or the extent of the legislative or executive authority of the federation, or on a question which arises under an agreement under Part VI of the Act relating to administration by the state of federal laws. In such cases the mode of procedure is by case stated either by the high court or required to be stated by the federal court.[1]

Appeal[2] lies to the King in Council from the federal court without leave from any decision of the federal court in its original jurisdiction dealing with the interpretation of the Act or Order in Council thereunder, or the extent of legislative or executive jurisdiction of the federation in any state or an agreement made under Part VI of the Act; in any other case leave of the court or the Privy Council is requisite.

It may be assumed that in granting special leave the Privy Council will act on its usual principle and grant leave mainly where some important question of law or matter of public interest is involved,[3] and that it will adhere to its principle that it does not act as a normal court of criminal appeal but intervenes only to vindicate the law where there has been a miscarriage of justice by neglect of essential legal principles.[4]

The federal court in allowing an appeal shall indicate the judgment to be substituted and the court below shall give effect to it; it shall also, where it orders costs, transmit the order for payment of the sum ascertained to be due to the court for execution. It may stay execution pending hearing of an appeal on such terms as it thinks fit.[5] All authorities, civil and judicial, throughout the federation must act in aid of the court, which can make orders for attendance of witnesses, production of documents, and punish contempts which shall be given effect in British India, and any federated state. In the case of the states the court shall act through letters of request to the ruler who shall secure their effect.[6]

The law declared by the court or the Privy Council shall

[1] S. 207.

[2] S. 208.

[3] *Prince* v. *Gagnon* (1882), 8 App. Cas. 103; *Clergue* v. *Murray*, [1903] A.C. 521; cf. *Raghunath Prasad Singh* v. *Partabgash Deputy Commrs.* (1927), L.R. 54 Ind. App. 126; *Jivangiri Guru Chamelgiri* v. *Gajanan Narayan Patkar* (1926), 50 Bom. 673.

[4] *Dillet, In re* (1887), 12 App. Cas. 459; *Arnold* v. *King Emperor*, [1914] A.C. 644; *Mohindar Singh* v. *King Emperor* (1932), L.R. 59 Ind. App. 233; *Ras Behari Lal* v. *King Emperor* (1934), 60 Ind. App. 354.

[5] S. 209.

[6] S. 210.

bind all courts in British India and state courts in respect to the interpretation of the Act or Order in Council thereunder or any matter with respect to which the federal legislature can bind the state.[1] The governor-general may in his discretion obtain opinions of the court on matters of law of public importance, but it is not stated that such opinions, though delivered in open court, shall have binding effect.[2]

The court in making pronouncement on such references will follow the analogy of the Privy Council itself, and of the Supreme Court of Canada, as contrasted with the High Court of Australia, which holds that this does not fall within the judicial function. In the case of Northern Ireland advisory opinions of the Privy Council are given binding force.

The court with the approval of the governor-general in his discretion may make rules of court, to determine the rights of practitioners, times of appeal, costs, fees, etc., and may provide for the summary disposal of appeals deemed frivolous or vexatious or dilatory. If its appellate jurisdiction is enlarged by the federal legislature, rules must provide for the constitution of a special division to hear causes which would have been within its jurisdiction without such addition.[3]

Three judges are made a minimum to decide any cause, and those to sit shall be determined by the chief justice. Judgments are to be delivered in open court with the concurrence of the majority present at the hearing, but minority judgments may be delivered. Apparently it is not intended that members of the majority should express differing views, thus giving the majority view greater weight. But it may be doubted if this compromise between the Privy Council system of a single judgment and the system of the final courts in Canada, Australia, and the United Kingdom of the views of all the judges is specially wise. Proceedings must be in English.

The administrative expenses of the court are charged on the federal revenues, to which fees of court accrue. The governor-general decides in his individual judgment the amount to be included in his financial statement for such expenses.[4]

The state courts to be deemed high courts for the purposes

[1] S. 212.
[2] S. 213. Cf. Keith, *Constitutional Law of the British Dominions*, p. 309.
[3] S. 214.
[4] S. 216.

of appeals are decided by the Crown and the ruler concerned.[1] The federal court is not given any jurisdiction to hear appeal from high courts when these exercise jurisdiction usually under the Foreign Jurisdiction Act, 1890, to hear appeals from courts outside India, and nothing in the Act affects any right of appeals with or without special leave to the Privy Council in such causes.[2]

The arrangements for the jurisdiction of the federal court assure as a rule that any question of the interpretation of the constitution or Orders in Council thereunder shall be finally decided for the provinces by the court subject to appeal to the Privy Council. There is left unprovided for the case where the high court refuses a certificate that such an issue is involved, in which case reference would have to be had to the Privy Council under the existing rules of appeal thither from the high court in question. It might have been desirable to confer on the federal court jurisdiction in all cases affecting the interpretation of federal laws, instead of leaving them to be dealt with by the high courts on the ground that uniformity of interpretation of such laws was desirable. But of course appellate jurisdiction in such cases can be granted by the federal legislature, and if the federal court had been given original jurisdiction in all such cases, it might have been given too much work. There is, however, the obvious difficulty that as matters stand it may have too little work to do. Moreover, there is given no power to the federal court to correct misinterpretations of federal laws in the state courts, except indirectly to the extent that, if the federal court decides the interpretation of such a law in a provincial cause, its judgment ought in future to guide the state court. It may be doubted if this is at all an effective assurance for uniformity.

(*b*) THE HIGH COURTS

The status of high court is conferred on the existing courts at Calcutta, Madras, Bombay, Allahabad, Lahore, and Patna,

[1] S. 217.

[2] S. 218. High Courts hear appeals from the Court of the Consul-General (Political Resident) for the Persian Gulf, coast and islands (Bombay), and the Kashgar Consular Court (Lahore).

the chief court in Oudh, the judicial commissioners' courts in the Central Provinces and Berar, the North-West Frontier Province and Sind, any other court constituted or reconstituted as a high court, and any comparable court which may be declared a high court for purposes of the Act by the Crown in Council.[1] Each court consists of a chief justice and such number of judges as may be deemed necessary by the Crown, subject to their not exceeding with additional judges appointed by the governor-general in case of pressure of business the maximum fixed by the Crown in Council, a provision which excludes any possibility of increasing the numbers of the court unduly. Tenure of office is until age sixty, but in other respects as is the case of federal judges. To be qualified as member a person must be a barrister or advocate of at least ten years' standing, or if a member of the Indian Civil Service of that standing have served for at least three years as district judge, have held for at least five years judicial office not inferior to that of subordinate judge or small causes court judge, or have been for at least ten years a pleader of a high court or courts. But to be chief justice of a high court created by Letters Patent any person who was not a barrister, advocate, or pleader when first appointed to judicial office must have served for three years as judge of a high court.[2] Judges are required to take the judicial oath; their salaries, pensions, and leave are regulated by Order in Council as in the case of federal judges.[3] Vacancies pending new appointments or resumption of duties are filled temporarily by the governor-general in his discretion.[4]

The Act abandons the rule that at least one-third of the judges of a high court should be barristers or advocates and at least a third members of the Indian Civil Service, but the joint committee while approving absence of rigidity asserted the importance of maintaining the Indian Civil Service element as source of strength to the courts.[5] The former provision that such a judge could not be permanent chief justice of a high court has been abandoned for a less drastic exclusion. The joint committee insisted on the importance of securing recruitment of barristers and advocates for the courts. The high

[1] S. 219. [2] S. 220. [3] S. 221. [4] S. 222.
[5] Report, i, 197, 198.

court at Calcutta, formerly under the control of the central government, is placed by the Act on the same footing as other high courts. The issue was disputed.

The jurisdiction of high courts is continued as before,[1] but it is expressly provided[2] that every high court shall have superintendence over every court subject to its appellate jurisdiction, and may call for returns, issues general rules of practice and proceedings in such courts, prescribe books and forms to be used, and settle fees for sheriff, attorneys, clerks, and officers. But this power is subject to existing law and the approval of the governor.

An important provision exists to facilitate issues of invalidity of any federal or provincial Act being decided. Where the high court has power to order a transfer of a case from an inferior court, the advocate-general of the federation or the province, as the case may be, may apply for such transfer if the issue of invalidity will arise, and the court shall then order it.[3]

As before, the high courts have no jurisdiction in matters affecting the revenue or acts done in the collection thereof in accordance with custom or law for the time being in force, until otherwise provided by the federal or provincial legislature, with the previous sanction of the governor-general or governor in his discretion.[4]

Proceedings of the high courts are in English;[5] their expenses are charged on provincial revenues and fixed in the individual discretion of the governor.[6]

On an address from a provincial legislature the Crown may constitute a high court, or reconstitute such a court or join two high courts. On agreement[7] of the governments concerned the Crown in Council may extend the jurisdiction of a high court to an area in British India outside the province. Existing arrangements under which a high court serves two provinces or one province and an area outside remain unaffected. The legislature of a province wherein is the chief seat of the court is not empowered to alter its jurisdiction outside the province, but the power to do so rests with the legislature having authority over the area in question. Similarly the power to

[1] S. 223. [2] S. 224. [3] S. 225.
[4] S. 226. [5] S. 227. [6] S. 228. [7] S. 229.

approve rules made by the high court for the area rests with the head of the executive thereover.[1]

An interesting survival is the power now given to the governor of Bengal to appoint the sheriff of Calcutta from a panel of three nominated by the high court; he shall hold office at the pleasure of the governor, who in his discretion fixes his remuneration.[2]

In the case of death sentences in provincial courts, the governor-general is given the powers of the governor-general in council as regards suspension or remission of sentence, and the general power of the Crown or by delegation of the governor-general to grant pardons is expressly reaffirmed.[3]

The law to be administered in the courts remains unaltered save that the King in Council may make such adaptations as may be desirable to meet the changed conditions consequent on territorial redistributions on the creation of new provinces.[4]

(c) DISTRICT JUDGES AND THE SUBORDINATE JUDICIAL SERVICE

The importance of securing judicial impartiality is recognized by giving to the governor of a province in his individual judgment the appointment, promotion, and posting of district judges, a term which includes additional, joint, and assistant judges, the chief judge of a small causes court, the chief presidency magistrate, and sessions judge, additional and assistant sessions judges. He must consult, before making appointments, the high court, and any person not already in the service of the Crown must have been a barrister, advocate, or pleader for five years and be recommended by the high court.[5]

The joint committee[6] was emphatic in favour of securing the independence of the subordinate judicial service in view of its close contact with the people, and rules are enacted for that end. The service is defined as consisting exclusively of persons intended to fill civil judicial posts inferior to that of district judge. Rules for entry thereto are to be made by the governor

[1] Ss. 230, 231.
[2] S. 303.
[3] S. 295. Cf. *Life of Maine*, pp. 301–5.
[4] Ss. 292, 293.
[5] S. 254.
[6] Report, i, 202, 203.

after consulting the Public Service Commission and the high court. The Commission is to hold such examinations as the governor thinks fit and to prepare lists of qualified persons whence the governor will make appointments, based on such rules as he may lay down regarding the number of posts to be awarded to the several communities. The promotion, posting, and grant of leave to officers shall rest with the high court, but without prejudice to such rights of appeal as officers enjoy under the general principles affecting servants of the Crown as provided in the Act, and mentioned above.[1] The communal character of appointments is inevitable, and the governor's action in this regard will be in his exercise of responsibility for minorities, and in accord with his Instructions.

In the case of criminal proceedings some security is provided by the rule that no recommendation is to be made—presumably by the government to the governor, for the grant of magisterial powers or increase or withdrawal of such powers except after consultation with the district magistrate or the chief presidency magistrate in whose area the person concerned is to work or is working.[2]

(*d*) REVENUE COURTS

It is expressly provided that no member of a legislature may be a member of a tribunal which deals with revenue appeals. Where prior to provincial autonomy the governor in council acted in such matters as a court of appeal, the governor-general in council is empowered in his discretion to constitute the court otherwise pending provincial legislation on the matter.[3]

(*e*) JUDICIAL CONTROL OF THE EXECUTIVE AND THE RULE OF LAW

Despite the inevitable tendency of government under Indian conditions, having regard to the origin of British power, to be dictatorial, the Courts have definitely asserted their control over the executive. It must, of course, be remembered that

[1] S. 255. [2] S. 256. [3] S. 296.

control merely means assertion of legal rights; if the existing law derived from the practice in Indian states before the attainment of sovereignty by the Crown permits high-handed action,[1] that is no breach of the rule of law in the strict sense. But in *Dhackjee Dadajee* v. *East India Co.*[2] it was definitely pointed out by the Chief Justice of Bombay that the governor in council had no power to lay aside the ordinary law; office carried with it necessary powers or such as were in practice regularly used, but actions contrary to these principles must be indemnified to be legal. A statutory exception, of course, exists under the Government of India Act,[3] which prevents a high court in its original jurisdiction refusing to accept a written order of the governor-general in council as justification of any act done against any person except a European British subject, but this limited exclusion disappears in the new Act. In *Ameer Khan's case*[4] in 1870 the right to investigate the case of arrest under order of the governor-general in council was denied on the score that it was an act of state, but this plea was rejected, and the arrest found valid simply because of its validity under Bengal Regulation III of 1818, whose existence, providing as it does for detention for reasons of state arising from internal commotions or external causes, negated any general executive authority to imprison without judicial process. Any action of the government under a municipal statute may be investigated in the courts.[5]

Officers of the government therefore are unable to excuse action which is contrary to law by any appeal to the orders of superiors, save in so far as by existing statutes and the new Act the heads of governments are exempt from the jurisdiction of Indian courts.[6] The liability is personal; the company was never held liable for negligence of police officers or their trespasses,[7] nor is the secretary of state in council.[8] No claim can be sustained if a man be arrested and convicted for

[1] *Regina* v. *Shaik Boodin* (1846), Perry's Or. Cas. 435, 459.
[2] (1843) Morley's *Digest*, ii, 307, 311.
[3] S. 111, re-enacting provisions dating from 1781.
[4] 6 Ben. L.R. 392.
[5] *Vijaya Ragava* v. *Secretary of State for India in Council* (1884), 7 Mad. 466.
[6] Government of India Act, s. 110; Act of 1935, s. 306.
[7] *Dhackjee Dadajee's case*, *u.s.*
[8] *Shivabhajan Durgaprasad* v. *Secretary of State* (1904), I.L.R. 28 Bomb. 314; *Ross* v. *Secretary of State* (1913), 37 Mad. 55.

embezzlement, for such action is a matter of judicial procedure.[1] Where, however, an official may be liable, he is afforded a considerable measure of protection by statute[2] for acts done in good faith, and no gazetted officer can be proceeded against without the sanction of the relevant government,[3] an important immunity preserved in the Act of 1935.

In certain cases of tortious action by its officers the company and now the government is liable to suit, where no action would lie in England. This is due in some cases to statute, in others to the distinction between the governmental functions of the Crown and its carrying on non-sovereign activities; thus in the case of the *Peninsular and Oriental Steam Navigation Co.* v. *Secretary of State for India*,[4] it was ruled that damages could be claimed for injury done by the negligence of the dockyard officials at Kidderpore. On the other hand, it has been held that the making of roads is a governmental function, so that no action lies for the negligence of public works officers in such construction.[5] The difference between the two kinds of case is a narrow one.

In matters of contract, officers who contract are not liable, since they are acting for the government, not for themselves.[6] In India direct suit lies against the secretary of state in council in the courts, and will continue to lie against the government concerned and in certain cases the secretary of state may be sued in England.[7] Such cases include contracts dealing with land, for though the title to land may rest on sovereignty, that does not affect the attitude of the Crown in contracting in regard to it.[8] An action may also be brought to recover sums which have reached the hands of the government because improperly levied by a collector of revenue.[9] There is an

[1] *Mata Prasad* v. *Secretary of State* (1930), 5 Luck. 157.

[2] Eggar, *Government of India*, p. 47.

[3] Criminal Procedure Code, s. 197.

[4] (1861), 5 Bom. H.C.R. App. A; *Jehangir M. Cursetji* v. *Secretary of State* (1902), 27 Bom. 189.

[5] Wallis, C. J. (1914), 39 Mad. 351. There is much conflict of views. For liability of individuals as a normal rule cf. 46 All. 884 (1924); 51 Bom. 749 (1926); 6 Ran. 263 (1928).

[6] *Macbeath* v. *Haldimand* (1786), 1 T.R. 172: *Gidley* v. *Lord Palmerston* (1822), 3 Brod. v. Bing. 275.

[7] See § 13 above.

[8] *Kishen Chand* v. *Secretary of State* (1881), 3 All. 829; *Forester* v. *Secretary of State* (1872), L.R. Ind. App. Supp. Vol. 10.

[9] *Hari Bhanji* v. *Secretary of State* (1882), 5 Mad. 273.

analogy to cases in which a petition of right may be brought in England for sums which have reached the treasury without due cause.

Apart from these cases, the action of the courts is excluded in respect of those state proceedings which are technically called Acts of State, matters arising out of political relations with foreign states such as treaties or annexations. In 1793 the case of the *Nabob of the Carnatic* v. *East India Co.*[1] established that no English court would deal with a claim based not on a business contract but on a treaty with a sovereign state, which fell outside municipal jurisdiction. It has equally been held that there is no jurisdiction in respect of claims against the Crown as the successor to a state annexed[2] or on the score of the annexation.[3] When the Punjab was annexed the promise of a pension by the company to the deposed ruler and the taking possession of his property both lay outside the sphere of jurisdiction of the English courts.[4] On the same principle political dealings with Indian states have been held to lie outside the sphere of the courts, and it has been ruled that the court will not intervene against the action of the Indian government in removing from office the Maharaja of Panna.[5] In the same way the Privy Council has ruled that the jurisdiction exercised by political officers in the Kathiawar states is political and not judicial.[6]

Doubt, it must be admitted, still exists as to the extent to which actions of the Company can be made the subject of legal proceedings. The matter was formerly of greater importance than it now is, for it was laid down in the *Secretary of State* v. *Moment*[7] that Indian legislation could not override the right to sue the secretary of state in council in cases in

[1] 1 Ves. Jr. 371; 2 Ves. Jr. 56.

[2] *East India Co.* v. *Syed Ally* (1827), 7 Moo. Ind. App. 555; *Doss* v. *Secretary of State* (1875), L.R. 19 Eq. 509; *Raja Salig Ram* v. *Secretary of State* (1872), L.R. Ind. App. Supp. Vol. 119.

[3] *Elphinstone* v. *Bedreechund* (1830), 1 Knapp P.C. 316; *Secretary of State* v. *Kamachee Boye Sahaba* (1859), 13 Moo. P.C. 22; *Raja of Coorg* v. *East India Co.* (1860), 29 Beav. 300; *Sirdar Bhagwan Singh* v. *Secretary of State* (1874), L.R. 2 Ind. App. 38.

[4] *Salaman* v. *Secretary of State*, [1906] 1 K.B. 613.

[5] *Maharajah Madhava Singh* v. *Secretary of State* (1904), L.R. 31 Ind. App. 239.

[6] *Hemchand Devchand* v. *Azam Sakarlal Chhotamlal*, [1906] A.C. 212.

[7] (1912), 40 Ind. App. 48. Cf. Eggar, *Government of India* (2nd ed.), pp. 17 ff.

which the Company was liable to suit. The matter is now, however, open to regulation by Indian legislation.

It has already been noted that matters affecting the revenue are in such circumstances excluded from the consideration of the ordinary courts and these cases are dealt with under special statutory provisions in the various parts of India.

In general the rule of law is applicable in India subject to those exceptions which have been noted above. While martial law has not seldom been applied in India, in accordance with Indian practice which tends to reduce to writing all general powers, action has usually been authorized by express regulations with legislative authority. Thus Bengal Regulation X of 1804[1] authorized the governor-general in council to suspend the operation of the criminal courts and to establish martial law during the existence of open rebellion. Similar provisions existed in Madras.[2] The proceedings taken in the rebellion in the Punjab in 1919 were based on the regulation of 1804, martial law being established and trial by court martial directed in the case of the offences against the state specified in the regulation. By Ordinance 1 of 1919 trial by commissioners was substituted, but procedure by court martial powers under the Indian Army Act, 1911, was ordered. In *Bugga* v. *The King Emperor*[3] it was held that it was perfectly legal by ordinance thus to deprive a subject of trial by the ordinary courts. By Ordinance 2 the régime was extended to Gujranwala, by Ordinance 3 the death penalty of the regulations was modified, and by 6 continuation of trials after withdrawal of martial law was provided for. An Indemnity Act, 1919, indemnified officers civil and military for acts done in good faith, and provided for payment of compensation for property taken by them. In 1921 an ordinance provided for the proclamation of martial law in Malabar, and authorized the military commander to make regulations for the restoration of order and to establish summary courts; the Madras high court[4] construed the powers given strictly, held that the provisions of the Criminal Procedure Code as to police officers were not

[1] Repealed by Act IV of 1922. [2] Regulation VII of 1808; Act XI of 1857.
[3] (1920), 47 Ind. App. 128.
[4] 45 Mad. 14 and (1922) 45 Mad. 922.

overridden, that the new courts could sit only in the martial law area to try crimes committed therein, and that the power to issue habeas corpus remained. In 1930 again it was necessary to provide for the exercise of martial law in Peshawar and Sholapur.

In view of terrorism it has been necessary to provide by special legislation for the grant of extraordinary powers of arrest, detention, and trial to supplement the right of detention and deportation which is given by Bengal Regulation III of 1818. This was effected by a large number of ordinances especially from 1930 onwards directed at the non-co-operation movement and the terrorism and oppression of public servants attending it. Part of the substance of these measures was enacted for three years by the central legislature in 1932,[1] but in 1935 the Assembly declined to renew the measure, and it had to be certified by the governor-general. The Press was dealt with by the Indian Press (Emergency Powers) Act, 1931, reinforced by later legislation. The Bengal legislature also passed several Acts without certification,[2] as the revolutionary activities of terrorists had there excited general dissatisfaction. The measures taken included extended powers of detention without trial, of summary trial, of taking possession of property of associations declared illegal, etc. Severe penalties were imposed for boycotting of recruitment to the services, tampering with the loyalty of the police, spreading false rumours, and on Press publications bringing the administration into contempt, preaching nonpayment of rent or taxes, and similar misdemeanours, for which the security furnished by the printing press responsible may be forfeited. It was found necessary also to legislate in 1930 to defeat the attempts of those accused in the Meerut trial indefinitely to prolong the proceedings, though the measures taken to that end did not secure the result desired. It is clear that the fundamental rights of the liberty of the subject, of freedom of speech, of freedom of assembly and of the Press were subjected to drastic

[1] XXIII of 1932. Cf. Ordinance 10 of 1932.

[2] Criminal Law Amendment Act, 1925, extended for five years by Act III of 1930 and Act VI. See also Acts XII, XIX, XXII of 1932. Power to detain without trial terrorists outside Bengal is given by the Bengal Criminal Law Supplementary (Extending) Act, 1934, of the Indian legislature, as it is impossible in Bengal to prevent detenus inciting fresh conspiracies.

28

restriction, for which the only, though sufficient, defence lies in the existence of organized terrorism which at Chittagong in 1930 (April) and 1932 (September) passed over into deliberate rebellious onslaughts on the government, supplementing assassination in perpetrating which women were pressed into service. It is fair to note that efforts have been consistently made to safeguard persons dealt with under these emergency measures, for example, under Ordinance 1 of 1931 against revolutionary crime in Burma in connexion with the rebellion there, special tribunals were set up and the local government was authorized to issue orders in regard to suspects restricting their movements, or committing them to custody. But such orders had to be submitted for the scrutiny of two judges. Some of the measures were necessary for the protection of Indian states, thus Ordinance 10 of 1931 was issued to prevent assemblies of men intending to proceed from the Punjab into Kashmir in order to create disorder in that state.

The power of the courts to compel the performance of executive functions is limited. By this Specific Relief Act of 1877 the High Courts at Fort William, Madras, Bombay, and Rangoon[1] may require any specific act to be done or forborne by any person holding a public office where such doing or forbearing is under any law for the time being in force clearly incumbent on such person in his public character and the order is applied for by a person whose property, franchise, or personal right is in danger and no other remedy is available. The court will not compel the performance in a particular manner of an act left to the discretion of an officer, but it may compel such discretion to be exercised fairly and in a proper manner.[2] But no such order can be made[3] against the secretary of state in council or any local government. This procedure takes the place of action by mandamus.

It must be noted that under the constitution of 1919 the courts claimed the right to make orders binding the presidents of the legislative councils.[4] This view was contrary to the

[1] Added by Burma Act XI of 1922. The other courts seem not to have this power; cf. 4 Pat. 224, 229 (1924).

[2] (1901), 26 Bom. 396; (1903), 28 Bom. 253.

[3] S. 45.

[4] (1924), 51 Cal. 874. An injunction was desired to prevent the submission of a supplementary demand for ministerial salaries.

practice both of the United Kingdom and the Dominions and the Act of 1935 negatives the interference of the courts.[1]

20. THE HOME GOVERNMENT OF INDIA

(a) THE SECRETARY OF STATE

The authority of the secretary of state in council over India is vested under the Act in the Crown, and is exercised under responsible government on the advice of the secretary of state, who is controlled by constitutional convention by the Cabinet, while the Prime Minister has the right to select the governor-general, and to be consulted as regards other high appointments.

The secretary of state, however, is to be aided by advisers,[2] with special duties in certain cases. They are to be not less than three or more than six, of whom one half at least must have served for ten years in India and must be appointed within two years of ceasing to work in India. The maximum duration of office is five years, and to prevent staleness reappointment is forbidden, and the secretary of state may remove any member on the score of infirmity of mind or body, a power given for the first time. Payment is due at the rate of £1,350 with £600 a year extra for those of Indian domicile. The secretary of state is at liberty to consult them individually or collectively or to ignore them, and he may act or refuse to act as they advise, except in certain specified matters, namely, those duties conferred as regard the services of the Crown by Part X of the Act as set out above. The advisers may not be members of either House of Parliament, thus reproducing a provision which prevented the employment of Lord Cromer as at one time contemplated by Lord Morley, and ended the services of Lord Inchcape.

The secretary of state's staff is now brought into the normal position of British civil servants, with due saving of existing rights and provision for charging on Indian revenues a part of costs incurred before transfer.[3]

The stock and money of the secretary of state in council at the Bank of England is transferred to the secretary of state.[4] Note has already been made[5] as to the provisions as to contracts

[1] Ss. 41, 87. [2] Ss. 278, 279. Cf. my view in 1919, Cmd. 207, pp. 37 ff.
[3] Ss. 280–4. [4] S. 279. [5] See § 13 above.

of the secretary of state in council, and property formerly vested in him. Under these arrangements the India Office falls under the control of the British Government, and arrangements may be made to give the secretary of state full power over its contents, including its valuable library and other possessions.[1]

Mention has already been made of the legal liability to which the secretary of state shall continue to be subject[2] contrary to the otherwise regular exemption of any secretary of state from liability in the courts.

(b) THE KING IN COUNCIL

Mention has already been made of the many cases in which authority is given to the King in Council to regulate matters under the constitution, and in the next section will be noted his constituent power. Moreover,[3] a very important power is conferred to cover the period of transition to the new system, including that which must elapse between the operation of provincial autonomy and federation when the central government must operate under new conditions. It is then lawful to provide for modifications in the Act and in the provisions of the Government of India Act still in force; to provide for a limited period that sufficient funds shall be available to all the governments in India and Burma; and to make other temporary provisions to remove difficulties which emerge. But the power cannot be exercised in respect of the transition from the central government to federation more than six months after federation or in other matters more than six months after provincial autonomy.

As regards all Orders in Council, save those referring to appeals to the King in Council or sanctioning proceedings against the governor-general, the representative of the Crown in relation to the states, the governors and the secretary of state, it is provided that a draft must be laid before both Houses of Parliament and an Order can only issue after approval by both Houses with or without amendment. In emergency, if Parliament is dissolved or prorogued or both Houses are

[1] S. 172 (4). [2] See §§ 13 (*d*), 19 (*e*) above. [3] S. 310.

adjourned for more than fourteen days, the secretary of state may secure the immediate issue of an Order, but it falls unless approved by both Houses with twenty-eight days after the next meeting of the Commons. The control of Parliament is thus ensured, and the House of Lords receives full recognition as of equal concern in this regard with the Commons.[1]

(c) THE HIGH COMMISSIONER FOR INDIA.

The office of High Commissioner was provided for in the Act of 1919 and established by Order in Council of August 18th 1920. The functions assigned to him were to act as agent of the central government and of the provincial governments and to perform any functions hitherto carried out in the office of the secretary of state which might be assigned to him by that officer. The work undertaken is essentially non-political. Normally all political issues are conducted through the India Office, and the chief use of the High Commissioner in this regard has been in connexion with international conferences where he has been deputed to act as representative of India. In the case of the Ottawa Conference in 1932, however, the exceptional step was taken of making the office of the High Commissioner the centre of the activities of the Indian delegation, which negotiated with the British Government. This exceptional step was based on the desire to emphasize the independence of India in fiscal policy.

In addition to the duty of procuring stores for Indian governments, furnishing trade information and promoting the welfare of Indian trade, the High Commissioner deals with the education in this country of Indian students, and supplies information on India to inquirers.

Under the new régime he will be controlled by the governor-general in his individual judgment, and may be authorized to act for a province, a federated state, or Burma.[2]

Mention has been made above of the auditor of Indian home accounts[3] who is likewise under the control of the governor-general, and by whom the accounts of the High Commissioner are audited.

[1] S. 309. [2] S. 302. [3] S. 170 (2), (3).

21. THE AMENDMENT OF THE CONSTITUTION

As was inevitable in the circumstances, the Act confers on the federation no general constituent power, nor does it give any authority to the provinces, such as is enjoyed by the provinces of Canada and the states of the Commonwealth, to mould their own constitutions in detail, within the federal framework. The only power of change is vested in the Imperial Parliament with the exception that in a number of minor points change by the Crown in Council is permitted. These are: (*a*) Any amendment relating to the size or composition of the chambers of the federal legislature, or to the methods of choosing or to the qualifications of members of that legislature, not being an amendment which would vary the proportion between the number of seats in the Council of State and the number of seats in the Federal Assembly, or would vary, either as regards the Council of State or the Federal Assembly, the proportion between the number of seats allotted to British India and the number of seats allotted to Indian states; (*b*) any amendment relating to the number of chambers in a provincial legislature, or the size or composition of the chambers, or of either chamber, of a provincial legislature, or to the method of choosing or the qualifications of members of a provincial legislature, (*c*) any amendment providing that in the case of women literacy shall be substituted for any higher educational qualification standard for the time being required as a qualification for the franchise, or providing that women if duly qualified shall be entered on electoral rolls without any application being made for the purpose by them or on their behalf; and (*d*) any other amendment of the provisions relating to the qualifications enabling persons to be registered as voters for the purpose of elections.

The procedure is elaborate. Addresses must be passed by the federal or provincial legislature on motions moved in either chamber by a minister on behalf of the Council of Ministers, recommending such amendment; then an address must be passed in like manner asking for the communication of any such resolution to Parliament, and within six months after such communication the secretary of state must lay before the Houses a statement of the action which it is proposed to take. The governor-general or governor is required to send with the address a statement of his opinion on the proposed amendment, its effect on any minority, the view of that minority, and a statement of the attitude of the majority of that minority's representatives in the legislature, and this must be laid before Parliament. Moreover, no amendment other than one of type (c) from a province may be suggested sooner than ten years from federation or provincial autonomy as the case may be.

The King in Council may make any of the specified amendments at any time and even without any address. But if no address is presented before the draft is laid before Parliament, the secretary of state must take such steps as His Majesty may direct for ascertaining the views of the governments and legislatures affected, of any minority, and the attitude of the majority of the representatives of the minority in the legislature affected. In any case, the provisions of Part II of the first schedule of the Act dealing with the representation of the states is not to be affected without the consent of any ruler affected.[1]

The explanation of the powers given, offered on July 3rd 1935, by the government, was the impossiblity of foreseeing points of detail as to the franchise or constitution which required amendment, and the undesirability of having to secure an Act for matters of that type; further, any agreement between communities as to the communal award might have to be given effect, without the delay of an Act. It was realized that the Muhammadan community in particular feared any interference with the communal settlement, and it was explained that it was not intended to deal with it save by agreement. It must, however, be admitted that the power to affect it is now given, and that in view of the expressed intention of the government it should have been easy to safeguard from change without consent that part of the constitution.

[1] S. 308.

22. THE TRANSITION TO THE FEDERATION

It is clear that there cannot be immediate provincial autonomy and federation, and accordingly the Act contemplates that after provincial autonomy has been established—perhaps in 1936–7—there shall be a period when the federation will be non-existent.[1] During this time the Indian legislature, as constituted under the Act of 1919, shall exercise the functions of the federal legislature so far as British India is concerned, and executive power such as the federation will possess will vest in the governor-general in council, or in matters under the federation placed in his discretion, in the governor-general, in respect of British India. The governor-general will have special responsibilities similar to those which are provided under federation, but the provisions as to action in his individual judgment will naturally not apply, since responsible government does not exist. But the rules as to prior sanction of legislation, as to broadcasting, as to directions to and principles to be observed by the federal railway authority, and the services recruited by the secretary of state shall have effect in regard to defence, external affairs, ecclesiastical affairs and tribal areas as they have effect in relation to matters in which the governor-general is required by the Act to exercise his discretion.[2] In all matters the governor-general and the governor-general in council remains subject to the secretary of state, who in questions of the grant or appropriation of revenue of the governor-general in council must have the concurrence of a majority of his advisers who are to number between eight and twelve.[3]

While this part of the Act is in force, no sterling loans shall be raised by the governor-general in council, but under the authority of Parliament a loan may be raised by the secretary of state, with the concurrence of a majority of his advisers; such loans shall be free from Indian taxation, rank as trustee stocks, and claims in respect of them may be brought against the secretary of state, but without imposing any liability on the British Exchequer.[4] The Indian legislature is forbidden

[1] Act, Part XIII and Sched. 9.
[2] S. 313.
[3] S. 314.
[4] S. 316.

to limit the borrowing powers of the governor-general in council.

The federal court, the public service commission, and federal railway authority may be brought into being for purposes connected with British India before federation, either together with or later than provincial autonomy.[1]

Subject to these important changes the whole structure of the central government shall remain unaltered pending federation.[2]

23. THE POSITION OF THE STATES

Reference has already[3] been made to the position of the states in regard to federation. But states need not federate, and apart from that there will remain many matters in which the states are not concerned with the federation but have relations with the Crown through his representative.

Under the advice of the Montagu-Chelmsford Report[4] the relations of the states, formerly often conducted through the local governments, have been in the great majority of cases rendered direct with the governor-general. But the control of the Crown is exercised in most cases through an agent. In immediate political relations with the government of India are Hyderabad, Mysore, Baroda, Jammu and Kashmir, Gwalior, as well as Bhutan and Sikkim, whose connexion is slightly different from that of the ordinary state. The agent of the governor-general in Baluchistan is concerned with relations with Kalat and Las Bela. The Central Indian Agency whose agent resides at Indore with political agents in Bhopal, Bundelkhand, and Malwa, includes twenty-eight major states, marked by the possession of salutes by their rulers, and sixty-nine non-salute states. The Deccan States Agency was formed in 1933 by detaching the states controlled by Bombay; the agent is resident at Kolhapur; there are sixteen other states, mostly small. The Eastern States Agency was created in 1933 by detaching the states in connexion with the Central Provinces,

[1] S. 318. [2] S. 317 and Sched. 9.

[3] See § 3 above. In the Muslim states, all told, there are only some 3,000,000 Muslims, with 8,000,000 in other states.

[4] Parl. Paper, Cd. 9109, pp. 247, 248.

Bihar and Orissa. Of the forty states Mayurabhanj, Patna, Bastar, and Kalahandi are the most important; the agent resides at Ranchi with a secretary and political agent at Sambalpur. In the same year the Gujarat States Agency, with eleven greater and seventy non-salute states and estates, was created at the expense of Bombay, the resident at Baroda being made agent; the leading state is Rajpipla, and subordinate to the agency is the Rewa Kantha Agency. In 1923 the states in communication with Madras were detached and formed into the Madras States Agency, including Travancore, where the agent resides, and Cochin. The governor of the North-West Frontier Province is agent for five states, including Chitral. The Punjab States Agency was formed in 1921; it includes fourteen states, the Muslim Bahawalpur and the Sikh Patiala being the more important; in 1933 Khairpur was added. The Rajputana States Agency has its headquarters at Mount Abu, where the agent, the chief commissioner of Ajmer-Merwara, resides; Bikaner and Sirohi are directly under him; the twenty-two others fall under the resident at Jaipur, the resident in Mewar and political agent Southern Rajputana States, the political agent Eastern Rajputana States, and the resident Western Rajputana States. Tonk and Palanpur are under Muslim, Bharatpur and Dholpur under Jat rulers; the others include Udaipur, the premier Rajput State, Jaipur, Jodhpur, and Bikaner. The Western India States Agency was created in 1924, when the states of the Kathiawar, Cutch, and Palanpur Agencies under the Bombay government were placed under the governor-general, Mahi Kantha Agency being added in 1933. The agent resides at Rajkot; under him are political agents for the Sabar Kantha, Western and Eastern Kathiawar Agencies. There are sixteen salute states, including Cutch, Junagadh, Nawanagar, and Bhavnagar, and 236 non-salute states and estates.

There remain in direct relations with local governments a small number of states. Assam is connected with Manipur and sixteen small states of the Khasi and Jaintia hills; Bengal has the states of Cooch Behar and Tripura, whose population is largely mongoloid; the Punjab is connected with eighteen Simla hill states of which Bashahr is the largest and three other small states. The United Provinces deals with Rampur, Benares, created afresh in 1911, and the Himalayan Tehri-Garhwal.

The governor-general in dealing with the states is aided by the political department, already referred to, which in its work in this respect is subordinate to the governor-general in his capacity as representative of the Crown in its relations with the states. The extent of the authority of the Crown, as we have seen, varies very greatly from state to state.

In these states constitutional government has made very slight progress. Since 1907 there has existed in Mysore a legislative council now consisting of fifty members with an elective majority, in addition to the diwan and the other members of the Maharaja's council. This body has wide legislative and financial powers but has no authority over the executive government.[1] More importance appears in popular opinion to attach to the representative assembly created in 1881 consisting of between 250 and 275 members, though its functions, modelled on the traditional Indian usage, are mainly consultative and interpellative. In Baroda administration is conducted on modern lines by the diwan, who presides over the executive council subject to the control of the Maharaja; for legislation there is a legislative council partly nominated, partly elected. A similar council was established in Kashmir as part of the reforms undertaken in 1933–4. There are councils also in the states of Bhopal, Travancore, and Cochin, and similar institutions in twenty-five other states. On the other hand, it was only under pressure from the British Government that in 1919 Hyderabad set up an executive council of eight members with a view to diminishing the immediate intervention of the Nizam in the affairs of state.[2] The legislative council established in 1893 contains twenty members in addition to the president, and of these eleven are officials.

In no case is there a state constitution which is binding on the rulers. There are still many instances in which no distinction is made between the privy purse of the rulers and the

[1] Matters affecting the princely family and relations with the Crown, and certain financial issues are reserved.

[2] Cf. Barton, *Princes of India*, pp. 199 f., 209 f.

state revenues, with the result that insufficient consideration has been shown in many states for the needs of the people, but 56 of the 109 princes who are directly represented in the Chamber of Princes have fixed privy purses. In the great majority of states executive and judicial functions are not separated, but thirty-four of these states have made this distinction. In many states the judiciary remains under the complete control of the ruler, but in forty states high courts more or less on British models have come into being, and in some of them no doubt justice is administered with due regard to law. But it must be remembered that the ruler of a state is not subject to law, and that officials acting on his instructions are not normally amenable to the jurisdiction of the courts. There is no system of law definitely laid down in the great majority of the states, a fact which leaves too wide discretion to the executive and the judiciary. There is nothing corresponding to the rule of law as it prevails in British India, and when the Government of India Act was drafted[1] it was found impossible to provide for a statement of fundamental rights since these could not be accepted by the states. Moreover, it must be pointed out that only in forty-six states has there been started a regular graded civil list of officials, though a larger number have established pension funds or provident funds.

With the advance of political rights in British India it is inevitable that the autocracy of the states should become more and more anomalous. The paramount power, having decided that it is proper that the people of British India should be encouraged to exercise political power, cannot logically maintain the view that the Indian states should deny their subjects the right to advance in political status. It seems clear, therefore, that the Crown should endeavour by the use of its authority to secure the gradual extension of political rights to the people.

The states are represented in accordance with the Montagu-Chelmsford scheme in the Chamber of Princes.[2] Under its constitution[3] it is a consultative body, to be consulted freely by the Viceroy in matters relating to the territories of Indian

[1] Joint Committee Report, i, 216.
[2] Parl. Paper, Cmd. 3568, pp. 88–91.
[3] Notification 262 R, February 8th 1921, as amended.

states and in matters affecting these territories jointly with British India or with the rest of the Empire. It has no concern with the internal affairs of individual states or their rulers, or the relations with the Crown, and it interferes in no way with the existing rights of states or their freedom of action. Its constitution is of some interest as marking the distinctions between the classes of states. There are (1) those with full legislative and jurisdictional power; (2) those which have such power partially subject to superintendence, such as the right of intervention in internal affairs, supervision of criminal jurisdiction, in some cases limitation of judicial authority and restriction of the right of legislation or even, as in the case of the Simla hill states, the reservation of residuary rights to the British Government; (3) states with very limited authority, now usually called estates and jagirs. The Chamber consists of 109 princes represented separately, and 12 chosen to represent 127 states of the second class. It must be added that, perhaps naturally, the greater states have shown dislike of thus being ranked with states of minor importance and have not sent representatives to the Chamber. That body, however, has taken advantage of its position to press for preservation and extension of the rights of the states. It has served to enable them to express views on tariff and defence issues, though British Indian legislators have not had a like right to discuss state issues, and it was by it that claims were put forward for the recognition of state rights as regards wireless telegraphy and air transport.

The Chamber took up the proposal for the reduction to regular rules of political practice in issues concerning the states, which had been mooted earlier and had led in September 1919 to the meeting of a codification committee to consider some twenty-three points on which difficulties had arisen, according to replies to an invitation for criticisms addressed to the states. Certain matters had already been taken up and adjusted before it became the business of the standing committee of the Chamber to investigate. Thus by a resolution of August 27th 1917 it was admitted that the government of India was the trustee and custodian of the rights, interests, and traditions of the state during a minority, and that therefore in future instead of entrusting control to a political officer—who in the past had often effected important changes during his tenure of office—a council of regency should be established: old traditions should be respected, radical changes avoided, local men employed, treaty rights respected, no jagirs should be granted, no state territories exchanged or sold, and no long-term commercial concessions or monopolies should be given to individuals or companies. In the same way it has been agreed that, where the succession to a ruler is regular, the government does not sanction as formerly the accession, but merely accords it recognition. But the government remains admittedly the necessary arbitrator where the succession is not regular or its regularity is disputed; thus it declined (1925) to permit the late Maharaja of Kashmir to pass over the heir in descent in favour of his adopted son. Accord has also been reached on such issues as the rules affecting the employment of Europeans by the states; the settlement of boundary disputes, and the payment of compensation to the states for land taken for irrigation, navigation, and other purposes.

The right, however, of the Crown in the exercise of paramount power to determine the extent of its sovereignty, asserted at Bahawalpur by Lord Curzon,[1] was reasserted in the most conclusive terms in 1926 by Lord Reading[2] when he closed the controversy over Berar with the Nizam and stands unaltered; the way for the rulers to acquire authority is through federation. It has remained necessary to intervene with decisive authority in state affairs. The Nizam was reminded of the desirability of orderly administration and pressed to employ British officers to bring order into the administration of the state under the executive council system.[3] The Maharana of Udaipur was required after a rising against his government in 1921 to rectify causes of complaint and to delegate power to his son.[4] It has been necessary to secure the absence from his state of the ruler of Alwar and to place a British officer in charge temporarily (1933). In 1926 the murder of a British Indian

[1] *Curzon in India*, p. 226; cf. p. 228.

[2] Parl. Paper, Cmd. 3302, pp. 56–8, reaffirmed by the Indian States Committee (ibid., pp. 18, 19).

[3] Barton, *The Princes of India*, p. 210.

[4] Barton, p. 94. Jaipur also was in need of a British administrator (p. 96).

merchant in Bombay was alleged to have been instigated by the ruler of Indore, who was therefore offered an impartial commission of inquiry on the lines suggested by the Montagu-Chelmsford Report as the best means of deciding issues of this kind through effective investigation.[1] Declining to face such investigation, he resigned in favour of his son. In 1922 the nawab of Nabha was found by the investigation of a special commissioner to have used the judicial machinery of his state to secure illegal convictions against subjects and officials of Patiala, with the deliberate intention of injuring a neighbouring state; he was permitted, with some hesitation, to abdicate,[2] but in 1928 on charges of disloyalty and seditious associations he was removed to Kodaikanal and placed under restraint. Prolonged absence from the state has occasioned the necessity of relieving the ruler of Dewas (senior) from the administration of his territory.

The position of the states in matters of titles has been recently made more clear. The government has no objection in principle to rulers of the states bestowing on their subjects titles which the British Government does not bestow, but it objects to their grant to British subjects, though in some cases it appears that recognition has not been wholly refused. The rulers of Baroda, Gwalior, Mysore, and other states have orders of chivalry, which may be worn after those conferred by the Crown. On the other hand, rulers receive membership of the British Orders of the Star of India or the Indian Empire, the omission of the ruler of Nabha being regarded as a signal mark of royal displeasure. They may not accept without permission any foreign title. They may not assume any new Indian title without recognition. The style of the heir-apparent is normally adopted from Indian usage; permission has been given for the adoption of new styles in certain cases. The Crown confines the term 'Highness' to the reigning head of the state and his wife; only in exceptional cases is it accorded to the heir-apparent as in Mysore. The term 'Prince' is recognized only of the rulers, and of the Prince of Arcot and the son of the last King of Oudh. The Indian princes are not royalty, nor their

[1] Parl. Paper, Cmd. 9109, s. 309.
[2] Panikkar, *Indian States*, pp. 60–3.

families royal, but ruling families. Their salutes and precedence are determined by the Crown.[1]

Apart from these vital questions of status, the princes have largely by assent been brought into economic relations of a close kind with the British Crown. The attainment of direct rule in 1858 was the prelude to the systematic bringing of the states into the railway planning of the period. The states were induced to provide land, and sometimes materials, to surrender jurisdiction, and transit duties, in some cases even to lend money, to further construction of lines which remained under British control; they gained no doubt from facilities for trade though the routes followed and rates imposed may have been chosen for reasons of military convenience and the interests of British India. The right to construct new railways in the states has naturally been subject to British intervention[2] in order to prevent competition with the established lines, a fact which explains the terms of the railway section of the new constitution. Certain rights with regard to railways are granted to Jodhpur, Bikaner, and Hyderabad, and Kashmir and Cutch are not included in the general railway system. Military considerations are of course sufficient to justify this claim of control.

Telegraph lines, telephone system, and postal arrangements have been established by the government of India. Telegraphs being essential for military purposes are under the government of India in all cases, though certain privileges are accorded to states where offices are established. Kashmir alone has a separate system, but the British Indian system also operates in this state. It has been agreed in 1924 as a result of negotiations that states may construct internal telegraph lines, but special arrangements are requisite for connexion with the Indian system. The same principle has been applied to telephones.[3]

In most states the Indian government has introduced its postal system. In Gwalior, Patiala, Jind, and Nabha there is a system based on a postal convention under which letters posted in the state post offices are carried throughout India. In other states the Indian post office has exclusive rights in respect of

[1] Panikkar, *Indian States*, pp. 68–72.
[2] Agreement on principles was reached in 1923.
[3] Parl. Paper, Cmd. 3302, p. 49.

All-India mail services, and only ten states, of which Hyderabad, Travancore, and Cochin are the most important, have the right of internal services. The states are also required to pay compensation in respect of robbery of mails within state territory,[1] a subject which has raised protests when the robberies have not been caused by lack of care in the state.

As regards customs duty British authority has extended mainly to seaborne trade, the states[2] being permitted to levy land customs and transit duties. Special arrangements have been made with the maritime states of Travancore and Cochin, under which Indian import duties are enforced in the port of Cochin and proceeds are shared. Certain minor states[3] levy import duties on seaborne goods, but the government of India claims a refund of duties in respect of such goods consumed in British territory, but it has not conceded the claims of states to be paid sums in respect of imports consumed in the states. Here again federation is proposed to meet the difficulty. Kashmir, however, not only levies its own customs duties but under a treaty of 1870 receives duties collected at British Indian ports on goods imported into the state in bond. The duties charged by Hyderabad are controlled by treaty.

In currency matters the British rupee has become everywhere legal tender, the process being assisted by the work of the Presidency Banks and the Imperial Bank of India. Hyderabad has its own rupee and has issued since the war currency notes. Travancore keeps accounts in its own rupee and coins half and quarter silver rupees. In Rajputana each state has its own rupee, a most inconvenient position, which justifies the action taken during minorities in the states of Alwar (1905) and Bikaner (1893) to introduce British coins. The government discourages the state mints, restricting them as far as possible to the state capital and to the production of sufficient coinage only to meet the needs of the state.

In the vital matter of salt British policy has succeeded in securing control of the production even in the states and the

[1] Rules of 1866, revised in 1885; condemned by the States Committee (p. 50).
[2] Mysore is the chief exception.
[3] Bhavnagar is a free port and keeps customs even on goods passed into British India.

fixing of a regular price, determined by the government, which depends on the duty charged.[1]

In a similar manner considerable success was attained in establishing monopoly in opium. In 1907 a convention with China provided for the closing of that market to Indian opium, and the states, though they were not consulted regarding the treaty, are of course bound by its terms.

In all these matters the Indian States Committee of 1928–9[2] found that the state had no serious grievances to be remedied, insisting that the states could not expect British India which suffered severely from the opium policy, to recompense them for a common sacrifice in international moral interests, while uniform currency was a boon to all concerned, and only confusion could arise from reopening the old treaties regulating salt production. But federation no doubt renders it fair to consider the claims of states which pay tribute or have ceded lands for protection and which would in federation be paying twice over for security.[3] Hyderabad, however, prefers to insist on her treaty rights for the maintenance in her borders of a British force.

The states have been brought into inextricable relations of unity with British India by the establishment, through roads, railways, posts, telegraphs, telephone, and wireless systems, of through communications. They have interests in British Indian currency and banking, and are vitally affected by the development of Indian industrialism and by the growth of oversea commerce. Tariff policy affects them deeply. All these factors operate in much the same way on all the states and help to create in their rulers the sense of common interests which rendered possible the creation and partial operation of the Chamber of Princes. In like manner their subjects have ceased to feel so intense a personal loyalty and have begun to conceive of themselves as Indian citizens, an idea which the Round Table Conference mooted but without reaching agreement on its practicability. The influence of the Press and the

[1] Travancore and Kathiawar do not pay salt duty. The value of immunities now is forty-six lakhs.

[2] Cmd. 3302, pp. 48, 50. Cmd. 4103 is more favourable to state claims, no doubt in the desire to promote federation, the concessions deemed just being made conditional on federation, a position naturally criticized as illogical.

[3] e.g., Mysore, Baroda, Gwalior; Barton, *The Princes of India*, pp. 301, 302.

universities has propagated demands for a minimum of rights. The Indian National Congress has recognized the unity of India by permitting Congress organization in the states; those connected with Madras and Mysore have such organizations to send representatives to Congress. The States' Peoples' Conference[1] represents the doctrine of the common interests of the peoples of the states as against their rulers, and it is in vain that the Maharaja of Bikaner contends that the Conference is in principle unconstitutional and illegal, and that at most the people of each state may organize to make suggestions to the ruler. But the essential fact of unity must prevail, and the demands put forward by the spokesmen of the people, though doubtless in advance of the great majority of those concerned, are all of an easily defended nature. They demand a share in legislation and taxation; the fixing at a reasonable sum of the privy purse of the ruler; the enactment of a code of law with securities for person[2] and property, administered by a judiciary independent of the executive; the declaration of fundamental rights of freedom of speech, of the Press, and of the right to engage in political agitation; they ask that the state representatives to any federal legislature should be elected; they desire to see the civil services placed on a definite footing with proper security of tenure, and their subjection to independent judicial control.[3] Some urge that the states should co-operate with British India in dealing with the appalling evils of child marriage, instead of affording facilities for evasion of the Sarda Act.

[1] For other organizations, etc., see D. V. Gundappa, *The States and their People in the Indian Constitution* (1931).

[2] Domestic slavery still lingers; Barton, *The Princes of India*, p. 63. See also the case of a subject of the ruler of Sirohi imprisoned in a bungalow; Bombay High Court, June 22nd 1935.

[3] Protection against the organization of activities in British India directed against state authority or mass movements into a state is given by the Indian States (Protection) Act, 1934, which also imposes penalties on Press statements exciting hatred, contempt, or disaffection for state administrations, though statements of fact are allowed. The Act dangerously limits criticism of maladministration. It must be admitted that the very necessary reforms in Kashmir were compelled by action in British India. Unfortunately there has been blackmailing of states.

24. BRITISH BURMA

The separation of Burma from India involves the creation of a distinctive constitution,[1] which is based on combining in the hands of the governor the powers of the governor-general and of the governors of the provinces, so far as is practicable, and in all matters of legislative concern giving the full authority of the federal and provincial legislatures to the Burmese legislature. There is, of course, as a result a constitution of a very remarkable type, presenting the possibility of the rise of effective responsible government in a manner without parallel in India. The provinces there are of restricted power, while the federation is shut out from many vital activities deeply affecting the life of the people, and the unity of its legislature is seriously lessened by the fact that it represents the nominees of autocratic rulers who disbelieve in democracy and the elected representatives of British India. In Burma the majority of the legislature is Burmese, so that, if it is desired, there is the possibility of a strong and united party, which is the necessary presupposition of responsible government. Moreover, there is nothing parallel to the weight of conservatism lent to the federal legislature by the states, though the power of the governor to nominate half the second chamber will doubtless be used to secure some measure of conservative support to a government which may tend to fall under the control of the majority in the lower house in an inconvenient degree.

In the main the constitution is a transcript from that of the federation and provinces, but the governor, who is normally to act on the advice of his council of ministers not exceeding ten in number,[2] is to act in his discretion with the aid of three counsellors in matters of defence, external affairs, other than relations with other parts of the dominions of the Crown, ecclesiastical affairs, the control of monetary policy, currency and coinage, certain areas including the Shan states, and areas in Burma which are not British territory,[3] Burma denoting those parts of India east of Bengal, Manipur, and areas attached to Assam. His special responsibilities[4] included

[1] Act, Part XIV, reprinted as Government of Burma Act, 1935. See Joint Committee Report, i, 245 ff., 381 ff.; ii, 1 ff.
[2] S. 5. [3] S. 7. [4] S. 8.

prevention o' grave menace to peace or tranquillity; the safeguarding of the financial stability and credit of Burma; the safeguarding of the legitimate interests of minorities; the securing to and to the dependants of members of the public services of the rights accorded by the Act and the safeguarding of their legitimate interests; the securing in the executive sphere of the prevention of discrimination; the preventing of discriminatory treatment or penalization of goods imported from the United Kingdom and India; the securing of the peace and government of certain areas specified in the Act,[1] and the securing that the due discharge of functions in respect of which he is to act in discretion or individual judgment is not prejudiced by action taken in other matters. He has to aid him a financial adviser and an advocate-general, and is required to exercise the same powers as in India in respect of police rules, the prevention of crimes of violence, and the safeguarding of information, and to make rules securing that ministers and secretaries give him information where any special responsibility may be involved.

The legislature in which the governor represents the King is composed of a Senate, half of whose members are nominated by the governor, half elected by the House of Representatives on the system of proportional representation.[2] Senators are qualified by a high property qualification or by ministerial or official service or other public service. Its duration is seven years, but it may be dissolved either with the lower house or by itself. The House of Representatives, which lasts for five years, consists of 132 members; there are 91 general non-communal seats, 12 Karen seats; 8 Indian,[3] 2 Anglo-Burman, and 3 European seats; 11 for representatives of commerce and industry, one for the university, and two each for Indian and non-Indian labour. The franchise is given at age eighteen, and is based on property, taxation, rent payment, and other qualifications wider than those in India, resulting it is anticipated in a wide representation.

The powers of the governor, the organization of the houses,

[1] Sched. 2, Part II. [2] S. 17 and Sched. 3.

[3] i.e., persons born or domiciled in India, or whose fathers or grandfathers were so born or domiciled.

privileges, pay, and so forth follow the lines indicated; there is close similarity in the disqualifications of members, and the general rules of procedure. The legislature is given extra-territorial authority in respect of British subjects and subjects of the Crown in any part of Burma; of British subjects domiciled in Burma wherever they are; of ships and aircraft and persons on them, if registered in Burma; and of the personnel of naval, military, and air forces raised in Burma and their followers.[1] The rules of legislative procedure follow the Indian model; the governor's prior assent is required in like cases, differences of view are solved after twelve months normally by joint sittings; Bills may be assented to, reserved, or refused assent. The governor[2] may promulgate ordinances at the instance of ministers, or in certain cases on his own motion, and may enact permanent Acts; moreover, for the scheduled areas he may make regulations,[3] and no Act applies save in so far as he makes it effective with or without modifications. He may also, if the constitutional machinery breaks down, take over the administration, subject to approval by Parliament, but the period shall not exceed three years.[4]

The financial provisions follow the Indian model.[5] Grants are the concern of the House of Representatives only, and the governor has the same power of restoring grants that exists in India, while similar exceptions from the necessity of voting grants are provided. Audit is entrusted to an auditor-general, but home accounts may be audited by the auditor of Indian home accounts.

Provision is made for a Burma railway board, and a rates committee may be appointed, but there is no provision for a tribunal, as the issues involved in India do not arise for Burma.[6]

The provisions regarding the high court are as in India. A new appeal is accorded to the Privy Council on the interpretation of the Act or any Order in Council under it.[7]

The services of the Crown are protected as in India. The secretary of state shall recruit for the Burma civil service (Class I), the Burma police (Class I), any Burma medical service,

[1] S. 33 [2] Ss. 41–3. [3] S. 40. [4] S. 139.
[5] Ss. 55–67. [6] Ss. 69–80. [7] Ss. 81–90.

and if necessary for irrigation. The security of the subordinate judiciary is provided for, and the governor is given full discretion to appoint a Burma frontier service, which is normally exempt from control by the legislature. A public service commission is provided for, and security against unfair prosecutions, and as to pensions and other matters are regulated as in India. The appointment of chaplains is authorized. Only British subjects are normally eligible to serve the Crown, but the governor may extend eligibility to areas in Burma, and to natives of specified Indian states or territories adjacent to India. Sex is not generally to disqualify.[1]

Lands and buildings held in Burma for the purposes of the government of India now fall to the Crown in Burma, as does other property, excluding property held for the Indian forces stationed in Burma, not being raised in Burma. Contracts pass to the government of Burma which is made able to sue and be sued, while liabilities of the secretary of state in council may be enforced against the secretary of state.[2] The secretary of state is to be advised by not more than three advisers on conditions similar to those in respect of India, but only one adviser need have had ten years' service in Burma.[3]

As in the case of India, there are restrictions[4] on the power of the legislature, including restrictions[5] to prevent discrimination against the United Kingdom; there is a prohibition of discrimination on grounds of religion, etc.;[6] property if taken must be paid for, and pensions and grants are safeguarded.[7] The existing law is to continue subject to adjustments by Order in Council.[8] The governor is to be immune from legal process while in office, and a like immunity is accorded to the secretary of state, and after leaving office only by permission of the King in Council may proceedings be taken for official actions.[9] A High Commissioner for Burma may be appointed if desired.[10]

There is no general power to amend the constitution. On a procedure[11] similar to that in India after ten years amendments may be asked for by the legislature as regards the composition of the legislature, or the method of choosing or the qualification of members, or the franchise, and at any time amendments may

[1] Ss. 91–129. [2] Ss. 130–3. [3] S. 140. [4] S. 34.
[5] Ss. 44–54. [6] S. 144. [7] Ss. 145, 146. [8] Ss. 149, 157.
[9] S. 152. [10] S. 150. [11] S. 154.

be made by Order in Council after due consultation of the government, the legislature, any minority; and after ascertaining the views of the majority of the representatives of the minority in the legislature.

The procedure by Order in Council is subject to the control of Parliament,[1] and there is power to make adjustments by Order in Council within six months after the coming into force of the constitution.[2]

As in India, there is power to remove partially exempted areas from that category and to place exempted areas into the category of partially exempted areas.[3]

The problem presented by the states in India is unknown in effect in Burma, for the only substantial non-British area is presented by the Karenni states, and they are of negligible proportions. One further area is non-British, the Namwan Assigned Area, which is held on perpetual lease from China in order to facilitate border transit. It is sufficient in their case to treat them on the model of excluded areas, but as they are not British territory, they have to be dealt with on the procedure of the Foreign Jurisdiction Act, 1890.

An exceptional position is occupied by the federated Shan states which are British territory but which are governed by their own chiefs with full powers. The governor acts in his discretion in relation to these states, and until otherwise provided by the King in Council he will continue to control the Federal Fund of this state. The King by Order in Council may require contributions to be made to the fund by the states; may require payments representing the share of the receipts of the Burmese government accruing on account of the states to be made from Burmese funds to the Federal Fund; may require payments to be made to Burmese revenues from the fund, representing the proper share of the states in the general expenses of Burma, and may make such other provisions as he thinks fit in respect of the fund.[4] Only the payments from and to Burmese revenue shall be brought before the Burma legislature. The accounts of the fund shall be kept as directed by the auditor-general of Burma, by whom they are audited.

The separation of Burma involves the allocation as between

[1] S. 157. [2] S. 156. [3] S. 155. [4] S. 68.

India and Burma of responsibility for Indian debt. An advisory tribunal recommended that as a general principle the proper ratio in which Burma should contribute in respect of the liabilities outstanding at the date of separation should be 7·5 per cent.[1] The King in Council is authorized to require payments from Burmese revenues of such sums as he may judge fit.[2]

The question of currency falls to be regulated by Order in Council,[3] but it has been agreed between the two governments that for a period of at least three years after separation the currency and exchange shall continue to be managed by the Reserve Bank of India and the currency system of the two countries will remain unified. Provision, however, is made for the issue of distinctive bank-notes for Burma in order to facilitate the adjustments consequent on the joint use of the Reserve Bank, and a local coinage of different design from the Indian may, if desired, be introduced in Burma.[4]

Power also is given to regulate by Order in Council the customs duties to be levied on trade between India and Burma.[5] It has been agreed[6] that in general Indian goods shall enter Burma duty free and without restriction, subject to the power to levy countervailing duties corresponding to excise duties. Special arrangements are provided as to similarity of treatment of goods imported from other countries. The agreement is to operate for three years after separation subject to termination by notice of twelve months. Immigration[7] likewise is to be continued for three years on the existing basis and is not subject to any restrictions other than those of general application in the interests of public health and safety or necessary for the exclusion of undesirable individuals, or considered necessary by the head of either government in the exercise of his special responsibility for the prevention of any grave menace to the peace or tranquillity of the territory under his government. Provision is made for India states to be placed in the same position as British India on a basis of reciprocity.

[1] Parl. Paper, Cmd. 4902, p. 20. [2] S. 134. [3] S. 137.
[4] Parl. Paper, Cmd. 4901. [5] S. 135. [6] Parl. Paper, Cmd. 4985.
[7] Ibid. and s. 138.

25. NATIONALITY AND ALIENAGE

The rules of nationality in force in India need not be discussed at length because they are those enacted by the British Parliament and they cannot be varied by the Indian legislature.[1] It is sufficient to note that under the statutes of 1914–33[2] British nationality is acquired by birth on British territory and by marriage to a British subject, and in certain cases by descent from a person of British nationality. Further, nationality can be acquired by naturalization under the scheme of the Act of 1914, which provides for the creation of naturalization which produces the status of a British subject throughout the Empire. In India this provision is operative, but there is also provision by Act VII of 1926, for the grant of naturalization to certain persons not being subjects of any state in Europe or America nor of any state of which an Indian British subject is prevented by law from becoming a national by naturalization; such nationality is valid in British India and the states and British protection is accorded in foreign countries.

Aliens in India owe temporary allegiance to the Crown and are entitled to the protection of Indian laws;[3] they are triable in the same manner as natural-born subjects. They are subjected to certain minor discriminations in respect of membership of local authorities, but the common law provision forbidding the ownership of real property was never introduced into India.[4]

Power was given by the Foreigners Act of 1864,[5] which was amended in 1915, to prevent aliens from residing in British India. The central and local governments have power to order any foreigner to remove himself from British India, and a foreigner who refuses to remove himself or returns after removal may be apprehended and detained. Power is also given to bring

[1] Government of India Act, 1935, s. 110 (*b*) (i).

[2] British Nationality and Status of Aliens Acts, 1914–33. See Dicey and Keith, *Conflict of Laws* (ed. 5), pp. 141–89; British Nationality and Status of Aliens Regulations (India), 1934.

[3] Cf. *Johnstone* v. *Pedlar*, [1921] 2 A.C. 262; *De Jager* v. *Att.-Gen. for Natal*, [1907] A.C. 326.

[4] *Mayor of Lyons* v. *East India Co.* (1836), 1 Moo. Ind. App. 175.

[5] Act III of 1864; III of 1915.

into effect when desired for any area provisions requiring aliens to report their arrival, to obtain licences for travel, etc.[1]

The position of the people of Burma is exactly similar to that of Indians. Only those born within the limits of British Burma as determined from time to time by the Crown in Council[2] are *ipso facto* British subjects, and the Burmese legislature will be able to modify the Indian legislation as to naturalization within the same limits as that can be done in India. But it will equally be unable to affect the general principles of that legislation.[3] Persons born in Karenni states and other non-British possessions will be aliens.

The question has, indeed, been raised whether the subjects of rulers of the Indian states may not be deemed to be British subjects.[4] The position is anomalous, for the rulers themselves unquestionably owe allegiance, and have accepted that position. Allegiance, of course, normally means subjecthood, and it is true that the subjects of the states have for all foreign purposes to be treated as British subjects.[5] So high an authority as Sir C. Ilbert has expressed himself in rather inconsistent ways[6] as to the national status of states subjects in respect of their capacity for naturalization under the Indian legislation. But it must be taken that they are not British subjects, seeing that their territory is not strictly speaking British. This view has been acted on in India where they have been deemed eligible for naturalization, and in several recent cases decided in the courts.[7] It accords with the treatment of Indian rulers as exempt from the jurisdiction of municipal courts in England,[8] though not in Scotland,[9] and while the position is anomalous, for no such complete exemption is given in India itself, the result must be accepted, despite its anomalous character. The status of the subjects of the states, therefore, is in some degree similar to that of the subjects of the Malay states and those of Zanzibar.

[1] Power exists to regulate entry and residence of British subjects domiciled in other British possessions on the basis of reciprocity; Act III of 1924.

[2] S. 44 (*b*) (i).

[3] Act of 1935, s. 142.

[4] Cf. D. K. Sen, *The Indian States*, pp. 129 ff.

[5] Cf. 53 & 54 Vict., c. 37, s. 15.

[6] *The Government of India* (3rd ed.), p. 292, compared with p. 422.

[7] Cited by Sen, op. cit., p. 130.

[8] *Statham* v. *Statham and Gaekwar of Baroda*, [1912] P. 92.

[9] *Ross* v. *H.H. Sir Bhagvat Sinhjee* (1891), 19 R. 31.

CHAPTER XI

DOMINION STATUS: THE PLACE OF INDIA IN THE COMMONWEALTH

1. THE MEANING OF DOMINION STATUS

THE term Dominion status has only become familiar within the period from 1919, but its justification lies in the decision of the Colonial Conference of 1907 to confer on the self-governing colonies the style of Dominions in order to mark them out from the other parts of the Empire. India was excluded from the Imperial Conference whose constitution was then decided upon; that body was to be the formal bond of connexion between His Majesty's governments in the United Kingdom and the Dominions, and was to consist of the Prime Ministers of the Dominions and of the United Kingdom, the latter of whom was to preside. The marking out of the position of the Dominions was continued by the Imperial Conference itself in 1911 when it insisted on the principle that not only should the Dominions continue to be consulted on all matters of foreign policy affecting them, but should also be given the opportunity of associating themselves with the United Kingdom in determining the broad lines of British foreign policy. At that date, however, it was recognized that the final voice in war and peace and alliances must rest with the British Government, whose army, fleet, and diplomatic service afforded the essential basis for active participation in world politics.[1]

The further development of the status thus acquired was greatly furthered by the part played by the Dominions in the Great War, and by the determination of the Prime Minister of Canada that the sacrifices of his people should be rewarded by the recognition of the birth of a new nation worthy to rank in power and place with all save the great powers of Europe and the United States of America.[2] The British Government readily conceded the justice of Sir Robert Borden's claim

[1] Keith, *Responsible Government in the Dominions*, Part V, ch. v.
[2] Keith, *War Government of the British Dominions*, ch. vii.

supported as it was by all the Dominions except Newfoundland whose inadequate resources precluded any attempt to assert individuality in external relations. The hesitation of foreign powers yielded to the earnest request of the British Government and the Peace Conference saw the Dominions granted distinct representation as on the footing of the minor allies in the war, while they still participated in the British Peace Delegation, the successor of the Imperial War Cabinet of 1917–18 in which Dominion representatives had sat to determine the conduct of the war and the terms on which the allies might accept peace. Moreover, the League of Nations Covenant was framed to admit as separate members besides the United Kingdom each of the great Dominions, and it was expressly recognized that the Dominions would be entitled to election to membership of the League Council despite the fact that to the British Empire was allotted a permanent seat in the Council. As early as 1927 this claim was given effect and the Dominions have almost established the right to having one representative on the Council. Finally the Peace treaties were not merely, as Canada demanded, signed separately for the Dominions, but ratification was delayed until each Dominion Parliament had had the opportunity to give its approval to ratification.

Achieved amid the turmoil of the post-war settlement, the solution left much still to be done to establish on a clear footing the position of the Dominions. But the principle was definitely asserted that the Dominions had attained the right to the same measure of autonomy in external affairs as they had long enjoyed in internal matters, and that it was the duty of the British Government to give effect in due course to the doctrine accepted.

Canada took the lead in further advance. In 1920 it secured from the British Government the vital concession that it might be separately represented at Washington, if the United States would agree, by a minister plenipotentiary, who should be under the direct instructions and control of the Dominion government, though in close relations with the British Ambassador, whose place he was to take in the absence of the latter on leave. The arrangement was not to infringe the diplomatic unity of the Empire. Though this concession was not acted on at the time, it was followed by the insistence by Canada on two doctrines. In the first place in the matter of the treaty with the United States regarding the halibut fisheries in the Pacific of 1923 Canada successfully enunciated the doctrine that a treaty which affected one Dominion only should be signed for the King by a Dominion representative alone; and secondly, in connexion with the treaty of Lausanne of 1923 Canada asserted that, without denying the power of the King on the advice of British ministers to conclude a treaty of peace binding the whole of the Empire, Canada would accept no moral obligation to participate in any measures necessary to vindicate the terms of any treaty which it had not assisted in framing. Virtually, therefore, Canada asserted the principle that, if a treaty were to be of any effect as regards Canada, Canada must be responsible for making it. The position adopted by Canada was accepted in substance as correct by the Imperial Conferences of 1923 and 1926.[1]

The efforts of Canada were ably seconded by those of the Irish Free State and the Union of South Africa. The former rested its Dominion status not on a British grant but on a treaty extorted by armed rebellion, and thus claimed to be absolutely autonomous except in so far as it had voluntarily limited its powers by convention. The latter under General Hertzog developed as essential the doctrines of the divisibility of the British Empire or Commonwealth which it asserted was a mere name for a number of distinct sovereignties, and the rights of neutrality and secession. These claims were not formally conceded by the British Government; it eschewed any discussion of the theory of the Union, which was not accepted by the Imperial Conferences of 1926 and 1930 attended by General Hertzog, while it consistently insisted, as against the Irish Free State, that its relation to that body was not governed by international law, and that by the treaty itself the Free State was absolutely bound to accept the status of a Dominion on the same footing as Canada, which, it must be noted, has never asserted the doctrines of the divisibility of the Crown, or of the rights of neutrality and secession.

[1] Keith, *Constitutional Law of the British Dominions*, ch. xvi; *The Governments of the British Empire*, Part I, ch. iii and iv.

On the other hand, the British Government was most willing to assure the Dominions of all the autonomy which was possible within the free association of the Commonwealth. The declaration of Dominion status by the Conference of 1926 was of British draftmanship: it declared of Great Britain and the Dominions that 'they are autonomous communities within the British Empire, equal in status, in no way subordinate one to another in any aspect of their domestic or external affairs, though united by a common allegiance to the Crown, and freely associated as members of the British Commonwealth of Nations'. This assertion was gradually made more explicit, and forms devised to give it full force.

In external affairs legislation was not requisite on the part of the British Parliament to give full effect to the principle of equality and autonomy. All that was necessary was to agree that each part of the Commonwealth might make such treaties as it pleased, and that it might make its treaties in the form it pleased. Thus the Irish Free State since 1931 and the Union of South Africa since 1934, the former without local legislation, the latter under the Royal Executive Functions and Seals Act, 1934, have made treaties and accredited ministers directly through their right of access to the King, who issues full powers to sign and ratify treaties on the advice of the ministry concerned and signs letters of credence in like manner. In other cases the formal procedure of acting through the British Foreign Office and the Dominions Office is maintained as a matter of convenience, but these departments are ready to act on the wishes of the Dominion concerned. The only restriction on freedom of action are those derived from the fact that the King, while he acts constitutionally on the advice of ministers, is yet entitled to place before ministers his own views, and that, as the head of sister states, he might have to urge considerations affecting such states on the government of any one of them, should it meditate action inconsistent with the maintenance of the Commonwealth, and that the Dominions by agreements at the Imperial Conferences from 1923 to 1930 are pledged to full communications with one another in matters of external relations, so that each part may be aware of the actions of the others and may express its views on contemplated action.

The issue of neutrality in a British war on the part of a Dominion remains unsolved. It has never been formally conceded by the Imperial Conference, and it is not claimed by Canada, Australia, or New Zealand. The Prime Minister of the Union asserts the right, but the Union is bound under the accord of 1921, under which the British Admiralty transferred to it valuable properties for defence purposes to aid in the defence of Simonstown, the British naval base in the Union. Despite the assertions of the Prime Minister, it is incredible that such a duty if performed would be compatible with neutrality under international law; the authorities on which he relies are wholly antiquated.[1] Mr. de Valera, who would desire to claim for the Free State the right of neutrality, has admitted that the obligations of the state to afford facilities to the British forces in war are incompatible with any international claim to have neutrality, even if proclaimed, respected by any foreign power.

In internal affairs it was found necessary by the Statute of Westminster 1931 to sweep away the formal remnants of imperial paramount power.[2] The statute therefore abolished for those Dominions who desire to accept the grant—so far Canada, the Free State, and the Union only—the principle that legislation contrary to imperial legislation applying to the Dominion is invalid, and has recognized their power to legislate with extra-territorial effect, and to render their freedom more indisputable has declared that no Imperial Act shall extend to any Dominion after December 11th 1931 unless it is declared therein that the Dominion in question has requested and assented to the enactment. It is perfectly true as the Privy Council said in deciding the case of *British Coal Corporation* v. *The King*[3] that the Imperial Parliament in theory, being incapable of parting with its sovereignty, could repeal the provision of the statute itself, but such action may be ruled out of the bounds of possibility.

The extent of the powers given has recently been stated by the Privy Council in reference to the question of the right of the

[1] Keith, *Journ. Comp. Leg.*, xvii (1935), 273, 274.

[2] 22 Geo. V, c. 4; Keith, *Speeches and Documents on the British Dominions, 1918–1931*, pp. 231–307.

[3] 51 T.L.R. 504; [1935] A.C. 500.

Canadian Parliament to abolish the appeal from the Supreme Court of Canada and other courts in criminal matters and of the Irish Free State Parliament to eliminate the appeal, civil and criminal alike, from the Free State constitution.[1] It ruled that both legislative enactments were valid in law, and it thus negated the view that the legislature of a Dominion is unable to affect vital royal prerogatives applicable to that Dominion.

There are in the case of Canada limits on the authority conferred by the statute, for it is clear that the constitution of a federation cannot be changed lightly, and the framers of the Canadian constitution intended that in all vital matters it should remain unaltered. The new powers, therefore, do not permit the alteration at the pleasure of the federation of the Canadian constitution, and the power to change remains vested in the Imperial Parliament, which could only act if the desire for change were supported by the provinces as well as the federation.[2]

The Commonwealth of Australia and New Zealand have not adopted the operative clauses of the Statute of Westminster; if they do, they will still remain bound by existing restrictions on constitutional change.

There remains to be considered the power of disallowance of Dominion Acts, which is provided for in their constitutions. Under the new powers which they enjoy this power has been eliminated from the constitution of the Union, while disallowance never was included in the Free State constitution. But that Dominion has, like the Union, removed the power of reservation of Bills, with the one exception in the Union that Bills to affect the prerogative right of the Crown to grant leave to appeal from the Appellate Division of the Supreme Court of the Union must be reserved. The power to remove even this restriction, of course, exists and may be exercised.

The plenitude of power thus accorded has raised in the Union the question of the right of secession by unilateral action. The Union by the Status of the Union Act, 1934, has adopted the Statute of Westminster as part of her constitution

[1] *Moore* v. *Att.-Gen. for the Irish Free State*, 51 T.L.R. 508; [1935] A.C. 484.

[2] Cf. the refusal of Parliament even to receive the Western Australian petition for secession from the Commonwealth; May 22nd 1935; H.C. 88 of 1935; Keith, *Journ. Comp. Leg.*, xvii, 269.

and claims to be a sovereign and independent state as explained by the Conference of 1926. It is also asserted that under the Royal Executive Functions and Seals Act, 1934, the governor-general might legally assent to an Act terminating the connexion of the Union with the British Crown or establishing a new dynasty. This speculation is of minor importance, because whatever the Union may decree it cannot deprive persons born therein of their status as British subjects while outside the Union, even should it repeal its own legislation, the British Nationality in the Union, Naturalization and Status of Aliens Act, 1926, and also the imperial legislation of 1914 which declares for the whole Empire the status of British subjects. It is therefore clear that secession could be effectively accomplished only by bilateral action, and in the light of this fact the theoretic right of secession assumes little importance.

At the same time it should be noted that none of the Dominions could possibly stand alone in present world conditions, without running grave risks. Canada, indeed, by reliance on the Monroe doctrine and American protection might preserve independence, but rather as a client of the United States than as a state of full authority in the sphere of international politics. Her position *vis-à-vis* the United States has always been greatly strengthened by the fact that she is part of a great Empire. Australia and New Zealand have avoided any defiant assertion of personality which might deprive them of British protection against the growth of Japanese power and the possible revival of Chinese authority in the Pacific. The Union is dependent on British sea-power for the security of her exports, especially of those of gold, and the Irish Free State is so geographically situated that her defence will always be assured by British interests.

2. THE POSITION OF INDIA IN THE COMMONWEALTH

Viewed historically, it is clear that the action of the Colonial Conference of 1907 in excluding India from representation thereat as an equal member denied to India the status of a Dominion. It is true that in fact the interests of India were adequately conserved by the representations of the secretary of state at the Imperial Conference of 1911, but it was not until the services of India in the Great War were realized and the necessity of meeting Indian aspirations was recognized that the necessary steps were taken to undo a serious blunder. On April 13th 1917[1] the Imperial War Conference resolved that the resolution of the Conference of 1907 regarding the constitution of the Conference should be modified so that India could be fully represented at all future Conferences, and that arrangements with the members of the Conference should be made to permit this being done. This resolution was early given effect. India *de facto* had been represented at that Conference and took her full place at the Imperial War Cabinet of that year and at the Cabinet and Conference of 1918. The Conference of 1917 further recognized the desirability of the readjustment of the constitutional relations of the parts of the Empire 'based upon a full recognition of the Dominions as autonomous nations of an Imperial Commonwealth and of India as an important portion of the same' and the recognition of the right of the Dominions and India to an adequate voice in foreign policy. Moreover, it gave effect to its views on the position of India by accepting the principle of reciprocity of treatment between India and the Dominions. It was accordingly entirely in harmony with this doctrine that the British Government in the announcement of August 20th 1917 spoke of the progressive realization of responsible government in India as the goal of its policy. India, it is clear, was in 1917 recognized as potentially a Dominion.

The decision to confer Dominion status on India, however, was finally confirmed by the events of 1919. It was open to the British Government to insist on treating India as an integral part of the Empire for foreign policy. Instead, without any coercion, and rather to the surprise of those immediately concerned with Indian affairs, it was decided to treat India as a Dominion, to give India a distinct place in the negotiotion of the treaty and its signature, and to secure for India separate membership of the League of Nations. Until that was done it might perfectly well have been argued that all that was promised

[1] Keith, *Speeches and Documents on Indian Policy*, ii, 132.

to India as the ultimate goal of its endeavours was responsible government of the type understood in 1917, at a time when the developments of Dominion autonomy in external affairs were only slowly being realized, and were quite unknown to the vast mass of British and Dominion opinion. But by securing admission of India to the League, the British Government virtually, though not technically, bound itself to the task of creating a self-governing India which would be entitled on the same basis as the Dominions to vote freely in the business of the League. In the long run an India which was merely a duplicate of the British Government would be an anomaly in League proceedings.

The implications of the position were naturally enough recognized in India, and it was no accident or inadvertence which led the Labour Government of 1929 to sanction the announcement by Lord Irwin of their view that it was implicit in the declaration of 1917 that the natural issue of India's constitutional progress as there contemplated was the attainment of Dominion status. The phraseology was probably unfortunate, because in 1917 the term 'Dominion status' was yet to attain currency, and it is quite certain that no one in 1917 foresaw the complete change in reference to international affairs which was achieved in 1919. It would have no doubt been wiser to adopt a more simple form of declaration, and it was no doubt unwise to make the statement at all at a time when the Statutory Commission had not reported, and when neither of the other two great political parties was prepared to approve the terms of the declaration. Moreover, as was natural, the interpretation put on Dominion status by many Indians was the widest possible; Srinivasa Sastri was reported as holding that it connoted the right of secession and that accordingly it could be accepted as the goal by those Indian politicians whose ideal was full self-government as an independent state. Nevertheless, it must be admitted that it did not lie with the government which secured the admission of India to the League of Nations to deny that the goal of India was Dominion status.

In the acrimonious discussion in the House of Commons[1] on

[1] December 18th 1929; also November 7th.

the declaration stress was laid by the secretary of state on the steps taken towards giving India the realities of such status. He pointed to the right of India under the fiscal convention to fix her fiscal policy as desired by the Indian government and legislature free from British control; to the decision permitted in 1921 to purchase stores without regard to British interests; to the presence of an Indian High Commissioner in London; to the distinct representation of India on the Labour Organization of the League, to its independent voice in labour questions; to the fact that the Indian delegation to the League Assembly had been headed in 1929 by an Indian and that India was represented with the Dominions on the Imperial Conference summoned to discuss the legislation to secure the status of the Dominions. For the Liberal Party Lord Reading made it clear that there was willingness to accept Dominion status as the ultimate goal, but that it was essential to bear in mind the limitations in the declaration of 1917[1] and the preamble to the Act of 1919. Mr. Lloyd George shared the same view, pointing out that the declaration had already produced misunderstandings, a view verified by the insistence of Mr. Fenner Brockway that the conference which was to meet to discuss the constitution must embody the principle of Dominion status in its report. The least favourable view was that of Lord Salisbury, who insisted that Dominion status was not a goal to which they were pledged, but a conditional purpose, and that it depended on the fulfilment of the conditions.

In the debate of December 2nd and 3rd 1931, after the formation of the National Government, Mr. Churchill, who had earlier expressed himself incautiously as looking forward to the addition of India to the Dominions, explained his position. India during the Great War had attained Dominion status as far as rank, honour, and ceremony were concerned, but he did not foresee any reasonable time within which India could have the same constitutional freedom as Canada. The sense in which Dominion status was used ten or fifteen years ago did not imply, in his view, Dominion structure or Dominion rights. The Statutory Commission had deliberately excluded Dominion

[1] Keith, *Speeches and Documents on Indian Policy*, ii, 133, 134; House of Lords, November 5th 1929.

status from its epoch-making report. Moreover, the character and definition of Dominion status had been fundamentally altered by the Imperial Conference of 1926 and the Statute of Westminster, and he therefore urged the House to agree that nothing in the Indian policy of the government should commit the House to the establishment of a Dominion constitution as defined by the Statute of Westminster. His amendment was defeated in favour of the governmental policy, but the government was careful not to reiterate the doctrine of Dominion status as the ultimate goal. Its silence was not unnatural, as the passing of the Statute of Westminster, 1931, had rendered it very difficult to say what bounds could be set to that autonomy which it furthered. It was, however, made amply clear that the governmental policy insisted on the doctrine of 1917 and 1919 that the aim was progressive realization of responsible government as an integral part of the British Empire. At no time since has the government deviated from that attitude.

In March 1933, when the White Paper proposals were commended for the acceptance of the House of Commons, Mr. Attlee objected that Dominion status had disappeared even as a goal, but Sir H. Samuel contended that the measure would bring Dominion status very close, a view as optimistic as the other was pessimistic. The government then and later, despite a rather informal reaffirmation of Dominion status as the goal by Lord Willingdon, maintained a remarkable silence, doubtless in view of the claims as to Dominion status urged and acted on by the government of Mr. de Valera in the Irish Free State, and by the action of the Union Parliament in 1934 in passing the Status of the Union Act which its Prime Minister asserted was intended to establish the doctrines of the divisibility of the Crown and the rights of neutrality and secession by unilateral action. It was not until the Government of India Bill was actually before the Commons that the government explained its attitude, when asked to insert in a preamble a declaration of Dominion status as the ultimate goal. It had naturally aroused doubts in India of the intentions of the government when it was realized that the joint committee had sedulously and rather absurdly avoided a vital issue.

The ministerial explanation was that no preamble was required as no new policy was contemplated; the preamble of 1919, as the committee had said, had set out definitely and finally the aims of British rule in India. It was not proposed to repeal the preamble, but the government reiterated its agreement with the interpretation of the preamble given by Lord Irwin in 1929 on the authority of the government of the day. The obstacles to Dominion status were not created by the British Government: they depended on the differences in India of race, caste, religion, and on the inability of India to undertake the burden of her own defence. These difficulties could not be removed by any British Parliament or Government, but sympathetic help and co-operation would be available to enable India to overcome these difficulties and ultimately to take her place among the fully self-governing members of the British Commonwealth of Nations.[1] Mr. Attlee[2] in reply moved an amendment for the rejection of the Bill on the ground that it did not explicitly recognize the right of India to Dominion status, and that it did not by its provisions as to franchise and representation assure to the workers and peasants of India the possibility of securing by constitutional means their social and economic emancipation. The government, however, refused both in the Commons and the Lords to do more than to retain the preamble of the Act of 1919 while wiping out all else. The Attorney-General deprecated inserting the words Dominion status because they were open to varying interpretation and their insertion would raise the issue, Was the status of 1935 referred to or that of some subsequent period? He himself, however, deprived this rather unsatisfactory apologia of some of its sting by asserting that he looked forward to India taking her place in full and free association with the other members of the British Commonwealth of Nations. In the Lords, Lord Crewe insisted on the fact that India already enjoyed Dominion status, though she did not yet exercise Dominion functions, but the contention is hardly of much weight, for by Dominion status men understood the exercise of functions; the effort of Lord Balfour in 1926 to

[1] Cf. the Committee's Report, i, 100, 101.

[2] Similarly Mr. Morgan Jones moved rejection at the third reading in June 1935.

induce the Dominions to accept equality of status as opposed to function, though expressed in the comment on the Conference definition, had never received any effect. It must be held a mistake to refrain from including the words in the preamble. Inserted there, they would, as Sir T. Inskip insisted, have just the same weight as a formal declaration in Parliament of the governmental intention. Neither preamble nor declaration can bind a succeeding government, and it was inevitable that omission from the preamble would be resented in India, nor was the attitude of the government approved by many of its own convinced supporters.

The omission of reference to Dominion status was one of the many reasons urged against the acceptance of the joint committee's scheme in February 1935 in the Indian legislature. Even a supporter of the scheme like Mr. H. P. Mody, a spokesman of Indian commerce, condemned the omission, and the Assembly finally resolved that the scheme of provincial government was unsatisfactory inasmuch as it included various objectionable principles, particularly the establishment of second chambers, the extraordinary and special powers of the governors, provisions relating to police rules, secret service and intelligence departments, which rendered the real control and responsibility of the legislature and executive ineffective. But All-India federation it held to be totally bad and totally unacceptable to the people of British India, and recommended instead the grant of responsible government in British India alone. These resolutions, carried by seventy-four to fifty-eight votes, were followed by intimations of the intention of the Congress party, when provincial autonomy was established, to use entry into the legislatures as a means to prevent the functioning of the constitution in the mode intended by its framers.

It is easy to see that on the whole the conception of Dominion status has worked harm in Indian politics. The fundamental mistake was that of 1919, when India was given a place in the League of Nations at a time when her policy internal and external was wholly dominated by the British Government. The justification for League membership was autonomy; it could fairly be predicated of the great Dominions; of India it had no present truth, and it could hardly be said that its early fulfilment was possible. In these circumstances it would have been wiser candidly to admit that India could not be given then a place in the League, while leaving it open for her when autonomous to be accorded distinct membership. It would have been just to assure India membership of the Labour Organization, for it was possible to permit India self-determination in that regard. As it is, in the League India's position is frankly anomalous, for her policy is determined and is to remain determined indefinitely by the British Government.

As regards internal issues the expectation of Dominion status at an early date, fostered unquestionably by the action of the Labour Government in 1929, has worked unhappily, encouraging in India hopes which the British Government of 1929 must have known were premature, and which certainly were not shared by the National Government of 1931. It is quite legitimate to hold that the action of 1917 was based on the failure to realize that responsible government of the British type was not a wise promise to make to India. The essence of responsible government, it may be held, is the existence of a people sufficiently homogeneous to be governed by majority rule; where caste, race, religion intervene, majority government becomes difficult or impracticable, and it is perfectly arguable that what was due to India was the chance of government by Indians on such lines as might be found appropriate to Indian conditions. At any rate, all British constitution-building for India has been carried on under grave difficulties. It has been realized that majority rule is impossible, but with the safeguarding of minorities the essence of responsible government is seriously if not fatally compromised. If the governors of the provinces were seriously to act on their special responsibilities, it is certain that responsible government would never emerge; but if they do not, much injustice may be done to those classes too little advanced politically to make use of the franchise, or too poor to enjoy it. It is difficult to resist the impression that either responsible government should have been frankly declared impossible or the reality conceded; it is not surprising that neither gratitude nor co-operation is readily forthcoming for a hybrid product such as is the provincial system of special responsibilities and acts to be done according to individual judgment. It is easy to see how the present proposals have developed themselves from the announcement of 1917 and the Act of 1919; but, if the source was tainted, it cannot be a matter of surprise that the stream is poisoned. It is, of course, to be hoped that the plan will develop into true responsible government through the wise disuse of the theoretical powers of the governor; it might do so if Congress gave co-operation in the sense of working the scheme in order to demonstrate that it was only by accepting ministerial advice that the wheels of government could be made to revolve smoothly.

For the federal scheme it is difficult to feel any satisfaction. The units of which it is composed are too disparate to be joined suitably together, and it is too obvious that on the British side the scheme is favoured in order to provide an element of pure conservatism in order to combat any dangerous elements of democracy contributed by British India. On the side of the rulers it is patent that their essential preoccupation is with the effort to secure immunity from pressure in regard to the improvement of the internal administration of their states. Particularly unsatisfactory is the effort made to obtain a definition of paramountcy which would acknowledge the right of the ruler to misgovern his state, assured of British support to put down any resistance to his régime. It is difficult to deny the justice of the contention in India that federation was largely evoked by the desire to evade the issue of extending responsible government to the central government of British India. Moreover, the withholding of defence and external affairs from federal control, inevitable as the course is, renders the alleged concession of responsibility all but meaningless. Further, it is impossible to ignore the fact that, if the state representatives intervene in discussions of issues in which the provinces are alone concerned, their action will be justly resented by the representatives of British India, while, if they do not, there may arise the spectacle of a government which when the states intervene has a majority, only to fall into a minority when they abstain. Whether a federation built on incoherent lines can operate successfully is wholly conjectural; if it does, it will probably be due to the virtual disappearance of responsibility and the assertion of the controlling power of the governor-general backed by the conservative elements of the states and of British India.

One essential requisite, moreover, for the working of responsible government is the existence of effective political parties. These, however, have not yet fully developed even in British India. The Indian National Congress, now freed by the collapse of non-co-operation from the governmental ban, which possesses organization of a widespread character and considerable financial resources, won 44 out of 106 seats at the Assembly election of 1934, but it is disabled from constructive operation by its determined refusal to accept the reform scheme. In itself it contains very disparate elements which work together only because of their negative policy. The Hindu Mahasabha, though it has co-operated with Congress in the ideal of Swaraj, is opposed to it in so far as its aims are essentially communal. There has also developed a strong left wing element in the Congress, which is definitely Socialist[1] and which stresses the necessity of winning social and economic freedom for the masses, in opposition to Mr. Gandhi's policy which has endeavoured to secure the co-operation of landlord and peasant, capitalist and workers, rich and poor. Much more in harmony with Congress is the Congress Nationalist party, whose chief difference with the main body lies in its opposition to the communal award of 1932.

The depressed classes—some forty to forty-five million strong—have their own separate interests and the Justice, or non-Brahman, party in Madras, Bombay, and the Central Provinces is prepared for constructive work in the political sphere. The Indian Liberal federation, representing the revolt in 1918 of the moderate elements from Congress, is strong in the ability of its leaders, but has little popular appeal; its chief divergence from Congress is due not to lack of Nationalist feeling but to belief that Indian self-government can best be achieved within the British Commonwealth. The Muhammadans for the main accept the communal award and desire to work the constitution, but a section favours co-operation

[1] S. C. Bose, *The Indian Struggle*, pp. 344 ff., stands for a synthesis of communism and fascism, anti-democratic, authoritarian, and under strict party discipline.

with Congress. Europeans in India have recently improved their organization in order to defend their interests, and the Anglo-Indians and the Indian Christians[1] have also found organization essential, while provincial associations of landholders have been formed to safeguard their interests. Nationalist sentiment and communal feeling still dominate the situation, and the rise of true political parties cannot be expected until the emergence of more general issues of division to which religious and social differences may be subordinated. It may be noted that the Justice party is open to include all those who wish to join it on the basis of a policy of social and economic reform, and accepts Brahmans, Europeans, Muslims, and Anglo-Indians, though it is still partly a communal party inside the Hindu community. There is clearly better hope in the provinces than in the federation for the evolution of effective parties. An essential part of such evolution must be the forming of real bonds between electorate and member, a matter yet to be accomplished, as the Simon Commission showed.[2]

There remains to be considered the position of India with regard to the Dominions and colonies. It seems impossible for the Dominions to permit immigration, and this bars any intimate association between an autonomous India and the Dominions; it may ultimately preclude even co-operation within the Commonwealth. In the case of the colonies India now controls absolutely emigration and permits it only under fair conditions, approved not only by the government but also by the central legislature;[3] such emigration is permitted to Ceylon and Malaya. Some feeling has been raised by the refusal of the franchise in Ceylon to immigrants save after five years' residence and proof of intention to settle.[4] The Kenya issue has abated in seriousness in view of the prospect of the maintenance of British control for a considerable period under

[1] On August 9th 1934 the Assembly supported the claim of the community—rapidly growing and literate in unusual degree, to a fair share of appointments.

[2] Parl. Paper, Cmd. 3568, pp. 199–202. The party supports rather than selects the candidates. Only political responsibility will produce contact of members and electors. The Communist movement, now illegal, is bent on destruction of all government; Legislative Assembly Debates, August 14th 1934.

[3] Act VII of 1922. The numbers abroad were, about 1931, Ceylon, 800,000; Malaya, 628,000; Mauritius, 281,000; West Indies, 279,000; South Africa, 165,000; Fiji, 73,000; East Africa, 69,000.

[4] Ceylon (State Council Elections) Order in Council, 1931, ss. 7, 9.

the decision of the British Government in 1932,[1] but the refusal to place Indians there and in Fiji[2] on a footing of electoral equality remains a serious practical as well as theoretical grievance which the British Government can hardly be excused for failing to remedy. Federation, it may be hoped, may secure at least the removal of this injustice, against which all elements in India have united in protest,[3] but which was initiated by Lord Elgin, an ex-Viceroy.[4]

[1] Parl. Paper, Cmd. 4141; H. of C. Paper, 156 of 1931.

[2] Emigration thither was stopped in 1916. Representation is communal under the Letters Patent, February 9th 1929 (amended March 24th 1932).

[3] Assembly debate, March 27th 1935; Viceroy's speech, September 16th 1935. In 1934–5 marketing legislation in Uganda, Tanganyika, Kenya and Zanzibar evoked protests, and a mission by Mr. Menon to investigate the issue.

[4] Lord Elgin was also responsible for the complete surrender of Indian interests in South Africa in 1906–8. But the blame for ignoring Indian rights must be shared by the Cabinet.

TABLE OF CASES

INDEX

Published by

Facsimile Publisher
Ashok Vihar, Delhi-110052 (India)
Website: www.facsimilepublisher.com

Distributed by

Gyan Books Pvt. Ltd.
5, Ansari Road, Daryaganj, New Delhi-110002 (India)
E-mail: books@gyanbooks.com, Website: www.gyanbooks.com

2 222000 000271